ROUTLEDGE LIBRARY EDITIONS:
PHILOSOPHY OF MIND

Volume 2

VALUES AND INTENTIONS

VALUES AND INTENTIONS
A Study in Value-theory and Philosophy of Mind

J. N. FINDLAY

LONDON AND NEW YORK

First published in 1961

This edition first published in 2015
by Routledge

2 Park Square, Milton Park, Abingdon, Oxon, OX14 4RN
and by Routledge
711 Third Avenue, New York, NY 10017

Routledge is an imprint of the Taylor & Francis Group, an informa business

© 1961 George Allen & Unwin Ltd

All rights reserved. No part of this book may be reprinted or reproduced or utilised in any form or by any electronic, mechanical, or other means, now known or hereafter invented, including photocopying and recording, or in any information storage or retrieval system, without permission in writing from the publishers.

Trademark notice: Product or corporate names may be trademarks or registered trademarks, and are used only for identification and explanation without intent to infringe.

British Library Cataloguing in Publication Data
A catalogue record for this book is available from the British Library

ISBN: 978-1-138-82464-5 (Set)
eISBN: 978-1-315-74048-5 (Set)
ISBN: 978-1-138-82563-5 (Volume 2)
eISBN: 978-1-315-73932-8 (Volume 2)
Pb ISBN: 978-1-138-82568-0 (Volume 2)

Publisher's Note
The publisher has gone to great lengths to ensure the quality of this book but points out that some imperfections from the original may be apparent.

Disclaimer
The publisher has made every effort to trace copyright holders and would welcome correspondence from those they have been unable to trace.

VALUES AND INTENTIONS

A STUDY IN VALUE-THEORY AND
PHILOSOPHY OF MIND

BY

J. N. FINDLAY

M.A., PH.D., F.B.A.

LONDON: GEORGE ALLEN & UNWIN LTD

FIRST PUBLISHED IN 1961

This book is copyright under the Berne Convention. Apart from any fair dealing for the purposes of private study, research, criticism, or review, as permitted under the Copyright Act, 1956, no portion may be reproduced by any process without written permission. Enquiries should be addressed to the publisher

© *George Allen & Unwin Ltd, 1961*

PRINTED IN GREAT BRITAIN
in 11 on 12 point Imprint type
BY UNWIN BROTHERS LIMITED
WOKING AND LONDON

αἰσχρὸν τὰ μέν σε θεῖα πάντ' ἐξειδέναι,
τά τ'ὄντα καὶ μέλλοντα, τὰ δὲ δίκαα μή

Euripides, *Helen*, 11. 922–3.

For my yoke is easy, and my burden is light.

The Divine Logos according to
Matthew xi. 30.

TO DENIS RICKETT

CONTENTS

PREFACE   15

I. INTRODUCTORY AND PROGRAMMATIC   19

    (i) Plea for a Teleological Ethics of Value
    (ii) The Outward and the Inward Approaches to Mind
    (iii) On Intentionality as the Mark of the Mental

II. THE BASIC MODES OF CONSCIOUSNESS   45

    (i) General Consideration of 'Cognition' and 'Consciousness'
    (ii) The Modes of the Clear and the Obscure and of the Fulfilled and Unfulfilled
    (iii) The Variations of Conscious 'Light' or Sense
    (iv) The Reflexive and Projective Modes of Consciousness
    (v) The Essential 'Drifts' of Consciousness

III. THE MODES OF BELIEF   93

    (i) General Characterization of Belief
    (ii) The Approvability of Belief

IV. THE MODES OF ACTION AND ENDEAVOUR   135

    (i) The General Nature of Mental Activity
    (ii) The Nature of Wanting and Trying
    (iii) The Dimensions of Wanting
    (iv) The Role of Emotion and Feeling

V. THE MODES OF WISH AND WILL   179

    (i) The Nature of Willing
    (ii) The Freedom of the Will
    (iii) The Firmament of Values and Disvalues
    (iv) The Approvability of Valuations and Values

VI. THE VALUES OF WELFARE   227

    (i) The Values of Satisfaction and Dissatisfaction
    (ii) The Values of Apprehension and Contemplation
    (iii) The Values of Belief and Knowledge
    (iv) The Values of Personal Transcendence
    (v) The Values of Power and Freedom

14 VALUES AND INTENTIONS

VII. INJUSTICE AND ITS DISVALUES   286

    (i) The Just and Unjust in General
    (ii) The Justice of Distributions and Understandings
    (iii) Corrective Justice
    (iv) Platonic Justice

II. DUTY AND MORAL VALUE   332

    (i) The Notion of 'Ought': Hortatory and Minatory
         Imperatives
    (ii) The Detailed Determination of Duty: Generalities
    (iii) Blue-Print for Practice
    (iv) Moral Goodness and Badness
    (v) Developments of the Above Principles
    (vi) Virtue and Vice: Duty and Moral Value

IX. EPILOGUE ON RELIGION   395

APPENDIX

    Henriette Hertz Lecture (British Academy) entitled *The Structure of the Kingdom of Ends*

INDEX   436

PREFACE

This book is the attempted elaboration of ideas and themes very briefly set forth in my Henriette Hertz Trust Philosophical Lecture, read to the British Academy on March 20, 1957, and entitled *The Structure of the Kingdom of Ends*. For convenience of reference, and by kind permission of the British Academy, in whose *Proceedings* (Vol. XLIII) the lecture first appeared, the lecture has been reprinted as an Appendix to the book.

Unsatisfactory as my exposition of the themes of my book undoubtedly is—chiefly on account of their extreme magnitude and diversity—I have felt in writing it that I was being true to the shapes and alignments of my cloudy material, and was making a groping use of the sort of method that really fits them. All philosophy has been bedevilled by the methods and ideals of formal logic—which may be summed up as the attempt to draw sharp lines round all concepts and to make all inferences rigorously deductive—and increasingly so with the improved formalization of recent times, but in no field of philosophy has this bedevilment worked more direly than in the field of moral thinking. It may be said almost to have conjured the whole subject out of existence. For the logical relations interesting to moral philosophy are all what may be called 'family relations': they are relations of *kinship* among concepts, all differing in kind and among concepts differing in kind, and yet drawing the mind and will on from one to the other in a manner not necessary nor obligatory, and yet somehow resting on the nature of what is considered. 'What is sauce for the goose is sauce for the gander' is an aphorism representing the very soul of moral philosophy, yet with absolutely no standing in formal logic. The concepts, too, which preside over this whole region of discourse must be flexible concepts, capable always of being shifted and pushed in new directions, and never achieving more than a provisional circumscription. And the 'family relations' among values and ends can be seen to reflect family relations among our various acts and attitudes of mind, and among their characteristic objects, so that we tread countless bridges between the natural order of fact and the 'non-natural' order of values, in a manner that recent moral philosophy has taught us utterly to forswear. What I have done

16 VALUES AND INTENTIONS

in this book has been faulty because the old analytic Adam is still strong in me, but the extent to which I have broken loose from him is a matter for pride and not for shame. I am not abashed that my basic concept of 'impersonality' should be shifting and nebulous: it hits off and sums up the complex family relations of various psychological and value-concepts, rather than something narrowly common to them all. I hope too that, while my book is crammed with inferences, they all involve a genuine advance and a subtle change of ground, and that there are none in which conclusions merely *follow* from premises. (Not that this is not a good thing in certain sorts of discussion.) I hope, however, that in avoiding the Scylla of deductive rigour I have also steered clear of the Charybdis of empiricism or of mere positivism: the family relations studied in this book are either such as would be felt (though not always obeyed) in every possible world, or my whole treatment is a mistake. I have also tried to push into the background of moral philosophy the whole notion of obligation, which has practically no application once one moves out of the sphere of formulated contract and legal prescription. The sort of relations studied in this book ground endlessly varied desirabilities and undesirabilities: they furnish no basis for the clearly demarcated 'right' and 'wrong', or 'ought' and 'ought not', etc., on which law-inspired theories of morality principally insist. In adopting this stand, I have been true to my own moral experience. Perhaps I am singular in not understanding what it is for something to be or not to be my absolute duty—perhaps even in suspecting those who address me in such terms—and yet in feeling great clearness as to what is more desirable or undesirable that I or anyone or anything should do or should be.

The debts of this book are most numerous and very obvious. They amount almost to plagiarism in my taking over of certain doctrines of Meinong regarding the relations of value to aesthetic and logical dignity. I have restated these doctrines fully, both because they are almost wholly neglected, and because they seem to me to be the last words of truth on these matters. I am also obviously in debt to Brentano and Husserl, particularly the latter, both for the intentional view of the mind, and for the constant appeal to a non-formal, non-tautological *a priori*. I also owe much to the moral theorizing of Scheler and Hartmann, and of Moore, Rashdall and Ross. I have been much influenced by the British

PREFACE

Moralists, particularly by Adam Smith, an influence which goes back to a memorable series of lectures of Sir David Ross, heard in my undergraduate days. My basic methodological concept of 'family relations' is an apotheosized version of a notion rather deprecatingly used by Wittgenstein, who has in other respects played the role of Cartesian demon to my thought. His unacceptable bifurcation into the tautological and the empirical, characteristic of the *Tractatus*, and his behaviouristic-naturalistic account of meaning and sensationalistic analysis of experience, characteristic of the *Philosophical Investigations*, have seemed to me to furnish the fruitful errors that have driven me towards the truth. Of the linguistic methods employed by certain post-Wittgensteinian philosophers, I have made little use: I admire the treatments of Austin and Hare, but have not found, in general, that they shed light on my particular problems. My greatest and most positive debts are to Kant and Hegel. Professor Popper rightly characterized the design of this book as an attempt to give a transcendental deduction of the whole field of moral and other values. My own studies of the practice (rather than the professions) of Hegel have given me a completely new insight into the significance of his dialectic: of this dialectic, as I understand it, I regard my book as a specimen. Once or twice I have borrowed notions from Heidegger, and there are also, I find, resemblances between some of my views and the 'ontology' of Sartre. These last stem, however, from the common inspiration of our views, rather than from any actual influence.

I wish to thank the Leverhulme Research Awards for the grant of a Fellowship which relieved me from lecturing during the session of 1959–60, and made the writing of this book possible. This grant and this relief have been one of the great uncovenanted kindnesses of my existence.

J. N. FINDLAY

Carleton College, Minnesota
March 1961

CHAPTER I

INTRODUCTORY AND PROGRAMMATIC

(I) PLEA FOR A TELEOLOGICAL ETHICS OF VALUE

The aim of this book is to discuss the old question of the general pattern of the ends and counter-ends of rational wish and endeavour. It proceeds on the assumption that, while there may be vast disagreement on the relative choiceworthiness of various characters of activity, experience or states of affairs, and extremely great disagreement as to what is to be sought, chosen or preferred in the individual case, there is none the less a consensus—remarkable or unremarkable as one chooses to regard it—as to the *characters* of things that confer on them their desirability or worthwhileness, or the reverse. While the detailed content of desirable living may be infinitely debatable, or open to personal decision, its general direction (or range of directions) seems much more uncontroversial. We seem always ready to justify our preferences by appealing to a relatively small number of 'reasons', all of which show much interconnection and mutual kinship, and are as readily appealed to by other persons as by ourselves. Thus we might successfully justify our preference of A to B by holding A to be more agreeable to someone, or to afford greater insight and mastery in some field, or to involve less arbitrariness than its rival: we should not try to justify it by holding it to be more nearly a square, or to require a greater amount of chewing than B, or to be a considerably greater distance west of Greenwich. Or if we did give such reasons we should feel it obligatory to justify them by bringing in further grounds. While our *first* reasons in justification of our preferences vary immensely, and are not necessarily acceptable or intelligible to others, they are for that reason also felt to be insufficient, and we are soon ready to justify them by falling back on one or other of a comparatively small range of reasons, which are in general acknowledged by others as well as ourselves. And this general acknowledgement has a queer air of the self-justifying and self-evident, just as its refusal would have a strange air of the absurd. While the last reasons cited are not mere synonyms of desirability, and while

20 VALUES AND INTENTIONS

there is consequently no mere tautology in holding something to be desirable on their account, they seem none the less to have more than a merely factual or customary foundation. It is not, it would seem, merely because we belong to a certain species, or to a certain social group, that certain reasons strike us as compelling or at least relevant: they seem to have a not readily *avoidable* appeal. That things strike us in this manner is undeniable: to say otherwise would be to be (as Hume would say) a disingenuous disputant. It is for philosophy to probe these beguiling appearances to the bottom, and to see what foundations (if any) they may have. This task remains obligatory even if contemporary philosophy largely evades it.

This contemporary ignoring of the question of the last grounds of desirability has itself a large number of grounds. It is founded, first of all, on the long predominance in philosophy of an *ethics of rule*, which sought to prescribe what it is proper for the individual to *do*, or bring about by his doing, rather than with what it is proper and desirable for him to aim at, or wish for, or prefer. This ethics of rule, while not denying that questions concerning the desirabilities of conduct must be set in a context, and that it is impossible to decide them without *some* consideration of circumstances or remoter results, none the less sought to narrow this context down as far as possible, so as to involve the minimum of disturbance and uncertainty in the rules it wished to set up. And while it was doubtless right in recognizing that questions of practical desirability always have an *horizon*, beyond which it is neither profitable, obligatory nor even allowable to inquire, they none the less made this horizon very much narrower than they had any reason to do. The manifest obligations of, e.g., truth-telling or keeping faith could hardly be set aside in any circumstances whatsoever. In so doing, they ignored the fact that questions as to the propriety or desirability of the immediate aspects, adjuncts or inward preliminaries of an act were questions entirely of the same sort as questions of the desirability of states of affairs lying quite beyond the bounds of action, even if, as was obvious, they were not of the same *practical* importance. And they ignored the further fact that the interstices of our action are crammed with unfruitful or not immediately fruitful *wishes* directed to such remoter objectives, such wishes being often as seriously conceived and as carefully cherished as those which have an immediate

INTRODUCTORY AND PROGRAMMATIC 21

practical relevance, and that it is in a soil of such surrounding wishes that our practical motions usually grow. What a man prays for or earnestly approves is plainly as significant as what he practically sets about to achieve.

Another equally strong ground for this ignoring of wider issues of desirability lay in the one-sided stress on what is *obligatory* in our conduct, rather than on what is desirable or undesirable in it. In this stress it was forgotten that the obligatory in conduct derives most of its ordinary significance from its opposition to what is permitted, and that, in the wide field of what is *non-*obligatory in our conduct there are none the less deep distinctions between what it is more or less desirable or undesirable to do. That it would be 'rather fine' or 'somewhat shabby' to do something, which it is none the less not a matter of strict obligation to do or avoid, is an idea as common in ordinary ethical discussion as it is ignored by philosophers. The obligatory, moreover, is a notion having one prime application in situations involving complex social relations between persons exercising authority, on the one hand, and persons pledged to obedience, on the other. It also has a prime application in situations involving complex relations of commitment and mutual faith among persons, such as do not and need not always obtain. Such relationships may come to have a reflex in a man's attitude to his own possible actions—he may, after a fashion, issue commands to, or exact pledges from, himself—but, in default of the special social relationships involved, the notion loses its force. It remains fairly clear always what it would be *better* or *worse* to seek to realize, while it is always maddeningly unclear what one is *obliged* to do. The obligatory, moreover, has a much closer relationship with the undesirable and the evil than with the desirable or the good. We are obliged to do things mainly because certain grave evils would otherwise befall, and not merely to realize what is positively good. We have no doubt some obligation to provide or secure what is good, but mainly in cases where such goods would be *missed*, where their absence would be undesirable or bad. For an obligation to provide a dispensable good there is no plain warrant in the ordinary use of the notion, much less for an obligation to secure the greatest possible sum of good that lies within our power. Some obligation there may be to seek spontaneously to achieve some goods which are not as such matters of obligation,

22 VALUES AND INTENTIONS

but this obligation is by its nature self-limiting, and presupposes the non-obligatory. Plainly the voice of strict duty represents only a single tone in the complex utterance of Practical Reason, which not only enjoins or forbids, but also beseeches, grumbles and sometimes simply asks, and which also sets various winning or repelling possibilities before us, which it may be possible to hunger and thirst after, and possibly also to groan over, but not practically to effect.

Of the vast realm of the desirable and the undesirable obligation, therefore, touches only an inconsiderable portion. The main question is why practically all philosophers, with the exception of a few Jesuit moralists, should have thought otherwise. Possibly the ambiguity of the verbs 'ought' and 'should' (or their equivalents in other languages) which not only express the exaction of obligation, but also the very mildest of exhortations, have played their part in this confusion. For we say that we ought to adhere to truth in our communications just as we say that we ought at times to cut our hair. Possibly, too, a deep cowardice and unwillingness to exercise responsible choice has no little share in it. It is often painful to face a choice between better and worse, and easier to feel that there is 'only one thing that we can do'. And an even stronger ground for repudiating an investigation of the grounds of goodness or desirability lies in the monstrous exaggerations of Utilitarianism, which not only puts all desirable things on a level, recognizing only quantitative distinctions among them, but which adds to this the further enormity of obliging us to sweat and strain after the *maximum of attainable good*, a requirement so senseless that it would condemn deity to an endless multiplication of excellence, and would burden man with a conscience so greedy for good, and so ruthless in lacerating those who necessarily flag in their zeal for it, as to be far worse than the rigoristic conscience of an ascetic system. Better the haunting fear of having violated the strait but limited commandments of an authoritarian deity, than the certainty of having failed to live up to the Benthamite requirement to squeeze out the last possible ounce of pleasure for everyone. These monstrous Utilitarian exaggerations deserve to be opposed by the equally valid counter-intuition that it is not our duty to seek to realize the least particle of *mere* good in any case whatsoever.

Another source for the contemporary disregard of the final

INTRODUCTORY AND PROGRAMMATIC 23

ends of action lies in an excessive preoccupation with the new discipline of meta-ethics, and a consequent neglect of the old discipline of ethics. The main task of the moral philosopher is thought to be the analysis of the meaning of such ethical terms as 'right', 'good', 'ought', etc., rather than in the consideration of the kinds of things to which one might possibly apply them. It has been thought that the two questions were quite separate, and that, since to say that something is good does not simply *mean* that it has one or other of the properties that are recognized grounds for calling it good, such grounds therefore lie entirely outside its meaning, and that it is possible to explore that meaning without taking them into account at all.

Moore's famous indictment of the naturalistic fallacy may have shown that the meaning of 'good' does not consist merely in our reasons for thinking something good, and perhaps does not include these as its parts, but it has not shown that it does not include them in some manner, as things pointed to, or pre-supposed, or involved, if the central notion of good is to have any content whatever. For the goodness of anything may, among other aspects, be essentially such as to be a goodness *for* this or *for* that, a goodness on one account or another, a goodness specified according to the varying grounds we give for it, and having no residual kernel of meaning separable from such specifications. The notion of goodness may be, in short, a place or point in dis-course, and, like a point in space, have no inner content beyond being a position in that kind of discourse, with defined relations to other positions. All this was in a sense conceded by Moore when he acknowledged synthetic *a priori* connections between certain properties and their consequent goodness, but the force of this concession was made null by the tacit assumptions of the analysis that he practised: that whatever is many-sided is a 'complex' of distinct elements, and that it arises by the cementing of 'con-stituents' into a characteristic relational whole. This determined application of a whole-part logic vitiated Moore's recognition of necessary connections: they became arbitrary and external, not 'built-in' to the nature of what they connected, even when said to be 'internal' and necessary. And so it came to seem that the meaning of 'good', in ethical contexts, was something which could be studied apart from the reasons for holding something to be good, and that it could be linked to the latter only by a remarkable

24 VALUES AND INTENTIONS

exercise of intuition. And since intuition is a highly personal faculty, which different viewers use to quite different effect, the result was to throw into the arena of controversy and obscurity the whole question of the grounds for holding anything to be good.

All this does not mean that Moore did not make many valuable contributions to the theory of the grounds of goodness, and that other contemporary thinkers did not do likewise. But the manner in which such inquiries were pursued had a fatal defect: though styled 'intuitive', it was in reality dogmatic. It fell into what we may call the 'quasi-empiricism' characteristic of all modern realism, in that it treated as a mere matter of fact, discernible only by detached, separate acts of observing, what could be acceptable only if given some sort of a 'deduction', some showing that it 'flowed' inescapably from the whole 'spirit' and frame of mind characteristic of morality. And so Moore said that personal affection and the enjoyment of beauty were by far the greatest of goods, Ross held virtue to be infinitely more precious than knowledge or pleasure, Rashdall held just distribution to be of value only as expressing the virtue of just distributors, etc. etc. These high-minded pronouncements were a heap of disconnected insights, incapable of coherent colligation, and much less of higher order explanation. And their effect was to lead inevitably to the doctrine which makes the content of ethics a matter wholly for personal 'decisions', which in no sense *accords* them with the formal pattern of our moral utterances, nor with the 'spirit' behind them. It is not necessary that we should here trouble to refute this doctrine, save to say that it would never have won the smallest acceptance save for subtle ambiguities in the word 'decision'. We can decide *that* certain things are good and proper, and we can decide *to* follow or implement such decisions, but the former sense of 'decision' involves a submission to fixed canons of settlement which is quite absent from the latter.

We have suggested *where* the source of our value-pronouncements is to be sought and by *what* they are to be tested. It is to be sought in the general 'spirit' or attitude of mind lying behind our varying value-determinations. To this 'spirit' some kinds of judgement may come more 'natural' than others, and some judgements framed hastily or initially may tend to pass over into others that fit it better. This 'spirit' may, further, have a natural developmental history, through the customary, the legalistic, the

INTRODUCTORY AND PROGRAMMATIC   25

impulsively libertarian, the personally conscientious and such-like stages, to a stage which brings out its implications adequately, and which is best accommodated to it. And there may be a definite absurdity in certain evaluations which is not the absurdity of self-contradiction or of a violation of convention: it is the absurdity pinned down in the 'pragmatic paradoxes' studied by recent thinkers, as where a man affirms his belief in what he knows to be against the evidence, or impartially recommends the most narrow partiality. Of all thinkers on ethical questions the idealists alone have shown explanatory mastery over the detail of our value-pronouncements: others may have developed this detail more brilliantly, but they alone have rendered it intelligible. And it would seem that their success was due to the *subjective* foundations of their explanations, though this lay rather in a universal than an empirical subjectivity. We, having had bitter experience of the realistic, emotivistic and personal-decision treatments of ethics, may do well to follow this idealistic lead, even if not following all their epistemological errors. We must attempt something in the nature of a 'transcendental deduction' of our varying ethical slants of mind, without falling into the many muddled absurdities of Kant's mighty performance.

To study the 'spirit' or attitude lying behind our ethical pronouncements involves, however, a study of our attitudes and frames of mind in general: we must supplement the transcendental approaches of Kant and Hegel with the detailed classification and ordering of states of mind characteristic of such systems as the 'psychognosy' of Brentano, the 'phenomenology' of thinkers like Husserl, and the 'logical geography' applied to mind by Ryle. We must deal with our subjective life not empirically but conceptually, ranging its specific forms under notions of wider generality, and establishing varied logical relations among them, of which some will be the relations of entailment and exclusion interesting to modern analysis, while others will be the more subtle, penumbral relations of favouring and unfavourableness among our notions in which their inferential force and their true 'content' may be said principally to consist. The 'reasonableness' and the 'consistency' which leads those who are in one frame of mind to pass over into another which is akin, or which leads those who are conceiving of the one frame of mind to conceive also of the other, may have nothing that savours of purely

26 VALUES AND INTENTIONS

formal rigour. They are none the less among the most important influences in the life of the mind, and as much deserving of the title of 'logical' as any other.

(II) THE OUTWARD AND INWARD APPROACHES TO MIND

Having decided that the study of the ultimate objects of choice and preference must be by way of a study of 'the mind', we may now ask how 'the mind' should be studied. We have said that it should be studied conceptually, in terms of general *types* of frames of mind, rather than particular mental states, but this leaves unsettled whether the whole study shall proceed 'from within' or 'from without', whether it shall deal with frames of mind as concentrated into transitory personal episodes or 'experiences', or spread out, not only over many such episodes, but also over episodes that are physical and public, the individual's 'overt responses', the many things that he publicly does or says. Such a question would not have seemed to merit much discussion in the past. It would have been assumed that the life of mind consists of strictly unsharable, private 'experiences', each of which is how things seem to or are felt by a particular conscious individual, and that what such an individual openly did could have interest only as betokening such experiences, as throwing light on them, or providing the evidence for them, while lying quite outside their special circle. Such an approach is one that has now fallen into the discard. For it has become plain that in many of the activities most distinctive of mind, e.g. the execution of a task or design or the solving of a practical or intellectual problem, there is often little of significance in the items of momentary personal experience. Our possession of mind is shown more in the *organization* and *sequence* of our outward doings, and of our inward sensings and reviewings, than in the content of the latter taken alone. A man carrying out some difficult design does not need ever fresh mandates or thrusts of the will to keep him to his task, just as he does not need fresh experiences of illumination to guide him at every point. Nor does he need private imaginative rehearsals before he actually carries out each stage. There appears, in fact, to be some economy in the occurrence of the types of experience just mentioned: they appear when the situation is difficult and crucial, and vanish at once when it falls within an accepted programme. All these are facts well known to ordinary self-observation and elaborately demonstrated in the laboratory, when the net let down to make a haul of countless expected 'judgements', 'volitions', 'images', etc., came repeatedly empty to the surface. If the possession of mind is shown by the ability to respond sensitively and adaptively then it is shown as much in the plastic course of our doing and saying, as in the single experiences that accompany its unfolding. And the whole tendency to place separate acts of understanding, judgement, decision, etc., behind each turn in our intelligent performance, would seem, in fact, to be no more than a misguided mythology, inspired perhaps by a simplifying misinterpretation of the words of our mental vocabulary. Words like 'understanding', 'judgement', etc., seem to mean something simple and uniform though they in fact cover widely various sorts of situation. The prejudice that they mean something simple and uniform then leads us to look for that simple, uniform thing in the queer twilight of personal experience, rather than in the public daylight where it is obviously not there.

It has become clear, further, that, so far from its being the case that we pick out various intelligent performances, and apply to them various words in our mental vocabulary, because we think of them as betokening various types of personal experience, we rather approach the latter through the former, and pin them down as being the sort of private experience that is naturally 'acted out' in this or that public performance. Our various terms for emotional disarray were first (it would seem) given employment in connection with disturbances of public action, and only afterwards transferred to cover the experiences and feelings which go with these. And we can in fact only characterize them, even to ourselves, by an analogical or transferred use of the expressions used to characterize disturbed action. The burstings, the sinkings, the chillings, the quiverings, the heavings, the hardenings and the meltings so inevitably referred to in accounts of emotional experience have all obviously their source in the observation and experience of action. In much the same way the whole vocabulary by which we speak of imagery and the imaginary derives from our normal exploration of public objects. And our approach to such higher experiences as those of referring, judging,

28 VALUES AND INTENTIONS

wishing, resolving, etc., involves obvious comparison with significant speech. In one experience it is as if a man were pointing out something, in another as if he were uttering a pronouncement, in yet another as if he were voicing a wish, in yet another as if he were pledging himself to carry out a certain line of action, etc. etc. It is not, it would seem, through the clear structure of the frames of mind behind them that we can throw light on the words used to express them: it is rather through the clear use of those words that we can throw what light we may on the character and structure of attendant experiences.

There is yet another grave objection to the whole attempt to approach mind through personal experience rather than through outward action and significant speech. This lies in the consideration that, if the content of experience be limited to what strictly forms part of it, it can embrace no more than simple affections of sense, or that other kind of simple affection known as personal feelings: acts of understanding, meaning, inference, etc., cannot form part of it. Experiences may no doubt be said to be *of* this or *of* that, experiences of tension, of harmony, of frustration and what not: they may even be said to be experiences of seeing a number to be divisible by seven without remainder, of making up of one's mind to act more cautiously in future, of feeling that one has the right to ask a certain question, etc. etc. But what makes them be *of* this or *of* that, can be nothing intrinsic to them as experiences, but can appear only when we look upon the full setting in which they arise and the full set of personal responses and attitudes into which they develop. We are subject to what Wittgenstein considers to be the *strange* temptation to incorporate into our experiences, and to treat as if they actually were parts of them, and so also could proceed from them, what in effect belong only to their setting or future developments. We are in a sense right in thus incorporating setting and developments into our notion of the contents of our experiences, since this is the way in which we actually do talk and think, but in another sense we proceed misleadingly, since it misleads to put into an experience what it only has by virtue of what surrounds it or of what it leads up to.

The views we have been examining rest, however, on the basic assumption that the relation between what may be called the outer and inner sides of a frame of mind is in all respects *a relation*

INTRODUCTORY AND PROGRAMMATIC

of fact, that each has its independent character and structure, and that it merely *happens* to be associated, perhaps regularly, with that of the other. Neither is then such as intrinsically to shed light on the other, though it may cast a confusing verbal shadow of itself on the other, which makes it hard to see what either actually contains. These doctrines rest upon a view of completely free association among entities genuinely distinct, all necessary relationships being tautological reflections of linguistic rules, views supposedly derived from Wittgenstein's *Tractatus Logico-philosophicus*, though this work seems in fact to have taught quite a different doctrine, objects being held to be of differing *forms*, which in a sense fix their possibilities of combination. It is to this latter type of doctrine that we shall have to recur if we are to make sense of the relation between 'experiences' and the external situations and outward pantomimes that 'fit' them. The 'form' of the experience, to use the suggested terminology, must be such as to favour certain forms of outward manifestation, if we are to grasp how we can pin down experiences through their manifestations, how we can describe the former by analogy with the latter, and how we can properly employ the same words to cover either.

That we do feel it to be quite wrong to treat the relation between an experience and all the outward things it is *of*, or that it prompts us to do and say, as merely casual and external, can be shown by considering an example. I am carrying some luggage in a customs shed, I put it down to show my passport to an official, an interrogation results to which I reply in harried anger, the official is satisfied and stamps my passport, I lift up my burden and totter further—all this is from one point of view a complex physical transaction, while from another point of view, and with only a nuance of difference, it is an 'experience'. In both cases it is something undergone by me, but at one time described in neutral fashion, special to no definite observer, at another time considered as it seems and feels to me, with the overtones, emphases and omissions peculiar to my personal standpoint, as well as with the unity and detachment from context which stamps it as an experience. An experience in the sense given to it by certain philosophers, consisting merely of detached throbs, thrills, sensations and feelings, is as remote from an experience in the ordinary sense of the term, as it is remote from the actual transaction in which it originates.

VALUES AND INTENTIONS

The situation is not altered if we go on to the situation in which I recall my first 'experience', now tranquilly resting my head on the lace of my railway carriage, a situation which itself represents a second 'experience' that I undergo. Now I say that it is 'as if' I were back in the customs house, subject to those past indignities, not of course exactly as if it were so, but in some ways as if it were the case. That such an 'experience' is quite different from a physical transaction is of course evident, and that it does not even resemble it as one physical transaction resembles another. It is, however, not casual but *unavoidable* that we should liken it to the physical situation in which it had its origin, while also using metaphors which bring out the deep gulf between the two sorts of situation. The same applies if we pursue the situation a stage further to where the 'experience' I have had is present only as an 'atmosphere' or a 'background', something I feel when I refer pointedly to *that* experience without actually reviving it. Can it be doubted that this new 'experience' must inevitably be described as in some sense the appropriate 'concentrate' of the original experience, as that into which the original experience 'condenses', and from which, by a natural expansion, something like the original experience can be derived? The 'atmosphere' precipitated by my encounter with the customs is (when it does occur) as specifically fitting to just that encounter, and as necessarily expansive into something just like that encounter, as it is also quite different in its character as an actual happening. We may describe this situation by saying that it is as if future (or past) developments are in some manner contained or summed up in what now occurs, and it is suggested that there is something gravely misleading in this way of speaking. And so there is, if we are led to think that the sense in which these developments are present in the condensed thought of them is the same as the sense in which they are present when actually there. But apart from such a gross confusion, our way of speaking represents exactly what we do and must say if our description is not to be an inventory of inessentials but to do full justice to the situation. And the strange unwillingness to accept such descriptions, or the determination to give them unplausible translations, can rest only on a deep unwillingness to face the (from a physical point of view) queer, but none the less quite basic and ordinary properties of our mental life. For if natural existence is precisely characterized by an

INTRODUCTORY AND PROGRAMMATIC

Aussereinander or mutual outsideness of parts, what we call the life of mind is as correctly characterizable by a tendency towards an ever increasing *Ineinander* or interpenetration of aspects, which none the less preserve a residual distinction by virtue of the *Aussereinander* to which they correspond.

Let us approach the same point from an opposite direction. It seems plain that our various experiences, while in one sense complete expressions of a given frame of mind, in another sense allow of and require an indefinite further completion, and this both in further experiences of various sorts and in physical situations and actions. Each experience, we may say, *fulfils* itself in further experiences (to borrow an invaluable term of Edmund Husserl's), as well as in physical conditions and acts relating to such experiences, and the relation between an experience and its 'fulfilments' is again felt to be not merely factual and empirical, but in some sense intrinsic and necessary. Thus such a personal experience as regretfully concluding something to be the case, though perhaps drily verbal in its occurrence, and though requiring no further development to have the character and direction that it has, none the less naturally explicates itself into experiences in which the thing deplored will be more palpably present, and our own reaction to it more concretely carried out. And such 'fulfilment' tends to a limit where there will not be a merely fanciful or hallucinatory encounter with the regrettable situation, but a fully physical mourning over what physically is. In much the same manner the inner state called a decision or a wish, though in a sense whole and complete in the instant of its occurrence, none the less intrinsically seems to point to a whole range of further developments, in which the thing wished for or decided upon will be brought about by our own agency and in the full concretion of physical presence. And even the actual sensory confrontation with something, though in some ways the most satiated of experiences, none the less points to many other confrontations that will accord with it or confirm it, as well as to other less palpable reconstitutions which will suffice to place it in wider contexts. To reflect on our experiences and on various kinds of physical conditions and activity, is therefore to see various relations of relevance among them, which, though they may not be relations of strict logical entailment, none the less deserve the name of 'logical'. They are 'logical' in the sense that a form

VALUES AND INTENTIONS

of speech which ignored them or ran counter to them would involve surd expressions difficult of application not unlike the expression 'orange but not between red and yellow in hue' or the expression 'physically real but vanishing as soon as one looks hard at it'. And they are logical in that the one provides some reason to expect the other, and favours the other as a natural and reasonable continuation, and this not on account of experienced frequencies of concomitance, but because our terms are the terms they are. If our devotion to what notions strictly include or exclude is such as to cause us to ignore all these looser connections among them, some necessary without being analytic, and some probable without being empirical, we shall not get far in our study of 'the mind', where they encounter us at every step.

It is these relations of 'kinship' or of 'natural affinity' between what we may call the outer and inner sides of a frame of mind, which both explain and justify the analogical way in which we approach our inner states. It is because a felt spasm of anger has such a relation of 'kinship' with various kinds of explosive and demolishing behaviour that we can describe it by saying 'I felt ready to burst, I felt my gorge rising, I could have killed him,' etc. etc. It is likewise because certain cognitive states have similar internal bonds with situations involving confronting, manipulating, illuminating, etc., that we find it natural to describe them in such ways. So close indeed do we sometimes feel the fit to be between certain experiences and certain physical motions, that we may be said to *show* the one by showing the other (much as we might teach the meaning of a term by exhibiting a diagram or a model). There is a sense in which we can show someone what it feels like to be completely carefree by pointing to a lamb leaping or a colt rolling, a demonstration that may be highly successful even if the man himself has never felt in this manner. Such relations may not wholly remove all the tangled difficulties concerned with 'other minds' but they at least attenuate it to vanishing point.

The evident kinship between inner experience and external behaviour likewise explains our use of the same terms to cover both, and our treatment of mind in general, and of particular frames of mind, as being *radically amphibious*, as functioning in two media, and as being able to switch from one to the other without loss of continuity or identity. At one moment, we say,

INTRODUCTORY AND PROGRAMMATIC 33

we enact something physically, at the next we continue it in fantasy, at one moment something physically impinges upon us, at the next there is only the faint felt 'impression' left by this impact, etc. etc. And so intimately do we conceive of the two 'sides' as being geared to one another, that we see something of an inverse relation among them, the one being thought to take up more vigorously as the other declines. If our 'soul' be taken to be that portion of ourselves at any time active on the plane of pure experience, then we are willing to echo the Heraclitean phrase and to say that external activity is constantly being bought 'at the cost of soul'.

In all this there is nothing of Cartesian dualism, and as little is there any in our constant use of the deliverances of outer action to check those of personal report, and the other way about. The precise content of certain very condensed experiences can often only be assessed by trying to utter their content in words, or to illustrate it by examples or models, or to carry it out in detailed action, and it is commonplace that one may sometimes decide that its content and direction were somewhat different from what one would at first have described them as being. One may have felt that one grasped the 'principle' of something, which one had in fact really not grasped at all, or which was perhaps not there to grasp. This procedure is not the absurd one of trying to find what is in an experience by going on to something which is quite different: it is like tasting a *strong* solution of some substance in order to detect its overlaid presence in a diluted mixture. But though there are all these cases in which outer performance corrects our view of the content and direction of an experience, there are more salient cases where the reverse obtains. There is, e.g., a conclusiveness and a clearness in what a man says about what was explicitly present to his thought, how he felt, what he intended, etc. etc., that have made some people doubt whether we can even be said to *know* such matters, since it is not clear how we can be *wrong* about them. Beside such clear assurance the characterization of frames of mind as evinced in outward action can be no more than a well-grounded hypothesis, since it involves to an indefinite extent what a man *would* do if certain circumstances were thus or thus, and on the assumption of countless other prior states of mind, themselves hypothetical and in need of supporting evidence. There is an irremovable inconclusiveness

B

34 VALUES AND INTENTIONS

in the self-deliverance of frames of mind in action beside which their self-deliverance in the form of experiences usually seems conclusive and complete.

We may maintain, further, in the case of all those forms of intelligent activity which are *not* accompanied by distinctive experiences, that it is not a *mere* mythology which imagines them to be guided by a continuous stream of judgements, decisions and other appropriate experiences. Though such experiences certainly do not exist in most cases, it is none the less *as if* they existed, and to stress this fact is to improve one's understanding of what happens. The philosophy of mind is to this extent 'teleological' that in it we do not understand a frame of mind by considering the *minimum* necessary or sufficient conditions for its occurrence: we must consider the conditions that would realize it in its *fullest* form. The mythology which locates conscious experiences behind each turn in our intelligent performance may be said to be a necessary and valuable mythology since we can only understand such performatory intelligence by regarding it as in some way existing in the interstices of, or as doing duty for, or as moving towards an intelligence that is fully conscious. For the intelligence manifest in action is essentially *dispersed* over a large number of successive acts, which need not be close or continuous in time: though it falls under co-ordinating plans or concepts these are nowhere brought to a focus, not present in their entirety in a single instant of time. It is only as subject to such a concentrated unity that a dispersed unity can be fully intelligible: there is a mystery about intelligent action unsteered by guiding experiences that we seek to lessen by mythically postulating the existence of such experiences. We can at least say that a being whose performances show consistent domination by *very* high-level projects and concepts, must *at times* be capable of consciously grasping such projects and concepts, and that it is only as doing duty for such moments of grasp that its less conscious performances can be adequately understood.

We shall in what follows therefore deal with 'frames of mind' without implying that such frames of mind are necessarily present in the form of conscious experience, or of outward situations and behaviour. A frame of mind, like a Spinozistic mode, straddles two attributes, but may from time to time be more strongly operative in the one than in the other. We shall, however, tend to

INTRODUCTORY AND PROGRAMMATIC 35

lay greater stress on the form taken by frames of mind in experience, since their main properties will be found to be much clearer there.

(III) ON INTENTIONALITY AS THE MARK OF THE MENTAL

We may conclude the present chapter by considering the classical characterization of the mental that we owe to Franz Brentano. This is the view that what is strictly peculiar to states of mind or 'psychic phenomena', is what Brentano variously called the 'directedness to an object' or the 'intentional inexistence of a content' or an 'immanent objectivity'. 'Every mental state possesses in itself something which stands as object, although not all possess their objects in the same way. In a presentation something is presented, in a judgement something is acknowledged or rejected, in love something is loved, in hate hated, in desire desired, etc.'[1] A mere sense of grammatical propriety would in fact teach us Brentano's doctrine, would tell us that most of our mental activities must be said to be *of* something.

Brentano's doctrine, however, goes farther in refusing to admit any class of mental state that is *not* thus of something or other: the thrills, pangs, twitches, etc., which are for some paradigms of 'experience', would be for him not experiences, not 'psychic phenomena' at all. And he goes still farther, in the important first section of the Appendix to his *Psychology from the Empirical Standpoint* in holding the intentionality of mental states to be a case of a unique logical category: the category of a determination which is *relation-like* without being a proper case of a relation. Intentionality, we may say, is a relational property which is one-sided, which does not involve the being of a corresponding relation or related term as it has seemed to many axiomatic that it should. In maintaining this, Brentano is doing justice to the incontestable fact that in describing a state of mind as being *of* this or *of* that, we must not be taken to imply that there *is* anything having the character attributed to our object. That this would be an illicit transformation is of course clear to all ordinary speakers: from the fact that X is striking an F one can infer that something *is* an F, but from the fact that X is thinking of an F one cannot infer that there is some F of which X is thinking. What is peculiar to Brentano is not, however, the simple recognition of this truism,

[1] *Psychology from the Empirical Standpoint*, Bk. II, Ch. 1, §5.

36 VALUES AND INTENTIONS

but the fact that he does not try to offer any explanation or analysis of it. He assumes it to be as intelligible as it is abundantly illustrated, and proceeds to understand mental life in terms of it. What was for Moore and for many others an insoluble problem becomes for him a basic principle of explanation.

To Brentano's doctrine of intentionality we may here give a preliminary assent, though the full justification for doing so must lie in the problems it eliminates and the simplifications it affords. This is not the only case where the way round some seemingly desperate difficulty may lie in recognizing it to be, not really difficult, but illuminating and explanatory, and our difficulties as due to an obstinate determination to assimilate one basic category to another. The category of relations which occasioned so many headaches for philosophers by seeming to hover neutrally *between* entities without inhering *in* any of them, or which seemed to require an infinity of other relations to cement them to their terms, became wholly unmystifying once philosophers had ceased to try to assimilate them to qualities or to particular entities, and had become clear as to their unique conceptual status. The characteristic 'being' of a relation becomes wholly unproblematic once one accepts it, with Aristotle, as being merely the way in which something may stand to something else, and not as something quite different. In much the same way one may become content to treat the being of what may be called 'conscious reference' as being simply the manner in which states of mind are *of* this or that thing or state of affairs, this manner having the unique but not puzzling peculiarity that what a state of mind is *of* need not be held to *be* in any other sense or way than that there are (or may be) states of mind *of* it, and whose properties only enter into the description of such states of mind to the extent that they are thought of or acknowledged.

The difficulties attendant on this conception may all then be seen as arising out of a failure to recognize the categorially unique status of intentional directedness, and out of the attempt to assimilate it to a *bona fide* relation. Because a term occupying the *object*-position in an ordinary relational statement can by a suitable transformation be shifted into a corresponding *subject*-position—'Brutus killed a bald man' being transformed into 'A bald man was killed by Brutus'—it is thought that a similar transformation should be possible in the case of a statement

INTRODUCTORY AND PROGRAMMATIC 37

involving mental reference—e.g. 'Brutus dreamt of a bald man' should yield 'Some bald man was dreamt of by Brutus'—and, because this proves not to be allowable, it is thought that the whole statement requires reformulation, or an 'analysis' into terms that will not yield these objectionable inferences. And because a term occupying an object-position in an ordinary relational statement can be replaced by another term having an identical reference—'Brutus killed the author of *De Bello Gallico*' being replaceable by 'Brutus killed the husband of Calpurnia'—it is thought that the same should be possible in a statement concerning mental reference—e.g. 'Brutus thought of the author of *De Bello Gallico*' and 'Brutus thought of the husband of Calpurnia'—and when such a replacement yields unallowable consequences, an object referred to under one title not being necessarily referred to under another, complaint is made of 'referential opacity', and recourse is had to various reductive or analytical devices. Whereas, if Brentano is right, 'referential opacity' merely signalizes the fact that truly mental categories have entered into one's discourse, and any attempt to reduce this or to analyse it away would simply be to free one's talk of any reference to the mental. Such a liberation would indeed be a simplification, but scarcely one that can be philosophically admired. If an object accordingly occurs in the description of a mental state, we must not try to take it out of its place in that description and refer to it independently, nor must we take more liberties and latitudes in speaking of it than are permitted by the mental state in question. All this, as remarked before, is entirely in accord with ordinary thought and usage, which never is guilty of the inference 'I think of a bald man, therefore a bald man is' or 'He thought about the author of *De Bello Gallico*, therefore he thought about the husband of Calpurnia', and which never thinks that it *should* perform such inferences till taught to think so by philosophers. This would appear really to be a case where the true task of the philosopher is to lead us back to the clarities of ordinary speech rather than to exacerbate difficulties resting on fundamental misunderstandings.

If this be the outcome, in modern terms, of Brentano's penetrating doctrine, then it is from the outset plain that *no* analysis or description of a mental state will be adequate that is in terms of *existent contents* or *elements*, however these may be interrelated or arranged, and whether they are thought of as mental or

38 VALUES AND INTENTIONS

physical. No mental state can be exhaustively described in terms of images, sensations, feelings, objects, universals, intelligible species, words, bodily movements, neural changes, etc. etc., however these may be thought of as qualified or compounded, for to accept or even propose such an analysis is to ignore the touchstone of the mental, its built-in reference to what is not part of it and to what need not exist anywhere else at all. And the impossibility of such an analysis is what we do in fact intuitively accept and acknowledge, for quite plainly no whole of elements that are merely 'there', however put together or modified, could ever amount to the *consciousness* of anything, whether of the elements themselves or of anything else. And without an account of consciousness or awareness there can plainly be no satisfactory account of anything mental.

If Brentano's view is correct, modern treatments of 'experience' as consisting of sounds, smells, the waxing and waning of pains, etc. etc., are wholly to be repudiated, though such elements may indeed be held to play a part in such experiences, being, as it were, the items which condense or carry our references. In holding this we are not running counter to accepted usage. For the sensory contents it recognizes are all stamped with the seal *of* something or other: they are odours *of* roses, pangs *of* remorse, etc. etc. They are the most palpable part of an experience which cannot be adequately described except in terms of what it is *of*. And even when we attempt to 'isolate' such contents, and to concentrate on them separately, they are never *all* that there is to our state of mind: this includes also such things as attention to parts, emphasis on aspects, etc. etc.

If Brentano's doctrine thus forbids any exhaustive description of a mental state in terms of related constituents, it forbids also any description or analysis of it in terms merely *dispositional*, though here it is much harder to show up the inadequacy of the proposed description or analysis. For it might well seem that in some *readiness* to perform certain appropriate acts in the right circumstances, or in a readiness to feel appropriate surprise or unsurprise, or in a readiness to utter appropriate words or a readiness to have appropriate mental pictures, one might in fact have found 'the essence' of mental reference, a view to this extent confirmatory of Brentano's analysis that the things one is ready to do, or is ready *for*, need not as yet exist, and need not

INTRODUCTORY AND PROGRAMMATIC   39

ever be likely to come into existence. And the proposed analysis does hit something 'of the essence' of mental reference, since, if a man is mentally directed to X, and his reference has the specific form of belief, then he will in appropriate circumstances be likely to satisfy his wishes in ways influenced by his belief in X, and he will also very probably in appropriate circumstances be surprised if what he takes to be X fails to behave in an X-like manner, and he will very probably be ready to use appropriate words on such occasions, e.g. 'There's X', etc. etc., and to form mental pictures of X which conform to his past experience. All this can be seen *a priori* by anyone who reflects on what it is to be mentally directed to X, and on its affiliation with the other notions concerned. But though thus capable of being seen *a priori*, and so having something of a 'logical' connection with mental directedness, the dispositions in question should not be held to be more than a sort of consequent penumbra of such mental directedness, since they are infinite in their variety, since they depend on circumstances which need not obtain, and which cannot in fact be conceived exhaustively, and since it is only by understanding what it is to be mentally directed to something (and also to believe in it) that we can see them to be likely. Mental directedness is *explanatory* of all these indefinitely various, hypothetical, merely probable outcomes, only because it has some simple, categorical side independent of them all: if it merely consisted in them all, or were itself some other sort of readiness or disposition, the whole of mental life would rush apart into dispersed nullity.

To accept Brentano's analysis means to locate intentionality more essentially in the introspectively reported poses of the mind than in what is outwardly done or said. For a man's words refer to objects only in a conventional manner, and what their precise reference is, is determined by usages of great complexity which may indeed be simply formulated in grammars, etc., but in phrases whose sense is determined by usages of great complexity, illustrated indeed in a man's actual utterances, but not conclusively and exhaustively so. There is therefore never a plain illustration of mental directness in a man's words. Whereas what may be called the internal conscious reference to something is thought to have its sense intrinsically and not conventionally, and by means of this sense to refer simply and unambiguously to objects. If the inner life of the mind can be called a 'discourse',

40 VALUES AND INTENTIONS

then it must paradoxically be conceived as a discourse whose words are meanings, rather than signs having a meaning. And a man's acts in the same manner only presuppose a completing conscious reference to certain objects, which is filled in more or less hypothetically, and never with final confidence and clearness. A man acts *as if* certain considerations weighed with him, but he acts as if many alternative considerations were thus operative, and which really is operative never can be clear. The mere request for what he is conceiving or thinking of may, however, receive a decisive answer, an answer decisive only because we believe there to be a conscious act behind the words, whose direction is not (except abnormally) a matter of doubt or inference.

The notion of a conscious reference to something must therefore be held to occupy a position in understanding which it does not occupy in linguistic instruction. We must have been *taught* the use of the terms 'understand', 'believe', 'think of', etc., in situations where we or other persons employed words in a suitable manner, or behaved in a manner and setting which suggested that we might, if provoked, have made use of certain words. It is on account of this origin that our talk about thoughts, decisions, etc., is always largely an 'interiorization' of our talk about words, the same oblique or direct forms of diction serving for both, and the mental reference being as it were a shadow of the verbal. But (if our present approach is correct) we only fully *understood* the use of such mental terms by ourselves executing certain directed conscious acts, by having knowledge of thus executing them, and by supposing others to do likewise. In understanding, therefore, we in a sense *reverse* the relation obtaining in linguistic instruction: the thought, brought into discourse by the word, serves to explain and illuminate the latter. This, the accepted, ancient view of the priorities need not be taken as overthrown by modern linguistic researches. That the processes which give a sense to expressions should also go beyond what is in the grossest sense ostensible is by no means absurd: it is indeed necessary to say this, since the line between showable and unshowable is vague and arbitrary, and since nothing is more inapplicable than the notion of a private box in which each individual carries matters he cannot show to others, while outside of it *all* can be freely displayed.

Brentano's doctrine of intentionality will no doubt require

INTRODUCTORY AND PROGRAMMATIC   41

much supplementation in many directions, and we shall attempt to provide this in what follows. Its concept of 'reference to objects' employs no clear distinction parallel to Frege's distinction between Sense and Reference, between an object *as* thought of in a given thought-reference, and the same object as possibly functioning in many quite different references, a distinction plainly basic to the intentional life of the mind. Equally clearly it fails to distinguish between objects in the pregnant sense as the continuing *themes, topics, subject-matters* or *logical subjects* of a series of references as opposed to any and every sort of item appearing in such a series. This notion also is central in mental philosophy, it being doubtful whether there can be anything deserving the name of a consciousness of something where nothing is examined, even fleetingly, from a number of distinct sides, no topic is dwelt on, no theme developed, etc. etc. Objectivity in this pregnant sense derives genealogically from the hard, lasting objects of our first intention, the physical things that we handled, looked over, smelt, sucked and learnt to locate in an orderly environment, and our thought-relations even to the most tenuous abstraction or the most fleeting datum of sense must retain something of this original many-sidedness, shift of viewpoint, varied experimentation, etc. etc. And Brentano's doctrine has plainly not indicated a place for all those *non*-conscious approximations to fully conscious mental directedness, where we find that it throws light on what happens to treat it *as if* involving conscious direction to this or that object.

As the intentional doctrine of Brentano was framed to deal, among other things, with our ability to refer mentally to the non-existent, we may here advert briefly to Russell's famous 'theory of descriptions' which has something of the same purpose. This theory had its origin in the strange view of a proposition as being a relational complex made up of a number of 'constituents', and in the natural unwillingness to hold that something which did not exist could be a constituent of anything. Propositions which appeared to concern objects which did not exist, e.g. the proposition expressed by the words 'Centaurs do not exist', were accordingly held to have as their constituents only the separate *properties* of such non-existent objects, as well, perhaps, as the somewhat suspect property of 'applying to something' or 'having application'. Thus 'Centaurs do not exist' means that

B*

42   VALUES AND INTENTIONS

centaur-properties jointly lack the property of applying to any-thing. (This is only one way of reading Russell's astonishing rigmarole.) As a resolution of difficulties due to an astonishingly crude theory of conscious references this theory has perhaps some merit. Plainly it must not be possible to conjure up a centaur out of the true judgement that there are no centaurs, or even out of the existence of the false judgement that there are such things. But the theory contrived to give the impression that references to centaurs were not really directed to centaurs but only to certain disjointed properties, and perhaps also to the whole assemblage of actual things in the world, some of which exhibited centaur-properties separately but none together, and that so our 'robust sense of reality' might be satisfied. Whereas to talk or think about centaurs is plainly to conceive of centaur-properties as exemplified *together*, and as exemplified in cases which need not be thought identical with *any* of the actual objects in the world, so that there is plainly a going beyond existent boundaries. And the supposedly innocuous 'Centaur-properties-as-applying-to-something' which Russell proposes as an alternative to non-existent centaurs is as much a content unembodied in the existent world as a centaur, and is in fact merely a higher-order variant of the same content. It is not profitable to devote further atten-tion to a theory as obscure and confused as Russell's, nor to consider the implications of his 'polyadic' treatment of belief, etc. etc. We may here only deplore the general effect: the com-plete corruption of the study of thought and meaning by the notion that there is something intrinsically different between thinking or talking of what does, and of what does not exist, that thought or talk about what does not exist, should be said to be *about* something, or to refer to something, only in some derived, secondary or 'Pickwickian' fashion, and that once it can be shown that there is *not* something of a certain sort, both it, and the thought of it, are deprived of all interest and importance. Whereas there is absolutely no *intrinsic* difference between thinking or talking about what does, and what does not really exist—in so far, that is, as the issue of real existence is not specifically raised in thought—and there are, in consequence, few distinctions of less importance for a philosophy of *mind*. Provided two objects are conceived in the same way, whether believingly or not believingly, it does not matter that the one is, and the other is not, a denizen

INTRODUCTORY AND PROGRAMMATIC   43

of the real world. And while all thought-reference no doubt goes back genetically to the direct intercourse with, and cognitive pinning down of environmental realities, and bears traces of this origin in its make-up, this origin is not as such of vast importance for a philosophy of mind (despite much opinion to the contrary), only *that* relation to reality counting for it as interesting and important that the mind itself acknowledges, and by standards intrinsic to itself.

We have given reasons for espousing a view of mental life basically in harmony with that of Brentano. That we shall have convinced those pledged to reductive existential analyses of various sorts, and particularly such as have a strong flavour of naturalism, is to be doubted: we must rest our case on a basic appeal to the simple. Our untutored reports of our thoughts, wishes, decisions, imaginings, etc., even of such as condense wordless perception and practical response, are all intentional in form: they are *of* the most vastly complex matters, such as sometimes require pages to unravel, and that without either the actuality or the plain promise of a satisfactory carrying out. For such untutored accounts the tutored reports of the laboratory have not succeeded in substituting anything more illuminating. The most legitimate ground for disliking intentional concepts lies, perhaps, in our deep distrust for 'internal', 'built-in' forms of conception, which seem not to square with the looseness and openness favoured by empirical and experimental approaches. If we conceive of a state of mind as encapsulating references to remote things that are not part of it, and perhaps tending to produce them or be produced by them, we seem well on the way towards a dissolving monism like that of the Anglo-Hegelians, where everything in the world is held to be internally geared to everything else. The defect of this Anglo-Hegelian internality lay, however, in its universality and its engulfing necessity, which together rendered it practically meaningless: to build absolutely everything, however remote and seemingly irrelevant, into the being of everything else, is to turn such internality into a mere phrase, little different from the most universal and absolute externality. The strictest empiricism is not, however, irreconcilable with the recognition of many and varied forms of intrinsic connection, not projected by verbal convention, but rather helping to shape the latter, which provide the framework,

44 VALUES AND INTENTIONS

the 'logical space' within which empirical discoveries may be made. And many of their connections may be probabilistic in form, rather than necessitating, indicating A as an intrinsically likely complement of B, rather than as what *must* go with it in its actual being. The idealism of Hegel made great use of this relatively loose, probabilistic *a priori*, and succeeded thereby in throwing great light on many mental facts. However this may be, we shall attempt to show, in detailed elaboration, that an intentional approach to the facts of mind is conceptually fruitful, and that, above all, it will help us to understand and connect together the various basic 'values' which serve as the ends of practice and living, and to relate them all to the life of the mind.

CHAPTER II

THE BASIC MODES OF CONSCIOUSNESS

(I) GENERAL CONSIDERATION OF 'COGNITION' AND 'CONSCIOUSNESS'

Having reached an accommodation between the 'outward' and observational, and the 'inward' or directly 'experiential' approaches to frames of mind, and having considered the 'directedness' or 'intentionality' which for some philosophers is the distinguishing mark of the mental, we shall in the present chapter limit our view to the mental orientations traditionally known as 'cognitive', the orientations in which things (in the widest sense of the word) are in some manner made themes or objects of examination or awareness, or become 'present' or 'apparent' to thought or perception, in which they are 'brought' or 'laid' before the mind, in which they are treated of, weighed, dealt with, turned over, pointed to or variously regarded and illuminated, whatever the metaphor derived from primitive confrontation and manipulation may best please us.

The word 'cognition' is, of course, a philosopher's word, and hence suspect from the point of view of all those who like to range concepts in 'families' without necessarily looking for, or believing in, a Platonic thread of identity that runs through them all. We shall, however, presume that the word genuinely distils a significant affinity resting at least on a common relation to a single basic type of situation, which all in varying degrees and ways reinstate and condense. To have before one some coloured dots on a grey ground or to see the point or truth of some abstract theorum, may be profoundly different mental postures: they have, however, a deeply felt affinity marked by the natural use of the words 'looking' and 'seeing' which ranges them over against urgings, surgings, promptings, stirrings, reverberations and other states naturally spoken of in more dynamic terms. 'Cognition' is of course a term fraught with many disadvantages. By its connections with 'knowledge' it tends to stress the often adventitious success of a state of mind in hitting its target in the 'real' or 'true', so making intrinsic what is to a large extent extrinsic: it tends also to suppress or under-emphasize

46 VALUES AND INTENTIONS

our wholly normal and fruitful mental intercourse with the unreal, and to make its very existence somewhat of a puzzle. And it has the further disadvantage of meaning *both* an orientation of mind which may be merely an element in such richer frames of mind as those of choosing, preferring, wishing, liking, etc., and which are more essentially relevant for our purpose, and *also* a more or less complete frame of mind, opposed in respect of its 'coldly' detached, contemplative character to states involving warmth, movement and commitment. In either case, however, some study of the mental orientations covered by the word 'cognitive' is essential to the study of the frames of mind more closely concerned with the good and the bad, or with the better and the worse. For not only are the real or possible facts or objects cognitively brought before us the indispensable target or background for our evaluative responses, but our cognitive pursuits and achievements themselves involve valuations analogous to those we are about to study, and are themselves the objects of an impersonal 'prizing' of the most deeply felt 'absoluteness'.

In seeking to deal with what is peculiar to cognitive frames of mind, we seem to be involved in the traditional obscurities of the notion of 'consciousness', the difficulties of a medium whose total transparency renders it unapparent, of a phosphorescence so universal as to cast no revealing shadow, or of a presenting activity whose fate is to be hidden behind what it presents. It is the postulated elusiveness of the supposed action or passion involved in being conscious that has rendered it so suspect, and that has led to nonsense-questions as to its 'existence' or to nonsense-analyses of that existence in terms solely of 'directed response'. We shall hold, however, that this postulated elusiveness is a mere consequence of a postulated invariance, the invariant being such as to provide no point of salience by means of which it can be picked out. And this postulated invariance would seem genuinely to spring from a philosopher's misunderstanding of a word which, while it may bring out a profound analogy, has its use only in *varied* and *variable* situations, where there is a continual *becoming* alive to all sorts of things and features, and this necessarily on a *background* to which one is differently and less fully alive. It is an analytic truth, fully acknowledged in eastern systems of mental concentration, that to succeed wholly in checking the 'transformations

THE BASIC MODES OF CONSCIOUSNESS   47

of the thinking principle' is to succeed also in extinguishing thought and consciousness altogether.

'Consciousness' is not therefore the name of some perfectly pellucid medium, nor of a universal phosphorescence or shadowy activity, but a term systematically covering all the forms and guises of *esse apparens* (to use a pregnant expression of Ockham's), the ways in which things may appear *differently* without thereby necessarily appearing *as* different. Alternatively it embraces the ways in which frames of mind may vary independently of what they are *of*, and which show that there is something *more* to such frames of mind than what they are *of*. It is by considering all the dimensions of variability in our frames of mind that are not primarily concerned with what they are *of*, that we may hope to rise to a satisfactory notion of consciousness as such, which, like the light to which it is so readily compared, is never discernible *in vacuo* but only in so far as it is interrupted by, and illuminates varied objects, and illuminates them *variously*. It need scarcely be said that such differences are primarily brought out by reflection on the manner of our experience, on how things feel and seem to us personally, than by the mere consideration of what we outwardly do.

(II) THE MODES OF THE CLEAR AND THE OBSCURE AND OF THE FULFILLED AND UNFULFILLED

We may begin, therefore, and say that any state that we should wish to call the consciousness of this or that, a frame of mind in which something was 'apparent to us' or 'there for us', must involve at least one salient opposition, between the two poles of which there must also necessarily be, for all conceivable 'objects' or 'contents', an uninterrupted shuttling to and fro. This opposition is that between what, with varying metaphor, may be said to be consciously clear, central, focal, relieved, regarded or emphasized, and what may by contrast be said to be obscure, marginal, in the background, half-regarded or under-emphasized. Alternatively we may state the opposition in terms of our own full conscious aliveness to certain things and features of things, and our own ancillary half-aliveness to other things and features which are, in no necessarily physical sense, merely neighbouring. The opposition is simply illustrated by the differing mode of impact or appearance

VALUES AND INTENTIONS

of a sound or visible flash to which we 'attend', and its context of other sounds or visible forms which do not thus 'engage our attention'; it is as well illustrated by the way in which certain considerations press on us insistently in thought, while others contribute merely to their general background. To be conscious of anything essentially involves a difference: something must be singled out, taken note of, especially emphasized, and it must be opposed to other things not thus singled out, not specially noted, not emphasized, which serve as its context.

This difference between what is clearly and what is obscurely present to mind must not be confused with the all-important difference between what is *actually* and what is only *facultatively* or *dispositionally* present to mind, though the two types of distinction shade into one another and are not always readily kept apart. The interior of a church may be *ready* to come to mind when I look steadily at its façade, but this is not the same as the actual presence to my mind of its contrasting pattern of black and white layers, which I nevertheless do not explicitly 'notice'. In the same way it is possible, though by no means so easy, to draw a line between the innumerable things I was only *ready* to think, and the comparatively few things that I really *did* think, even if only in an obscure fashion. In thinking of Jeremiah I may, e.g., think definitely, though obscurely, of Hebrew prophets and prophecy: I may, however, only be *ready* to think of the prophet Amos or of the prophetess Joanna Southcott. And though there are some hard cases such as those of the just past strokes of the clock, then not noticed but now recalled, or of the lost objects glimpsed by some 'corner of the eye' and recalled in dreams, in which there is really only a doubtful *inference* to the obscure past presence of some content to our minds—an inference doubtful since the inference to some merely physiological registration would be equally apt—there are none the less countless cases where the obscure presence of something to our minds is not at all inferential and in no way open to doubt.

The difference between being clearly and being obscurely present to mind is likewise not to be confused with the difference between clear-cut definiteness and hazy obscurity in the structure and character of what is thus present to mind. Thus an exceedingly nebulous form or muffled and indeterminate sound may be maximally present to mind, while the surrounding background of clear

THE BASIC MODES OF CONSCIOUSNESS 49

shapes and loud noises may be almost wholly disregarded. What is clear, in the sense of being consciously central and thematic, is in fact more often and more naturally what is indeterminate and problematic, rather than what comes before us with sharp outlines or with readily classifiable character. And the change we call one from being obscurely, to being clearly present to mind, is quite different from the change we should call one from having vague outlines or nebulous articulations to having more definite outlines or articulations. A landscape merely taken note of and studied, only changes in the former manner, whereas the same landscape first seen with the naked eye, and then looked at through a telescope, changes in the latter fashion. In the same way there are cases where we feel that some thought or notion is merely being more consciously and explicitly enjoyed, whereas in other cases we feel that we are replacing it by some other more developed and specific thought or notion.

We may here note the grave temptation to reject the whole distinction we have been drawing, and to refuse to distinguish a change in presented clarity from a change in a thing's presented or intended properties. When the speckled hen's presented speckles cease to be separately noted, they cease also, it may be plausibly argued, to be presented either as distinct or as definitely numerous, and it represents no more than an intrusion of irrelevant knowledge to suppose that they *must* have been either. Such a thesis would, however, override the plainest of phenomenal differences. We must in some way register and signalize the difference between situations in which a thing's structure becomes literally blurred and confused, however much we attend to it, and situations where the blurring and confusion is no more than a metaphor, and means a quite different vanishing of stress, or relaxation of grip, which is a much less gross, obtrusive phenomenon. In attributing the one kind of difference to what is consciously objective, and the other kind of difference to the subjective function of 'consciousness', we do nothing arbitrary and misleading, since it is in terms precisely of this second sort of less palpable, metaphorical variability that 'consciousness' as a discriminable function achieves its distinction and its definitory pinning down. That by a metaphorical use of the words 'clear', 'obscure', etc., we should succeed in directing attention to the most basic feature of conscious experience is not at all remarkable: it is through the

50 VALUES AND INTENTIONS

medium of metaphor that discourse first penetrates what are the unshowable reaches of the mind, though, once broached by metaphor, the unshowables lose their unshowability and the metaphors their metaphorical character. We reach a point where we can direct attention to what was previously unshowable—'Note how when you concentrate on X, Y faded from view, etc.'—and can even command their presence—'Now make X clear, now concentrate on Y', etc. etc. All that is to be regretted is that the lesson has been so thoroughly learnt that we no longer know that (or how) we learnt it.

The distinction between being clearly and obscurely present is likewise independent of the distinction between the active and the passive, with which, however, it has intimate inter-relations. The clear presence of something to mind seems at times to be something pre-eminently brought about or sustained by our own activity, whereas at other times it seems wholly brought about by factors external to ourselves, by the things we mind rather than by our own minding of them. It is also not to be confused with the various distinct, outwardly observable manifestations and consequences into which, however, it naturally develops, and with which it has more than a merely adventitious or empirical connection. That I have something much or little in mind, may be of all things the most withdrawn and 'spiritual', the most independent of anything that can be outwardly observed, the most independent, even, of what lies beyond the immediate occasion. I can turn my mind to the state of my knee-cap, or to the posture of things in China, without betraying the precise shift in my regard by as much as the flicker of an eyelid or the quiver of a muscle. But though this is so, my interior state is always felt to have a recognizable *affinity* with states which are manifest and overt, by analogy with which it must, in the first instance, be described and characterized. Though I am not now turning my gaze in the direction of my knee-cap or of affairs in China, and can perhaps not actually do so, it is none the less *as if* I were so turning and adjusting my various sense- and motor-organs, and I therefore naturally speak in terms of metaphorical eye-swivellings and muscular manipulations. It is also *as if* my sense-organs were receiving a better and stronger impression, and I therefore naturally speak in metaphors derived from such sensible strengthening, sometimes aiding my talk by reference to metaphorical lights,

THE BASIC MODES OF CONSCIOUSNESS 51

pressures, etc. We may, in fact, say that we describe our various inner states of 'attending' or 'heeding' in terms of forms of sensory and motor adjustment, only because they represent what we have called 'condensations' or 'telescopings' of the latter, carryings over or projections into an alien medium which none the less preserve much topological analogy. All this does not, of course, mean that, the bridge of analogy having once been forged, it may not be trodden in the reverse direction, and that we may not use the mind's spiritual heed to help illuminate the outward pantomime and results of heeding.

It is evident, therefore, that there will be something appropriate, and in an absolute sense 'natural', in the 'expansion' of an interior act of regard into an outward pantomime of heeding: the turning of the gaze in an actually or symbolically suitable direction, a real or symbolic manual exploration, an increase in the force and accuracy of acts inspired by what we heed and a corresponding decrease in irrevelant activities, the profounder, more lasting effect on the subsequent course of our performance, etc. etc. This external pantomime may not be connected with variations in interior clearness in the tautological manner covered by the term 'logical entailment': it is thinkable, and sometimes is the case, that there should be the clearness without the pantomime and the pantomime without the clearness. But the pantomime is none the less connected with the clearness in an entirely 'internal' manner, one of the countless interlacing *a priori* connections from which no segment of mental life seems free: either is such as intrinsically to favour the other and to find in the other a suitable and likely complement.

If being consciously alive to anything involves, therefore, some position between the twin poles of the consciously clear and obscure, it involves also a position between the twin poles of yet another antithesis, which, following Husserl, we may call that between a *fulfilled* and an *unfulfilled* awareness.[1] Conscious orientations have as their one extreme a state in which that of which they are conscious is fully and concretely present, actually apprehended or 'given': at their other extreme they have a state in which what they are *of* is merely indicated, foreshadowed, vestigially suggested, present merely in a reduced, attenuated or surrogative form. Husserl's metaphor of an 'empty' conscious

[1] See *Logische Untersuchungen*, VI.

52 VALUES AND INTENTIONS

intention to which certain intuitive materials provide the appropriate 'filling', hits the distinction as well as possible. For in both cases we have fundamentally the *same* consciousness, with the same scope and the same range of near or remote application, but in the one case it grasps, as it were, vainly in the void, whereas in the other case it is 'fulfilled' or 'satisfied'. What it is important to stress is that *both* poles of the above antithesis are essential to anything that we should care to call 'consciousness' or 'awareness', and not only both poles, but also a continuous, restless shuttling between them. To be consciously alive to anything is to move constantly, at least in intention or by approximation, towards a pole where *all* that we are conscious of will be adequately displayed, illustrated or envisaged: it is equally a state in which the shown is always surrounded by a great deal that is merely prefigured or foreshadowed. Without some limit of fully realized presence or authentic givenness towards which we at least always aspire, and at which we at least in some partial or fragmented fashion at times arrive, our states of mind could not be said to be really *of* anything, nor could they in consequence merit the designation of 'conscious'. This is true even of our thoughts of the absurd and the infinite, which exist as thoughts only because of the fragmented or approximate fulfilment of which they alone admit, and beyond which they unceasingly and fruitlessly press. Equally well it may be said that the life of the mind would lose its varied conscious direction, its peculiar intention to this or to that, if *all* that it was *of* could be completely and concretely present, without anything for which it might look, and which it might at length find. The movement that we call 'conscious cognition' can exist neither in a plenum nor a void: it presupposes fullnesses that are forever being emptied, and emptinesses that are for ever being filled.

The antithesis we are now studying is not the same as the antithesis of the clear and the obscure, even though the two frequently vary together, and are in their general form inseparable. What is more clearly present to mind is more often than not what is actually exhibited or illustrated, but this need not be the case. It is possible to be maximally mindful of things merely prefigured or indicated, and to have the most richly fulfilled awareness of what one barely minds at all. Nor is it the same as the antithesis between what is directly and what is indirectly or

THE BASIC MODES OF CONSCIOUSNESS 53

discursively apprehended by way of general concepts or notions. My awareness of the notes I have just heard may be as precise and individual and unmediated by generalities as my awareness of the notes I am now hearing, yet it may lack a pictorial 'carrying out'. By contrast, my generalized thought of 'something picturesque' may be well fulfilled by some decayed villa before me, without for that reason becoming less general and discursive. Nor must our antithesis be confounded with the distinction between what is only 'symbolically' present, and what is more 'directly' or non-symbolically given, since experience abounds in empty awarenesses which, while arising in a context of many fulfilled awarenesses, none the less have nothing in the latter which either represents or symbolizes them.

The paradigm case of fulfilment is of course the case of the direct 'presence to sense'. I most definitely fulfil my references to a village green in Essex, or to the contents of the left drawer of my desk, by having the actual objects displayed before me and laid open to visual and other forms of exploration. There is a sense, too, in which sensory fulfilment may be said to be more 'basic' and 'fundamental' than fulfilment of any other sort, inasmuch as the most removed mental orientations all 'point back', perhaps after a large number of intermediate stages, to possible illustration in terms of the deliverances of sense. The least palpable features of our inner experience have a bond, tenuous and analogical, but essential, with what can be sensuously shown, and it is likewise obvious that there must be such bonds even in the case of the most refined abstractions of the natural and the philosophical sciences. The particular form of our 'sensibility' may be an empirical accident, but without something which at least in an analogous manner can fulfil our conscious references, there can be no such thing as 'consciousness' at all.

The 'presence to sense' is further paradigmatic and basic, inasmuch as it plainly provides the foundation for all identifications, for the notion of the *same* thing as the subject of a large number of distinct attributions, and hence, in the last resort, of the very notion of an *object* of thought or perception. For it is plain that it is in some sense possible to satisfy a large number of distinct mental references by means of what may be called the *same* sensory situation: while the impact on our senses remains in some sense unaltered, we can fulfil such varied intentions as those

54 VALUES AND INTENTIONS

of 'something green', 'something smooth', 'a fine piece of lawn', etc. etc. (which may, but need not, be expressed in words). This possibility may be distorted into the notion of a fixed mass of sensory materials upon which varying interpretations are put: it may even be distorted into Moore's strange view of 'sense-data' as in some sense the true logical subjects of all judgements of perception. Such views are unacceptable since the 'materials' common to our various fulfilled sensory awarenesses can as little be isolated from the latter as can Aristotelian prime matter from the four elements: attempts at separation merely substitute a simpler intention for one more complex. However this may be, it is still proper to speak in terms of a genuine sensory *community* among a whole series of fulfilled sensory awarenesses, which makes possible the intersection of several distinct and possibly successive awarenesses in an identical object. Such an intersection may then be 'carried over' into the most abstract regions of discourse, but remains moored to this primary community: it is not for nothing that the word 'sense' applies both in the regions of the sensory and the significant.

But though thus basic and paradigmatic, a 'presence to sense' must not be regarded as the one and only form of fulfilled consciousness. There is a very good sort of fulfilment of one's awareness of this or that by way of mental pictures or images, and also by way of physical pictures, models, simulacra or diagrams. A sufficiently vivid and detailed mental picture might perfectly show what a certain thing would be like, and would demand no further sensory illustration. A diagram or model might likewise illustrate some abstract pattern of relations more clearly than any sensible instance. There are further matters of which one's fulfilled awareness could not take the form of a presence to sense, e.g. the fulfilled consciousness of being happy when one actually *is* happy, or the fulfilled consciousness of an absence when something really *is* absent. Husserl has here shown, with admirable elaboration, how many cases of 'categorial' or 'improper' fulfilment must be set beside the standard case of encountering something in sense-perception. There is, e.g., a fulfilment of a higher-order consciousness that operates mainly by means of words, when an abbreviated symbolic reference, e.g. 8^4, is replaced by another more analysed variant, e.g. $8 \times 8 \times 8 \times 8$.

THE BASIC MODES OF CONSCIOUSNESS 55

The antithesis between a fulfilled and an unfulfilled awareness must, further, be kept apart from the distinction between *actual* and merely *dispositional* awareness, however much sensationally minded philosophers may have been inclined to confuse them. It is true that, when I have an unfulfilled understanding of some general pattern or some verbal meaning, all sorts of appropriate images may be ready to 'crowd in' on me (in the phrase of Hume); I may likewise be ready for many sensory confrontations or active performances. But this readiness for a more fulfilled awareness does not mean that an unfulfilled awareness is in any sense less genuinely an awareness: it may in a sense be more rounded out and perfect because the wide scope of what is intended remains unblurred by irrelevant specifications. There is a whole world of difference between actually grasping a pattern or meaning, even if not carried out illustratively, and being merely *able* to find one's way about it, or to develop it correctly, though the whole life-work of Wittgenstein has been devoted to its obscuration. It must, however, be conceded that the two states shade over into one another, and that it is sometimes impossible to say with accuracy whether some content was actually present to mind, though unillustrated, or if it was merely *ready* to become present. As to the conundrums concerning people who feel that they understand something yet cannot go on appropriately, they may be countered by equally puzzling conundrums of those who always do and say the right thing, yet are never sure of its rightness. Such examples merely show that things which belong together profoundly, do not necessarily always go together in their actual existence, a proposition basic in a philosophy of mind.

We may note, further, that just as the wide range of what we are aware of is chequered over by a constantly changing pattern of conscious clearness and obscurity, so it is also chequered over by a complex, ever-changing pattern of fulfilment and non-fulfilment. This is true even of the immediate situation present to our senses. When we *see* an object before us, there is a more or less clear segment of its features and dimensions of which we enjoy a *fulfilled* consciousness, while there remains a wide range of further features and dimensions of which we have only an *unfulfilled* awareness, a fact which may be the basis of many misleading sense-datum analyses, but which is none the less

VALUES AND INTENTIONS

fundamental for all that. In the same way, the sensory situation before us provides as it were the 'matter', in the sense of the real possibility of fulfilling countless awarenesses which might be, but are not actually, formed. And the life of consciousness consists in continually turning real but empty awarenesses, or the sensory possibilities for such awarenesses, into awarenesses both actual and fulfilled, while the latter continually lapse back into emptiness or into mere possibility. And we may note further that, while of some mental orientations fulfilment may be *perfect*, in the case of others it is necessarily always *imperfect*, as in our ideas of all physical realities.

We may here note, in general, that to recognize a close and necessary connection between unfulfilled conscious approaches and the corresponding fulfilment, is not to hold, with an earlier empiricism, that every unfulfilled notional awareness necessarily has an origin, at least as regards its elementary components, in some wholly fulfilled, empirical awareness. Much less will it commit us to that modern form of empiricism which not only holds that every unfulfilled notional awareness, at the price of having definite content, must necessarily terminate in a thinkable fulfilment, but which even goes further and holds that we must be able to *verify*, or go some distance towards verifying, every assertion involving an unfulfilled awareness. The content of an unfulfilled awareness is in fact, on this view, identified with all the infinitely many circumstances which bear on its verification, an extension which so strains the notion of meaning or significance as to destroy it altogether. As against this type of view, we shall hold, without here troubling to argue it in detail, that there may be many notions or meanings which by their very nature do not admit of exhaustive fulfilment, and assertions involving which even less admit of complete verification, by the individual concerned. The 'no longer' or 'not yet' of past or future time afford a good illustration. But that there are limiting notions incapable of fulfilment is only the case because this is *not* the case in regard to the *main* body of our notions.

We may hold, lastly, that just as there is a not merely empirical or contingent relation between an inner state of conscious clearness and the outer pantomime of attending, so also there is a not merely empirical and contingent relation between the interior distinction of fulfilment and non-fulfilment, and the outer

THE BASIC MODES OF CONSCIOUSNESS   57

distinction between unsurprised and satisfied encounter on the one hand, and the half-fledged adjustment to what is absent on the other. It is by analogy with an actual encounter and its opposite, that our conscious states of fulfilment and non-fulfilment are naturally introduced into discourse, and our interior states of fulfilled and unfulfilled awareness naturally adopt a corresponding pantomime.

We may now claim to have studied two of the ways in which mental orientations may vary without corresponding variation in what they are 'of'. We may thereby claim to have pinned down, at least in preliminary fashion, the elusive figure of 'consciousness'.

(III) THE VARIATIONS OF CONSCIOUS 'LIGHT' OR SENSE

If our consciousness of anything may be distinguished from that *of* which we are conscious by its position relatively to the two pairs of antithetical poles we have mentioned, it may also be distinguished by a third type of variability, boundless in range, which may be called variously a variability in respect of 'conscious light', 'conscious approach', 'conscious intent', etc. etc. This is the sort of variability brought out by asking the somewhat sophisticated question '*As* what are you conscious of whatever thing or set of things or field of things you are conscious of?' The question may be sophisticated, but the kind of datum it is intended to elicit is anything but recondite: such data are alike characteristic of the most commonplacely observational as of the most remotely discursive situation. Obviously it makes a world of difference whether we see what is before us as merely being there, or as being a number of solid material objects, or as consisting of brick houses interspersed with persons, or as being different from what we saw the moment before, or as being likely to collapse on attack, etc. etc. Equally obviously it makes a difference if we merely think of some object or territory of objects as being free from dodos, as being a case of the number 10, as exemplifying parsimony, etc. etc. Such differences are at least to some extent not differences in what we are minding, and are to that extent rightly attributed to our 'consciousness'. The things of which we are aware may in some cases be held to co-operate in, or to provoke, or to justify our being thus or thus

58 VALUES AND INTENTIONS

conscious of them, and we may like to say that they do so on account of corresponding 'features' in themselves. Such talk of 'features' is, however, largely artificial, there being a 'feature' presupposed wherever things can be seen in a given conscious light. It has, however, this amount of justification: that what we are minding is more intimately concerned in the dimension now to be investigated than it was in the two conscious dimensions previously studied.

The range of conscious variability now under examination must be kept apart from the two dimensions previously treated. It is not to be thought of as necessarily bound up with an unfulfilled as opposed to a fulfilled awareness, as in the traditional opposition of the conceptual and the intuitive. For it seems clear, as we saw previously, that an unfulfilled awareness may be of something wholly particular, e.g. the note just heard, without being of it *as* this or *as* that. A fulfilled intention, likewise, may be quite as much an awareness of something *as* being something or other as one that is unfulfilled: we *apply* our notions to the things before us, and we find the things honouring or fulfilling this application.

With equal emphasis we must affirm the independence of the variability of conscious light from the distinction between the consciously clear and obscure. Philosophers have often sought to make differences in conceptual angle differences in *attention*: our minds, it is said, can vary their apprehension of objects by attending now to one of their aspects, now to another, a procedure which, as Frege remarks, makes of attention a highly convenient faculty. They are to this extent right, that our attention *may* be said to shift when we pass from considering shape to considering colour or number, etc. etc. But it may likewise be said to shift when we pass from considering a man's feet to considering his head, and yet the change differs utterly in the two cases. In both cases there may be said to be a shift in clearness, but in the former case it rests on a different shift which we have called a shift in conscious 'light' or 'approach'. It is only because we pass from looking at objects in *one* light to looking at them in another that the focal point of attention can be said to vary. All this can be seemingly evaded by connecting the 'lights' in which objects are viewed with 'aspects' or 'moments' actually present in them: we may, after the fashion of the early

THE BASIC MODES OF CONSCIOUSNESS 59

Moore, equate them with certain of their *parts*. Parts, however, they are not, in any ordinary sense of the word: there is no such part of an object as its being two metres in diameter, or as its being a thing that would reverberate if struck. There is undoubtedly a genuine legitimacy, afterwards to be considered, in erecting such 'sides' or 'aspects' of objects into objects in their own right, but they are not so erected in the ordinary consciousness. It is not, therefore, by some modification in attention, but by some quite different variation in consciousness, that such changes of 'aspect' come about. We may further observe that not only do differences of angle and aspect go together with conscious clearness: they may go together with profound conscious obscurity. The background of what we consider contains much that is a matter of interpretation, of conceptual approach: we may, e.g., be *half*-aware of the likeness of a painting to the paintings of a certain painter or school.

It would be misleading, further, to identify variations in conscious light with anything merely dispositional, though dispositions may be held to 'flow' from such variations, and to enter into any *full* account of their nature, and though we may also recognize imperfect or degenerate cases of them in which there is nothing beyond the dispositional. If something comes before me in a certain light, I am certainly ready to pass over to the thought or picturing of countless other things in the same light, and I am also ready to pass over to the thought or picturing of my object in many other congruous lights, which will complete my general notion of it, and which accord with the sort of object I take it to be. To view X as A is to be ready to view other objects as A, or to view X as having properties complementary to A: in neither case are we dealing with some mere empirical 'law of association', whether by similarity or contiguity, but with tendencies basic to conscious life, and to its capacity to be *of* objects at all. But though thus basic and essential, the tendencies in question presuppose for their full understanding the possibility of conscious lights in some other, non-tendentious sense, even if there are many cases in which they exist unaccompanied by conscious lights in this sense, where we proceed rather *as if* we were viewing matters in a certain light, than actually putting any conscious emphasis on anything. Such routinized cases are best regarded as degenerate instances of fully conscious viewing,

60 VALUES AND INTENTIONS

understandable only because they *sometimes* rise to the latter, and not as rendering the latter redundant for understanding.

Much the same applies to the indefinitely complex dispositional development of 'conscious lights' in external behaviour. To envisage things in this or that light, and to do so in a context involving appropriate wants and beliefs—the desire, e.g. that a thing should *be* as we projectively envisage it, and the belief that it *will* be so if this or that is done—is undoubtedly to be ready to engage in various lines of practical endeavour, and that on grounds not merely contingent or empirical. Through such practical endeavour it may become clear to the outside observer in what light we view the situation and our own part in it. Such interpretation of behaviour is, however, a problem of severe difficulty, since it involves several variables of which conscious approach is only one, and since there is no situation where all variables but conscious approach have such firm values that the last named can be simply determined. In behaviour it is only more or less *as if* one were conscious of something *as* this or *as* that, an ambiguity to which the direct verbal expression of conscious orientation alone provides a clear answer. All this does not of course exclude routinized behaviour unguided by any non-tendentious form of conscious light: it does not even preclude us from saying that such behaviour is in a sense actually so guided. Mental concepts are nothing if not infinitely flexible, extensible and contractible, but in all their change they maintain allegiance to the fully rounded, maximal case rather than to the impoverished, minimal one. This maximal case, however, involves conscious lights in a sense not definable in terms of outer behaviour.

Conscious lights cannot, however, be adequately studied except in terms of the single words or verbal combinations which are felt to be their appropriate expressions. I cannot say *how* something is appearing to my senses, or how it is being approached in my thought, except by making use of the words I would have applied to it, or used to describe it, had such application or description been called for. I must say, e.g., that I am seeing something *as* a series of thin black lines on a green background, or that I am thinking of something as a clash between economic determinism and social idealism, etc. etc. Though verbal expressions are not normally used to talk about conscious lights, and though it is possible to use words appropriately without actually

THE BASIC MODES OF CONSCIOUSNESS 61

viewing anything in a corresponding light, it is none the less possible to use words in a peculiar *reflex* manner to refer to the conscious lights that *may* accompany their use (i.e. in what the Middle Ages called *suppositio simplex*), and there would not in fact seem to be any *other* than this peculiar reflex manner in which they may successfully be 'pinned down'. This reflex use of words may be compared to the abnormal reflex use of a telescope, not to give us information about the heavenly bodies, but to reveal the limitations and peculiarities of its own field of view.

When we use words ordinarily, we may be viewing objects in certain lights, but we do not concern ourselves with the lights in which we view them. Our concern is with our object as such, and we accordingly go on to supplement each one-sided approach with countless other similar approaches, all of which may be said to intersect in, and to illuminate, an identical object. If we have seen and described something as consisting of a set of thin black lines on a green ground, we may go on to seeing and describing it as consisting of lines about an inch apart, etc. etc. Our conscious attitude is thus essentially *open* and incomplete. But if we are using the words 'a series of thin black lines, etc.', to stand for the light in which an object is viewed, we are not free to supplement it in this manner: we must live in one conscious pose exclusively, it must become frozen, closed, complete. (Perhaps this is what Hegel meant when he spoke of the abstract Understanding as freezing, fixing and cutting adrift the fluid concepts of ordinary thought.) Words used in this fixed, frozen manner are functioning much as they also function when used to state the *sense* of other expressions, as when we say that the expression *le maître d'Alexandre* means the teacher of Alexander. Here the English phrase 'the teacher of Alexander' does not function as it normally does: we cannot, e.g., replace it or supplement it by the name 'Aristotle', or by the phrase 'the pupil of Plato'. As stating the sense of the French expression it in effect states its own sense, and as so functioning it ceases to be capable of the substitutions and supplementations of which it is normally capable.

It may in fact be argued that the meaning of a set of words, in at least one widely used sense of 'meaning', that which coincides with the sense given to the word *Sinn* (sense) by Frege, is no other than the conscious light in which users regard objects

62 VALUES AND INTENTIONS

when they employ such words. Frege's celebrated studies of Sense (*Sinn*) and Reference (*Bedeutung*) are on this view fundamental contributions to mental philosophy as well as to the study of language. A conscious light, like a word, is universal or general, and so naturally extends itself to a wide range of cases: the 'light' may in fact be said to condense and 'telescope' the whole use of the word. In studying the sense of an expression, we may therefore be said, in quite traditional fashion, to be studying the thoughts, the conscious lights of those who make use of it. This does not mean, as remarked previously, that everyone who employs words necessarily views matters in a peculiar light: there may be no more to his utterance than a mere utterance. One of the blessed advantages of words is precisely that they are economical of consciousness, that they achieve the effect of seeing things in certain lights without seeing them in any light at all. A correct use of words can, however, only derive its unity from the fact that the person who employs them is *at times* capable of regarding things in an appropriate conscious light, and it is only as held together by such a facultative light that a whole range of usage becomes understandable. In a conscious light we in a sense cross our bridges before we reach them, and we in a sense really have a 'reservoir' from which the details of usage 'flow'.

Since our conscious lights must be spoken of by a reflex use of linguistic expressions, there is undoubtedly great artificiality in speaking about conscious lights in the case of those who are not speaking, or who are perhaps not capable of speech at all. This artificiality is at a minimum where we are dealing with a mature human adult, who might find words to fit the ways in which he is regarding things, even if he does not happen to be finding them at the time. It is much more artificial to attribute such a conscious light to an infant or an animal. Here as elsewhere, however, the fact that certain extrapolations involve inadequate data or instruments, does not mean that they should not be made at all. However small their significance for science, they may remain significant for philosophy.

It is plain, further, that the use of verbal expressions not only enables us to refer to our conscious lights, but that it also, in almost all complex cases, enables us to *have* them. The use of verbal expressions is therefore an ineliminable element in the advanced life of consciousness. For it is by the use of such

THE BASIC MODES OF CONSCIOUSNESS 63

expressions that the shifting lights in which we regard things acquire something of the same fixity as the things we regard in them, and can be summoned up, referred to and manipulated at will. The use of verbal expressions further enables us to express the precise scope of our conscious states, and thereby not only renders them accessible to our references, but also, through their manifold internal relations to the things of a common world, to the references of others. More than all this, however, the use of verbal expressions enables us to 'seal off', and to erect into quasi-objects, the precise zone, feature or segment of objects which can be thought of as lit up by a given conscious light. We saw before that we could use verbal expressions reflexly to express the particular conscious light implied by their use, but we can also, after a fashion, *project* this light outwards, by which device we come to have before us the mere abstracts or schemata or maps of possible objects, or objects *as* caught in a particular ray of thought. This is what we do when we think abstractly of the *property* corresponding to the expression ' . . . is blue', the proposition expressed by the phrase '*A* being to the left of *B*', etc. etc. Such entities of reason enjoy an 'intentional inexistence' inasmuch as there are certain verbally inspired, artificially frozen conscious approaches which remain within their limits, and resist supplementation by their normal complements. Such an 'intentional inexistence', and the verbal usages which go with it, may be productive of philosophical confusion, but they remain important as enabling us to apprehend clearly, and state succinctly, what would otherwise require an intolerably complex apparatus of 'in so far ases' and adverbial qualifications. The use of words further enters, not only into the knowledge, but into the being of consciousness, inasmuch as our awareness of many things is an awareness mediated by many layers of words. The scope of our thoughts is often more immediately given by exchanging them for other verbalized thoughts, than by exchanging them for the smaller coin of actions and situations. Many a thought merely telescopes and concentrates words, rather than the remoter things and performances that would justify the use of such words.

If we now ask to what extent variations in verbal form correspond to possible variations in the conscious lights in which things are regarded, the right answer would appear to lie rather in admitting as many as, or more variations in conscious light

64 VALUES AND INTENTIONS

than are suggested by our words, than in holding them to be fewer. Philosophical tradition has made much play with the notion of 'merely grammatical differences' which do not correspond to 'real differences in thought'. The analogy is that of puffed and exaggerated court-fashions masking the uniform facts of human anatomy, whereas the analogy should arguably be that of a number of stock sizes and shapes which do not always accord with anatomical variety. There are plainly many 'real differences in thought' which correspond to no grammatical variations, but are indicated by context, stress, pausation, etc. etc. The attempt to iron out all these subtler differences stems largely from the corrupting influence of logic, the desire to stress only those features of our thought-approaches which are important in deductive inference. Because we can draw precisely the same conclusions from p doubly denied as from p alone, there is a temptation to deny a difference in thought in the two cases, to hold we have an identical meaning dressed in different verbal forms. This mode of speech, with its pretended deference for logic, is in the end destructive of logic itself, since logical connections only signify anything as long as there are intrinsically *different* modes of conscious approach and expression which can be legitimately equated or interchanged. When all logical principles say the same thing, and that nothing, logic has plainly committed *felo de se*. It is only because thoughts differ in their conscious approach, that it is worth saying that they *must* agree in their application. We may hold in fact that each difference of verbal stress registers a difference in meaning, that '*James* murdered John' expresses something different from 'James *murdered* John'. Even the mere fact that we employ different expressions to express an identical content, will soon succeed in making their meanings distinct, since a reference to the words themselves will creep into their sense. The thought of a botanically classified antirrhinum is not the same as the thought of a homely snapdragon. All this does not mean that we may not regard expressions as synonymous in all contexts where difference of thought-approach may conveniently be ignored.

We may accordingly hold, without going into vast detail, that there are at least as many types of conscious approach as there are distinct sentence-forms, and that most of these, as Husserl has wonderfully shown in his *Erfahrung und Urteil*, can plausibly

THE BASIC MODES OF CONSCIOUSNESS 65

be held to be exemplified in 'pre-predicative', i.e. non-verbalized experience. There will be conscious approaches to what is immediately present, of which the simplest is probably the mere acknowledgement of particular existence ('There's this') which finds no place in Russellian logic. There will also be more elaborate sort- or character- or relation-attributive awarenesses, or individually recognitive awarenesses of different sorts ('That's a man', 'That's James', 'That's bigger than that', etc. etc.). On such awarenesses may be built such consciousnesses as those of a negation or a conjunction, the former at first where some intention is disappointed by the situation offered to sense, and where the mind engineers a conceptual advance out of the very stuff of its defeat, the latter in situations where two intentions find satisfaction in one and the same sense-encounter, a situation which may also in certain circumstances mediate a consciousness of *identity*. There will also obviously be, even in the most primitive experience, awarenesses of things as like or unlike, or as merely diverse, or as indefinitely or more definitely numerous. And we need not hesitate to admit, even in the most primitive experience, those consciousnesses of the 'not yet' and the 'no longer' of which tenses and time-concepts are an elaborate development, as well as rudimentary 'mays', 'musts', 'woulds', 'coulds' and 'likelies' which can be crystallized into the clear concepts of a modal logic. Fashionable timidity may utter warnings as to the inadmissibility of bringing in 'pre-existent meanings' prior to the organized usages of speech, and may content itself with an external, naturalistic account of the way in which such usages are taught: in so doing it ignores the mind's capacity to concentrate and dissolve multitude in unity in a variety of ways, which certainly antedates the learning of words, and through which alone the learning of words is made possible. To use the word 'after' when something has happened is not, we may say, to understand 'afterness', unless the precise sense of the word can be present to and 'savoured' by the mind, and this it may be *before* the word has been learnt at all.

We must also plainly admit, even in quite elementary experience, those forms of *general* awareness expressible by means of such quantifying expressions as 'some', 'something', 'somewhat', 'there are', etc. etc. Even without words we can experience a desire, and therefore a conscious intention, directed to *a* stream

C

66 VALUES AND INTENTIONS

that will slake our thirst. The universal approaches, which represent the negations of our ordinary general awarenesses, and which exploit such words as 'any', 'all', etc., probably require the aid of verbal symbols to fix them: it is only by formulating them verbally that we can come to have them. Without speech one might think thoughts of limited, but certainly not of unlimited, universality. The same certainly applies to higher order approaches involving 'entities of reason', as well as almost all our thought about the interior life of the mind. Only one, e.g., who can employ the adjective 'blue', and can artificially limit its sense to its precise coverage, leaving it open to no normal supplementation, can come to make reference to the mental concept, and to the property, of blueness, and to view this concept and this property in various higher-order 'lights'.

The edifice of our conscious approaches therefore rises, in steady gradations, from 'lights' that do not require words at all, to 'lights' that could not exist without the fixing power of words, and then on to 'lights' that are essentially verbal (even if pointing back to others of a non-verbal character), 'lights' in which we see things and situations primarily as requiring us to *say* this or that, rather than as *being* this or that. The whole structure of approaches, with its ascent from non-verbal to verbal storeys, and with its endless proliferation at the top is, however, more a theme for painstaking, detailed examination of the sort in which Husserl was so uniquely skilled, than for dogmatic, overall pronouncement. We cannot pursue the topic further here.

We may conclude this section by observing that, just as it is essential to being consciously alive that there should be constant *change* in the clearness and obscurity, and in the fulfilled or unfulfilled character of our awareness, so too it is essential to conscious aliveness that we should continually vary the 'light' in which we view objects. To regard things continuously from one unvarying angle, must as obviously be a quick road to total unconsciousness as to seek to regard them from no angle at all.

(IV) THE REFLEXIVE AND PROJECTIVE MODES OF CONSCIOUSNESS

After the three sorts of conscious variability we have dealt with we may now briefly deal with what is practically a fourth: that

THE BASIC MODES OF CONSCIOUSNESS 67

of the 'ecstatic', outward turned, object-absorbed direction, on the one hand, and of the reflexive, self-directed, inward-turned awareness on the other. This, though perhaps strictly a difference in the *object* of our awareness, is yet so fundamental and so peculiar, as also legitimately to be made part of its manner. Obviously, as the above sections witness, it is not only possible for there to *be* variations in the manner of our consciousness— clear, obscure, fulfilled, unfulfilled, infinitely various as to 'approach'—it is also possible for these differences to become *apparent*, and to be specifically marked down and commented upon.

This presence of consciousness to consciousness must not, however, be thought of as something that always *must* occur, as being part and parcel of our being conscious at all. A reflex illumination so universal would really be a redundancy: it is only because we can be so deeply *unaware* of the forms of our conscious life that we can also become significantly alive to them. And it would obviously involve, as has been demonstrated to weariness, either a vicious circularity or an incredible infinity. Equally well, however, we must not regard the reflexiveness we have mentioned as something rare and adventitious, a difficult contortion performed only by the sophisticated, and comparable to biting one's posterior or swallowing one's toes. To conceive it thus is to make its existence as dubious as it is in fact indubitable and of most frequent occurrence, our whole experience being an oscillation between states in which things other than our consciousness are made principally apparent, and states in which the *way* in which we are conscious of these acquires emphasis. The capacity for this sort of transformation must, if it exists at all, be present not only in our sophisticated, but also in our most ordinary frames of mind. We must, e.g., have as clear a conscious commerce with conscious clearness and obscurity as we have with the objects that are given in these ways. And the capacity to switch from an 'ecstatic' to a reflexive pose of consciousness must be so easy and natural, as to be plausibly listed among the definitory properties of consciousness, as it has been by many philosophers.

That such reflexiveness really does enter into quite ordinary states of mind can be seen if we consider the many definite experiences that can only be described as experiences *of* a relation between experiences. Thus to experience surprise or shock is

68   VALUES AND INTENTIONS

not merely to *be* surprised, not merely to pass from one bodily state or frame of mind to another, which suddenly disrupts the first: it is to have an experience of, to be aware of, the sudden shocking transition between the two experiences. It involves, that is, the awareness of an experiential transition, and is not merely a transition among experiences. The same is the case when we have the consciousness *of* spontaneous ease and naturalness in the sequence of our experiences, and the opposed experience of having certain experiences *forced* on us from without. The same holds of the experience *of* being interested in or absorbed by some object, which is not the same as, and does not always coincide with, the actual state of being absorbedly interested, in which there may be too much absorption for the absorption itself to be revealed. Paradoxically, one must not be too absolutely absorbed if one is to have the *experience* of absorption. And it holds, above all, of the crucially important experience *of* satisfaction, which is quite distinct from having a satisfying experience. Absorbing experiences arising out of mental and bodily activity may be satisfying experiences, they may appease deep bodily and conscious trends, without being for that reason experiences *of* satisfaction. It is generally only in our more reposeful states of mind that their satisfying character is itself evident. Rudimentary reflexive awarenesses of the sorts just mentioned may quite rationally be attributed to animals. A cat purring peacefully before the fire may enjoy the reflexive consciousness of being appeased, and some of its sex-experiences may likewise have a reflexive as well as a first-order character.

The reflexiveness of consciousness is, of course, something that cannot be indefinitely reiterated: it is doubtful, in fact, whether it can ever be carried beyond the second stage. The presence to mind of X may be itself present to mind, and so perhaps may be the presence of this presence: of the higher stages of the hierarchy we can have at best an unfulfilled awareness, as of something possibly enjoyable by beings with a more finely divisible awareness than our own. There is necessarily, in such reflexive situations, a *last* presence to mind which is not itself further present to mind. The further question, as to whether the presence of something to mind can be present to a *simultaneous* awareness, or only present to a later, *retrospective* consciousness, is plainly detailed and empirical: sometimes the consciousness of a consciousness will

THE BASIC MODES OF CONSCIOUSNESS 69

accompany that consciousness, as where we are conscious of our relaxed enjoyment of a bath, more often it will be necessary for such a consciousness to come *after*. States of mind which absorb us fully can be brought to mind only in immediate retrospect: states of mind which leave our energies largely undrained can be appreciated as they pass. All this can only seem surprising to those unpractised in systematic reflection on the manner and scope of their consciousness—its points of clearness and obscurity, its empty understandings and imaginally fulfilled references—and who have not realized what firm and readily communicable results are to be achieved by such means. Only the perverse requirement that the language of natural reflection should be transformed into some queer analogue of our talk about physical objects can explain why our talk about our own minds should ever have been thought puzzling.

The fulfilled consciousness of a state of consciousness has been frequently spoken of under a metaphor of sensory confrontation: our states of mind are present to 'inner sense'. This metaphor is only usable if its metaphorical character is confessed. That my just past clear awareness of X illustrates, realizes my thought of such a clear awareness is a situation analogous to the one in which the presence of X to my senses illustrates, realizes my thought of X. To that extent talk of a sense has good analogical foundation. In other respects, however, there is a profound lack of analogy. For it is my being *actually* aware of X, rather than my being as it were sensationally affected by this awareness, which fulfils my awareness of such an awareness, and it is clear, further, that the possibility of my misconstruing this fulfilment or of my seeing it in a wrong light—though this cannot be entirely discounted—is not as it is in the case of sense-perception. I may correct my first impression as to the clarity, sensuous detail and precise 'angle' of some just past experience, but such correction falls within comparatively narrow limits.

The presence of one's own awareness to mind has, further, its appropriate behavioural analogue in those slow, self-savouring, self-inhibiting activities to which it is natural to give the name 'self-conscious'. It is in terms of these that our self-awareness tends to be described, and it is into these that it naturally expands. There is more than a merely adventitious connection between activities over-scrupulously or luxuriously performed and the

70 VALUES AND INTENTIONS

form of self-interference known as conscious reflection. In either case there is the difficulty of sustaining an activity while trying, with a more passive adjustment, to 'take it in'.

We may note, finally, that there is much reflection concerned, not with the immediate pose of a man's conscious life, but with his long-term motives, virtues, beliefs, tendencies, etc.: this is not the reflexive awareness we have been considering, though it is to this rather than the reflection considered by us that the philosophically misused term 'introspection' is appropriate. There are also many betrayals of orientation and attitude—sometimes verbally couched in reflexive language—which none the less do not express the presence of anything genuinely reflex. To say 'I think', 'I hope', 'I see', etc., is in countless cases *not* to betray the presence of consciousness to consciousness. The same will be found to apply to our 'practical knowledge' of what we are doing or trying to do: our knowledge of the direction in which our conscious or bodily performance is *tending* is reflexive in a quite different manner from our knowledge of *conscious* direction, what our state of mind is *of*. It is, however, in virtue of their arrangement in a series whose limit is the explicit presence of consciousness to consciousness that all these cases can be spoken of as reflexive, as the inward turning of the mind upon itself.

We may now maintain, with considerably more openness to question, that just as we may reasonably make it 'of the essence' of conscious experience to shuttle continually from an 'ecstatic', outward turned pose to one that is inward turned and reflexive, so too we may reasonably make it 'of the essence' of conscious experience to tend repeatedly to 'project' the findings of its inward turned researches 'outwards', to surround itself, in short, with a supporting circle of 'other minds'. To be aware of objects *as* objects of consciousness, as we always are in reflection, may be held to lead, by a logic real because not based on formal entailments, to the thought of the possible presence of such objects to other possible conscious intentions, which are not to be found among those we now execute, and hence to the thought of other possible consciousnesses themselves. What other consciousnesses there may be, and what precise frames of mind they may be in, can be suggested only by experience, but in being conscious of anything we are, on this view, implicitly conscious of it as being a

THE BASIC MODES OF CONSCIOUSNESS 71

possible object of other possible minds and states of mind. We sit, as it were, in a theatre with a stage always before us, even if it is not clear what drama will be played on it: we sit likewise in an auditorium, surrounded with *places* for countless other spectators and hearers, though it is not clear who, if anyone, will occupy them. Kant held that space always hung like some empty screen before the perceiving mind on to which experience projected its detailed contents: he might with as much justice have believed in a *space of persons* into which actual social intercourse breathes detailed life and content.

To accept such a space of persons as a dimension into which conscious life naturally extends itself, is by no means the wildly *a priori* fantasy it might appear to be. It involves little more than holding that the mind which reflects on its own awareness of an object, is thereby made ready to think of countless other appearances of or references to the same object, differing in their occasion and their manner, and this seems plainly implied (even if not narrowly entailed) by the very notions of consciousness and its object. For an object is nothing if not a focus of coincidence of countless possible rays of mental reference, many of which will not be among those that are here and now being executed. The profound puzzle of the situation lies, however, in the fact that the consciousnesses that we postulate in conceiving of other minds are not mere imagined *possibilities* of consciousness, but consciousnesses accepted as *actual*, and that they are also thought of as consciousnesses *not* to be had together with those here and now executed, of which there is a direct reflex awareness. They can be emptily thought of or intended, but not had or taken note of, and yet, from another point of view, it is taken to be the case that they are indeed had and taken note of. The convenient words 'our own' and 'someone else's' throw a plausible gloss over a deeply difficult situation, where it is not only unclear how we would or could come to know that *someone else* is in some way conscious of something, but in what the mentioned situation could consist. For it involves the paradox of something actually had, that is also not had, and something present that is also not present, without any seizable distinction to tone down this contradiction.

The situation is, however, simpler than philosophical obfuscation, in love with its own beautiful difficulty, might lead one to suppose. For the notion of a *foreign* ownership of a mental

72   VALUES AND INTENTIONS

orientation is no more than a special case of the disjunction, the negation of togetherness, well known to us in the case of experiences separated in time which, however much thought of or remembered together, are yet not thought of *as* having been themselves together, as having been components of a single embracing experience. Whereas the states of mind that are synchronous and spanned by a single reflex regard, are all patently united and intimately fused, so as to resemble rather a set of qualities manifested in a single place than the separateness of those manifested at long distances. To conceive of a state of mind as *not* being my own, is to conceive of it merely as being disjoined from, *not* together with *these* experiences, whose mutual togetherness is in every way so manifest. And to conceive of a plurality of minds is to conceive merely of sets of mutually conjoined experiences each of which sets is *disjoined* from other similar sets of mutually conjoined experiences. This purely negative disjunction of minds carries with it the support of the much more positive, showable disjunction of bodies in space, since it is to living bodies more or less widely disjoined in space that disjoined minds actually are (and probably only fruitfully can be) attributed. And it also carries with it the support, not only of many empirical arguments from analogy, but also of relations of 'logical completion' between the situations and responses which are the natural 'expansions' of certain interior postures, and the interior postures which 'condense' the former.

All this support would, however, be without weight and vain were the notion of a disjoined subjectivity without any *prior* foundation or legitimation, a legitimation which it can obviously *not* derive from concrete illustration, since such illustration would contradict the very notion of disjoined experiences. The difficulty may be surmounted, as so often in philosophy, by disputing the whole approach that makes it seem difficult, by holding that just this unillustrable contrast is *required* in all reflex experience, in which certain conjoined, reflexly noted experiences stand in a necessary contrast to other not reflexly noted, emptily intended experiences disjoined from themselves. If it be held that the conceived contrast is nugatory, since it can plainly have no illustration nor direct verification, then the fact that it is *not* nugatory puts an end to the contention that illustration or direct verification are essential to significance. We are after all more

THE BASIC MODES OF CONSCIOUSNESS 73

sure of the substantial character of the contrast under examination than we are of any analysis of meaning thought up in post-1918 Vienna. The unillustrable character of the contrast between disjoined mental states is plainly no result of internal contradiction: it is a perfectly understood consequence of a contrast we perfectly understand. And being thus understood, it may provide the pegs on which to hang all those inferences, constructions, divinations, those exercises of empathy and sympathy, on which psychologists and philosophers have dwelt so elaborately, and which help only to explain the detail, not to illuminate the foundation of our consciousness of other minds.

If we hold that, in the reflex consciousness of an object *as* an object of consciousness, the thought of other possibly disjoined consciousness of the same object is implicit, we must hold too that, for the reflex consciousness in question, the objective is necessarily the public, that it is objective not only for *me* but also for *us*. This is true obviously of public objects *par excellence*, the things and doings of the physical world, on to which, as on to some busy central square, the windows of the senses are perpetually thought to open. It is true likewise of the various abstract quasi-objects which correspond to the scope of our conceptual approaches, and which are given hardness of outline by a special reflex use of words: these too are thought of as objects of a common regard to all who have been trained in the use of the same words. But it is thought to be true also of the most recondite details of the inner life. For these too are thought of as tied to the world of our common references by links of inner fittingness and analogy, so that there can be none of them which is *intrinsically*—not accidentally—a private datum. The one thing strictly incommunicable among disjoined minds is thought to be the *particularity* of their conscious references: what is 'this experience' for one can only be 'such and such an experience' for another. Even this limitation could be overcome could the disjoined experiences be brought together in unity, a supposition not at all absurd, but which would unfortunately abolish the distinction of minds which poses the problem. To *be* someone else is not to know someone *else*. And we may observe, lastly, that even within the close-knit unity of the single person there are voices for and voices against, memories and observations that testify in one direction and others testifying in another. We must not regard this inner

c*

74 VALUES AND INTENTIONS

multiplication of voices as the mere introjection of our social relations with others: these social relations could with as much justice be regarded as a mere projection of our own inner diversities. Other persons are, in fact, a supreme convenience since they give hardness and body to the interior society that we carry about with us, and that we each intrinsically are.

We may maintain, lastly, that not only is our reflex awareness of states of mind implicitly an awareness of them as disjoined from other possible states of mind, but that it is also implicitly an awareness of them as having possible extensions beyond the present occasion, as at least requiring a continuation by means of other states of mind which each prospectively or retrospectively acknowledges, and as themselves capable of being commented on and illuminated from *their* standpoint. Descartes may have been wrong in assuming that he *knew* of the existence of a perduring thinker who would outlive the passing thought: he was not wrong in holding that he knew of the existence of a life of thought intrinsically *capable* of outliving the present idea, and continuing into the future and the past. For the passing thought, being the thought of an *object*, and itself the object of a reflex awareness, must appear to the latter as having countless facultative couplings which will link it to many other possible awarenesses, by which its *theme* may be further developed and its object more fully given. It will also appear to the latter as having many facultative couplings with possible bodily manifestations which would 'express' it appropriately. In all these cases experience may fill in the detail, but the general pattern is part of the 'form' of consciousness. Our reflex awareness is always of a fragmentary *excerpt* of a personal conscious life, whose extension in past or future time, or into physical being, is a matter for further thought or inquiry.

(v) THE ESSENTIAL 'DRIFTS' OF CONSCIOUSNESS

We shall in the present section develop a theme touched on in much of the foregoing treatment: that a conscious orientation has not merely what we may call an explicit scope, which comes out when we inquire what the words used to express it precisely *mean*, but that it also has what may be called an *implicit scope* which spreads out widely, perhaps indefinitely, beyond these limits. And this implicit scope is to be understood in terms of

THE BASIC MODES OF CONSCIOUSNESS 75

origin and *tendency*, particularly the latter: it includes the scope of the orientations out of which an orientation has arisen, and to which, as its relevant context, it may be said to look back, and it also includes the scope of the orientations into which, for some motive or other, it is ready to pass over, which would develop or carry it farther. This latter category really includes the former, since the background out of which an orientation arises is also one to which it tends to recur. If I conceive of something as green, the explicit scope of my thought is certainly of the narrowest, but its implicit scope includes the exclusion of other colours, the possession of other properties besides colour, a resemblance or non-resemblance to many objects, the being thought of as green by me and possibly so thought of by others, etc. etc. There are, it is plain, a large number of directions in which my thought may relevantly develop, some following up logical entailments, some pursuing logical tracks of less stringency, some tracks in which the logical and the empirical are combined, and perhaps a few following tracks beaten out purely by experience, the last being rather an unreachable limit than the normal case.

These varying directions of relevant development constitute a sort of sidelong intentionality additional to the straightforward: our states of mind are not only of this or that directly, but also of many things *implicitly* or *indirectly*. Of this we are sometimes aware reflexively: we may *feel* how our thought presses on beyond the bounds of what it principally illuminates. But since, for the most part, we neither feel nor know how our mind puts forth its 'cognitive energies', we judge of this sidelong intentionality only through its outcome, from the things and aspects that it brings to light. The mind's sidelong intentionality is accordingly readily ignored, and whole philosophies have been built on this ignoring: the abstract psychological atomisms which build experience out of self-complete, externally related sense-contents, and the logical atomisms which exclude from a notion whatever is not *entailed* by its application. Such an ignoring may, however, be gravely disastrous, since on *some* of the directions along which our thoughts tend to develop, depends their whole character as conscious intentions, and their power to be *of* any object at all. A conscious orientation self-enclosed in its own blinkered field of regard, without a tendency to look forth in countless directions is, in fact, an unthinkable absurdity. It will

76 VALUES AND INTENTIONS

therefore be by showing that certain sorts of *coupling* among our awarenesses, certain 'hooks' which fasten them on to other completing awarenesses, are both necessary to their character as awarenesses, and to their direction to objects, that we may hope to gain light on the implicit ideals and standards which shape our endeavours on the plane of thought, and whose analogues will be shown to shape our endeavours on all planes of conscious life. It is to the task of distinguishing and describing what may be called the essential *nisus* of our conscious life that we accordingly address ourselves. Much that we shall say will be commonplace, though not so for philosophers: the philosophical treatment to which we shall have most kinship will be to Kant's treatment in the *Transcendental Deduction*.

We have emphasized in our previous treatment the tendency towards *variation* in mode and content which is essential to all consciousness. To be consciously alive to things means to be alive to them *changingly*, and to be confronted quite steadily by something itself unchanging must of necessity induce a swoon. Hence new items must be for ever coming into view, new sensory situations must be forever suggesting interpretations, the obscure must be becoming the clear, and the clear the obscure, the emptily foreshadowed becoming the fulfilled perception and *vice versa*, and the 'angles' from which things display themselves must be perpetually changing. To be conscious is, however, not merely to vary, but also in some measure to continue to live less energetically in at least *some* of the orientations through which one has just passed, and to be ready to relive others, so that the objects and aspects given in such phases are as it were *together* with, and form an enriching background to what is now clearly present. Consciousness necessarily has the *synthetic* character predicated of it by Kant, and the result of such synthesis must at least be a tendency towards an *enriched* conscious field. We may be said (metaphorically) to expect such an enrichment as we look towards our future, and to enjoy its realization as we sum up our past. It may be unfashionable to believe in progress, but progress is in an elementary sense *logically inevitable* wherever consciousness works without impediment. That the obliterating touch of forgetfulness may at times leave us as unenriched by what we have been through as we are unenriched by what we have yet to experience, makes no difference. Past experience remains such as

THE BASIC MODES OF CONSCIOUSNESS 77

to enrich, even if on a given occasion it may fail to do so. This is not learnt from experience: in default of it nothing could be learnt from experience, nor could there be experience to learn from.

With the enriching synthesis of conscious experience there must always go, it is plain, a *nisus* towards *comparing* the new with the old, and with this a further *nisus* towards becoming clearly conscious of likenesses and differences and of countless other *relations*. What relations are thus elicited will obviously depend as much on what things are brought singly to mind, and in what character they are brought to mind, as on the summing up which brings out their relations: those idealists were therefore plainly wrong who made relations the mere work of the mind, but not so wrong as those who denied that work to be necessary for their apprehension. Consciousness is such as to view what it views *together*, and when things are thus viewed together, their relations necessarily make their presence plain. And some such relations will undoubtedly have a superior obviousness to consciousness which is not a matter of habit, or attitude, or actual mental constitution, nor founded on any vagaries of linguistic usage. Thus the relation of being opposed in colour, or of being exactly equal in size, are in some sense *absolutely* obvious, and absolutely more so than the relations of being next but three, or of being greater only when above. And with this tendency to elicit relations there will also necessarily go a tendency to bring out *wholes* of various sorts, some obvious and natural, others far-fetched and arbitrary, some presented as prior unities out of which elements and relations must be carved, while others must be more or less elaborately pieced together by consciousness. It is not so important to distinguish all these cases as to be clear that they *are* numerous and different.

If conscious experience thus involves a *nisus* towards the eliciting of relations, we may with the same justice recognize in it a *nisus* towards the *eliciting* and ever sharper *distinction of parts and aspects*. To be aware of anything is, as we saw, to be aware of it *as* something or other; the life of consciousness, like that of journalism, involves a perpetual quest for 'angles', and, if one may so put it, an endeavour to make these *more* angular. To draw ever finer and more numerous distinctions, and to remove all vagueness and borderline overlap from among them, is merely to carry farther a process essential to consciousness, it

78   VALUES AND INTENTIONS

is merely to be *more* conscious in a certain direction. And that being conscious at least involves a *nisus* towards being ever *more* conscious in every possible direction is a proposition that pleads powerfully for acceptance. The formal laws of Contradiction and Excluded Middle, with their extreme sharpening of the ordinary notion of negation, so as to effect precise dichotomies in every field, which can be further dichotomized without end, certainly formulate an ideal towards which all conscious life is committed, even if it at times pursues conflicting ideals as well. This endeavour we satisfy also by reifying or hypostatizing 'entities of reason': it is the *nisus* towards one-sided angularity which leads us to 'cut off' each conscious light or angle from its normal supplementation by countless other lights or angles, and to make these mutilated fragments, enjoying no more than an intentional or semantic inexistence, the subjects of many higher-order predications. These remarkable hypostatizations, capable of an indefinite hierarchical extension, are in no sense a diseased growth upon the body of thought and discourse, but the mere carrying farther of a tendency essential to conscious life.

We may say, further, that, if consciousness has a 'rooted' tendency to dirempt things into 'aspects', it may equally well be held to have a rooted tendency to undo this diremption, to put the dirempted aspects together so as to reconstitute what can be properly called a *thing*: it is in fact only as having this tendency that it can be said to be *of* objects at all. The precise manner of this putting or fitting together will of course differ vastly from object to object, and will involve such things as the further extension of space and time, the synthesis of quality with position, the synthesis of perspective with perspective, etc. etc. Much in such syntheses stems simply from empirical confrontation, though *how* much is a matter for detailed research in each case. We cannot therefore attempt to discuss fully how the aspects of objects cohere together in each specific case, nor how we learn of their characteristic form of coherence. As Aristotle says, the bond constitutive of 'substance' or specific essence may be vastly various: it may be one of place, time, common origin, even merely of nails and glue. What it is important to stress here is the all-pervasive work of *analogy*. If consciousness, by virtue of what it is, has a tendency to live pointedly in distinct aspects, it will also have a tendency, by virtue of what it is, to pass over to things in

THE BASIC MODES OF CONSCIOUSNESS 79

which like aspects can be distinguished, and which count, from its special angle, as 'the same'. To see things in a given conscious light is to be implicitly ready for items which, though different, can, with perhaps some shift of light, be regarded as 'more of the same'. This tendency inspires the humblest interpolations and extrapolations of ordinary perception, but it is present also in the most advanced inductions and constructions of science. We may here take up the point so greatly emphasized by Kant, that without some measure of 'rule', of recognizable and repeated (if sometimes complex) analogy and affinity among the items distinguishable in our experience, there could be no such thing as an object of consciousness and hence no such thing as consciousness at all. For to be conscious is to have some *subject-matter* or *theme* before one in which many distinct references may intersect, which can be carried farther, which is undetermined in ways that can be determined further, etc. etc.; where there is absolutely no possibility of such analogical extension there can be nothing that corresponds to such a subject-matter or theme. And, while much inconsequence in the items of which one is conscious is both permissible and essential, consciousness will obviously have *less* and *less* of an object the more tenuous the links of analogy connecting its various successively presented aspects become, until, when they cease to be discernible, it will have no object at all. It was not merely a *verbal* decision which determined Kant to deny the name of 'experience' to a mere 'rhapsody of impressions', as if such a rhapsody might well exist though beneath the level of Kantian notice. It is plain that the term 'rhapsody of impressions' names a limit at which consciousness would have to lapse, since there would be nothing for it to describe, no subject-matter for it to refer to, and no 'angle' from which it might even momentarily view it, no possible consciousness even of confusion. All this has been thoroughly explored by Plato in the early part of the *Theaetetus*. Kant was of course deeply wrong in making the regularity necessary for an object of consciousness the highly specific regularity necessary for an object of Newtonian physics.

The 'reconstitutive' tendency of consciousness shows itself, further, in the manifest *incompleteness* of the varying aspects in which it views its objects, and in their consequent manifest need for supplementation by further aspects. This incompleteness we admit readily in the case of an unfulfilled notion, but the whole

80 VALUES AND INTENTIONS

modern treatment of 'sense-data' involves setting it aside in the case of what is present to sense and introduces physical things. For sense-data are conceived as completed entities, not fragmentary abstracts from these, and as accordingly requiring other sense-data only through the adventitious bonds of custom. Whereas the 'sense-datum' corresponding to the sofa before me, if it is to mean anything discriminable, means the sofa *in so far as*, and precisely *as*, it is now being seen by me (in an entirely ordinary sense of 'seen'), and with *omission* of all parts and features which are not now being seen by me (again in an ordinary sense of 'seen'), and this recipe yields, not a surface or part of a sofa, but a queer, insideless, backless, bottomless, oddly distorted and in many respects indeterminate *abstractum*, a 'thing' not merely 'mutilated', but with mutilation written large on its face, and which can only yield a complete object if we fill in its indefinitenesses and discount its distortions with the help of further sense-fulfilments. Sense-datum theorists operate with atoms of experience which are rounded and smooth and assembled only by accident: they should have borrowed a leaf from the ancients and endowed their atoms with hooks. The tendency to complete sensory excerpts rests on the fact that they are *presented as* excerpts and cannot be presented otherwise: the 'tendency' flows from what they are.

A similar tendency to completion flows from every conscious experience as given to reflection, or as projected into the interior life of others: as remarked before, we cannot be aware of a passing thought or perception, except as pointing to a possible completion in thoughts or perceptions which precede it or which follow it, and which can also look back to their predecessors or forward to their successors. The thoughts of a mind fit into and continue each other, not accidentally, but because they are mutilated and imperfect without such continuation. They may be, and often are, violently discontinued, but such violence presupposes their natural continuity. This, as we saw, is the justification of the Cartesian claim that reflection shows us a thinker and not merely a thought: it is also the basis of many claims to immortality. One's conscious life, like a straight line, may be produced infinitely in either direction: it remains so producible even if, through the actual arrangements, it continues only a little way.

THE BASIC MODES OF CONSCIOUSNESS 81

We may now also recur to another tendency previously mentioned which is certainly basic to consciousness, that of pressing on to a state of *fulfilled* awareness, a state in which an object is concretely present (in a manner appropriate to the particular object) rather than merely intended or thought of. An 'empty' thought-reference necessarily presses on towards some degree of fulfilment, and a fulfilled thought necessarily presses on to a richer, or at least to a different, fulfilment. My thought of something blue has an objective direction only because it leads to my *seeing* something as blue, and my seeing something as blue tends towards the seeing of countless other things as blue or seeing things as blue in other manners or ways. A state of fulfilled awareness has, we feel, an object in a more *proper* sense than a state of unfulfilled awareness, a superiority also acknowledged when we say of a state of fulfilled awareness that in it the thing *itself* is present, the thing is *actually before us*, is *really given*, etc. etc. This superiority appears also in the fact that we hesitate to say that a self-contradictory thought has an object, what it intends being obviously incapable of being fully carried out. And it appears also in our unwillingness to classify the things and persons of fiction, imperfectly fulfilled through discrete private images, as persons and things in the same sense as those of history and geography. Though the gulf between the 'objective' and the imaginary is much less clear-cut in personal experience than realistically minded thinkers have tended to make it, yet it does correspond to a gulf in that experience, the gulf being mainly one of 'fulfilment'. The notion of 'fulfilment', as we have seen, covers a wide family of differing cases: the fulfilment of a negative thought, e.g., is quite different from the fulfilment of a positive one. There is, as we saw, a fulfilment through sense-perception, and a fulfilment, not necessarily less perfect, through imagery: there is also a partial or surrogative fulfilment by way of pictures, models, copies, or any sort of close or remote likeness. There is a fulfilment of inner-life references when we reflect on experiences we are actually having, or project them, in imagined fullness, into the outward pantomime of others. In all these cases what we mean or intend becomes present in a more pregnant, heightened manner, and some measure of pressure towards such heightened presence must be included among the basic *nisus* of consciousness.

If it is basic to consciousness to press on towards the fulfilment

82   VALUES AND INTENTIONS

of its orientations, it is basic to it also to make its orientations such as are, or can be fulfilled, in other words, to *conform* to the given. To conceive of something as blue, and to have experiences which frustrate this conception, is certainly a disarraying experience, from which one avenue of escape is to 'adjust one's thought to the thing', to think of it so that it *does* fulfil one's thought of it. The so-called 'material of sense', though not, as we saw, anything genuinely isolable, but rather performing the Aristotelian function of being the common possibility of a large number of alternative thought-references and fulfilments, may be said, in metaphor, to prompt or press us away from such thoughts as fall outside of its capacity to fulfil, and towards such thoughts as lie within this capacity. To this pressure we yield when we say such things as: 'No, this is not really blue: it is really greenish-blue in colour', etc. etc. Our idea now conforms to our experience, it is *true to* what is given—this *truth to something* is a notion different from and more elementary than that of simple truth—the craving for fulfilment which is basic to consciousness has been appeased. This appeasement is due, however, rather to a surrender of a preconception than to a victorious carrying of it through. To conform to the 'given', to be 'true' to it, may accordingly be held to be a deeply rooted, if derived, goal of conscious experience, the fruit of its bifurcation into two modes, one of which 'fulfils' the other. And from the pursuit of this goal flow ultimately all those higher thought-surrenders which are part of the pursuit of 'truth' and 'knowledge'. The adjustment to fact may of course take forms widely different from the adjustment of notions to what is present to sense. It may consist in framing notions to fit what we carefully picture, as when we ask what *would* happen in certain circumstances; it may consist also in framing notions to occupy a precise place among a set of other systematically interconnected notions so as to answer some precise question, e.g. the number of edges of a cube, the highest perfect square less than 100, etc. etc. In these last cases the conforming of notions to the 'given' may take the form of 'seeing' what notion thus conforms, or it may take the form of arriving at this by way of imagined illustrations or a symbolical 'working-out'. All these procedures, elaborate and sophisticated as they may be, have a profound analogy with, as well as a stepwise descent to, the basic performance of finding a notion to fit what is present to sense.

THE BASIC MODES OF CONSCIOUSNESS 83

It is an error when the higher forms of conformity are interpreted as involving no more than a manipulation of counters according to approved rules, even if this is, in degenerate cases, what they may become.

Conscious orientations, with their pressure towards fulfilment, necessarily also involve, we plainly perceive, a *nisus* away from all internal conflict and discrepancy. These last are what we discover when we try in vain to fulfil certain thought-orientations, e.g. that of being coloured and that of being unextended, in the same sensory or other intuitive situation, when our failure inspires a peculiar hopelessness, which we refer to what we think of, and not to ourselves, and which so mediates the consciousness of what is impossible in itself and not merely for us. (That this consciousness may not, on reflection, be found to fit the material to which we apply it, goes without saying.) This consciousness of a conflict does not rest on our linguistic conventions, but our linguistic conventions rest upon it. This is true alike of more specific incompatibilities, such as those we discover between being red and being green all over, and also of the generic incompatibility of being X and not being X, or of being the case and not being the case, which sums up all these cases of incompatibility and other simpler cases besides (those where a mere absence or lack is opposed to a presence). For in the peculiar experience of disappointed intention which seems the basis of the awareness of a negation, there is as yet no clear thought of the *conjunction* of that negation with the corresponding positive state, and it is only by trying to fulfil such a conjunction that its impossibility becomes obvious. So little is the thought of incompatibility explicitly part of the thought of a negation, that there is even a class of cases where we fail to discover it, cases which in a perplexing manner both fulfil and frustrate an intention, and where we prefer to employ an 'inexact' use of negation rather than one sanctioned by formal logic. It is, in fact, by trying to fulfil and disappoint the same reference, that we find out *where* our conflict is of the unfulfillable type interesting to the formal logician, and where its fulfilment would be 'queer', monstrous, equivocal or anomalous but not in the strict sense impossible. Since our conscious references press onwards towards fulfilment, they must, however, shrink from or shun thought-conjunctions whose fulfilment is altogether excluded, and also, in a lesser degree, those which

84   VALUES AND INTENTIONS

involve considerable internal discrepancy or anomaly. There may
of course be powerful motives which may compel an acceptance
of the latter, or which may lead us to reclassify the impossible
per se as the merely anomalous, or the impossible in relation to
ourselves. It is thus, e.g., that we may assuage our sense of the
unfulfillable character of our references to other minds, by
making it a mere consequence of the sheer apartness of our
experiences from theirs, or the unfulfillable character of our
reference to the infinite by making it a mere consequence of
successive, piecemeal approaches. There may also be motives,
not strictly classifiable as 'cognitive', e.g. religious or aesthetic
ones, which may make it seem interesting or profitable to dwell in
notions whose rich discrepancy makes them incapable of fulfilment. And there can plainly be nothing more profoundly appeasing
in our conscious approach, because more compounded of provocation and relief, than a conflict which turns out not to be a
conflict at all, whose discrepancy vanishes in a wider context.
Hegel may have been right in making the resolution rather than the
avoidance of conflict the true goal of our conscious endeavours.

   If our conscious experience in its urge towards fulfilment
tends to steer clear of overt conflict or uneasy near-conflict, it
must also, and for the same motive, tend to move in a direction
most opposed to that of conflict, the direction of mutual requirement and belongingness, whether in the sense of strictly formal
entailment or in that of the looser kinds of consequence characteristic of science and philosophy. Consciousness by its nature
seeks to piece things together so as to fulfil them in a common
thing or situation: it must therefore be almost headily happy
where what we may call its fulfilling base is reduced to a minimum
or vanishes altogether, and the aspects it distinguishes *necessarily*
belong together merely because they are varying modes of
approach to the same possible range of things and situations.
Relations of formal entailment produce an almost over-poignant
sense of the intersection of distinct thought-approaches in the
same object, since in their case the distinction of aspects becomes
altogether transparent, remaining a distinction only for us and
for our conscious approaches, and involving steps which prove
on examination not to be steps at all. But consciousness must also
tend to appease its love of fulfilment along lines involving only
imperfect transparency in the mutual belongingness of distinct

THE BASIC MODES OF CONSCIOUSNESS 85

aspects, where they hang together by analogy or some other sort of non-formal continuity, and where the passage from one to the other always involves a genuine step. Such appeasement, though less heady, is in a sense more solidly based, since in its case fulfilment is genuinely important, and is not a mere reflection of the transparent interchangeability of a number of distinct mental approaches. And it is also important since it may span a wide variety and genuine disparity of cases. Both formal entailment and looser forms of implication, however, have it in common that they vastly reduce what may be called the fulfilling base of a wide number of thought-references. Formal entailment reduces it to nothing or to anything, but looser forms of implication also reduce it immensely. Where a thought-pattern involves a high degree of mutual belongingness and systematic relevance among its elements, it may be illustrated, in all its divergent variety, in a very small specimen, and the whole character of a system may be decisively manifest in a crucial excerpt. Consciousness, with its *nisus* towards fulfilment, necessarily shuns the loosely coherent, whose fulfilment is hopelessly endless, and which must necessarily muddle and finally extinguish it altogether, whereas it must tend to direct itself to the case where a variety of references can be simply fulfilled in the single crucial sample, and must feel that, alone in such cases, it has a provoking, arresting and unifying theme or object.

Conscious experience, further, and just because it is conscious experience, may be said to involve a *nisus* towards *exhaustive determination*, towards a complete filling in of the indefiniteness in the pattern it is developing or the object that it is envisaging. It aspires, in the case of any conceivable angle of regard, to decide how its object stands in respect of that angle, an aspiration which is one of the many which gives point to the Law of Excluded Middle. The aspiration in question is simply a form of the basic urge of consciousness to enter more deeply into its object. It seems clear that, in a sense, the less definite the object of consciousness, the less consciousness has an object at all. To think merely of something-one-knows-not-what has always been recognized as being next door to not thinking of anything. This aspiration, like many other of the fundamental aspirations of consciousness, may have bounds set to it by many factors, e.g. the essential indiscernibility of the future by an active being, the interference by

86 VALUES AND INTENTIONS

investigation in the behaviour of sub-atomic particles, etc. In such cases thought may find a new definiteness in first-order undecidability. But, however much frustrated and impeded, the aspiration towards complete closure in every direction of determination remains fundamental to consciousness, and even the constructions of fantasy show some deference to it. We do not like the irreducible ambiguities of the novels of Henry James.

We have so far stressed only the tendencies of consciousness which pertain to it *qua* the consciousness of something, not those which pertain to it *qua* the consciousness of itself. We held, however, that all consciousness must tend to pass from the 'ecstatic' dwelling in certain conscious poses to dwelling in the consciousness *of* them, and must tend also to project such attitudes outwards, to surround itself with actual and possible conscious attitudes disjoined from *these* which are its own. Neither of these tendencies is a mere case of the tendencies previously mentioned, and it is therefore *thinkable*, though deeply anomalous and monstrous, that the other tendencies should exist without these. But it would be hard to make sense of what we are conscious of could we not refer some of its shifts and variations to the manner in which we are conscious of it, and this is possible since we know of our conscious life through reflection: it would also be harder and more hypothetical to interpret our own and other people's behaviour could we not fill in gaps with data derived from or extrapolated from this source. And if consciousness has a natural *nisus* towards reflection and projection, it will have also, we may hold, a tendency to use these to *sharpen* its notion of objectivity by rendering to the object the things that are the object's, and to its own activity those that are its own. Since it is of the essence of consciousness to be capable of variation without variation in its object, it is also a necessary, if outlying, property of an object of consciousness to be capable of being *variously* minded or intended, and that not merely by the mind that is conscious but by other minds as well.

While, therefore, there may be a purely 'ecstatic' consciousness of objects which lives merely in the continued fitting together of the aspects which constitute them (and the dropping of those that do not), there will also be a more 'pregnant', half-reflexive view of objects, in which we *oppose* them to the ways in which we may be conscious of them. An object of consciousness is then seen as something *indifferent* to the ways in which we may be conscious of

THE BASIC MODES OF CONSCIOUSNESS 87

it, and which develops its characteristic unity and pattern *in the face of* conscious variations. We are most pregnantly conscious of an object when we are conscious of it as unaffected by, or even resisting our conscious approaches to it: there is, as a well-known idealist once said, a connection between the 'objective' and the objectionable. This objectionableness is of course at its most plain when we adjust notions to the material of sense, but it is encountered also when we transform thoughts according to strict logic or even develop fantasies in a coherent manner. Consciousness, with its essential orientation towards objects, must positively *care* for what heightens or brings out the independence of its object, very much as a sexually obsessed person likes everything that stresses the marks of sex. There will even in consciousness, as in sex, be a tendency towards an exaggerated submission to the objective, a love of what goes against its own grain: this natural 'masochism' in fact enters into all the higher forms of judgement and knowledge, and also colours our attitude in art and morals, where we crave an order we can conform to instead of one that we can decide on or construct.

Kant, in the *Critique of Pure Reason*, emphasizes both the unity and pattern necessary for an 'ecstatic' awareness of an object, and the additional indifference and opposition to our subjective approaches and tendencies necessary for its more pregnant apprehension. The former is the theme of the *Transcendental Deduction* proper, the latter of the *Analytic of Principles*. If the former stresses the minimum regularity and unity needed to make of something a connected theme or object of thought or knowledge, the latter stresses the necessary *opposition* of such regularity to the arbitrary variation of our conscious approaches. We must, e.g., be able to distinguish objective successions which are irreversible, from subjective successions which depend only on our conscious approaches and are accordingly reversible.

If consciousness thus presses towards experiences where the pattern of objects resists and quarrels with our own purely subjective tendencies, and so makes conformity to the object's pattern a curious mixture of painful constraint and overriding satisfaction, it must also necessarily seek to secure conformity with the conscious orientations of others. What is objective, in the sense of constraining us to think in a certain manner, and showing marked indifference to some of our conscious variations (clearness, fullness, angle, order, etc.), must also, we feel, constrain others as it does ourselves, and must show as marked an indifference to *their* conscious variations as it does to our own. In other words, we cannot help extending the objective pattern that constrains us to those with whom we people the social space around us, and we must make it constrain them as it constrains us. By so doing we not only satisfy the passion for analogical extension which, as we saw, is basic to the consciousness of objects: we also make the object of our consciousness be *more* of an object because indifferent and resistant to *more* conscious persons. Contrariwise, to conceive of a conscious orientation, however constraining, as *not* similarly constraining to others, is to weaken its hold even on ourselves. And a conscious orientation thought of as constraining others, must also tend to be thought of as constraining ourselves, and the more so the *more numerous* those others are thought of as being. All these are principles and tendencies of telling power, belonging together with, and yet not logically entailed by the other tendencies basic to consciousness, and themselves giving rise to other fundamental tendencies in a similar manner.

Most interesting of these last is a two-way *nisus* towards *communication*: a tendency on the one hand to *impose* our conscious orientations on others, and, on the other hand, to *conform* our orientations to theirs. By either route we achieve the characteristic goal of consciousness, the having of an object which is more of an object because it is an object for many or for all. Even vagrant fancy seeks to spread its notions to wider ranges of auditors or readers, and all speech subserves this single aim. Conscious experience may therefore be said by its very nature to pursue and prefer what is public and open: the real physical thing or situation which is patently there for many persons, as opposed to the private illusion or hallucination, which is only deviously connected with what is patently there, the thought-content that can be unambiguously communicated and readily applied, as opposed to the thought-content which is hard in either respect, the thought-development that follows clear rules, as opposed to the thought-development that seems arbitrary and idiosyncratic, etc. etc. Even in solitary discourse we must after a fashion pluralize ourselves: we vary viewpoints, we raise objections, we accommodate approaches that are independent and diverse. And what is most personal in our subjective life achieves importance, even for

THE BASIC MODES OF CONSCIOUSNESS 89

ourselves, to the extent that it can be widely communicated, brought down by analogy and metaphor into the arena of common discussion and shown to involve a predicament common to all. We value our inner life above everything not because it is unsharable, but because its sharing is so rewardingly difficult, because its communication represents the last victory of articulate universality over particular privacy. It in fact brings to full publicity the very privacy which characterizes us all.

If all conscious experience, to the extent that it is conscious, may be held to involve a *nisus* towards the open and common, it may be held also to involve a *nisus* away from all arbitrary one-sided dwelling in particular conscious approaches. Since an object is essentially such as to reveal itself through a multitude of approaches, and to be unaffected by many of their peculiarities, it would be running counter to the whole direction of consciousness to prefer one such approach arbitrarily to another. The manner in which something appears to one man's senses and on one occasion may indeed be preferred to the manner in which it appears on another occasion or to another person, but only because its *content* justifies the preference: it may, e.g., be more determinate, more free from internal discrepancy, more coherent with other appearances, etc. etc. Where no such superiority obtains, it would run counter to the direction of consciousness to dwell exclusively or predominantly in one of these appearances and to neglect others: it would mean, in fact, to make an object of this appearance, to see *it* from many angles, rather than the object that comes to light in it. (Such higher-order concern with appearances is not of course illegitimate.) In precisely the same manner the interest of consciousness in what is objective must tend to make it lay *equal* weight on, or make *equal* use of, all its impressions of one object, or all the impressions that different people form of the object, rather than concentrate this weight or use on some of them. Again, some may tend to be preferred to others on account of richness of content, greater truth to the given, coherence, harmony, etc., but where there are no such counter-vailing grounds, arbitrariness would be utterly out of place.

A tendency, therefore, towards an *impartial equalization* of the 'lights' in which things are viewed or thought of by different persons, or by the same person on different occasions, is accordingly to be reckoned as part and parcel of a conscious orientation to

90 VALUES AND INTENTIONS

objects. Other things being equal, consciousness, in so far as it sums up what is brought out in each of these conscious lights, must tend to base its view equally on each of them. That there is here an extraordinary degree of vagueness as to what counts as a single conscious impression and in the situation glibly covered by the phrase 'other things being equal', will not make the above statement wholly nugatory. We can point to instances of the rough conscious equity we are mentioning, not only in the exalted fields of law and science, but even in the humblest of our conscious performances. Even animals conscientiously manipulate objects and try to see them from several sides, and show no one-sided preference for a single approach. Men, too, conscientiously probe into objects and experiment with them, give heed to perplexing and unwelcome aspects as well as to those that are acceptable, and make almost as much use of the senses of other persons as they do of their own. This deference to the impression of the *orbis terrarum* is established even at the sensory level, from which it spreads upwards to the higher regions of thought and practice. Its authority may be rejected on many occasions, but not without special discrediting factors, and it sits in even on our fictions and our dreams. The creations of personal fantasy acquire their own natural drift of development, and their creators may well wish to defer to those to whom such fantasies have been communicated as to how they may most naturally be continued.

Having made tendencies towards abstraction, towards analogical extension, towards fulfilment and conformity with the given, etc. etc., fundamental to consciousness, we need not be over timid in crediting consciousness with what Bosanquet called a *nisus* towards totality, a tendency towards views with an unbounded horizon, that extend over all or everything that may come up for consideration, whether this 'all' or 'everything' be meant distributively, or, with an addition of strength, collectively. ('All' taken collectively is a whole, a single object of concern, into which we think of 'everything', taken distributively, as entering as a constituent: there may, of course, be very different conceptions of the *closeness* of the unity into which 'everything' is thus thought to enter.) The tendency we are now considering is not the same as the tendency towards enriched synthesis, exhaustive determination, etc. etc.; these are 'open' tendencies, pressing indefinitely onwards in a given direction, but not for that reason

THE BASIC MODES OF CONSCIOUSNESS 91

achieving the *consciousness* of such an indefinite openness. The tendency towards the conscious orientation will at first be exercised in restricted form: we may see *all* that lies before us, or *all* that has just been reviewed, in a certain conscious light, e.g. as being alternately white or black, or as consisting of small masses moving in regular orbits round a common centre, etc. etc. The force of 'all' is plainly negative: what is before us disappoints, excludes the thought of an exception, of something not fitting the light in which things are being viewed.

A higher flight of negation is involved in thoughts limited only by the scope of a conscious light (or, what is the same, by the meaning of a descriptive expression). Here there is not only a ruling out of anything not falling under the scope in question, but also a tacit removal of any restriction binding one's orientation down to any particular or indeed to any actual case. Our thought, e.g., is of anything blue *whatever*. In a still higher flight of negation there is even a removal of any narrowing or specific conscious light or meaning: our thought is of anything whatsoever, i.e. without any restriction at all. This rise to a wider and wider universality may further be carried out in the field of characters, relationships, etc., in the manner formalized in the higher functional calculus. (Such a rise, we may note, does not necessarily involve an 'ontology' or an erection of fragmentary meanings into 'entities': to think of A as in *all* respects like B is not to have an ontology of 'respects'.) It is a great fault of symbolic logic that it suggests that a restricted reference to all A's arises by adding a restriction to the reference to everything whatsoever, rather than that, the other way round, the unrestricted reference represents a last shedding of initial restrictions.

The whole line of advance we have been considering may be native to consciousness, but it could hardly be carried far without the use of symbols. It is absurd to think of an animal, even if its notions have the openness of our own, forming the notion of *anything whatever*. It would also seem to involve, in at least pregnant cases of understanding, a reflective and even a social element: the words 'whatever' or 'whatsoever' express an unbounded readiness for thoughts and perceptions on our own part, which we seek also to induce in others by such variants as *quodlibet* or 'anything you like'. But whatever may be condensed in the various forms of unrestrictedly distributive or collective references, it is not unreasonable to hold that all conscious life has a *nisus* towards them. Mind is nothing if not a viewing of things in lights that are general, which extend themselves naturally to ever further cases, and the thought of things in an explicitly universal perspective is in a sense merely a making plain of a spirit in which we have always operated, and a seeing of things in terms of it.

CHAPTER III

THE MODES OF BELIEF

(I) GENERAL CHARACTERIZATION OF BELIEF

We have so far dwelt exclusively on states of mind as being *of* this or *of* that, or of being of something *as* such and such, etc., without considering the further property, obviously present in many states of mind, of in some manner incorporating a 'built-in' endorsement (not necessarily a valid one), of being conscious of objects, not merely as objects, but as in some unqualified sense 'real' or 'existent', and in being conscious, not merely of particular circumstances, but of them as being *really* or *truly* or *actually* the case. We have, in the terminology of Brentano, considered only the 'ideas', the *Vorstellungen* or Presentations, in which things are diversely present to mind, without considering what it is that erects some of these into acts of *believing*, or, in more considered, verbalized and publicly oriented contexts, explicitly entertained *opinions* or *judgements*. To this difference, which presents almost insuperable problems for philosophical description, we now address ourselves.

The difficulties are great since, while we can assert without hesitation, and often without fear of question or controversion, that we believe this or that, and while others can often assert this of us and we of them, there does not appear to be any seizable trait or feature common to all the cases we want to cover, and there are moreover strong arguments tending to show that any particular manifest sign or outward or inward evidence of belief *cannot* be of its essence. Feelings, urges, practical preparations, verbal pronouncements, associative linkages and evidential bindings, all obviously play their part in belief, yet are obviously absent from many cases of it, and we can almost always imagine cases in which they *are* present *without* belief being there at all. This situation can be met by saying with Mill, Stout, Brentano and others, that belief is ultimate and unanalysable, a solution which is no solution, since it leaves quite mysterious why this simple something should have all the connections with feeling, action, assertion, evidence, etc., which it has and must have.

94 VALUES AND INTENTIONS

Alternatively it may be met by saying, with Wittgenstein, that the term 'belief' covers a wide 'family' of cases, through none of which any one pervasive resemblance runs, but which are linked together in series by a large number of overlapping resemblances. This solution also is no solution, since it merely seeks to repress our deep sense of a significant unity inadequately brought out in a range of cases, without *showing* this sense to be ill-founded. The pearl of great price may be lacking, but it will not do to be sure of this in advance, much less to pretend that mere sand and detritus *are* the pearl. Here as elsewhere, the solution would appear to lie in recognizing that the term 'belief' indicates a *place* in a complex notional field, a place filled by a large number of more or less closely interdependent features—features which really belong together, even though it is quite thinkable, and is in fact often the case, that some are present without the others—and which also shade gradually into an ambient neighbourhood of other notions, whose logical distance from belief fixes the character of the latter as much as what is unambiguously *in* it. And while belief may be manifest in a wide range of impoverished, blunted and denatured forms, such as some analysts have loved to dwell upon, they only qualify for membership in the belief-family because of their graded approximation to a form which is, as it were, the fountain and origin of the whole set, which exemplifies belief in the most perfect form, as the finished portrait of which they are merely the sketches. It is *this* portrait that we are now concerned to paint.

We may best begin work on the finished picture by considering what cannot possibly qualify as a full version of it, even though it has frequently been put forward as such. The believing orientation cannot, in the first place, be identified with the mere readiness to respond practically to something (or to respond practically *as if* to something) even though a relation to practice is plainly of its essence. Desires and wishes are, in their fullfledged and most characteristic form, of the *real* and not of the merely entertained and imaginary: what we desire or wish for, we desire or wish *to be*, and not merely to float before us as a prospect or a picture, and we are accordingly variously incited, appeased, relieved, satisfied or dissatisfied by what we believe to be actual or to be the case. If I believe you to be in want, and your want to be best capable of relief by the sending of a

THE MODES OF BELIEF

food parcel, which it is also in my power to send, then there is an almost logical necessity that I should go through the appropriate acts of purchase and posting, and it is from my performance of such acts that the judicious observer, who has reason to take my interest in your well-being for granted, will be able to gauge of my belief. It is, however, plain to the judicious observer that my activity is only an effect, albeit no merely factual or contingent effect, of my belief, and that it is as much an effect of what I *want* or *wish*, in the absence of which wanting or wishing I should perhaps do something different or nothing at all. It is a platitude, further, that we believe countless things to be the case which do not concern us practically, and it is most wantonly artificial to define such belief in terms of what we might have done had we had wishes that we do not in fact have, or had the situation been quite other than it in fact is. The condition is further quite conceivable, and in some psychic conditions actually realized (e.g. the 'waxy mobility' of schizophrenia) where there is absolutely no wish to adjust oneself practically even to situations normally thought of as most urgent, and yet there remains the most perfect *insight* regarding such situations, which can be well documented once the psychosis has been cured. It is likewise conceivable that, in a queer state, we should adjust ourselves systematically to what we did not believe to be true, and it would be merely perverse to analyse our state in terms of what we *should* have done had our state been less queer than it in fact was. It is clear, further, that no form of action, however well adjusted to circumstances and hypothetical needs, can afford a plain proof of what a man believes, and it seems absurd that something so clear-edged as belief, which in many cases so plainly exists, should be identified with what must be for ever in such doubt. It is not necessary, for our purposes, to pursue the argument further into the many subtle windings in which recent discussion has followed it.[1] For us it is clear that for something to be believed is for something to seem real (in a perfectly unqualified or unbracketed manner), or for something to seem undeniably the case, or to seem a plain and unquestionable fact, etc. etc., all of which 'seemings' are plainly cases of *cognition*, of the manner in which things appear or are given to the conscious

---

[1] See, e.g., Roderick Chisholm, 'Sentences about Believing', *Proceedings of the Aristotelian Society*, 1955–6.

96 VALUES AND INTENTIONS

individual, and not of any manner in which he responds practically to what is thus given.

If a purely practical account of belief cannot be rendered acceptable, equally little can we accept an analysis purely in terms of personal feeling or peculiar mental modulations, e.g. assent, seriousness, conviction, etc., whose character is complete in the instant of its occurrence, and which has no essential reference to *other* completing experiences or readiness for experience. (That the states classed as feelings and attitudes really have this psychic simplicity may be doubted. It may be doubted whether *any* description of a mental state merely predicates a *quality* of what is there. Simple feelings, in the sense believed in by many philosophers, are probably the offspring of a 'category-mistake', of an attempt to transfer qualitative talk to a field where it does not apply.) We cannot, like Hume, identify belief with a peculiar feeling of vividness or solidity which accompanies our ideas, and is descriptively complete on each occasion of its occurrence, since it is plain that such a feeling could as readily be attached to what we did not believe as to what we did, and Hume is in fact at pains to explain away cases, e.g. the case of the man suspended in a cage above a chasm, who vividly imagines but does not believe that he will fall, where such feelings go uncoupled with belief. The notion of belief as a self-contained personal feeling further encounters the same sort of objection as a parallel theory of ethical approval: that it renders mysterious why it should be wrong or bad to believe the false, and right or good to believe the true (as in the parallel case it renders it mysterious why it should be wrong or bad to approve the morally bad or wrong, and right or good to approve the morally right or good). There can be no shadow of a rational principle prescribing our attitude to a mere quality. And it is further at variance with the fact that we do not at all characterize beliefs, as we do colours, in terms of quality or intensity: of quality they exhibit no significant variations, and of the 'more and less' they in one dimension exhibit only a 'completeness' or 'fullness' and a companion 'partiality' or 'approach to completeness', which can only by a complete misunderstanding be regarded as a case of psychic intensity, and in another dimension only a variation in 'fixity' and 'firmness', which both obviously have a reference to the *other* beliefs in which a given belief is rooted, or to the other

THE MODES OF BELIEF

belief-tendencies that compete with it, and have some power to drive it from the field. The 'degrees of belief' are on the one hand degrees of approximation to a perfect type, and on the other degrees of ability to withstand attrition or destruction: they are in no sense proper cases of intensity.

To these unacceptable accounts of belief, we may add, thirdly, any account that makes it involve no more than the addition of some feature to what is brought to mind, or of some additional 'conscious light' in which things are seen. If to think of an X does not of itself qualify as an act of belief, then to think of an X as or with Y will not qualify as belief, no matter how unique and portentous an addition Y may be. This is even so if Y be made such things as the coherence of what is thought with all our knowledge or past experience or with what we now perceive, for it is as easy to think of what we do *not* believe as having such coherence as to do so in the case of what we believe. We may here take note of the strange dual role of such words as 'exists', 'real', 'actual', 'is the case', 'true', etc., which in *some* contexts give expression, not so much to any feature in what we think of, as to the momentous feature, whatever it is, which differentiates serious belief from mere entertainment or imagination, while in other contexts they as plainly indicate something which is part of what we conceive of, and which may not be believed *at all*, as where we *imagine* that the end of the world as conceived by some preposterous sect should one fine morning prove horribly to be *true*. They are words also which in one context are a redundant reinforcement of an already complete asseveration—there is no difference between asserting p and asserting p to be true—while in other contexts they express the whole difference between a mere idea and a fully fledged assertion. This dual role plainly indicates something of fundamental importance in the life of thought, how what does *not* enter into the content of what we are thinking, can none the less be made somehow to contribute to that content, and yet cannot do so without losing something in the process, which, once lost, it cannot by any means regain.

The answer we shall give to the request for a description of belief is an answer inspired by modern theory, even if it is not the answer that modern theory has given. Modern theory has been delighted to expand the meaning or significant content of a formulated assertion to all the circumstances that might help to

D

98 VALUES AND INTENTIONS

justify or invalidate the assertion in question, whether these circumstances enter into the relatively narrow scope of what would ordinarily be regarded as asserted, or whether they merely provide some reason, direct or indirect, close or remote, compelling or merely inclining, for putting forward the assertion in question. Such an expansion of the content or meaning of an assertion till it becomes infinitely wide in its spread may be regarded as thoroughly inexpedient: by the meaning or content of an assertion we generally mean something falling within fairly narrow bounds, even if it may not have precisely cut edges. To understand what it means or involves for something to be red or languid or a chaffinch, or to be the relative product of certain relations, is a comparatively simple matter: it only involves experiencing a few cases or considering or working out a few examples, or relating a few verbally pinned-down notions, and it can be done as readily with imaginary materials as with real ones. Whatever its marginal vagueness, this does not extend into considering, and even rules out as irrelevant, many of the circumstances that would bear on the use of a meaning in an assertion, and that would either weaken or strengthen the latter. But, on the other hand, to take something to be real or true, in contexts where these words express unqualified belief, does involve precisely such a readiness to go beyond the narrow bounds of content or meaning. It does mean being ready to consider what is asserted in the light of countless possible circumstances, however alien, that could possibly bear upon it, it does in short mean being ready to fit it into a context capable of indefinite expansion and in every possible direction. Thus a view which makes it wholly clear what it 'means' or is like for a thing to be salmon-pink, only gives a relatively weak ground for believing it to be salmon-pink, and requires supplementation by countless further tests, e.g. that the thing looks salmon-pink in certain 'good' lights and that it does *not* look salmon-pink in certain 'bad' ones, that it emits waves of certain regular frequencies, etc. etc., before we can say that the thing really *has* the character that it perfectly *exhibits*. To speak in this natural manner may involve the relatively slight paradox that a thing may illustrate, may show forth and acquaint us with a property that it does not possess, but it avoids the enormous paradox of saying that we never know the precise coverage of even the simplest qualifications that seem to apply to it, since each

THE MODES OF BELIEF

covers an infinity of validating tests. In the same manner, and for much the same reasons, the definitory account that satisfactorily circumscribes something cannot be stretched to include all that it logically entails, or all that is logically equivalent to it, and the proof of whose truth or reality establishes its own truth and reality as well. An essential omnidirectional *openness* may therefore as rightly be affirmed of belief as it is wrongly asserted of the detached idea or meaning. And what is true of belief will be more explicitly true of those publicly professed, verbally expressed beliefs which we call opinions or judgements.

What we have just said requires, however, a large number of weighty qualifications. In attributing 'openness' to belief we are not saying that all the infinite circumstances that might bear on an assertion enter surreptitiously into that assertion's content or meaning, so that the man who makes the assertion really asserts *them* as much as anything he would ordinarily be held to be asserting. To hold this would be precisely to widen the sense of 'content' or 'meaning' in the indefinite manner we found so objectionable. It would also be to ignore the principle, established above, that *no* addition to the content of what is believed can possibly constitute the essential differentia of believing. The 'reference' to the infinite circumstances that might bear on an assertion is a reference of the 'sidelong' sort previously distinguished, a reference shown in the readiness to continue what is thought of in certain directions, and a pained unreadiness and shock when one is forced to move in others, rather than in anything explicitly added to the content of one's thought. And, prior to definite experience (or to an actual working out), this readiness need not be for anything highly specific: it may merely be described as a general readiness for whatever will fit in with, will accord or harmonize with (or will positively follow from) what we have before us. And while the effect of experience (or of detailed calculation) is to some extent to give this readiness more definite form, it is also, to some extent, to render it more indefinite: we learn to continue our notion of a thing, not merely in what is felt intuitively to be appropriate and akin, but also in what at first seems most remote and alien, so that, in the end, in believing things in unfamiliar fields, we may not know to *what* completing tissue we are in fact committing ourselves, what precise circumstances will accord with or follow from or lend support to what

VALUES AND INTENTIONS

we say. A man, e.g., who assents to some proposition in modern physical theory—to the expansion of the whole universe, for example—may be as vague as to the considerations which might lead anyone to entertain anything so strange as he is perhaps vague as to its precise import.

In the respects mentioned the 'assent' involved in belief is not unlike the 'consent' involved in voluntary decision. Both involve the same indefinite openness to a completing context. If I determine to do X, I certainly determine to do it *with* all the infinite consequences it may have, and *in* all the infinite circumstances that surround it and lead up to it, without needing to have the least idea *what* these circumstances are. In exactly the same way, in believing something, I swallow with what I believe (as it were) the absence of all the things that would disallow it or exclude it, and am favourably disposed to all the things, not otherwise disallowed, that would bear favourably upon it, no matter how vague my conception of all such circumstances may be. This infinite openness is something of which we may at times be reflectively conscious, and appears then in our sense of the *unconditional*, wholly committed character of believing. It has been circumscribed in such metaphors as the closed grasp of the Stoics or the internal assent of Ockham, perhaps also in such doctrines as that of Newman regarding the 'indefectability' of certainty, etc. etc. A belief-attitude may be overthrown by untoward experience, but it cannot, *qua* the attitude it is, look forward to such an overthrow. But while such belief-experiences may be reckoned the crowning form of believing, they are so only because condensing and giving unified form to a readiness which would otherwise operate obscurely and dispersed among many distinct experiences. If we were to describe them merely in terms of passing 'feeling', their whole import would be irretrievably lost.

The unconditional character of believing means, further, not merely that we are ready for an indefinite contextual extension of what we have in mind, but also that this contextual extension must be unique and embracing, that it brooks no parallel infinite alongside of itself, nor an enclosing infinite which, in another dimension, encompasses it about. Belief has, in other words, the not simply, but the absolutely and exhaustively infinite character of a Spinozistic substance. If our thought and experience roved

THE MODES OF BELIEF

to and fro between two systematic contexts, neither of which was in any way continuous with the other, we could not be said to *believe* in the contexts of either context, except perhaps in some loose and derived sense. Only if both were somehow co-ordinated in a single picture (with links not necessarily very close or evident), or if the one were definitely *sub*ordinated to the other, being thought of as a dream or fiction or purpose of beings placed in the other, could the notion of belief have significant application. In the same way, if the context of something was thought of as having the indefinite openness of the contexts of 'convincing' works of fiction, we should not have a case of belief as long as the whole context remained framed or 'bracketed' in some other wider context, or was thought of, even marginally, as having no more than some sort of 'intentional inexistence', or an oblique life only in the cognitive acts and symbolic references of those who read and write about it, who perform it or see it performed, etc. etc. It could only be raised to belief were this encompassing framework to lapse, were the brackets of intentionality to vanish, if we ceased to think of something, together with its indefinite completing context, as no more than thought of, and were to live simply in the thought of the thing and the context themselves. When we treat fiction as fiction, we keep the notion of its purely fictional status at bay, so that it does not obtrude itself on our enjoyment, but it remains more or less ready to re-emerge, and contributes to the penumbra of the quasi-belief-experience. Could it be wholly banished from this experience, we should lose ourselves in our imagined creation, and should seriously believe in its creatures. The 'seriousness' which distinguishes genuine from factitious belief involves, therefore, at least the absence of those encompassing 'brackets' which demote the status of what we think of to a mere *esse apparens* or intentional inexistence; it will, however, be more fully present where there is also some consciousness of their absence, where doubt is not merely lacking, but consciously dismissed.

The absence of 'brackets' is, however, far more fundamental than the mere notion of their absence, for, as we have seen, we may have the latter *without* the former. There are, as we saw, cases where the thought of real existence, as opposed to intentional inexistence, can itself occur in brackets—the case, e.g., where we imagine that Joanna Southcott's absurd prophecies have come true.

VALUES AND INTENTIONS

Here the presence of wider brackets surrounding the thought of the total removal of brackets of narrower scope, makes the latter, like what is within them, a thing merely thought of or intended and in no sense believed. All these things make it plain that we can with difficulty speak of the beliefs, and even less of the opinions and judgements of animals, for though they may well be credited with the rudiments and materials for these higher-order performances, they cannot be thought to manipulate such materials with the requisite number of subtle contrasts. They may, however, like men, be governed by many unchallenged notions, and this may serve as a low-grade analogue of belief.

The open readiness basic to belief must, however, be qualified further as a readiness, not only for the *empty* conscious references characteristic of mere thought nor for the wholly *free* conscious references characteristic of mere fantasy. It is a readiness for references that are at once *fulfilled* or satisfied (in the precise Husserlian sense dealt with above), and which are further absolutely *compulsive* (to use a most illuminating term of Peirce's). To believe is to look to the concrete *carrying out* of one's thought in the manner appropriate to its content, but it is also to 'expect' this to occur compulsively, in a manner exacting submission on our part. The phrase 'readiness *for*', so often used in the present discussion, as opposed to the companion phrase 'readiness *to*', indicates the essential passivity of the disposition involved in belief. Belief is a sort of anticipatory bowing to anticipated violence which merges into the actual bowing to violence actually exerted. The paradigm case of what we are ready for in believing is provided by the deliverances of sense: seeing is the term of believing. If we believe there to be honey in the jar, then we are ready for all the compulsive experiences which would be said to show us the honey in the jar, or which would lead up to or fit in with such experiences. There are, however, *other* compulsive experiences besides those of sense-experience: a belief that such and such is the case in regard to certain inner life states, looks forward to, prepares for the actual having of certain experiences, which both fulfil and validate our expectations, but which need not be experiences of sense. In the same way, a belief in the correctness of an abstract analysis, or in some theorem connecting various classes of numbers, may reach establishment by the mere manipulation of notions or symbols, without recourse to the compulsive deliverances of sense.

THE MODES OF BELIEF 103

It may be held, however, that *all* cases of belief, have some relation, remote or direct, to the compulsions of sense-experience. For the inner life states which are not primarily those of sense have none the less a necessary connection with what is revealed through compulsive sense-experience, through which alone they acquire a fixed place in 'reality', and a being for other persons as well as ourselves. And the abstract truths that we establish directly by manipulating notions and symbols have also a necessary relevance to the things presented to sense, through which alone it is meaningful to *assert* them. That if equals are taken from equals the results are equal, may be established purely symbolically or conceptually, but to *believe* this is to look forward to what you will for that reason find in concrete sense-confrontation. Mathematical truths may not be true because of what we find in our pockets, but they certainly *apply* to what we find there—having spent equal sums out of equal sums in our pockets, the situation will necessarily be describable as one of equal sums in those pockets, excluding complications regarding vanishing, etc., not entering into the sense of normal talk about money and pockets. We may hold, accordingly, that without something like the hard compulsions of sense to look forward to, it would be impossible to have the sort of state of mind called belief. Belief essentially 'looks forward' to such sense-compulsions, or at least to something conceived on a remote analogy with these. There are undoubtedly metaphysical beliefs, as in the divine threefoldness or in the timeless blessedness of disembodied spirits, which do not look forward to sensory confrontations, but we can believe in them only in a fashion, by looking forward to something remotely akin to the compulsions of sense, through which this divine threefoldness of this disembodied existence might be brought home to *someone*, possibly to God Himself or to the blessed spirits in question, though not at present to ourselves. The validity of such beliefs is of course not here in question.

The readiness involved in belief must, further, be qualified as a readiness which not only, as it were, looks forward to compulsive sense-confrontations, but which also, as it were, looks *back* upon the latter, and which *builds* what it looks forward to upon this. One must hold, that is, that one cannot believe *in vacuo*, but that one must have had a prior store of remembered compulsions, woven into a fairly well-knit fabric, on to which

104 VALUES AND INTENTIONS

one's anticipation of fresh compulsions can be grafted, and of which it represents the continuation. Believing is like looking forward to the *next* stage of a story: when the story has got some distance under way, one can begin to anticipate how it will continue. When the story has just been started, there is as yet not enough to which such an anticipation can attach itself, and there can accordingly be no such thing as belief. Such a building on past confrontations may be the sort of building that, at a higher, formulated level, can be classified as an appeal to evidence, but it may equally well be a case of the intuitive induction, that leap to universal principles from particular *illustrations*, which is the psychological foundation, however much logically spurned, of our insight into abstract truths. Belief is therefore not accidentally, but essentially, something which build upon what, if formulated, would be premisses, evidence or illustrations: the words 'founded', 'firmly founded upon', etc., express this dependence. This is so even if in the particular case such evidence, premisses or illustration can be reasonably dispensed with, or if its use is irrational and bad, or even if, in pathological and perverse contexts, there is either a building on nothing, or on what is not really evidence or premisses or illustration at all. Having learnt to build beliefs on the main mass of compulsive experience in an orderly manner, I can now build them in an entirely wanton fashion: I can proceed as if I had a foundation to go on where such a foundation is lacking, or I can build on a genuine foundation in an arbitrary and perverse manner. It is, however, only because I have practised the art of building belief on a genuine basis and in a regular manner that these perverse performances are possible. Tertullian may have believed something *because* it was absurd, but he could only do so because he and countless others had formed most of their beliefs less abnormally.

We are now brought to a point central for an analysis of believing: its necessary relation to what certain idealists have spoken of as 'systematic coherence', or to what Peirce covered by the less imprecise concept of 'synechism'. Belief is only possible where there has been compulsive experience manifesting a fairly high degree of positive coherence or continuity of pattern, and belief is always, in principle a proposed extension of such continuity and pattern, a preparedness for it to be carried on or continued. The circumstances we *have* experienced must have

THE MODES OF BELIEF 105

'fitted together' to form a tolerably unified or coherent or continuous picture for us to build upon it, and belief is, in principle, a carrying farther of such unity or coherence or continuity. Belief is, on the analysis we are presenting, essentially *inferential* (however much it may have come to cover cases in which this inferential element is inexplicit or suppressed), only the inference is not from a small body of formulated premisses, but from a body of circumstances altogether too vast and vague to be formulated, some small segment of which may be represented as the condensed content of an explicit thought-reference, but most of which is present only in disposition, being something that *could* be thought of if we chose, or that could *have* been thought of if circumstances were favourable, or which operates *as if* it had been thought of, though it in fact neither was nor could be so. We are referring, that is, to the vast context of past experience and tacit acceptance, which serves as a background to our most trivial affirmations, and makes their verbal formulation so difficult: it is in relation to this, and as an extension to this, that belief alone is possible. And we must not be misled by the sophism that it is only if the *background* is believed that it is possible to build beliefs upon it. The background must have a certain massive extent, and a certain close cementing of separate parts, before it can serve as a base for believing anything. Before it achieves such a minimum extent and unified structure, neither it, nor what is built upon it, can properly be said to be believed, and when it has *just* achieved this extent and structure—if such a point can be singled out at all—only what is built on it, and not it, should be said to be believed. Only when this stage has been long passed, as it is in normal adult experience, can one be said to believe separate circumstances by attaching them, more or less tentatively, to a background which is itself believed. To put the whole matter crudely, and with some inexactness, it is only if one has had a sufficiency of compulsive experience, whose items did not fall apart into mutual irrelevance or sharp discrepancy, that one can have the notion of a 'reality' on to which some anticipated circumstance can be 'tacked on', and to believe in such a circumstance can mean nothing unless it means to tack it on firmly, and without *arrière pensée*, on to what has been thus experienced.

As to the nature of this 'tacking on' involved in belief, it is important not to limit it to the quasi-logical necessitation affirmed

D*

106 VALUES AND INTENTIONS

in Spinozism or in the doctrine of universal 'internal relations' held by certain British idealists. A logically necessary thought-development is, by its nature, a thought-development which hovers round one spot, which may illuminate it from a variety of angles, but which does not, in an important sense, move on to other points by transitions whose illumination and informative worth depends on the fact that they are *not* strictly necessary. Though few genuine thought-transitions, even the most obvious in their necessity, quite deserve the dispraise conveyed by the Wittgensteinian term 'tautological', yet there are some thought-transitions which, in an important sense, and by a vast expenditure of energy, contrive not to advance but to remain stationary, while others are, in a related sense, ampliative, engaged in covering new territory. It is a strange fact that the energy of philosophers has to a large extent been directed to the absurd project of trying to turn thought-changes which involve this kind of advance into those which are elaborately stationary, or to regarding the former as a *faute de mieux* for, or an approximation to, the latter, not the latter as a queer limiting case of the former. Even those who, like Hegel and the British idealists, have most stressed the systematic coherence involved in genuine thought-progressions and the deliberate stationariness of logistical and mathematical thinking, have still sought to give to the former the ineluctable character proper to the latter, failing to see that genuine movement generally involves a choice among a variety of directions. 'Coherence' no doubt has as its limit the complete suppression of diversity, so that what one advances to is only in conception different from what one advances from, but this limit, though it may condense all the unimagined riches of mathematics, none the less represents the self-destruction of the 'coherence' of which it also represents the limit. If, however, coherence is taken to involve genuine diversity among the cohering elements, it will tend to have a more and a less and a variety of possible directions: it will be an essentially vague principle, exemplified alike in the continuous passage from point to point in space and time, in the constancy, or more or less smooth change in character, of their contents, in the fragmented repetitiousness of specimens of the same natural kind, in the strange economy of diversity which marks off whole natural fields and whose breakdown defines their edges, perhaps even in the absence of *simple* coherence, in the

THE MODES OF BELIEF 107

sheer 'randomness' shown in certain kinds of juxtaposition among certain sorts of object, which we readily carry over into new cases, and in the odd statistical sameness which pervades such randomness. Apart from a small range of genuinely inescapable though content-bound necessities—one has in mind the 'synthetic *a priori*' of colours, etc. etc.—compulsive experience alone shows us the extent and manner in which it is unified and continuous, alone shows us the extent to which we inhabit a 'world' and what manner of world we inhabit, and thereby shows us how and what we may believe. The 'coherence' or 'synechism' presupposed by belief is therefore a notion capable of infinite forms and degrees, all of which are reduced to common emptiness and meaninglessness by a general assertion of 'internal relations', which amounts really to a blanket determination to incorporate a reference to everything, however disparate and irrelevant, into the account given of any single thing.

That belief has this ampliative, cohesive character does not involve denying that we believe many things without specifically conceiving *how* they fit on to or continue the 'pattern' of reality: there are many facts of immediate compulsive experience which are obviously in this position. It is only, however, by connecting them (in a manner not 'bracketed' by considerations which demote them to fancies or uncertainties) with the coherent background deposit of compulsive experience, that we can be held to believe in them, and it is also obviously by their capacity to fit continuously into its growing pattern that our faith in them can be sustained. In the same way there are doubtless many abstract *a priori* 'truths' which we can believe or demonstrate solely by immersing our minds in their contents, or by the steady transformation of other similar 'truths'. Some such 'truths' were, however, believed in the first instance as a result of an intuitive induction in which all indirectly share, and they all, as we saw, look forward to an application to compulsive experience, by which alone they can qualify as beliefs, and which is such at times, by forcing us to apply them to uncontemplated cases, as to modify our confidence in their truth. There are likewise many intuitive convictions, detached from past experience and not issuing at any definite point in what we anticipate, which we can cherish only because they can be put side by side with other convictions not formed in this intuitive manner. And there are

108 VALUES AND INTENTIONS

further, as we saw, metaphysical convictions going altogether beyond anything in our possible experience, which we none the less cherish by analogy, behaving *as if* they had their roots in some coherent system of compulsive experience, and as if they could provide the basis for further extending this system (as they, or something in some sense 'corresponding' to them, may well do for an experience other than our own).

The unconditioned character of belief implies further that we 'expect' what we believe to continue to fit the fabric formed by extending compulsive experience, *however* far such extension may be carried, and that, being true, it will be found 'at the bottom of the well', in the limiting view of things to which our imperfect views are thought of as tending. And we expect further that the fit will be better the farther the fabric is extended, that what we believe will be tied in by increasingly many threads to a fixed place in the whole. The 'real structure' of things is, in short, thought of as revealing itself more and more the more the manners in which something is experienced, a proposition of a profound non-formal plausibility that required the genius of a Peirce to prize it out.

It is clear further that the unconditioned character of belief cannot be satisfied with the mere survival of what we believe through the unbounded projection of our own future experience: it as naturally demands that it should be perpetuated *sideways* into experiences disjoined from and parallel to its own. The 'real structure of things' towards which, as a limit, each addition to, and each thought-extension of, compulsive experience brings us closer, must also be a limit for a whole scientific community of persons, to make use of a Kantian illumination of C. S. Peirce. That belief involves in itself this limiting ideal is shown in the fact that to believe anything naturally involves the wish to communicate such belief to others, and to 'expect' that they will have the experiences (in proper circumstances) that will lead them to share it, as also in the fact that belief tends to be shaken by other people's incredulity, or by their not having experiences confirmatory of, or having experiences which run counter to, the beliefs in question. That it is likely that what is real or the case should be revealed in like manner to like persons, and the more so the more the persons and the occasions of revelation, is *almost* a tautology. To regard it as a mere fact of human psychology that

THE MODES OF BELIEF 109

we seek to impose our convictions on others, or that we consult them and are ready to modify our convictions to accord with theirs, shows a total inability to penetrate deeply into the close linkage of traits making up the notion of belief, which must tend ultimately to make its nature wholly mysterious.

If belief is thus unconditional, it can exhibit degrees only in so far as it is hindered from achieving its complete status, by having its objects bracketed or demoted by some other similar would-be belief, whose objects it in its turn demotes and brackets. Partiality is accordingly no phenomenon that can characterize an isolated belief or belief-tendency. Belief, incorporating what it believes into an ultimate, limiting view of the world, can be diminished to something partial and imperfect only by encountering something as absolute in its claims as itself, something whose view it would demote and bracket in its own, while the contending view would demote and bracket *its* view in similar fashion. Out of this clash of absolute claims a new balance arises, in which each claim is diminished to a would-be approximation to belief since it lacks the *uniqueness* essential to belief. Partial belief resembles the situation in which Pope and Anti-pope confronted each other at Avignon and Rome. Partial belief is accordingly no merely lessened degree of belief, but a mental phenomenon of a new and more complex kind: it measures, we may say, the inability to achieve belief, due to the clash of competing belief-claims. That partial belief thus arises out of complete alternative world-views, explains why, even in its least reflective form, it naturally assumes the numerical structure which at a higher level it achieves once more: we are *half*-minded or a *third*-minded or a *quarter*-minded to believe X as against the other complete 'alternatives' which offer themselves to our thought. It is a more sophisticated, rather than a less developed attitude than belief: it represents, we may say, the degree to which our attitude falls short of, and by the same token approaches belief. And it represents this degree, not as something based on the independent characters of the competing partial beliefs, and elicited only by an external comparison—much as we elicit a thing's degree of loudness or saturation or temperature—but rather as something essentially pertaining to the partial beliefs taken *conjointly*, in their very competition and mutual attrition, and shown in the extent to which each succeeds in driving the others from the field. All this may be

110   VALUES AND INTENTIONS

a vivid event in the life of the mind, taken note of by its own immediate self-reflection, but it will of course also register itself in countless blunted and imperfect forms, which may have more palpability from a behavioural or linguistic point of view. It is thus no mere empirical accident, but a circumstance arising out of the very structure of partial belief, that, to the same extent that our belief in one alternative increases, our belief in what are felt to be *other* alternatives tends to wane. This is not, even here, something that by a mere definition *must* happen, since the mind can, in a remarkable manner, fail to practise self-collection, and to let its right hand know what its left hand is doing: it is something that must, however, always *tend* to happen where consciousness becomes comprehensive and clear.

We may note further that, while partial belief is a subjective phenomenon, representing a man's readiness to extend his picture of the 'real' in a given direction, it is also, for that person, a quasi-objective phenomenon, a seeming readiness of the things thought of, and thought of as having their roots in what was or could be compulsively experienced, to complete themselves in a given manner. We are, in short, saying that the 'likely' or the 'probable', in a sense as yet free from anything 'standard' or intersubjective, enters into the very description of partial belief, that to believe something partially is to see it as a likely continuation of one's growing picture of the real, and as composing, with other likely continuations, the full round of what unambiguously is or will be. Likelihood, in fact, like negation or disjunction, or like its own sister modalities, is, in its fullest development, a peculiar conscious 'light' in which things may be regarded, a 'light' which may not exist on sea or land but which none the less *inexists* in the mind's own vision of things. To think rain likely is to see, not oneself, but the weather as inclining in various directions, but preponderantly towards rain, and this 'vision' is plainly as much 'objective' as 'subjective', since it as much grows out of what the weather has done or is doing (or does so in all but the abnormal or perverse case) as it grows out of what one oneself is or has been. Such a vision of things is one to which the thinking person, with his readiness to continue his experience in given directions, essentially contributes, but it is also one to which the 'things' of his past experience and knowledge have contributed, and it is to *these* that the alternative leanings seem principally to

THE MODES OF BELIEF

pertain, which seem in a sense, likely to complete themselves in alternative ways. This peculiar vision is not even confined to situations in which belief, with its unconditioned claims enters: it seems present rudimentarily even at the level of the cut-off meaning or detached idea, in so far as this presses to its appropriate sensuous or other fulfilment. The 'risky' and the 'safe' are certainly characters of the experienced world which we may, without great courage, attribute even to the world of animals, who certainly give every sign of appreciating them.

Partial belief has one sort of magnitude, essentially relative and fractional, representing the extent to which it *is* partial, the degree to which it is near to or far from ousting competing claims from the field. To the partial believer this shows in the degree to which an alternative 'looms large' on the horizon of the possible, like the moon on the physical horizon, the extent to which it appears to coincide with a wider spread of difference among distinct alternatives, and so in a sense to come on him from more directions than alternative possibilities. What we believe *more* in this sense, we feel liable to encounter in a greater number or range of ways than other alternatives, whether this persuasion may rest on a simple comparison of character, or on long experience of natural frequencies, or on mere personal predilection. It is impossible to express this sort of magnitude of belief in any wholly non-metaphorical manner: the image of a *Spielraum* or space of possibilities seems as indispensable to the full development of partial belief as does the image of a spatialized past and future to the fully developed consciousness of time, or the image of an inner personal world to the full development of our consciousness of other persons and even of ourselves. It is a mistake to look on all pictures and likenesses as dispensable and to seek graspingly for their 'cash-values'; in their incomplete cashability their very use may consist.

Partial belief also will have a second sort of magnitude, generally covered by such terms as 'strength', 'firmness' or 'fixity', which depend on the general power of a partial belief to resist reduction or modification by other partial beliefs: this too may depend on the volume and range of considerations, or merely on personal predilection. It will be a magnitude distinct from the first, for what we believe *more* we need not believe very *firmly*, as is shown by the rapid yielding to novel alternatives or considerations,

VALUES AND INTENTIONS

whereas a belief inconsiderable in its spread may also be stable and firm. Both magnitudes of partial belief may at times make themselves reflectively evident: we are then said to 'feel' the degree and the solidity of the conviction inspired by certain alternatives. But such 'feelings' are what they are only as the crowning condensation of countless other manifestations: the varied energy of our practical preparations or the energy we *should* show if the occasion and our own wishes warranted it, the vivid imaginative and emotional working out of alternatives which make belief 'real' and not merely 'notional', the varied necessary images of the *Spielraum* occupied by different possibilities, the problematic 'lights' playing over our world-picture and variegating it with mysteries and questions, the dry, verbal estimates that may be given of range and number of alternatives, weight of grounds, etc. etc. The whole 'evolution' of belief represents a passage from a crudely felt struggle between imaginatively and emotionally developed belief-tendencies towards a 'cool' assessment involving only the adduction of verbal reasons or the manipulation of fractions and numbers, a 'cool' development which would, however, be deprived of all sense could it not, on occasion, revert to its 'warmer' origins. All these states, tendencies and performances hang together, by bonds recognized but not forged by language, and in their complete, conjoint realization, or in their perpetual to and fro oscillation, lies the perfection of belief.

We have now completed our sketch of the anatomy of belief. It will be seen that it does not represent any mysterious addition to the conscious references which enter into it, but that it merely carries to a limit, and gives unconditional form to the tendencies present in any and every consciousness of objects. The 'reality' of which belief is the subjective correlative is merely the completely worked out, ideal form of an object. The existence of belief depends, further, on what may be called indifferently a great natural accident and blessed piece of good fortune, or a necessary requirement of reason: the presence in compulsive experience of continuities sufficiently simple to be recognized as such by us, and to be used for the further anticipation of compulsive experience. The ultimate thanks go to 'matter' that the demands of 'mind' exist and are met. Many will have felt it a defect that a phenomenon so humdrum as belief, which occurs among typists in offices and busmen in buses, and which is referred to quite

THE MODES OF BELIEF 113

unphilosophically by either, should have received at our hands so cumbersome and so portentous an analysis. We have acted, however, on the assumption that philosophical understanding always must involve a *rounding out* of notions into forms strange and complex from the point of view of their first use, that it must practise supplementation and not stripping, and that it must endeavour rather to look on each simple phenomenon as a rude sketch of some unimaginably complex, completely fulfilled manner of being or acting rather than to proceed reductively the other way round.

(II) THE APPROVABILITY OF BELIEF

Belief, as sketched by us in the foregoing section, can be seen to involve aspirations or directions of endeavour, directions which it can follow, or from which it can diverge more or less widely, thereby rendering itself *approvable* or *disapprovable* (or in one sense of the words 'probable' and 'improbable'), and this not merely to particularly oriented believers, but to all who see the goals involved in believing anything. Beliefs are, in short, subject to 'norms', 'standards' and 'values' which are not grafted extrinsically upon them, through reason of the chance responses of particular believing persons. They enter into the description of belief as such, since some regard for them colours any act of believing, and they accordingly tend to win recognition and approval from all who have ever believed anything. Were belief a merely natural phenomenon, in the sense of being part of the mere contingent detail of organic or conscious existence, a feeling, attitude, state of mind or what not to which certain living beings were disposed, then there would be little sense in discussing the approvability of such a phenomenon. Such discussion would amount to little more than an analysis, already performed by certain thinkers with stupefying completeness, of the not very deep-going or interesting requirements of personal commendation. Now, however, belief has shown itself to be a phenomenon carrying to the limit certain features essential to and definitory of conscious aliveness as such, and so having intrinsic connections, however suppressed or implicit, not only with all forms of conscious aliveness, but also with all conditions that bind persons into a realm of communicating intelligences confronted with what deserves to be

VALUES AND INTENTIONS

called 'material nature' or a 'world'. Having all these momentous connections, belief cannot be characterized except as at all times *endeavouring* to do something in which it may either succeed or fail, so laying itself open to approbation or disapprobation by standards not arbitrary and escapable, but inescapable because intrinsic to itself. All this may seem unintelligible to those concerned to keep distinct concepts rigorously separate, but here as elsewhere the solution of philosophical difficulties consists in a conscious blurring of the boundaries that keep notions strictly apart.

The 'approvability' of a belief is, as we have said, its probability in one sense of the word, but it is not, nevertheless, its probability in the dominant and most straightforward sense. Probability, like negation and disjunction and its own sister modalities, is, in its dominant sense, a 'light' in which things may be regarded. It may depend on the presence of belief in the person to whom something seems likely, but it does not include such belief in its explicit purview, it does not regard what it thinks probable as believed, or as believed in a peculiar manner. To think something likely is to see the vaguely organized rump of things we take to be real, which has grown up around our compulsive experience, as extended in two or more manners, which are not such as to combine or fall together harmoniously, but to quarrel with one another and demand co-ordination in a complete circle of disjoined cases, occupying different amounts of 'room' in an imagined 'space' of possibilities. But as opposed to this complex 'light' in which things appear to the hesitant thinker or believer, the approvability of belief is a 'light' in which possible beliefs about things may themselves appear to him: it is a phenomenon of reflection or of 'second intention'. It is, in short, the degree to which a belief approves or justifies itself when measured against the intrinsic standards descriptive of its own endeavours. Such approvability will be independent of, and will behave in many ways quite differently from, the first-order probability and the correlative belief it endorses. When a low degree of belief and a low corresponding likelihood have a high degree of approvability, a high degree of belief and a high corresponding likelihood will normally have a low one. And while degree of belief and probability tend towards fixed limits in either direction—an upper limit where belief is perfect, and where what is believed covers the whole range of

THE MODES OF BELIEF 115

co-ordinated possibilities, and a lower limit where belief is extinct, and where what is thought of is extruded from this range—degree of approvability (and its converse disapprovability) varies quite without limit in either direction. A near-belief, e.g., or a correspondingly high assignment of probability, will become indefinitely more disapprovable, the more weighty and the more numerous the points that tell against it. In the same way, the firmness of a belief, which is itself capable of indefinite increase, is capable also, at all its levels, of an indefinite increase in approvability or disapprovability. The firmer belief at a disapprovable level becomes, the more disapprovable is its firmness. (We so use the term 'disapprovability' that, where approvability increases, disapprovability decreases, and *vice versa*. It would perhaps have been better *not* to reckon disapprovability as a mere negation of approvability, but as a positive contrary determination. We distinguish, e.g., between the disapprovability of running *counter* to evidence in forming highly confident beliefs and the lessened approvability of forming them on an inadequate basis. It is, however, convenient, to speak as if an increase in approvability meant the same as a decrease in disapprovability and *vice versa*.)

But though thus logically independent and different, approvability is none the less essentially bound up with probability. There is no sense in which a belief can be said to be approvable if what is believed cannot be said to be in any way probable. Approvability is in fact merely the seal set upon the probable light in which something appears to someone, and in the absence of such a probable light there is nothing that can be approved or disapproved. There is further no sense in which the likelihood in which a certain belief or near-belief makes us view the world, can have any 'objective status', or can itself be affirmed or believed in, except in so far as the belief or near belief which mediates it can be *approved*. The probable light in which things appear to a near-believer is no primary phenomenon of direct experience: it depends on the power of a thing to set quarrelling appearances before the same person, it is an iridescence in which *he*, as well as it, plays a part. This being the case, it can be a real or true light only in the sense of being a light for all believers, a light in which, in so far as a man detaches himself from all that is merely personal in the formation of his beliefs, things must of necessity appear. The probability which is objective and which can play an important role in the description of nature, is accordingly a probability which depends on the approvability of the belief to which it corresponds: it is, we may say, the probable light 'cast' by the most approvable or 'rational' degree of belief.

Approvability and probability being thus bound up with one another, we may here deprecate the strange usage of Professor Popper, according to which the laws and theories of science all have *zero* probability to start with, and remain of zero probability however much evidence accumulates in their favour, and yet manage to pile up an ever-increasing degree of *corroboration* or *Bewährung*, which in this usage certainly entails increased approvability. Professor Popper has indeed forged a queer, one-sided notion of probability of which these things become true by definition—the probable being determined exclusively by such things as the *number* of thinkable objects in a space-time region of the universe—but it remains inexcusably odd to speak of corroborating, i.e. strengthening, an assertion which is and remains indefinitely improbable. The view certainly *suggests* that we must confide in what we know to be wholly incredible, merely because its consequences have been repeatedly tested and have not been found to be false.

The approvability of a belief, and the probable light that it authorizes, must not be thought of as confined to matters of an empirico-scientific character. Though all belief points ultimately to the compulsions of sense, and the coherent picture they permit us to form, there are, as we saw, many arrests and stations on the way, and many beliefs which achieve fulfilment and justification at levels remote from the sensuous. There are beliefs concerning the correct solution of an equation, or the proper analysis of a notion, or the right description of a state of mind. There are also beliefs, as we shall have occasion to illustrate in more detail, concerning the approvability of beliefs, or the permissibility of lines of conduct or the desirability of ends. And there are beliefs of a metaphysical character, framed on an analogy with ordinary naturalistic beliefs, but going beyond the limits of nature and the senses. In all these cases, things appear in more or less plausible lights, in all of them there is a confidence ranging more or less firmly or broadly over a round of co-ordinated alternatives, and in all of them we assume there to be approvabilities and disapprovabilities that can be laid bare as nicely, and which follow analogous principles, to those

THE MODES OF BELIEF

governing theories concerning the natural world. The tendency to confine the term 'probability' to the latter, represents, therefore, an unfortunate and confusing debasement, calculated to blur our sense of the deep kinship between rules governing belief in these various fields. Even more serious is the restriction of the term 'probability' to the special issues belonging to the mathematicized 'theory of chances', the special class of case where we are concerned either with freely variable combinations of various abstract alternatives, finitely numerable or covering finitely numerable and abstractly equalized segments of qualitative difference, or belonging to fields characterized in our experience by random irregularity in the combined occurence of alternatives accompanied by increasing approximation to regularity in the *proportion* of their happening. The probabilities here are peculiar only in respect of the abstractly restricted or empirically random character of the basis from which they grow and of which they represent the extension, on their exclusive concern with states *indifferent* to one another, and having nothing that gives one the slightest prerogative over the other. There is no reason to regard beliefs resting on such a fragmented basis as in any way more or less approvable than beliefs resting on other types of basis, and hence no reason to discriminate between the 'probabilities' of their several subject-matters. As to the further proposal to make 'probability' *mean* either short-range frequency in the realization of a type of alternative in a certain actual series of cases, or the limiting frequency towards which such short-range frequencies may be taken as tending, it represents nothing but a disservice to language, since it robs a word of a sense for which another word must immediately be manufactured. It seems also to spring from a disreputable preference for immediately satisfiable, naturalistic notions over those whose fulfilment is more indirect and circuitous, a preference which produces its own nemesis, since the notion of the limiting frequency of the realization of a certain sort of alternative is a notion fraught with far more problems and obscurities than a notion of probability linked with the notion of approvable belief, and can be shown, further, to rest on and presuppose the latter.

That our beliefs are approvable or disapprovable, and that this approvability springs from their very nature as beliefs, can be shown only by considering in detail the qualifications that render beliefs approvable or disapprovable, or the conditions that make

VALUES AND INTENTIONS

them so. Here we may first emphasize the truism that a belief is approvable to the extent that it *submits* to the compulsive experience appropriate to it, and, in the paradigm case, to the compulsive experience of sense. Belief is, in its essence, a preparatory submission to what compulsive experience may offer, and is thereby differentiated from wish, fantasy and hypothesis which owe no such allegiance: it must therefore, to be 'true to itself', submit to the arbitrament of such experience. I may believe, or come close to believing, that A is B if I have no compulsive experience to back or thwart my belief: having had that experience I must suffer my belief to be strengthened, or weakened, or altered, according to what such experience brings forward. Such compulsive experience may also *fulfil* or realize the content of what I believe, in which case the notion of correspondence is applicable: a belief is approvable if it can be *seen* to correspond to the facts. This formula is, however, much more empty than it seems, since it is only the one compulsively fulfilled belief that establishes the correspondence. There can be no confrontation of beliefs with an uninformed, inarticulate piece of 'direct experience'. And it is also unsatisfactory, since the mere fulfilment of a belief, even if compulsive, may still leave it mistaken. To be fully approved, it must be found to 'fit in' with the whole coherent web tied to our compulsive experiences, and to do so however far this may be extended and developed, and to persist up to its limit. Seen in this connection, correspondence means no more than that a belief will correspond to a fact or to a reality if it can be sustained to the limit of inquiry, and will become ever firmer in the process, again a principle that we owe to the genius of Peirce. But the compulsive experience which renders a belief approvable need in no sense fulfil or illustrate it, and in some cases *cannot* do so. It may merely fit in with or continue what is believed, and so provide an *evidential basis* for it, without illustrating or carrying out its content. It is an obvious truism or 'predicament' (however we may choose to regard it) that the situations which best *fulfil* our beliefs about other people's experiences (i.e. comparable experiences of our own) provide little evidence of their existence or character, whereas the situations which best provide evidence for these beliefs (i.e. behavioural ones) also do nothing to fulfil them.

The submission of belief to compulsive experience which renders it approvable may also be several stages removed from the

THE MODES OF BELIEF

experience in question: it may be a submission to a belief (perhaps someone else's) based on a belief based on a belief . . . fulfilled by compulsive experience. And, as we have remarked before, it is only in the most elementary case that the compulsive experience which renders belief approvable is one of sense. The belief that the door is green is rendered approvable by actually observing the green door, but the belief that thoughts can occur unillustrated by images is rendered approvable by actually having and reflecting on such thoughts, the belief that there can be a lamina with but a single surface can be rendered approvable by successfully imagining such a lamina, the belief that X is not a prime number by actually carrying out appropriate divisions, etc. etc. The compulsive experiences by means of which ethical and aesthetic beliefs can be rendered approvable will concern us later. The submission to compulsive experience is, of course, not the only or final condition governing the approvability of beliefs, and may at times have to yield to others. It may also have to submit to our submission to *other* compulsive experiences. The compulsive experience which renders one belief approvable may fail to fit in smoothly with the compulsive experiences which render other beliefs appropriate, so that, whatever we believe, we may do violence to some items in our compulsive experience. In such situations submission to the main volume of compulsive experience may require a belief not readily geared to certain tracts of that experience: we may have, in deference to the overall plausibility of some opinion, to give an unplausible account of certain matters. All this has its analogues in the sphere of morals, and is a matter of such plain common sense, as to seem barely worthy of philosophical notice.

If belief, by its nature, seeks accommodations with compulsive experience, it must, by its nature, seek to make such accommodations as detailed and deep-going as possible. There is an accommodation with compulsive experience which consists merely in evading a clash with it, in believing things so broad and vague as to fit practically any pattern of experience, in nursing expectations which are *safe* merely because they are indiscriminately adjusted to practically anything in the wide round of the possible. Such beliefs may be approvable in holding what they hold in a very probable light, and yet have a *low* approvability in doing so, since they do so without deference to the detailed content of experience.

120　VALUES AND INTENTIONS

Whereas a belief insecure and disapprovable at the outset, because finely accommodated to a fairly narrow way of building on some presumed basis, and exceeded in variety by countless other feasible ways of building on the same basis, may yet win the laurels of the highest approvability, if found to fit the actual detail of experience. The fact that it *fails* to fit countless *other* possibilities of experience, that it runs the risk of being *falsified* by their realization, means that it does almost uniquely and closely fit the one possibility, or the one narrow range of possibility, whose realization accordingly confers on it the highest approvability. The matter can also be tautologically put by saying that the fact that certain unlikely experiences raise certain little approvable beliefs to a high degree of approvable confidence, shows that the beliefs in question *were* specifically adjusted to such experiences, and that *this* is the reason for their high approvability. As Popper would put the matter, that belief is most approvable which most risks falsification by adverse experience, and which best survives and triumphs over that risk, a position perhaps not deeply different from that of Hegel when he holds that what is positive in a worthwhile conscious state must of necessity be a negation of a negation, and must involve always the difficult triumph over some 'other'. To regard the self-immersion of belief in specific empirical detail as a submission to the risk of falsification represents, however, a somewhat artificial perspective. It is rather because belief *is* loyal to the positive particularity of experience that it risks greater falsification than the other way round, and it is this positive loyalty which grounds its approvability rather than its exposure to falsification. For risks do not confer honour unless undertaken for some worthy end.

The approvability conferred by deep sensitivity to experienced detail applies also to theories embraced because what is experienced would fit on smoothly to them, or because they would fit on smoothly to what is experienced. The supposition of which the experienced facts seem likely continuations is raised in approvability when they prove to be facts, and much more so according to the closeness and the uniqueness of the bond. If the supposition most naturally debouches into the experienced facts, and they into it, and no other supposition achieves the same overall naturalness of continuation, then the supposition achieves greater approvability from the experienced facts with which it is so

THE MODES OF BELIEF

closely and uniquely continuous. If the author of A wrote B, B could most approvably be expected to have the traits which it does have, and which continue the pattern of A, and more so than having the same authorship as C or D. Its having the traits it has will accordingly deepen the approvability of the first supposition of authorship to the extent that this supposition deepens its *own* approvability. Such derived strengthenings of approvability are affected, no doubt, by the *prior* approved likelihood of the view strengthened: the view having the closest bonds with some fact may, on account of its stark disconnection with other experience, have to yield in approvability to a view which continues it less well. This rightful deference to a prior probability must not, however, be construed as giving countenance to the strange opinion that experience cannot give an approvable likelihood to what continues it, unless what thus continues it has some not inconsiderable approvable likelihood *to start with* (or *a priori*) quite *apart* from all empirical strengthening. The circumstances which fit on to and continue a believed content are not, except for the deliberately narrow gaze of the formal 'theory of chances', really 'outside' and separable from this content, and the force of experience which gives approvability to the former is therefore necessarily communicated to the latter.

If belief is thus approvable in so far as it measures itself fully against compulsive experience and the evidence stemming from this, it will also be approvable in so far as it goes positively in quest of such experience, in so far as, in other words, it constantly invites and courts refutation. It is not necessary to stress how this sustained, gratuitous gallantry constitutes the heart and soul of scientific method: only the absurd attempt to imitate the dry talk of science and mathematics in a discipline essentially ethical has served to mask this fact. It is also clear that the approvability of a belief depends always on the use of the *widest possible* empirical and evidential basis: it is not approvable to believe something on a basis more selective and more abstract than the broadest one possesses. This principle can be justified in terms of the submission to compulsive experience characteristic of belief, but not on any more abstract basis. It will be found to have an analogue in the sphere of morals where a morally approvable volition necessarily adjusts itself to meet *all* the available and knowable facts.

VALUES AND INTENTIONS

If belief is rendered approvable by virtue of the completeness and depth of its submission to the verdict of compulsive experience, it will, as we have seen, be no less rendered approvable by its *synechism*, by its continuation of what is vouched for by such experience in the straightest and least varied manner. Belief, as we have seen, involves an *attachment* of what we believe to the main mass of coherent compulsive experience, together with all its coherent extensions and fillings, and attachment means nothing if not, in general, the supposition of more of the same sort, more related in the same manner, more following according to the same principle or rule, etc. etc. There may be beliefs in what is incongruous, extraordinary, unpredictable, miraculous, exceptional, incredible, etc., but not *all* or *most* of our beliefs could be of this sort, for this would leave us with no main mass of fixed reality to attach our suppositions to, and no fixed principles to govern such attachment. The belief in the incongruous and exceptional must itself be an incongruous and exceptional belief, one framed in the mere *hope*, whether relegated to this world or some other, of laying bare connections which are not now apparent.

As to the precise meaning of synechism, it is no doubt true that such formulae as 'more of the same sort', 'more related in the same manner', 'more following according to the same general principle' can be so twisted by clever wilfulness as to be quite void of content. There are *no* items added to some assemblage which cannot, in suitably chosen perspectives, be said to be *of the same sort* as those already in it, or as related to them and to each other *in the same manner*, or as following upon them and each other *according to the same general principle*. If a pumpkin is transformed into a coach it can be said to be as much a coach-or-pumpkin as it always was, if something is blue up to a certain moment of time and then for no reason whatever ever after green, it can be said, following Goodman, to have been continuously 'bleen', and if a man after successively doubling numbers up to 132 suddenly starts to triple them, it is no doubt possible to invent formulae which normalize his deviation, etc. etc. All this does not affect the fact that there are some sorts of sameness of quality or regular sequence which are more genuinely *same* than others, which represent a more genuine community, that our judgements on this matter have the most remarkable unanimity

THE MODES OF BELIEF 123

and security, and that, if to rely on this is to rely on a mere fact of psychology, then it is to rely on psychology in a sense in which all objects and themes of discourse reflect facts of psychology. The wisdom of Plato's Academy departed from the crude view of the Dialogues that there were 'forms' corresponding to every term covering a range of distinct entities, to a view which held that such forms only existed where there was a marked convergence to some simple natural type (geometrical solids, types of organism, etc.) and to the *virtues* characteristic of such types: it is the same wisdom which guides us in continuing the pattern of compulsive experience. We recognize that there is an absolute more and less of likeness, that some sorts of likeness are more remote and derivative than others, and that, beyond a certain degree, likeness in any important sense vanishes altogether. It is on such likeness that probability, not by accident spoken of as 'likeliness' (and in corresponding terms in other languages) both reposes and should repose. The precise likeness postulated in the individual case will of course defer to the course of compulsive experience. If I have experienced unbroken whiteness, it will satisfy continuity and the claims of compulsive experience to expect such whiteness to continue. To believe anything else, except in deference to past experience of sudden switches to other colours, would be gratuitous and logically disapprovable. If whiteness and blackness occur in uniform alteration, it will be approvable to expect similar alternation in the future, and disapprovable to invent freer formulae which bring in wider diversity. If white and black occur repeatedly in regular formations but at irregular intervals, it will be approvable to extrapolate similar irregular recurrences of regular patterned formations, etc. etc. Precisely what constitutes the simplest extension of experience, the one which genuinely minimizes diversity, may at times be unclear and ambiguous, and in such cases varied extensions will be alike approvable, but all this does not affect our great clearness, in the majority of cases, as to what is most like, and accordingly most likely. It is not right to say that such deference to likeness is a law for our minds only and not for things: one might say that without thoroughgoing deference to likeness there could be no 'things' at all.

It is all-important to stress, if it is not yet sufficiently clear, that the irregular and the random, which might seem the negation

124 VALUES AND INTENTIONS

of the regular and continuous, are merely eccentric cases of it: they apply in perfectly definite and quite circumscribed fields and could not apply everywhere, they affect specific characters and no others, and the *lack* of discoverable order is itself a definite empirical character, albeit a higher-order one, which we discover when induced to *give up* the quest for order in certain directions, a giving up which is as much an argument from like to like as the straightest inductive or analogical inference. (As to the disorder which masks itself in a perhaps indefinitely maintained semblance of order, or the order so complex as to be indistinguishable from disorder, neither are more than empty limiting concepts for which there cannot be illustration or use.) Thus we have all *given up* the picturesque quest for a law governing the distances of the planets from their centre, or the distribution of the stars in space: these things, like the more spectacular phenomena of the gaming table, have been found to be random, not falling under any repeating pattern that can count as a pattern for us. This *giving up* is, of course, as precarious, as much liable to revision, as is the acceptance of a pattern in other cases: the well-based regularity may turn out to have been an extraordinary chance, and the seeming play of chance to have masked deep-based regularity. The synechistic principle, the principle which argues from like to like is, however, the overriding principle in either case: it alone can ground chance, as it can ground continuity in the narrower sense. This principle therefore has the Hegelian property of outstripping and absorbing its opposite, since it makes of disorder a peculiar, higher case of order.

There is no sense, therefore, in which, from the logical think-ability of boundless random variety in the combinations of distinct entities or properties, we can proceed to find it mysterious that such variety should be more restricted. The assumption of limit-less independent variety is itself covertly synechistic: it involves both the persistence of the entities or qualities whose independence is thought to be so unlimited, as well as a *reliable*, discoverable absence of regularity in the modes of their sequence or combination. That there should be an irregularity that masks itself in unending regularity, or a deep-set regularity that is for us always masked as irregularity, are both, as we have seen, limiting possibilities that can be gratuitously entertained, but only in a synechistic framework, and whose nature is further such that they

THE MODES OF BELIEF

cannot *count* for our beliefs. Only where like is discoverably continued by like, at whatever level of likeness is in question, can there be any talk of believable existent things or properties, or of anything being the case at all. And the synechistic character of the random shows itself further in the approvable extension of the *proportionate* realization of randomly realized alternatives to further stretches of the same series. In the random series of cases fixed propensities, of constant but diverse strength, are divined, and are credited further with the Bernoullian property of showing themselves ever more clearly as the series grows longer. It would only be mysterious if this were *not* to happen, and if it did not, the mystery would have to be rendered orderly at some higher level.

Since belief only is what it is by virtue of its synechism, it will be approvable further according to the *depth* of that synechism: the more profound the unity and connection postulated among the things believed, the more food for belief in any part or in the whole of them. Hence the approvable search for ever furthergoing routes of explanation, which fly like *Autobahnen* over the twisted roads of ordinary thought, and establish straight tracks of likeness between territories seemingly separate. Each such link, to vary the metaphor, gives us more of a basis to believe upon, and the possibility of firmer building upon it. This approvable search points towards the limit of a system absolutely unified, and therefore in a sense self-explanatory, an ideal which, on account of its own inner conflicts, would seem incapable of fulfilment, and rightly to be classed among the transcendental, regulative Ideas of Kant. For belief is nothing if not submissive to an ineluctable, compulsive 'other', which both limits the possibility of, and gives precise form to, the quest for the continuous and the unified. And the system of thought, the Hegelian, which comes closest to explaining the very incongruity of the incongruous, the inexplicable, unideal particularity of such things as mud, hair and dirt, which Platonism finds so rebarbative, can do so only by postulating the *necessity* of the incongruous, compulsive 'other' for the unifying, universalizing life of reason.

If 'synechism', or the pursuit of the maximum of continuity, analogy and explanatory unity is one of the basic conditions of the approvability of belief, it is plain that 'equity', the avoidance of arbitrary and unwarranted discriminations, is as deeply fundamental. In believing, we seek to knit things together by the bonds

126 VALUES AND INTENTIONS

of affinity and likeness, and where likeness tends equally in different directions and permits competing completions, it can never be approvable to prefer one of these completions to the other. To choose arbitrarily, where reasons weigh equally in different directions, may be a proper thing in the magisterial realm of practice; it is excluded by the essentially self-humbling, submissive spirit of belief. To be guided by the bonds of reason and affinity is, therefore, necessarily to tend towards that *balance* among alternatives which finds a new, higher-order way of settling a problem where simple first-order settlement is impossible. The laying bare of this 'principle of indifference' among likelihoods—that where our basis affords no ground for approvable discrimination among alternatives, it is approvable to accord each an *equal* partial belief—may be regarded as one of the great steps in the advance of human reason, comparable to the early, gnomic formulations of justice, even if provoked by such unworthy perplexities as those of the Chevalier de Méré. That this principle leads to antinomies and contradictions if not repeatedly and sometimes artificially qualified is no disproof of its fundamental character: there is no non-trivial principle guiding judgement and conduct that is not in similar case.

In its most abstract form the principle of equity depends on our basic judgements of *qualitative difference or diversity*, on our judgement that the range of diversity covered by an alternative *A* is just equal to, or greater or less than, the range of diversity covered by an alternative *B*. Thus we judge intuitively that the *variety* of the incompatible ways in which a die can come to rest on one of its sides is, by reason of its approximate symmetry of construction, just about equal to the *variety* of the incompatible ways in which it can come to rest on any other of its sides, so that a fall on each side covers about the same range of *likeness* and *unlikeness*, and is for that reason equally likely. It is not the mere *number* of the various alternatives, but the apparent likeness or the unlikeness each covers, that determines this approvable judgement. In much the same way, where our basis allows something to be of any possible colour, we find it more likely to be green than emerald-green, since the range of variety comprised under the latter is less than, since falling under, that of the former, and equally we find it more likely to be green than salmon-pink, since the range of diversity comprised under the latter is judged

THE MODES OF BELIEF

to be less than, though *not* falling under, the former. Such judgements are among the clearest and least open to question of any we can form, even if belonging to a class having many undecidable and paradoxical members. If to accept such judgements is to be a mere slave to 'verbal magic', as some have contended, then the whole fabric of science is shot through and through with such 'magic'. There are, as the ingenuity of logicians has discovered, not merely cases where we *cannot say* whether an alternative *A* covers a wider range of incompatible diversity than an alternative *B*, and is accordingly to be judged more likely, but even cases where it seems approvable, in *one* way of regarding the matter, to consider *A* as covering the *same* range of diversity as *B*, and hence as *equally* likely, whereas, on other equally plausible ways of regarding the matter, *A* covers *more* or *less* incompatible diversity than *B*, and hence is *more* or *less* likely. Bertrand's problem of the chord drawn 'at random' in a circle, so as to be either more or less than, or just equal to, the side of the inscribed equilateral triangle, is set forth by Keynes and others as the classic case of such perplexity. Perplexities of this sort may dispose of the notion of a probability which is 'objective' in the sense of being simply 'out there', in which case they perform a welcome, necessary service such as is fulfilled also by other antinomies. They at least humble the factually arrogant theorist, and show that he has no better standing than the moralist. They do not, however, dispose of probability as reflecting an approvable disposition of belief, resting on tendencies inherent in belief as such, even if leading to difficulties in the particular case. The role of such perplexities is to challenge thought to higher-order accommodations of the same sort as those which gave rise to the whole notion of approvable probability itself. And that this challenge can be met, is shown by the excellent casuistry of certain recent solutions.

The abstract equity which estimates ranges of diversity can, however, only function in the framework provided by the demands of continuity, and the deliverances of compulsive experience. Since the supreme law of belief is submission to compulsive experience, it is to these demands and deliverances that it must defer. And in the field of repeatable happenings in time and space, this means a continual move from what may be called an alternative's abstract *range of realizability*, to its actually experienced *frequency of realization*. To be green is abstractly *realizable* in a

128   VALUES AND INTENTIONS

vastly wider range of ways than to be salmon-pink, and hence, abstractly, a certain sort of thing is more likely to be green than salmon-pink. If, however, experience has shown being salmon-pink to be realized in this sort of thing more frequently than being green, then it is to being salmon-pink that we must allot a wider sweep of the complete round of the likely. And deference to compulsive experience means, further, that the *latest* deliverance of frequency applied to the *narrowest* and *most heavily qualified class* to which a phenomenon can be allotted, must be allowed to determine the likelihood that it will be this or that. That the deference to compulsive experience thus modifies the abstract deliverances of equity does not mean, however, that the latter are ever done away with or nullified. Like the abstract claims of justice in morals, they continue to operate within the limiting framework provided by established fact, to ignore which would be to transform them into the greatest inequity.

Failure to accommodate the ideal of equity to the ideal of synechism in belief, is a source of one of the major false perplexities of philosophy, the so-called problem of induction. This problem arises through the attempt to treat the inductive extrapolation of pattern to unexperienced cases *within* the limits of the calculus of chances, to show it approvable that all cases of A should almost certainly be B, even though each new case of A stands poised between being B and as many possibilities other than that of being B, and just in the same way, as any case that preceded it. Obviously the task is impossible: if the cases of A are indefinitely numerous, and the possibilities of being other than B remain unalterably wide, and abstract equity remains our only principle, then, no matter *how* many cases of A have been observed to be B, the likelihood that *all* A's will be B's will remain as remote and negligible as before. Like the speed of light it will outstrip us in the same measure, no matter how much we spend ourselves to overtake it. Abstract equity is, however, seldom the only, and never the supreme principle governing our beliefs, and so the whole problem resolves itself as nugatory. It is a case of a determination to argue deductively, to energize vastly without stirring from the spot, where ampliative progress is demanded. For it is only when our basis is as yet void of particularized information as to the exact *realization* of certain alternatives, and involves nothing but their abstract *realizability*, that we can equate equal

THE MODES OF BELIEF

spreads of possibility with equal spreads of qualitative diversity. Abstract realizability is a 'caretaker' disposer of belief which approvably resigns as soon as data regarding realization becomes available. And the steady world of chance in which alternatives can be combined with unlimited freedom, and in which no repetition of *one* combination makes itself or another more or less likely, is a special sphere set aside and guaranteed by a long experience of irregularity, much as the unbiassed character of its gaming tables is guaranteed by the constitution of Monaco. It is only because we have *learnt* that certain types of phenomena are reliably irregular that we can prefer, to the narrowly based evidence of long uniform runs, the more broadly based claims of abstract equity. In so doing we are not really preferring equity to synechism, but a wider synechism to a narrower one. It is not, therefore, possible, without an unwarranted circle, to treat the whole of nature as a roulette table, and to argue as if no continued experience of certain combinations could reduce the likelihood of other thinkable possibilities. To argue thus is to use the independence of character found inductively in certain limited fields to argue to a corresponding universal independence, cunningly masked by fortuitous long runs. But to do this is to argue synechistically on a basis itself synechistic in order to refute the very principle of synechism itself, and to do so in the face of most indications of experience.

As to attempts to found arguments on what is 'logically thinkable' or the reverse, they are of necessity valueless and nugatory, since to abide by what is 'logically thinkable', or not logically thinkable, in the face of actual experience, is to opt for stationary and unprogressive thought. Logical possibility, like the meditative Celts, retains no more than a merely poetical or philosophical importance, when driven, as by Saxon invaders, from the territories that it once cultivated, and made to submit to the harsh pressure of empirical frequencies. The problem of induction retains its importance, however, as pointing to the distinctness of the strands woven into the approvability of belief, and to the non-automatic character of their harmony. An approvable determination of the probable, like an approvable determination of what is to be desired in conduct and life, has none of the passive registering involved in describing a landscape or the niceties of court etiquette. It involves the adjustment of claims whose mutual dovetailing is a desideratum rather than a datum, and its deference to principle

E

130 VALUES AND INTENTIONS

requires completion by a certain free flair which is certainly personal and subjective. If the problems of induction have destroyed a false positivism or a facile logical realism they will, however, have done much.

A final condition of the approvability of belief with obvious roots in its philosophical description, is its acceptability and communicability to as many persons as possible, and, in the limit, to all who are in any way prepared to defer to the criteria we have listed. *Securus iudicat orbis terrarum* is an indispensable principle of approvability, provided that the *orbis terrarum* is made both unbounded in its scope, so as to apply to possible as well as to actual judges, and provided that some desire to be 'impersonal', to rise above the peculiarities of a personal standpoint and to find something invariant with change of standpoint, is a condition of membership. The principle applies not merely to the deliverances of compulsive experience, where a compulsion only grounds full belief if it can be made a compulsion for all: it applies also to the much less compulsive common tendencies to belief. That there is a widespread, not readily explicable, tendency to think this or that, even if nothing fulfils this thought compulsively, is certainly an approvable, if not conclusive reason for thinking this or that. For what we *tend* to believe is in a degree compulsive, even if not fully so, and in fact surrounds like a penumbra what we cannot by any effort help believing. An ancient tradition has applied such names as 'common sense' or the 'teaching of nature' to tendencies which are not themselves compulsive, and which do not straightforwardly continue what is strictly compulsive in experience. Such 'common sense' certainly deserves profound respect in the theory of rational belief and is in fact the one corrective to the cult of the hard datum and the rigorous connection which is always liable to pulverize our notions and to paralyse all our inferences. It is of supreme importance to be able to say at many junctures that we are all much more sure of certain truths, and of their significant content, than we can be sure of any abstract arguments to discredit them or the reverse, or of analyses which leave out most of what they seem to involve. Only this principle must not be used, as by Moore, to support only a comparatively narrow circle of commonplace truisms—the existence of things in space, of a long past history of the earth, etc. etc.— and to permit almost any analysis of them, but to support, also,

THE MODES OF BELIEF 131

beliefs of a much vaguer character, and give inconclusive support to many, as well as perhaps leaning strongly to certain types of analysis. Thus we must accord respect to the widespread inclination to believe in a general *purposive* adjustment between the things in the world and our own intellectual and moral development, and also to our deep feeling that we are more sure that we do *not* mean certain things by our use of terms than we can be sure of any subtle, recently excogitated theory purporting to prove that we *must* mean just such things.

There would not appear to be any place in the theory of belief for any notion of 'knowledge', as something entirely different from sufficiently grounded and approvable belief, that will also *not* be overthrown as the fabric of belief is extended in an approvable manner. That there is a 'knowledge' inherently incapable of refutation, and differing in kind from a case of mere belief, is not an idea that can be squarely invalidated: it rather drops off as we think, and reveals itself as without a use and unprofitable. The supposed irrefragability of our judgements concerning abstract notional relations or the immediacies of personal experience can be sufficiently refuted: if there are any such irrefragable judgements they are either trivial and narrow beyond belief, or we are by no means clear when we are framing them, or their certainty, if actual, cannot go beyond the person or the occasion. If illuminations so fragmentary and transient can be held to exist, they can certainly serve as the foundation of nothing: their postulation represents merely the introduction of a queer, useless limiting concept. The beliefs that are important have the modifiability due to their membership of a continuous and growing system. Any stress of 'knowledge' in our treatment of thought and the world also tends to import an arbitrary and conventional element into our treatment of many topics, much as does the parallel emphasis on strict obligation in the consideration of action and the ends of life. For it is more or less arbitrary and unclear and dependent on convention when our belief, which automatically claims to be 'true', is *sufficiently* approvable for us to be said to *know* its content, though it is much more clear whether it is more or less approvable than another belief. In much the same way, it is more or less arbitrary and unclear, and dependent on particular social contexts and customs, whether or not we are strictly obliged to do something: it is much more clear whether it would be better or worse

132 VALUES AND INTENTIONS

to do it. Notions like obligation and knowledge, with their dangerous suggestions of an absoluteness and finality not attainable in actual enterprises or inquiries, have thrown up many gratuitous 'bunkers' in the fairways of theory and practice.

Our account of approvability might be criticized as being too idealistic, as having made beliefs good, bad or better, to be embraced, rejected or preferred, solely in so far as they satisfy certain subjective requirements, which have their root ultimately in the capacities and character of conscious experience. Such an approach, it may be held, delivers us over to the wild *hubris*, the 'constructivism', the ascription of natural law and order to the 'productive imagination', to all, in short, that is least credible and least creditable in the philosophy of Kant. It may, however, be argued that we have been idealistic only to the extent of holding that the standards by which we evaluate belief, like the standards by which we evaluate anything, must be our *own* standards, conforming to our own profound wants and wishes (including the wish to defer to compulsive experience), and capable of being 'objective' only in the sense that they spring necessarily from some detached, interpersonal segment of those wants and wishes which we cannot help sharing with others. That there are such central, definitory or nigh-definitory aspirations involved in all belief we have sought to argue. If there can be no such central segment, as many upholders of purely conventional views of definition and essence would no doubt maintain, then there can be no such objective evaluation. The fact that something exists, or is in fact there, can by itself, without some special power to bring itself home to us, and further to recommend or approve itself to us, mean nothing to us as believers. All this does not, however, commit us to a 'constructivist' view of experience or of the beliefs and judgements which grow out of it. For belief, as we have said, is nothing if not deferential to compulsive experience, of which sense-experience is the ultimate form. It therefore presupposes as its appropriate complement, the natural world in time and space, whose parts have a large measure of 'outsideness' and mutual indifference, and can therefore bring sharp strains and discontinuities into each other's lives, not least so in their action on the senses of living beings, in which all knowledge has its origin. The material world in time and space, with its fragmented patches of highly organized thinghood, scattered abroad and interacting with

THE MODES OF BELIEF

each other in a largely chance manner, has precisely that degree of independence among its parts, and of manageable simplicity within them, as to serve both as the source of our compulsive experiences and of the coherent beliefs built upon them. The external world, whose contents are so superbly indifferent to the wants, wishes and special characteristics of the conscious beings in them, and which buffets them *all* so impartially, is in fact the perfect complement of belief and knowledge. Belief in following its *own* tendencies may well be held to *re*construct for itself the independent, public, compulsive order which its own existence and development presupposes, and to reconstruct it largely as it is 'in itself'. For the world in which belief exists must itself be a believable world, and the structure it suggests to those relying on the compulsive experiences it produces in them, is likely to be like its own structure. These propositions, repudiated by Kant as involving an unwarrantable 'pre-established harmony' between belief and things in themselves, would seem to be almost truistic applications of the notions of the 'like' and the 'likely'.

There is therefore nothing idealistic in our account of belief; the standards intrinsic to belief are best met by a system of things having much realistic and materialistic indifference. Quite apart from the strong reasons for thinking that things are so, the world conceived by materialistic realism is the most intrinsically credible world. This does not mean that an account of the world that is fully credible may not go *beyond* the materialistic-naturalistic basis with which it necessarily commences. For the indifference of the material order to the immediate wants and ideas of the conscious person is not an indifference to the development of approvable belief and knowledge in him, but precisely the condition that makes these possible. And it can be shown that the other approvable activities of human beings also demand as a condition the same indifference and recalcitrance of the material order. It is therefore not absurd to claim that the external, largely fortuitous relations of ourselves to the material order must be subordinated to another set of purposive or teleological relations, the material order being taken to be as it is merely as leading up to the higher forms of conscious life. All this does not affect the fact that what is basically presupposed by belief is the indifferent mechanical, sensorily intrusive, material order, on which text everything else can be no more than a plausible gloss.

134 VALUES AND INTENTIONS

We have now completed our account of the approvability of belief. Our treatment has ranged over the sort of topics that should be included in treatises on probability, in a manner which these topics themselves demand and permit, and not as they are actually dealt with in such treatises. For the theory of probability is an eccentric branch of the theory of value, and has the mistiness and the liability to antinomy characteristic of all value-inquiries. It has sought to avoid these signs of nature by the shamefaced self-limitation to such seemingly scientific inquiries as the theory of chances or of statistical investigation. In so doing it has made itself incapable of understanding even what is done in such fields. By accepting its own limitations, it will not only be able to illuminate these exact developments, but also to shed light on the analogous problems of ethics, aesthetics and other value-disciplines.

CHAPTER IV

THE MODES OF ACTION AND ENDEAVOUR

(I) THE GENERAL NATURE OF MENTAL ACTIVITY

We have so far been dealing with orientations of mind that are concerned rather to dig down to things as they are, or as they may be, or to take the impress of their peculiar character, rather than to remould, press or push them on towards any purposed limit, or to see what they are in the light of such a limit. The orientations in question may have characteristic aims or goals of their own, revealed in the way in which they tend to develop, and in relation to which they may be judged approvable or the reverse, but such aims are in a sense not part of their purview, and are in fact normally excluded from it. It is irrelevant and in fact often ruinous to bring in considerations of the methods and aims of science into the actual application and use of such methods. The orientations of mind we have dealt with may have offered us the presuppositions, analogues and objects of the states of mind more narrowly concerned with the 'ends of life', but have remained relatively far from these last. Now, however, we shall be concerned with orientations more nearly related to such ends: the orientations of actively bringing objects and states of affairs into being, or of seeking or endeavouring to do so, and, in particular, those circuitous, perceptive seekings which aim at one object or state of affairs by realizing another. From blind wanting we shall have to ascend to cases of intended and chosen action, and, to what is most important for our purposes, the carefully framed rational *wish* and the assessment of what is desirable. Beside positive orientations we shall have to set down their opposing negatives: aversions, abstentions, inhibitions, submissions of varying type and level. And together with acts of bringing about and their appropriate contraries, and the various kinds of serious and semi-serious wantings and tryings which move in their direction, we shall have to study the various states of *satisfied endorsement* or dissatisfied rejection of objects or states of affairs, or of acquiescent abiding or pained squirming in certain doings or undergoings, which, while obviously not *the same* as our various doings, tryings

VALUES AND INTENTIONS

and purposings, none the less belong with them in the same 'family', and obviously stand to them in some deep 'relation of essence', a relation acknowledged alike in the exaggerations of certain forms of hedonism, as in Brentano's wise subsumption of them all under the one rubric of 'the phenomena of love and hate'. The machinery for our treatment has already, in large measure, been prepared for us by our doctrine of the secondary, 'sidelong' intentionality attributable to thought-references by virtue of their readiness to pass over into other thought-references. Now, however, we may hope more fully to understand and apply this machinery, seeing the anticipatory or the fully enacted *submission* characteristic of awareness and belief, as but one out of a complex, graded series of actively adopted mental poses or postures.

The first point to be clear about, then, is that an active mental orientation is not as such a case of the primary intentionality of consciousness, characterizable either by *what* something is conceived *as*, or *how* it is conceived, but rather, as we have said, a case of that secondary intentionality, characterizable in terms of what our state of mind is moving *towards*, and *how* it is moving towards this. This is so, because it is wholly possible to be mentally active, in the most fully deserved sense, without having anything that deserves the name of 'activity' present to one's mind, not even if one reflects deeply on one's own experience. The apex of achievement very often *feels* effortless: there is no close correlation between how much one judges to have been done, and how much one feels the doing of it. Were action, *per impossibile*, some self-contained feature of a mental phase, it must of necessity reveal itself to those reflecting upon this phase. This is not to deny, as has in fact already been conceded, that there are many experiences which deserve in themselves to be called experiences *of* action, or which can be said to involve a 'consciousness of action': considered decisions, tasks executed with some difficulty, performances done with continuous, supervisory care, physical acts involving the whole of one's musculature and straining this to the utmost, etc. etc.—all these obviously qualify for the description. But a consciousness *of* action is, as the word indicates, a state in some manner alive to, and presentative of action; it is what it is only by virtue of what it condenses and savours, to which it seems by no means essential that it should be thus condensed and savoured. Stout once wrote in a treatment

THE MODES OF ACTION AND ENDEAVOUR   137

still greatly worthy of being remembered: 'Mental activity exists in being felt. It is an immediate experience. The stream of consciousness feels its own current.'[1] If the last of these three sentences makes valuable sense, it being often the case that we are disposed to describe our state metaphorically as one of crashing mentally through the undergrowth of difficulty or ploughing slowly through the bog of tedium, the former two would seem to involve a mistake, which Moore would have styled a self-contradictory mistake. For the fact that a state B flows out of a state A—to adopt the 'current' metaphor—and that more or less vigorously, while it may certainly be said in some cases to be 'felt', 'experienced' or 'immediately known', has none the less the most complex analysable content, involving for its full exposition such extraneous considerations as that B would not have existed had A not first been there, that C, D, E though palpably present have *nothing to do* with the emergence of B, etc. etc. And while there is no reason why the most complex of analysable contents should not in fact be compressed or telescoped into the most simple and seamless of experiences, and while this is in fact a matter of the most routine occurrence in the life of men, and possibly too in the life of some of the higher animals, yet the complexity of such contents compels a differentiation between the simple, seamless experience and what it is *of*. That something is such as to owe its being to something else, and not in any degree to other attendant circumstances, may be something *of* which we can at times be said to have an 'immediate experience', but it cannot itself be called an 'immediate experience'. And feelings of mental activity depend for their arousal on such complex oppositions and contrasts that it is absurd to say that they 'exist only in being felt'.

If we now ask in what an active mental orientation can consist, it is obvious that it can consist in nothing beyond what we may call a steady prolongation of being necessarily bound up with and revealed in a more or less steady prolongation of identifiable pattern through a series of successive phases, in which conscious orientations play a dominant part. Activity is necessarily the outflow of an agent, and an agent is nothing if not manifest in a more or less characteristic, linked set of manifestations continuing each other over a fairly long period, and it can act only in

[1] *Analytic Psychology*, Vol. I, p. 110.

E*

138 VALUES AND INTENTIONS

prolonging its manifestations more or less characteristically—
the uncharacteristic being possible only as deviating from the
characteristic—such prolongation involving something more than
a mere inert maintenance of equilibrium, and including some
spilling over into the continuous life of other identifiable agents,
and some response to a similar spilling over from their side. Our
account is necessarily of embarrassing unclearness, since it covers
phenomena widely diverse and compounded together in widely
different ways. And *mental* activity will exist where such activity
constantly passes through a series of *conscious* orientations, held
together by such things as the primitive continuity of time, by
the constant overlapping of various objective fields, by the compulsive sensory presence of one and the same organized body, by
the constant looking back and forth to the contents of orientations
just past or to come as well as to the orientations themselves, and
also by the developing unity of various continuously growing,
interconnected *themes* or *stories*, to which each conscious orientation contributes a chapter. Without the basic continuity of
experienced time, the mutual overlapping of various successive
fields of awareness, the mutual recognition of experiences by one
another, and the appropriation of their contents, and without
interwoven threads of pattern or theme running through the
whole series, there can be no question of mental activity. Such
activity is mysterious only if sought for as for some *extra* phenomenon beside the close linkage of developing conscious phases,
a search readily inspired by the tendency to erect notional distinctness into atomistic independence, an independence without
application within the bounds of conscious life.

The activity that is rightly denominated 'mental', since conscious orientations play in it a governing part, may also be said
to be for a large part of its course physical, since it is always
passing over into and being carried on by processes that are
overtly physical. The same drifts that can be discovered, or can
exist undiscovered, in our unillustrated thoughts can further
be carried out in our developing fantasies: they can be seen still
more fully carried out in the movements of our bodies, and in
the movements of instruments and remotely affected objects by
means of which our bodily range is extended. Not only thoughts,
feelings and interior performances may therefore rightly be
classed as mental activities, and also the acts of walking, talking,

THE MODES OF ACTION AND ENDEAVOUR 139

signing documents, riding in vehicles, confining to prisons, attending church services and all the like moves in our personal and social life. In all such moves there is, for the most part, a consciousness of what we are doing that is continuous with other states of consciousness—thoughts, fantasies, etc.—that are not thus overtly enacted, and the doing is *rather an enriched, fulfilled way of being conscious of things* than something which supervenes upon the latter and completes it from without. This enriching overflow of the mental into the bodily has been exaggerated into the modern doctrine that mental activity is, in its *main* mode of manifestation, physical, that it represents no more than physical activity seen in a peculiar light, i.e. as tending to develop in this or that direction, that it requires for the most part no occult rehearsal nor briefing performed secretly 'in our heads', and that such occult performance, where actual, is the mere overflow or irrelevant side-reach of the main physical stream. These doctrines are valuable since they stress the *unity* of such performances as speaking, writing, etc., the impossibility of splitting them up into two lines of action mirroring one another, a prior writing in one's head followed by a mere copying out on paper, etc. etc. They have said importantly that it is as possible to do one's thinking on paper as to do it in one's head, that to perform it in the latter fashion is not necessarily to perform it better, and that to refuse to call an activity 'mental' unless first rehearsed or briefed in shadow-fashion is readily to fall into an infinite regress. Such views are, however, mistaken in ignoring the conscious orientations carried out in each bodily motion, and providing the right 'light' in which to regard or describe them, for which no adequate physical equivalent can be devised. For what I am doing at any moment, in the sense in which 'doing' represents *mental* activity, is what I *seem* to myself to be doing at that moment, or what I would seem if I gave the matter thought, such as minding the baby, preparing the supper, signing a hire-purchase agreement, etc. etc., and that some *other* account of my action, however true and revealing in a physical or other per-spective, such as, e.g., creating a new object-cathexis in the baby, giving my guests ptomaine poisoning, undermining the financial system of England, etc. etc., can play no part in describing my mental activity or in telling anyone what I am mindfully doing. And the activity which exists, realized or executed in my overt

140   VALUES AND INTENTIONS

performances, may exist less completely carried out in my fanciful enactments, and still less completely carried out in my momentary leanings and projectings. But while I am not necessarily conscious *of* this activity, and need in no way experience or 'feel' it, it may be constantly operative in my life, and principally in my consciousness of various matters, whether physically carried out or not, and may so rightly be spoken of as a 'conscious' or 'mental' activity.

Mental activity may be held, further, like all activity, to depend for its existence on a correlative passivity. It demands the possibility of constant attrition by alien irruption and incursion, whether from beyond the sphere of linked conscious phases or within it. No mental activity can exist except in so far as a conscious theme or developing trend can be at times *interfered with*, whether by the compulsions of sense, or the force of other developing conscious themes or trends. And the strength or force of an activity is one with its withstanding of such irruptions, its continuance in their despite: were all such irruptions removed, there would be no sense in speaking of mental activity or its degree. Activity, however, constantly shows itself as passivity and *vice versa*, wherever one has a case (as one almost always has a case) of one mental activity thwarted by another. Even the activities characterized as alien, those, e.g., of external physical things, soon become activities we partially understand, and are accordingly in a way our own activities. The most routine habits and associations, which often run athwart our main conscious drifts, and are accordingly seen as compulsive and passive, can in an unthwarted field be seen as simple activities that we easily perform. In the same manner high-minded resolves which, from one point of view, are supremely representative of the activity of the mind, from another point of view shackle and tie up many humbler activities, and so seem to hold us passively in their 'grip'. The contrast is, in fact, a matter of aspect: in every conscious drift we are, from the standpoint of that drift, active, from the standpoint of other drifts that it interferes with, passive, in every mutual interference among drifts we are, as interfering, active, as interfered with, passive. What we *feel* or fail to feel in such situations has almost no logic at all, but the conscious drifts and their mutual interferences have some solidity. There are, further, various subtle senses in which we can be said to be 'more truly active' or

THE MODES OF ACTION AND ENDEAVOUR   141

'more truly passive' in carrying out certain mental activities than others. Such usages, however, involve a fixing and remodelling of ordinary concepts into whose perhaps doubtful legitimacy we need not now enter.

It will have become plain from what we have said that there is not the opposition that has sometimes been believed in between mental activity and causality. Mental activity is, in fact, a special case of causality, causality in which conscious orientations play a dominant part. In mental activity, as in physical, something grows out of something, and this 'growing out of' in both cases reduces to a continuous prolongation of characteristic pattern (not necessarily in a manner which *excludes* the uncharacteristic or not readily to be expected), and though the manner in which such pattern is prolonged may differ profoundly in the two cases. The same prolongation we note when we reflect on a series of conscious references, we note too when we consider a bodily existent outside of us, and the way in which it exerts its peculiar style of being in a manner perhaps indifferent to and at variance to our own. The 'action' of some motor-car impinging loudly on our hearing in the silent night, does not differ fundamentally from our own action in flinging open the window and berating the driver. The main peculiarity of mental activity or causality lies, however, in the unique role played in it by the objects and circumstances which *inexist* in our conscious references, as things thought of or aimed at, and *which may be without a trace of actual existence*, or with an existence quite irrelevant to the activity in question. In a natural and proper sense, it is *these* intentional objects, rather than the intentions directed upon them, which *move* or *incite* or *provoke* or *cause* us to act in certain ways. Thus it was Nasser's 'resemblance' to Hitler, rather than his own belief in this, that plunged Eden into his 'Suez adventure'—his belief was not as such present to his mind at all—it was the 'infidelity' of Desdemona that moved Othello to strangle her rather than his own insane, credulous jealousy; it is poverty rather than the thought of poverty that terrifies us, and immortal fame rather than the hope or prospect of it that prompts us to starve in a garret or die on a battlefield. One might even have made it a distinguishing mark of the mental that it alone can be made to act by what does not exist anywhere, or by what exists elsewhere and irrelevantly.

The word 'cause' has, however, been so much pre-empted by

142 VALUES AND INTENTIONS

inductive science, and so much confined to what is palpable, existent and prior in time, that it would be odd to include among the causes of something an object which did not exist at all, or only irrelevantly. We therefore do not say that an act is *caused* by some non-existent or remote thing or consideration, but that it has such a thing or consideration as a *motive* or *reason*. The *cause* of such an act is then said to be the *thought of* (or the *desire for*) the thing or consideration in question, and mental activities then not only have the peculiarity of being moved by reasons, but also of having the thought of such reasons among their causes. The kind of causation is, however, deeply peculiar, since the way in which the thought of poverty issues in the acts which avert poverty, is quite different from the way in which the thought of poverty issues in the thought of such acts, or the actual poverty issues in the acts in question. There is a much more straightforward 'extension of pattern' in the latter cases than in the former. Obviously there is a μετάβασις εἰς αλλὸ γενὸς when a thought issues in a physical act or product, which does not occur when a thought issues in a thought, or a physical act in another physical act. It would, however, be misguided to see no more than an unintelligible empirical contingency in the causation of a physical state by a thought. Obviously there is an essential affinity between the thought of an *A* and an *A* itself or *vice versa*, and there is more than merely 'verbal magic' in seeing the one fitly *continued* in the other.

The causation involved in mental activity is further peculiar in that there is not in it the sharp contrast we elsewhere have between the *presence* of the causation in question and our *knowledge* of its presence. For we have what certain philosophers,[1] adapting the usage of Aristotle, have called 'practical knowledge', the clear awareness and ability to say how our experienced world will develop itself in and through our bodily movements, without *basing* such knowledge on our own previous thought and behaviour. A man who wants or intends to do X, or to produce Y, may be perfectly clear that he is going to do X or to produce Y, or that he is in fact doing or producing it, without needing to pay heed, as others must—and as he must in predicting the acts of others—to the detailed thoughts and actions that have led up to his act. His knowledge, in short, seems direct and non-inductive: if it involves,

[1] E.g. Miss Elizabeth Anscombe in her book *Intention*.

THE MODES OF ACTION AND ENDEAVOUR 143

as it indubitably does, a prolongation of the pattern exemplified in his past living, this is a different sort of prolongation from that which occurs when he develops a meaning, hazards a surmise or makes a probable prediction. It is, if one likes, a *practical* prolongation of his previous living, which does not involve that he brings that previous living to mind, and is in this respect quite different from the *theoretical* prolongation of what he has been through in compulsive experience and now takes as a basis for further building. The *same* pattern, in short, which is prolonged in the sequence of a man's deeds also often has an anticipatory prolongation in a programme or preview of those deeds: the man is clear as to what he is minded to do, without basing himself on anything that he has done. Such 'practical knowledge' is as much a direct *expression* of the trends dominating a man's life as a *registering* of their existence, and hence it is as readily expressed in the words 'Let me now take this vase from the shelf' or 'Shall I now take this vase from the shelf?' as in the indicative form 'I shall now take the vase from the shelf'. And, expressed indicatively, an expression of 'practical knowledge' is so little an ordinary prediction that its non-fulfilment leads us rather to say that we failed to carry out our intention than that we inaccurately predicted what we should do. Our non-practical knowledge looks forward to the test of compulsive experience, and defers to it in anticipation, but our 'practical knowledge' is quite free from a relation to present or future compulsion. So different are what we have called the theoretical and the practical prolongations that they tend actually to interfere with another: if I try to anticipate what I shall do, this may either prevent me from doing anything, or may make me do something different from what I should otherwise have done. If I try to determine practically what I shall do, this may either hinder me from making any predictions at all or may make them idle reflections of my actual decisions. But though thus non-inductive and non-extrapolatory, what we have called 'practical knowledge' can exist only in the interstices of the framework provided by observation and extrapolation. Having in the first instance blindly done certain things in certain situations, and having gropingly learnt what we then did and what it was like to do it, we now dispose of the materials that enable us to have a non-observational, non-extrapolative knowledge of what we are doing or about to do.

VALUES AND INTENTIONS

Shall we hold with Hume that the notions of action and efficacy belong primarily to the sphere of 'reflection', in the determination of our *minds* to pass on from one object or idea to the next, and are then wrongly referred to the objects or ideas themselves? Or shall we embrace the 'animism' of Stout according to which mental activity is an 'immediate experience', which we project behind the 'curtain' of phenomena, thereby adding a dimension of pressures, strains, stresses, resistances, impacts and energies to the inactive surface of things? Plainly such views are exaggerated, since prolongation of pattern is as much essential to the picking out of external things, and as much characteristic of their life, as it is of our own subjective being. There are, however, grounds for holding that we obtain *richer* and *more intimate* illustrations of action and causation by examining our own minds than by considering external things. For mental activity is revealed, not merely by looking to *what* we think of, but also by reflecting on our consciousness itself: reflectively we find, e.g., that there are sequences mediated more by the *manner* in which objects come before us, by the pressure, e.g., towards greater conscious clearness, than by the character of those objects themselves. It is clear also that we know our mental activities as circulating through the uniquely familiar part of the physical world known as our own bodies, whose state is in many cases revealed by quite distinctive sensations, not felt by us in connection with external objects, and which enjoys the further distinction of sometimes revealing its state in wholly non-observational fashion and without assistant sensations, as when we simply know how our bodies are disposed, oriented or moving in space. And it is clear, above all, as previously indicated that we often have a non-inferential, immediate knowledge of what we are doing or are about to do, which is a direct expression of the same pattern as issues in our action.

We may hold, further, that our own active life provides us with a more penetrating view, not merely of causation, but also of the *time* so closely interwined with causation, than could any study of 'external' things. For our knowledge of physical causation is theoretical, a matter of idea and belief. It proceeds from, and waits upon, outside compulsions, and is *re*constructive of an outside order, not, like practical knowledge, one with an actual self-extending construction. Being thus reconstructive, it can as readily move backwards as forwards in time: it can use the known

THE MODES OF ACTION AND ENDEAVOUR   145

present or future to reconstruct the past as readily as it can use the known past or present to construct the future. Hence for such mere theory it seems a mere matter of fact that we have determinate memory or other knowledge of the past and no similar knowledge of the future. All this might have been different: we might have had regular foreknowledge of the future and extrapolative knowledge only of the past, and might have progressed towards diminishing foresight and increased historical reconstruction as we now progress towards lengthening memories and diminished forecasting. That the past is said to determine the future, rather than the future the past, would be a linguistic asymmetry resting on a mere fact of nature. From the standpoint of practice all this is plainly absurd. For as agents we stand at the point where past pattern is growing into and determining what shall be present, regardless as to whether we can reconstruct its detailed content or not, and we are also at the point where future pattern is growing out of and being determined by what is present, and by ourselves as agents, and where it could not possibly be forecast exhaustively, nor seen as determining what we now do. The reversed world that we played with above would be a world in which there was, not doing, but *undoing*, a steady loss of definition and detail from an at first finished picture: there could not even be theorizing, only the evanescence of theory. And though, for the theorizing which ignores practice, including its own, such a state is conceivable, and can be significantly denied, yet, for the theorizing that takes account of practice, it can be seen not really to be possible at all. For practice, therefore, and for the theory which takes due account of practice, there are aspects of time and causation which are not accessible to *mere* theory.

(II) THE NATURE OF WANTING AND TRYING

From accomplished action we pass on to trying and wanting, both orientations of mind which stand to action as a mere thought-reference stands to its illustrations or concrete fulfilment: we have, by implication, dealt with both. Of trying we shall attempt no formal definition: it is, in fact, not to be elucidated without something of a circle. But we may say that it exists wherever action fails of its outcome, where a prolongation of pattern is carried out only to an extent judged *imperfect* in reference to some standard

146   VALUES AND INTENTIONS

intrinsic to itself, and where such imperfection of execution is seen as *fitting in* with the perfect or imperfect execution of other similar prolongations, which are seen as *resisting* it or *interfering* with it. And we have a case of *mental* trying or endeavour where the main part of this imperfect carrying out either has a place in, or constitutes an outflow from, the charmed circuit which passes again and again through the series of conscious orientations which form the history of a single person's 'mind'. It is here important to stress, in complete harmony with ordinary speech, that such conscious trying is *not* an 'immediate experience', though there may at times be an immediate experience or an immediate consciousness *of* it. We may be trying to do things without any sense of feeling of active endeavour, and this sense or feeling, when present, is not necessarily a proof of how *hard* we are trying. Trying may be estimated by such things as enlarged performance, elimination of alternatives from thought, absence of otherwise probable counter-endeavours, etc. etc., and not necessarily by any 'feeling' of virtue put forth. In the life of trying, as in the life of action, so-called feelings play a supernumerary, almost cognitive role: they register the presence of something in which they need play no part. We may likewise stress, in conformity with what was said about action, that while trying may come through to us by way of induction based on observation, and while it does in fact generally so come through to us in the case of the endeavours of other persons or animals, and the tendencies of things, it can come through to us also directly in non-extrapolative, non-observational form. A man trying to do A or to realize B knows of the presence and direction of his own endeavours, without basing himself on any examination of his present behaviour, physical state, feelings, etc. The same list or trend which would reach success in actions or in concrete results must be thought of as less fully carried out by the mere notion, or even verbal statement, that a man is trying for this or for that. We may stress, thirdly, that trying must not be conceived as some mysterious identifiable component present alike when an action succeeds or fails: if we fail in fact to do what we believe or think ourselves to be doing we say without more ado that we were trying to do whatever, if success-ful, we should say we were doing. In the same way, as demonstrated *ad nauseam*, there is no component of voluntary effort which passes over into such simple acts as moving one's hand, turning to the left,

THE MODES OF ACTION AND ENDEAVOUR 147

etc. etc. The splitting up of such activities into an inner exertion of trying followed by an outward performance is completely fabulous. We may note further that trying, like doing, involves a motivation by intentional objects, many of which need not exist anywhere, and that it is itself a case of such motivation: a man who tries is moved to realize something that does not exist, or at least not in the setting or way in which he tries to realize it.

From doing and trying we proceed to wanting, a notion more complex than either and which spans both. For we may want something when we try for it, and we generally want to do what we do. (We speak of 'wanting' rather than 'willing', 'wishing', etc., since we wish to cover low-grade mental activities as well as higher ones, the wanting to run away or to urinate as much as to keep Britain tidy or to free Europe from Communism, etc. etc.) What distinguishes wanting from mere trying would seem to be its contextual and concatenated character: it is trying ready to *deviate*, to spread to things like, to things regularly attendant on, or to things leading up to, the sort of things it is trying for, until it actually strikes a path or forges a chain of acts and states leading from some act of its own to what it is trying for, which path or chain then readily enters, with what it strives for, into a new pattern regularly to be followed. In wanting trying acquires an instrumental spread: it is pattern-prolongation characterized by an additional inventiveness which blazes out new trails through which it may be continued. This 'blazing out' may proceed on the level of full enactment, or on the less completely enacted levels of fantasy and mere thought. That what we have said bears some resemblance to the researches of certain animal psychologists is not to the point: those researches operate within the framework of a conception of what it is to want or to strive for which is then elaborately rediscovered in their outcome.

This kind of prolongation distinguishes the living and conscious from the unconscious and lifeless, and has a thoroughgoing intelligibility in the case of agents capable of conscious mental activity. For the spread of the thought of an A to the completer patterns in which this character is or might be embedded merely involves obedience to the fundamental tendencies of conscious life which we studied in our second chapter; the tendency to complete a thought-of object with every circumstance necessary to full-fledged or objective being, to realize it further in the material

148 VALUES AND INTENTIONS

of intuitive or compulsive experience, and to carry it out in fully believable fashion, so that it becomes part of a coherent order having a reality for others as well as ourselves. That we are trying to achieve an A merely puts force behind the tendencies intrinsic to consciousness, and makes their carrying out more likely than that of other similar tendencies, while to say, lastly, that a path to A once found will tend to be taken again, is merely to say that the completion towards which trying moves is also one that it tends to maintain and not move away from. There is no doubt a circle in what we have been saying, for we have explained the peculiarities of all kinds of endeavour in terms of the basic endeavours characteristic of conscious life: so much is, however, a unification and a simplification. The intelligibility of the instrumental spread is at its highest where the spread involves well-founded belief. If my whole weight of experience binds A in its actual existence with B, then it would only be by some monstrous artificial blindness, some deliberate not letting my right hand know what my left hand was doing, that I could fail to include B in what I strove for. This would of course be quite absurd if B could be realized by my own action: who wills the end 'must' (by logic neither empirical or merely tautological, since it admits of exceptions) will the means also.

We may now briefly repeat in relation to wanting the observations made in the case of doing and trying. First we may hold, in exact agreement with what is ordinarily said, that wanting is in no sense an 'immediate experience', though there may very well be experiences *of* wanting, in which our state of want is brought home to us in more or less poignant fashion. That wanting is not an experience is shown by the fact that there is no absurdity in saying, and that we in fact often truly say, that we want this or that, though we have absolutely no specific experiences of unease, longing, yearning, etc. etc. (That wants are not necessarily specifically experienced does not of course mean that they are 'repressed' or 'unconscious' in any psycho-analytic sense.) We may say, further, that while wants reveal themselves on an inductive examination of thought and behaviour, and are generally so discerned in our neighbours, they can be known also non-inductively and non-extrapolatively. By examining a man's or an animal's actions over a period we may satisfy ourselves that he is aiming primarily at A, that he is aiming at B, C, D merely as

THE MODES OF ACTION AND ENDEAVOUR 149

completing A, that he has taken cognizance of, and been guided by, facts F1, F2, F3, etc. etc. The investigations which establish these circumstances are, however, notoriously unreliable, and one has recourse, with relief, to the simple expedient of asking. A man knows, without studying himself, in many cases, that it is A he wants, and not B or C or D, which he is merely adopting as means: he can tell us also the reasons which determine him to pursue A by given routes or instruments. (Such non-observational 'desiderative knowledge' would of course not be possible without *some* prior acquaintance with himself and others, nor need the fact that we denominate it 'knowledge' imply it to be infallible.) There are many situations where our wants declare themselves with such firmness that it would be near-nonsensical to ask if we wanted what we thought we wanted, but there are many other cases where such facts as that the approach or presence of X awakened no zest would be taken as showing us to be in error as to our wants. That we ever use the term 'wanting' in so empty a sense that it would be *wholly* absurd to doubt whether we wanted what we said and thought we wanted, may perhaps be doubted. If such a use exists, it would deprive the notion of wanting of all significant content, or would be wholly parasitic upon other uses.

Since wanting is a case of conscious activity, it will be a case of activity guided throughout its course by how things are thought of or seen by someone, or by how they are believed to be (or about to be). Being thus dependent on ideas and beliefs, wants will in a sense be moved by the intentional objects of such ideas and beliefs, i.e. by things which need not exist anywhere, and certainly not in the context in which the wants arise. Such a movement by intentional objects must again not be confused with causality, though it depends on causality: without the conscious orientation which brings the intentional object before one, one would not be able to be moved or guided by it. The intentional objects connected with wants are all called 'reasons', at least in cases where they are *believed* to be the case. There may be reasons to the effect that something has or will have some property that we unconditionally want or do not want, reasons establishing the instrumental or causal relation of something to something that we unconditionally want or do not want, and there may be reasons expressing conditions, circumstances or consequences by which wanting is affected. It is characteristic of a

VALUES AND INTENTIONS

want, therefore, to be movable by reasons, and such movability is not a case of causality.

Since wants are by their nature moved and guided by 'reasons', it is difficult to apply the notion of a want to unconscious things and processes, or to things and processes to which conscious experience is irrelevant, or to things treated for certain theoretical purposes without relation to conscious experiences, e.g. animals in pure behaviour study. For apart from the comparatively narrow range of cases covered by mechanical maintenance of equilibrium or homoestasis, e.g. the orientation of insects towards light, it is not clear how, without anything like an idea extending itself in other ideas and guiding development, a peculiar bodily state should, when checked in its development towards a given outcome, explore and discover ways of circumventing the block, whereas to appeal merely to peculiar 'drives', dispositions or propensities is to have recourse to the asylum of ignorance. The attempts of a long line of theorists to remove or circumvent the theoretical block in question deserve our unstinted admiration: what we cannot allow is their success, or even remote hope of success. For it is not clear how *any* complex of merely existential elements, without any intrinsic 'direction' to this or to that, could ever do duty for states having such a direction. And until success is shown to be even conceivable, we must hold an explanation by way of wants not circulating through the sphere of ideas and conscious orientations, however much veiled in obscure symbolism, talk of dispositions, means-readinesses, etc. etc., to be merely an *as-if* explanation. It is, we are holding, *as if* an organism had some directive idea which develops towards various natural completions until one of them strikes through into action. Thus a man in a somnambulistic trance behaves *as if* his senses were mediating an awareness of chimney-pots, the edge of the roof, etc., and our senses function *as if* always on the watch for various interesting matters, our own name spoken, our waking child's first whimper, etc. etc. The various unconscious 'desires' of psycho-analysis, the desire, e.g., to keep matters out of consciousness or to preserve sleep, or the various 'mechanisms' of projection, reaction-formation, etc., through which such 'desires' are appeased, are likewise cases in which it is *as if* we had certain guiding ideas of ends and means, though in fact we have none at all. To call such explanations 'as-if explanations' is not to belittle them. It is to suggest that some

THE MODES OF ACTION AND ENDEAVOUR   151

things not fully intelligible as they stand, become more so when seen as approximating to other things more completely filled in and rounded out. The life of mind may not be as universally explanatory as some idealists have supposed, but it may provide the yardstick in terms of which many other phenomena may be measured and interpreted. We may lean towards a treatment of such phenomena on mildly Aristotelian lines, dominated by a sort of explanatory attraction of lower to higher forms. It is only when such a model is used extravagantly and without control from the compulsions of experience, and when it is used to supplant rather than fill in the interstices of non-purposive explanation, that it becomes the dangerous, facile thing the scientific conscience feels it to be.

The instrumental spread which is of the essence of wanting has other forms beside the *strictly* instrumental. There is also the form which is simply one of specification or individualization, the case where X is wanted simply because it is a species or an individual instance of Y. Wanting, being a mental activity, is always more or less universal, but what is universal not being realizable except in specific or individual form, there is a 'logic' which drives the mind from the one to the other. That I want food does not oblige me to eat what is put before me, but it gives this an attraction and a certain inevitability, well recognized by Aristotle in his 'practical syllogism'. There is likewise the form which is one of substitution or *faute de mieux*. We want X because it is very *like Y*, or the *nearest thing* to Y, etc. etc. It is not here necessary to advert to the tendency of wants to become tied up with or fixated upon the particular instruments, instances, substitutes, etc., that they instrumentally spread to, so that their instrumental, instantial, surrogative character vanishes altogether. To want X is to want the ways in which X is realized, and to tend to abide in them, and not to pass away from them. But it is equally characteristic of wants to seek to pass on to other things more or less *like* those which are immediately wanted: these tendencies work towards maintaining the merely instrumental, instantial, surrogative character of the particulars to which our wants are attached. The life of conscious endeavour must to a large extent be a struggle between tendencies towards fixated rigidity and wider tendencies seeking always to restore fluidity. These principles are widely illustrated in human behaviour, but it is important to realize that they are neither true by definition nor rest merely on experienced fact.

It is an all-important consequence of the instrumental spread of wants that they should move constantly towards a mutual integration and accommodation. The life of mind is single, and what is variously wanted tends to be brought together and *conjunctively* pursued. And as so conjunctively pursuant, the mind must tend to move away from the instruments, instances and surrogates which will satisfy one part of what it wants at the expense of another, and to move towards the instruments, instances and surrogates which will lead to, exemplify or do duty for all. Even the seemingly total sacrifice of one want to another may in a sense represent an accommodation of both: it is as where men draw lots for some honour or danger, and are equally satisfied that the best or lucky or unlucky man should win. This mutual accommodation of wants will, further, have the same tendency towards a systematic, coherent order of wants as ideas and beliefs have towards a systematic, coherent order of beliefs, a topic that will concern us later.

There is yet another direction beside the strictly instrumental in which a conscious want must tend to move: it must tend to surround and qualify what it wants with a gathering muster of circumstances and conditions. Wanting is not indiscriminate: it arises in a peculiar setting, both of things and conscious beliefs, some of the constituents or objects of which extend into distant regions of space and time. We want A because of its believed likeness to B which we liked and lost in the remote past, we want A as a complement or antidote to B, C and D, or in the absence of B, C, D whose presence would render it redundant or positively undesirable, etc. etc. We want A with seeming lack of discrimination until experimentation narrows our want down to cases in which B, C, D attend it, and M and N are absent, etc. etc. In all these cases there tends to be a progress from a state in which we want A, but do so only in the setting provided by B, C, D (or the consciousness of, or belief in these) to a state in which we consciously want A-only-if-B-C-D, etc., to a state, that is, in which the setting, though not consciously wanted, still plays the part of a setting *in the total intentional object* we have before us when the want circulates through conscious experience. The progress is not unlike the change from our readiness to believe X wherever circumstances B, C and D are believed, to the more

THE MODES OF ACTION AND ENDEAVOUR 153

complex belief that *if B, C* and *D* are the case *X* will be the case also. In both cases we have a sort of building into the object of the things conditioning our conscious attitude to it. Obviously as reflection progresses, there will be a tendency to further and future incorporation of the conditions in which something is wanted or not wanted into the theory itself, a fact that will be seen to be of great importance in the life of the 'will', where we learn to choose or prefer things *whatever* their outcome or complete setting may prove to be.

The life of wanting and endeavour admits of yet another kind of concatenated expansion beside the kind studied above. This is the expansion which occurs when the achievement of *A* serves as the occasion or stimulus for a new want directed to *B*, and so on, until in the end the whole sequence of ends becomes one concatenated policy in which no part is merely instrumental. There is something logical and inevitable in this sort of expansion too, since there is something queerly frustrating in the fulfilment of wants which leads on naturally to the development of substitute wants or goals. Satisfaction is frustrating in circumstances where, as we say, it comes too easy or too soon, and the want therefore in a sense survives its accomplishment and must transform itself into a new want with a different object. It is not clear whether the sequences known as habitual do not represent a particular case of the concatenated expansion in question, at a relatively low and fixated level. When I am habituated, I want to do *B* after *A*, and *C* after *B*, etc. etc., even if the wanting may have had its origin in relatively passive subjections to a series of compulsions, and even if it is now only a comparatively feeble want— which acquires strength only when inspired and used by some other more lively want. We discriminate habits from wants since in their case hideboundness and fixity predominate over inventive variability (though the latter is by no means absent), since their independent momentum is relatively feeble, and since they are to some extent mere abstractions, representing merely the hidebound, crystallized side of the manner in which our wants are carried out.

(III) THE DIMENSIONS OF WANTING

It will be our task, in the present section, to sketch something like the 'logical geography' of wanting, the whole territory

154 VALUES AND INTENTIONS

covered by the various specific forms that occur in it, the features that differentiate them from one another, and their varying relations of dependence and affinity. Here is a field of great complexity, not traditionally explored in a foot-by-foot manner. Our survey will be selective and impressionistic and suited to our general purpose, not exhaustive and exact.

Obviously the first point of importance is one often canvassed in the previous section, the variation of wants as regards *satisfaction*. It is of the essence of a want to press on, or prolong pattern, towards a certain *outcome*, which represents its satisfaction, and it may be distinguished according as (1) it has gone practically no distance towards its outcome, in which case we may call it *unsatisfied*; (2) it is *in process* of reaching its outcome, of being satisfied; (3) it is resting in its outcome, and is *perfectly satisfied*; (4) it is negatively satisfied or *frustrated*; (5) though not perfectly satisfied, it is satisfied in a *surrogative, as-if* fashion. Illustrations of these banal possibilities are not hard to come by: it may be the case, e.g., that I hope to meet some companionable philosophers at a conference, that I meet some philosophers who seem companionable, that I am experiencing the full happiness of philosophical companionship, that I meet only people with whom no such companionship is possible, that I solace myself by remembering some whom I met at another conference and imagine them present, etc. etc. Though not all linguistic usage is in our favour, it is enlightening to speak as if the *same* mental orientation ran through the whole series of cases. We want an outcome or object X (in whatever sense we do want it) whether this want is perfectly or partially or substitutively or not at all satisfied, and we want it too when the presence of its contrary is apparent. It is because the same sort of want is thought of as running through the whole series that its various members count as perfect, imperfect, negative, etc., satisfactions of the want in question.

It might seem paradoxical to hold to the persistence of a want in the actual state of satisfaction, yet nothing can be more necessary. Empirically the *exquisiteness* of a satisfaction consists in the fact that exactly as one wants a thing to be so it is, and there is even, as observed previously, a possible disproportion between a want and its satisfying outcome, which renders it disappointing to have what one has wanted too greatly, and forces one's wanting

THE MODES OF ACTION AND ENDEAVOUR 155

in some other direction. The connection is, however, logical and not factual: for if we should totally cease to want something when realized, it would make little sense to speak of it as satisfying us. A satisfied want is accordingly a want *perfected*, rather than a want abolished or externally supplemented, much as a thought accurately fulfilled in perception is a thought perfected rather than a thought done away with or supplied with some vacuously answering 'reality'. All this can be brought out by ordinary speech-forms. If the same declarative sentence 'That is a chaffinch' can be uttered with varying application where there are signs, or no signs, or where we have the conclusive presence or absence of the bird (in which last case it might be uttered in ironical dismay), so the sentences 'May that be a chaffinch' or 'Let that be chaffinch' can do duty in all these situations. We therefore in a sense agree with Brentano that the same mental orientation runs through 'sorrow—longing for the absent good—hope that it will fall to our share—desire to produce it for ourselves—decision to do the deed', to which series we may further add 'satisfaction that the deed is done' and 'satisfaction in the present good'. It is philosophically illuminating to see the same consciousness, or at least the readiness for it, as lying behind the whole sequence of cases, and having as its most natural verbal expression a *Fiat hoc* or a *Placet hoc* or their equivalents.

We may even go further and hold that a satisfied want or a want in process of being satisfied should be placed behind *all* cases of being pleased, even if, as in the Platonic cases of odours or mathematics, they do not involve any *previous* want or need. To be pleased with a smell is quite, or nearly, inseparable from wanting it to be there while it is there, or from wanting it to continue a little longer, even if this want does not *precede* the origin of the smell, and even if it will vanish when the smell vanishes. In much the same way there is a logical connection between negative or aversive want (to be considered presently) and the state of pain or unpleasure, however little there may have been a previous shrinking from what now pains us, or any subsequent aversion. All this is not to deny that to be pleased or displeased further involves a dimension of *feeling*, which will concern us later, and which is not exhausted by a determination of wanting or satisfaction.

Conscious wants may now be allowed to fall apart into a number of distinct classes according to the relation of the *object*

156 VALUES AND INTENTIONS

which concerns them to the *state* which affords them satisfaction. There is a temptation to think that all conscious wants press forward to the *realization* or *reality* of certain *objects* or *objectives*, and are satisfied once the reality of such objects or objectives is assured. As Brentano put the point: 'Every love is a love that something should *be*, and when one love gives rise to another, when one object is loved for the sake of another, such an occurrence involves a belief in certain relations between the one and the other. According to the judgement as regards the being or non-being, the probability or improbability of the thing one loves, the act of love is turned into joy, into sorrow, into hope, into fear, or into many other forms. And so it seems utterly impossible that a being should be endowed with the capacity of loving and hating, without sharing in that of the judgement.' The above passage sketches the profile of the most central, typical case of wanting, one in which the situation whose realization satisfies the want is also one in which the object or circumstance with which the want consciously concerns itself, is presented as 'real', or, in other words, believed in. There is indeed a paradigmatic sort of conscious wanting in which belief, total or partial, plays the decisive role, and which can be rightly characterized as a wanting that something should *be*. And such conscious wants have their best expression in various sentences in the subjunctive or imperative mood—'If only this were Tuesday', 'Long may he reign', 'Let this be our last meeting', etc. etc.—in which case we refer to them as *wishes*, the central category of the sphere now under consideration. One must, however, insist that there are forms of conscious wanting whose terminal satisfactions are not in believing, or at least not in believing anything specific, and so cannot be said to be concerned with the *real being* of what concerns them. The mere fact that such wants find their satisfaction in real conscious states must not be allowed to confuse us: we must distinguish between the sense in which the conscious state satisfies the want and the sense in which its object does so. The state satisfies the want as representing the completion towards which it presses, but the object satisfies the want only as thought of in a certain manner, which in some cases involves neither its reality nor our belief in its reality. A few examples will suffice to show the spread of the class of our belief-irrelevant, reality-indifferent wants.

THE MODES OF ACTION AND ENDEAVOUR 157

There are, it is plain, wants satisfied by the mere presence of certain objects to fulfilled awareness, by the bringing of their parts to conscious clearness, and by the seeing of them in a large number of different conscious lights. Such contemplative wants are not limited to the things believed to be real, nor need reality or unreality enter into their purview. It is as interesting to contemplate the swirling patterns or doubled pictures due to pressure on one's eyeballs, or the queerly significant attitudes adopted by ink-blobs, as a tract of farmland seen through a window in Wiltshire. Of such contemplative wants some aesthetic wants are a sub-species: it is notorious that the lover of beauty is interested only in the *seeming* straightness of columns, the seeming weight or stability of overhanging cornices, the seeming depth of Palladian vistas, etc. In the same way there are wants fully satisfied by the construction of something in imagination, without further translation to perceived reality. And there are wants satisfied by the mere building up or breaking down or ordered transformation of a set of notions in thought, or their execution in symbols. These wants and satisfactions have their natural verbal expression in questions and exclamatory utterances: 'What would that really be like?', 'How wonderful a thing!', 'How marvellously straight!', etc. etc. They can be *forced* into forms involving the verbs *to look* or *to seem*: 'If only that column looked straight!' etc. etc., but not without some untruth to the wants behind them. For the absorbed contemplator is not interested in the way things *seem* to him as an observer, nor in the way *he* is constructing them in imagination or thought, but in the very things themselves, and in what enters into their description.

Beside this family of contemplative wants, we may set a family of wants to be called scientific or epistemic, which are plainly not wants that anything should *be*. These are wants terminated and satisfied by well-founded beliefs, but which are none the less not specially interested in the reality of what is believed, since they would be as satisfied were the contrary found to be the case. As an historian I am interested in what happened, but from another point of view I set no store by what happened: I am as ready to accept A's murder or inspiration by B, as B's murder or inspiration by A, should the evidence compel either conclusion. My interest lies in 'the facts', not in the precise matters that happen to be facts. All this may be circumvented by saying that

158 VALUES AND INTENTIONS

my concern is only with knowledge or approvable belief, but this misrepresents the case, since an interest in science and its methodology is quite distinct from an interest in fact and truth: it burgeons, in fact, as an interest on the *decay* of science, and does not flourish in its bloomtide. Of the unsatisfied epistemic want the most natural verbal form is the question, just as its satisfied form is the assertion. It has no natural optative or subjunctive expression, since it does not demand that anything should *be*.

We may perhaps set beside the eccentric want-families just studied, two sets of wants for which the best names are possibly 'activity wants' and 'experience wants'. These are wants satisfied rather by the active endeavour towards certain ends, or the passive undergoing of certain experiences, rather than by the things or circumstances towards which they are officially directed. Such wants are in a sense indifferent to their consciously professed objectives, an indifference shown by their ready tolerance of other substituted objectives. But while they are satisfied by activity and experience, it is not these to which they are *consciously* directed. They might, in fact, be undermined were activity and experience brought into the conscious focus.

As opposed to all these eccentric forms of wanting or interest, the classic case of a want is certainly that where the object on which interest is concentrated is an object whose reality is consciously aimed at, where the want will be satisfied where the object is fully believed in. And it will, in a secondary manner, be the case where this belief has the best possible backing, and this is, as an ideal, the case where the idea of the object is *intuitively fulfilled* and stands actually before the desiring person. My desire that the garden should be full of bloom or the Prime Minister dead, is most fully satisfied, not only where there is good evidence for either state of affairs, but where this evidence is completed by seeing the bloom of the garden or the riddled body of the dead dictator. This last consummation is, of course, not always possible, sometimes owing to relatively chance circumstances, sometimes owing to the inescapable facts of my position in space and time, sometimes owing to the even more inexpugnable facts of my position in the 'space of persons'. Much as I desire certain Nazi atrocities not to have happened, or life to exist on other planets, or my remote descendants to lead sensible lives, or you to have the happiness of requited love, my desire cannot be satisfied by having

THE MODES OF ACTION AND ENDEAVOUR 159

the desired situation before me in the full concretion of perceived or felt reality. I must satisfy myself, on the one hand, by accumulating the right evidences for believing such matters, and, on the other hand, by achieving in personal experience and imagination, the most detailed and vivid view of what they, and their excluded contraries, are *like*. What is, however, essential to the kind of satisfaction in question is the firm *belief* in some object or objective's reality. The further carrying out in perception, feeling or fantasy is a relatively subsidiary matter, something that merely *rounds out* the satisfaction in question.

We have thus as the central category of our conscious wants the wants terminating in judgements, and which are wants that something should *be*. And though we have wants *not* falling under this pattern, we can conveniently, for many purposes, treat them as if they fell under it. Wants satisfied by contemplation, knowledge, activity, experience, etc., can be treated as if consciously directed to such states. As verbally expressed, the wants in question may all be called 'wishes', and their expression may be imperative, subjunctive, optative, quasi-ethical ('It would be good if . . .', 'You should . . .') or quasi-reporting ('I *wish* he were here!'). Such wishes are of central importance in considering the ends of life, since these ends are all things that we desire to see realized, that we wish to be. The use of the term 'being' in this context need not imply any narrowly conceived notion of existence: the desire for being is principally a desire for a being the case, and ranges over the whole spread of propositional forms and approaches. We may wish that A or B should win a prize, that all members of the class should win a prize, that A should win a prize if B does does not, etc. etc.; however things may be conceived, believed and spoken of, they can also be wished. Our wishes range also over every conceivable subject-matter: we can wish that Fermat's theorem should be true or that the analysis of the concept 'duty' should be simpler than it is. It is only if a form of words can be held to correspond to no conception or no possible belief, that it can be held to correspond to no possible wish. That the impossible and the nonsensical tend to be rubbed out in the natural development of our wants and wishes is of course obvious, but there is a level at which even such wishes can be entertained.

From the relation of wants and wishes to 'being' we proceed to elucidate the relations between wanting and *not*-wanting: we have

160 VALUES AND INTENTIONS

to clear up the nature of negative or aversive wants, the want, e.g., *not* to continue seated on a bed of spikes or *not* to go on listening to some intolerably complex, unenlightening exposition, etc. etc. Here there is a tempting path that we should not enter, the device of identifying *not-wanting* (in the pregnant sense in which it is *not* tantamount to the mere *absence* of want) with the mere wanting of an absence or negation: not-to-want fox-hunting to continue, in the pregnant sense distinguished, is merely to press towards the discontinuance or non-existence of such fox-hunting. This device may be likened to the device which identifies the disappointment of a thought-reference by some confronting intuition or the refutation of a belief-tendency by some piece of evidence, with the mere fulfilment or confirmation of a thought directed to the corresponding negation. To hold this is, however, to ignore one of the most interesting, if subtle, steps in human thought. For to have an idea or meaning *frustrated* by some object before me—to have, e.g., the faintly yellowish colour of some object disappointing our idea of it as white—is the uneasy foundation on which is reared the tranquil recognition of it as not-white, which counts for all the world as a new property of higher order. In the same way, to experience the collapse of a belief-tendency in an opposing tide of *dis*belief, is not yet to have advanced to the tranquil position of believing the contrary of what one previously believed, even if the one leads naturally on to the other, and involves no logical movement from the spot. For a frustrated thought or meaning is not as yet an accomplished counter-meaning, nor a disbelief an accomplished counter-belief, and it remains one of the remarkable properties of the life of thought that, like Christianity, it can thus wring triumph out of former defeat. In much the same way it is plain that *not*-wanting something, in the pregnant sense just indicated, is no mere wanting of a negation, but rather the stifling of wanting in the soul by an untoward thought or presentation, a sick withdrawal of self from a prolongation of pattern, the retreat of the active, conscious person from an outcome compulsively imposed on him from without (and sometimes from within). *Not*-wanting or aversion, like frustration of meaning or disbelief, is plainly a higher-order mental orientation, not co-ordinate with the wanting it withholds or refuses, and understandable only on the prior basis of such wanting. If the most natural result of any imposed prolongation of pattern, even if at first alien, is to create

THE MODES OF ACTION AND ENDEAVOUR 161

a spontaneous flow of mental activity in its direction—the familiar is *pro tanto* the satisfying—aversion or *not*-wanting is a simple shrinking from such prolongation, the perpetuation of its enforced character, the refusal to lend the forces of the soul to its furtherance. The metaphors we have used are those inevitable in our task, even if applying better to states rich in personal feeling, rather than the dry, brusque refusals we frequently practise.

There will be, further, a necessary tendency of mind to pass on from aversive *not*-wanting to the wanting of the corresponding absence: when sickened or wearied long enough by what we cannot stomach, we become inflamed with angry zeal for its removal or liquidation. In much the same way, when positively desirous of X, we may develop a profound distaste for its absence, and this distaste, as much as the positive want, may inspire our practical proceedings. It remains, however, an interesting fact, too deeply rooted to be merely empirical, and responsible for some of the most important distinctions in the field of morals, that the bond between the two attitudes remains a loose one, that the two do not march together closely in the conscious person, and that the one serves rather as the instrument ancillary of the other than as its mirror-duplicate. If we positively want X, and are deeply satisfied by its presence, we need not necessarily shrink deeply from, and experience dissatisfaction in its absence, and we do not in fact do so in many cases. There is a whole world of graces, ornaments and perfected flowers of existence which we most positively wish to accrue to the actual world, and which ravish us when actual, which we none the less do not gravely miss when absent, in whose absence we in fact acquiesce calmly as in something but to be expected. In the same manner, if we are deeply averse from X, and withdraw our soul's forces from its realization, we need not necessarily press urgently towards its removal, nor be deeply satisfied by its absence. There is a whole world of pains, horrors and corruptions, from dirt, lies and vulgarity, up to National Socialist diabolisms and infamies, which inspire many of us with a repugnance which lames, rather than inflames, our destructive energies, and the removal of whose objects brings relief, rather than ravishment, in its wake. It is not our concern at this moment to discuss the 'approvability' of this state of affairs. Certainly, however, it obtains, and its obtaining is a fact of great importance, hanging, as it does, together with the deep

F

162 VALUES AND INTENTIONS

gulf between good and evil, a gulf too little considered in current moral philosophy.

Having discussed the significance of *not*-wanting something, or of being averse from it, it remains to discuss the significance of wanting one thing *rather* than another, or of *preferring A to B*. Here, too, we have a feature fundamental to the life of conscious wanting but offering a like temptation to undue simplification as the *not*-wanting just considered. To want *A* rather than *B*, means, by a facile transformation, to want *A* more than *B*, and to want *A* more than *B*, is, by a transformation equally plausible, to have a stronger, more intense want for *A* than for *B*. From this it is but a step to the equation of the preferred with the strong, to the picture of choice and preference in terms of a pivoted lever, automatically inclining where the 'moments' are superior, to such strange things as the Hobbist identification of will with the 'last passion in deliberating'. It is, however, plain that there is a sense of wanting *A* rather than *B*, or of putting it *before B* in our wishes, in which it could not be the case that we did either if we had not considered *A* and *B together*, nor compared them as regards eligibility, no matter if our want for *A* were more clamant, and more deeply rooted in our personality than our want for *B*. My need to drop asleep in a given situation may be stronger than my desire to preserve the proprieties, or than my wish to hear about Ming pottery, and yet no one would say that I *preferred* sleeping to preserving the proprieties, or to hearing about Ming pottery. And when I do prefer one thing to another—as when I prefer the straight to the curved in furniture, or picnics by riversides to picnics on seashores—it may be artificial to picture me like a pivoted lever, automatically inclining where the 'moments' were heaviest.

Preferring *A* to *B*, or wanting *A* rather than *B*, occurs in its most pointed form in cases where there is an *accommodation* of distinct wants, and where this accommodation takes place in the daylight of full consciousness. It is in such pointed situations, in which we would definitely have one thing rather than another, that all less pointed cases of preference culminate, and by their relation to which they are all classed as cases of preferring. The important thing is that, in such pointed preferences, one want comes (not necessarily on grounds of independent 'strength') to be *subordinated* to another, in the sense *either* (if both wants are

THE MODES OF ACTION AND ENDEAVOUR 163

positive) that the object of one want comes to be *not*-wanted, i.e. sacrificed or foregone, for the sake of the other's object, while still being wanted in and for itself, *or* that (if both wants are negative, the object of one *not*-wanting or aversion comes to be relatively wanted), i.e. put up with or tolerated, in the service of the *not*-wanting of, or aversion from, the object of the other. Preference, it is plain, is in a wide sense *choice*, though not necessarily spreading out on the plane of action, or even on that of actual existence, and though not necessarily rising to the well-deliberated, cool, representative sort of preferring to which the word 'choice' is often restricted. The accommodation in question may be at times vividly 'felt', and we then have a definite *experience* of preferring. But, though operative *in* our conscious orientations, it may not announce itself *to* them, and may be manifest merely in such things as an ending of vacillation, a firm embarking on some course of thought and conduct, or in some verbal disclosures as '*A* rather than *B*', '*A* for me and not *B*', 'I should like *A* rather than *B*', which, despite wide seeming differences in thought-backing, really continue highly similar conscious approaches, of which, in the last impoverishment, words constitute the whole manifest be-all.

Since wants are not all reality- or existence-wants, satisfied by our belief that something is the case, our preferences will not all be reality- or existence-preferences, satisfied by our belief that one thing is and not another. There will be contemplative preferences, satisfied merely by *dwelling* on *A* rather than on *B*, and indifferent as to whether *A* or *B* are judged really to exist. There will be epistemic or scientific preferences, satisfied by the framing of judgements and surmises, in loyalty to remembered anticipations and compulsions, and without regard to non-compulsive trends and leanings. There will, lastly, be achievement- or experience-preferences, seemingly satisfied by certain actual actions or objects, but quite indifferent to their replacement by others. Reality- or existence-preferences may, however, be accorded the same primacy in philosophical treatments that was before accorded to reality-wants, since each merely aesthetic, scientific or other reality-indifferent preference must develop readily into a preference for one sort of conscious activity over another. And reality-preferences will exhibit the same range of surrogative and imperfect execution that we found previously in the case of reality-wants. While they may be completely executed when A is present in fulfilled, believed reality to the palpable exclusion of B, or when A is being actively carried out by one's musculature to the exclusion of B, they may be also carried out in the medium of fantasy or mere thought (and in some ways *more* perfectly since the exclusion of B still permits of its fantastic entertainment). The last types of execution are the natural vehicles for *general* preferences: we more readily advance to preferring *an A* to *a B*, rather than *this A* to *this B*, when an A or a B are imagined or thought of, rather than present in fulfilled awareness. From a general preference there is a decline to a merely habitual preference, to the established readiness to prefer an A to a B which may not be illustrated at a given moment. And from an habitual preference one may descend to the wider field of a preference *in posse*, which applies even where we have not actually preferred A to B, but *would* do so were the choice set before us whether in reality or imagination. In this sense we all prefer what is for us an exhilarating to what is for us a humdrum activity, though we may never have had occasion to compare them or to choose between them.

The notion of preference permits a further, somewhat vacuous extension to cases where one thing is positively wanted, and another thing is looked on with aversion or indifference. In such cases the doing-without the *not*-wanted for the wanted object, involves no conflict and represents no accommodation: it is a degenerate case, a preference by courtesy. Accepting such courtesy preferences, and accepting, too, our tendency to be transitive in our preferences—a readiness it would be *odd* rather than impossible to run against, the sacrifice of C made in our pursuit of B being in a sense retained in this pursuit, and so naturally subordinated to the further pursuit of A, to which B itself is subordinated —we arrive readily at an indefinitely extensible schema of preference, cut in twain by a central point of indifference, and embracing above wanted things arranged in an order of positive preference, and below unwanted things arranged in an order of increasing distaste. The schema represents an ideal rather than anything actual: its filling by a man's actual preferences is inconstant, inconsistent and full of lacunae. It provides, however, the framework or form into which our approvable preference may be cast, should they ever achieve enough harmony and stability.

THE MODES OF ACTION AND ENDEAVOUR 165

A preference of *A* over *B* is only in its crude origins a conflict of discriminable wants, of attractions and repulsions, which 'fight it out' in a man's conscious life, and achieve a new harmony of subordination and superordination, the victory going to the 'strongest' impulse, in some sense in which 'strength' means something other than the mere fact that an impulse wins. In most states of preference such struggle and accommodation are remote and vestigial, something at times present as a 'condensed meaning', sometimes only *ready* to make a conscious appearance, sometimes refining themselves to the mere verbalism of 'reasons' which shape conduct without crudely divagating into separate pushes and pulls. All this will concern us later. The whole passage from a determination by existentially distinct urges to a determination by logically distinct 'reasons' is characteristic of the higher development of the life of conscious endeavour.

We may complete our general profile of wants by considering briefly the status of unserious wants, the wants which govern thought and action in art, play, sympathetic understanding, etc., in which it is rather *as if* we wanted something than that we genuinely want it. Here there are several blind-alleys that we must avoid entering. We must not, on the one hand, make unserious wants, wants terminating in and conditioned by situations not believed in, and serious wants, wants terminating in and conditioned by things believed. Obviously there can be thoroughly serious wants terminating in situations *not* believed in, as in the deeply serious needs and satisfactions of imaginative art. In the same way there may be unserious wants terminating in things believed in: it is through an unserious want in myself that I may bring home to myself, and may succeed in dwelling upon, a serious want that I do not share. On the other hand, it would be wrong to regard the difference as one of 'feeling', in the sense in which 'feeling' involves a peculiar intensification of experience. Though we may say that an unserious want is 'not really felt', it may have all the raised intensity of the most profound emotional experience, while a quite serious want may have no such emotional appanages at all. I can want unseriously, yet emotionally, and I can want drily, yet with extreme seriousness.

The differentia of the unserious want would seem to lie, not in its connection with situations not believed in, nor yet in emotional coolness and poverty, but in its parasitic, shallowly

166 VALUES AND INTENTIONS

rooted, therefore unsustainable character. Much as a thing imagined, even if envisaged *as* of great intensity, touches 'the soul' but softly and in muffled fashion, without the 'attack' characteristic of the feeblest perception, just so unserious wants prolong patterns impinging relatively externally on the conscious person—as when we enter into other people's wants, or desire to impress them with our sympathy, etc. etc. Such shallowly rooted wants thrive in consciousness and behaviour while a parent impulse sustains them, but languish as soon as it languishes, and so are felt to be insincere, rootless in the personality. Merely instrumental wants are among these rootless, evanescent wants, and in all unseriousness and insincerity we in fact use a want as a mere means to something else. The parasitic character of an unserious want bears comparison with the bracketed character of unserious belief: what the encompassing framework of un-bracketed belief does in the latter case, the enclosing framework of independent wants does in the former. In both cases, likewise, there is a readily trodden path leading from the unserious to the serious.[1]

(IV) THE ROLE OF EMOTION AND FEELING

We have, in the present section, to consider two related dis-tinctions that have often casually arisen in the preceding dis-cussion: the distinction between *warm-blooded*, passionate, emotional wanting on the one hand, and unemotional, dis-passionate, *cold-blooded* wanting on the other, also the related distinction between the wanting which is, in an emphatic or pointed sense, *felt* and the wanting which exists in a wholly *unfelt* manner. The two distinctions are by no means coincident. Where we want warmly, we do not necessarily feel deeply—we may be much too 'engaged' to do so—and the deepest of human feelings may be notably cool in their temperature: the unruffled reasonable calm of the Stoics, the Buddhist freedom from craving, the simple mutual acceptance of profound love, etc. etc.

In the distinction between the warm-blooded and the cool we have one of those all-important differences, evident and interesting to ordinary thought and morals, which has seldom arrested the generalizing gaze of philosophers. David Hume is perhaps unique

[1] I owe much to Meinong in the distinctions of this section.

THE MODES OF ACTION AND ENDEAVOUR 167

in the attention he paid to it. It is plain, on the one hand, and intrinsically understandable, that a want unable to carry itself out completely, or with sufficient ease or swiftness, or with an intensity and emphasis perhaps not possible in the state in which it terminates, should 'burst forth' into a range of manifestations, exceeding in force but having perhaps only a slender instrumental or other relevance to the objective pursued. That wants should in certain conditions explode *widely*, and that we should know certain superficially irrelevant phases of thought and behaviour to be their expressions, and in our own case without profound study, is certainly a fact of experience: it is also much more than a fact of experience. The possibility of an irrelevant far-flung explosion, even if not built analytically into our notion of a want, would none the less be one that evidently 'belonged' with it, and tended to complete it. In knowing what it is to want greatly, we cannot but know the naturalness of being prepared to do practically *anything*, however little likely to secure what we want, in a sort of wild furtherance of it.

Such emotional furtherance will be likely, *a priori*, to assume forms at least resembling those which would genuinely further the wanted objective: it is not therefore a contingent 'vestige of evolution', or of anything else, that emotional scorn expresses itself in such things as bared teeth, emotional longing in outstretched arms, emotional hatred in various destructive gestures, etc. etc. There is logical virtuosity displayed in the choice of such useless expressions, not fundamentally different from the more useful virtuosity displayed in the appropriate selection of means to ends. But, in the limit, emotional expansion must be capable of *indefinite* extension, and just as a thought may attach itself full-fledged to the least likely image, so the driving inspiration of, e.g., frustrated love, must be capable of taking almost any expression. In this respect, methods like the psycho-analytic merely expand a sort of knowledge that we all intuitively possess. We know that in sighing we express our yearning for Sylvia, and on the analyst's couch we come to know that in so doing we are expressing our yearning for our mothers, or for worse. But if it is understandable that a want should be thus able to expand over a wide range of half-relevant manifestations, it is understandable too that it should be able to contract indefinitely, till its manifestation is simply the appropriate performance, e.g. putting a cross on a ballot paper,

168 VALUES AND INTENTIONS

or the dry acknowledgement of a personal attitude ('I always vote Conservative'). The movement towards coolness and contraction will, however, concern us later: here we are only concerned with developments towards warmth.

The development of wants towards emotional warmth has been seen *a priori* to have its roots in frustration, and to have a tendency towards wider, even less relevant *diffusion* of expression. But if emotionality is thus diffused, it will tend also to be less various: the emotional inflations of distinct wants will be so similar that it would be artificial to make them as numerous as the wants inflated in them. Thus we recognize many wants, but comparatively few major emotions. There are, e.g., aggressive, defensive, withdrawing, collapsing, deploring, agonized, voluptuous and acquiescent emotions (to name but a few), but hardly emotions specifically connected with stamp-collecting or the seduction of strawberry blondes. Precise strategies permit of infinite variety, whereas confused strategies fall under a few simple heads of offence, defence, withdrawal, help, etc. etc.: the same applies in the life of well-co-ordinated wants and ill-co-ordinated emotions.

There is yet another respect in which the empirical development of emotional wants is not without an *a priori* foundation: the tendency of emotional wants to have an unpractical expression in the inner economy of the body, in disturbances of the digestive, glandular, circulatory and other facts that represent the 'nightside' of conscious life, and in the sensations attendant on such disturbances. Obviously emotional life cannot be complete if its expansion ends in the voluntary, surface musculature: it must sink down to the deep, slow, hidden Lethe and Cocytus of our bodily life, and to the faint echoes which come up from their stirred depths. The direction towards emotionality is a direction towards *detachment* from the exactly cognized object and the well-regulated response: it is a direction towards the personal *immanence* in which Tetens saw the specific differentia of feeling. Being such a direction, it must tend to move towards the least practical, least object-bound of expressions, and these are no other than the disturbances of our internal bodily economy, and the barely describable sense-experiences issuing from them. It is in the queer language of the vitals, the formless changes of the breath, and the warm tides of the blood overstreaming their normal floodgates, that our emotional life has, and must have, its culminating

THE MODES OF ACTION AND ENDEAVOUR 169

expressions, even the preternatural calm of the religious ecstasy demanding an abnormal slowing down or arrest of these same processes. Were we the thoroughgoing teleologists that we sometimes wish to be, we should perhaps see in their emotional resonance (as men once saw in their prognostic significance) the supreme function of entrails, to which vital functions are merely subsidiary.

But though thus moving towards detachment from practice and lucidity, the core of an emotion must remain a practical policy, and one capable of some vague formulation in words. It is meaningless to speak of a fear (or even an *Angst*) which did not have at its heart a policy formulable in the words 'Let this not come upon me!', 'May this (Nothing) remain far from me!' or a wrath not formulable in some such phrase as 'Let this be utterly brought to nought!' or state of shame not expressible in some such words as 'Let me be utterly hidden from all eyes!' Even acquiescent pleasure could be expressed in some such phrase as 'Let this go on and on!', 'Let this engross me utterly and always!', while a state of squirming unease could be expressed in the phrases 'Oh for the surcease of this!', 'Oh let me not bear this an instant longer!', etc. etc. An emotion, to common psychological insight, stems from a specifically directed line of response: it is to be expected that it should condense this line of response in itself, and should describe itself, and be described by understanding observers, in terms of it. The policies embedded in our emotions are of course widely various—they are numerous shades of aggression, shame-facedness, etc.—and it is not suggested that anything but a fairly wide shading of verbal formulation could do justice to them all.

We may note further that not only must our emotions be thought of as incorporating policies, but that they must be thought of also as incorporating *presumptions* regarding the things that provoke them, or on which they seek to discharge themselves. Thus fear, with its policy of retreat and evasion, definitely presumes menace in its object: it has in such a presumption its natural complement. While it may not be logically impossible to have the fear-policy without the completing presumption, there must be something difficult, odd, exceptional in such a separation: we can see *a priori* that it cannot regularly be. This presumption will, in the most developed case, take the form of viewing the object in a certain light: it will appear dangerous, menacing,

F*

170 VALUES AND INTENTIONS

hostile, ready to harm or ruin us in some clear or unclear manner. Such a 'light' need not necessarily go with belief: it may in fact coincide with total disbelief. Thus a man beset with neurotic fears 'knows' that certain things involve no real menace: this still does not prevent them from coming before him as threatening, even if this whole presumption is bracketed in his wider knowledge. Even if there is no conscious light in the whole matter, the 'presumption' will still operate in a man's behaviour. A man afraid of something finds his fear dispersing if its object goes on behaving innocuously, while it is reinforced if there is an approach to actual harm. That there are empirical exceptions to this, proves nothing against the rule, which is neither a logical nor a merely natural law. To provide 'presumptions' for the various emotional attitudes is a scholastic exercise not further worth pursuing. What is noteworthy, however, is the fact of a rationality and an approvability pertaining even to the least rational of emotions: they may be held to be justified, or may be condemned as unjustified, by standards intrinsic to themselves. Fear and jealousy may be undesirable effects, but they may be evaluated both in relation to the actual occasion and to the precise means adopted to deal with it. Were emotions the featureless interior states that their surface divorce from objects and from practice sometimes makes them seem to be, there would be no sense in talking thus of their justifiability. Such talk is, however, necessary to their complete characterization, and prepares the way for the less narrowly relevant justifiability that will concern us later.

The policies and presumptions incorporated in our emotions are such as may be discovered inductively by considering our actions, and by prolonging and completing their pattern: they are so discovered by those who observe us from without, and in certain rare cases by ourselves. They may also be divined sympathetically by those prolonging in themselves in unserious fashion the trends suggested by the acts forced on their observation. But the emotional agent, like the agent generally, does not have the direction and presumed setting of his emotions made plain to him in this manner. The same want that diffuses itself in emotional activity will generally also blossom in what may be called 'emotional knowledge'. The emotionally seized man knows and can tell the sort of emotion he is having, and the wants and presumptions it embodies, and he can do so without meditating on his

THE MODES OF ACTION AND ENDEAVOUR 171

own actions: he can say, in most cases, that he is angry or dismayed or full of compassion or regret, and he can say in most cases with *what* he is thus emotionally concerned. And not only can the emotionally seized man give us this sort of information: he can tell us the precise sense of his varied gestures or his personal impression of things, that by such and such a wrinkle he was registering, not contempt, but simple puzzlement, that such and such an appearance was for him menacing, etc. Such 'emotional knowledge' is of course not possible except on a background of wide experience of past drifts in our own thought and behaviour, and in that of others: without this it could command no significant material. It can also fail us totally or lead us into error. The precise drift of our emotional state may not be at all evident, or it may be seen in a perspective afterwards felt to be inadequate and distorting. All this does not affect the fact that our emotional drifts can announce themselves to ourselves in a direct manner, that it is not through or by anything other than themselves, and their actual existence, that we come at times to have ideas and beliefs about them. This leads us on to the crucial topic of 'feeling', our second theme in the present section.

The whole identification of emotions with diffused wants, cut adrift from their normal moorings in objects and actions, and finding unpractical expression in half-framed gestures and obscure bodily resonances, obviously touches much that essentially pertains to them. It might seem, however, to have left out something central: the element of 'feeling', the mere quality or modality of our personal sufferance, which, however much it may depend on things thought of or wanted, yet has, as it were, a 'side' giving on a purely internal shaft, into which none of these relations may enter. That such an inner side exists, in the sense of an experience holding in dissolved unity what might otherwise spread over a wide array of actions and cognitions, is indeed central to the life of mind. It betrays, however, the most complete misunderstanding of this unique inner concentration and absorption of dispersed multitude in itself, to see in it a mere case of *quality*, to assimilate the dizzily packed plenitude of a feeling of sadness or an emotion of contrition to the mere presence to sense of something blue or noisy. Such shop-window exhibitions of plain characters in plain instances may be possible in the object of the senses: they certainly have no application to anything one might call an 'experience'.

172 VALUES AND INTENTIONS

That the category of indiscerptible, qualitative feeling has no plain instances has been recognized by thinkers who, like Titchener, reduce the life of feeling to two strange 'feeling-elements', of pleasure and unpleasure, distinguished from sensations only by their systematic insusceptibility to, and evasion of, conscious clearness, or who like Ryle operate with various twinges, tingles, throbs and other residua of emotional experience, held to resemble sensations and yet not be among them. These doctrines are a mistake, only abstracts torn from sensible objects have such a qualitative status, the whole placing of them 'in the mind' points to a confusion and misapplication of categories.

The word 'feeling' has of course a variety of uses, many of which belong rather to our bodily sense-experience than to our emotional life. We may be said to feel by way of, or *in* our bodies, how our bodies themselves are disposed or moved, or touched or pressed, or made warmer or cooler, or made to throb or vibrate or secretly squirm, or to be racked by those unique, disagreeable phantasms known as bodily pains. We may be said, secondly, to feel by way of the same bodies how *other* bodies are disposed, shaped, moved, arranged, in contact with our own or other bodies, and raised to various levels of temperature. And we may be said, thirdly, to feel certain bodily *sensations*, representing as it were the common material by means of which a large number of different bodily awarenesses may be satisfied, and which, though not strictly isolable, nor describable *per se*, yet represent the obscure limit of a natural abstraction. If we become less and less enterprising in perceiving the things around us as this or as that, we draw nearer and nearer to the pure 'matter' of all such interpretative perspectives, which, in Aristotelian fashion, is everything in potency and nothing in act. The route towards such an abstraction may be artificial and unnatural in the case of the other senses, but it is almost natural in the case of the bodily senses. For here the fulfilling sense-encounters are so inadequate to what we know or divine of the state of our body, as readily to ride loose of this. Frequently we simply have 'bodily knowledge' unmediated by specific sensations, as, e.g., of motion, position, orientation, etc., often likewise we seem to dwell in detached bodily sense-experiences whose relations to other completing sense-experiences, and to the things they help us to 'know', is largely obscure. Pains, particularly, carry almost no

THE MODES OF ACTION AND ENDEAVOUR 173

clear indication on their faces of any other phenomenal aspects necessary to their completion and to their secure location in reality. They come and go like phantasms haunting certain regions of the body, rather than like solidly backed appearances having a definite place in it. Hence one hesitates to locate pains elsewhere than in sentient bodies, and one hesitates to locate them even in one's own body, as one does not hesitate to locate temperatures, shapes, pressures, etc. The links they have with anything seem more with our conscious history than with anything else, and hence, though sensuous, they remain 'subjective', intentionally inexistent. Even here their links with our conscious orientations seem contingent rather than necessary: it is for instance unclear *why* sensory pains should be so very disagreeable, so much an object of aversion. This would seem a case where an obscure quasi-conscious aversion from bodily threats has found for itself an arbitrary conscious symbol: our hatred for pain is not *per se* intelligible, but can at best achieve a quasi-intelligibility when seen in the more general quasi-intelligibility of bodily 'purpose'.

The main emergent use of 'feeling' in connection with our own bodies, is therefore that of the largely obscure, sensorily fulfilled but fulfilled only with vanishing sketchiness, in an understandable sense *direct*, knowledge of our bodily state; it is the intimation the body itself gives us of its inner condition. It extends readily to the intimation the body gives us of the frustration or satisfaction of its own unconscious trends, the unmistakable sense, e.g. of bodily well-being illustrated perhaps by a few sketchy sensations, and the equally unmistakable sense of general bodily malaise illustrated perhaps by a few trifling aches and pains. From such uses it is but a step to the use of 'feeling' to cover our direct knowledge and understanding of our own emotionally diffused *conscious* trends, especially when surrogatively carried out in unconscious organic disturbances and in the sketchy sensations resultant therefrom. To feel in this sense is not merely to *be* emotionally seized, but also in a direct manner to *know* that, and how, one is emotionally seized. There are, we may note, in this all-important connection, two distinct uses of 'feeling', an *emphatic* and an *unemphatic* use. In the *unemphatic* use of the term 'feeling', to feel cross, sad, fatigued, dismayed, etc., does not differ from *being* cross, sad, fatigued, dismayed,

174 VALUES AND INTENTIONS

etc., without its needing to be in any way plain to one that one was so. But in the *emphatic* sense of 'feeling'—as when one searchingly asks 'But did you *feel* cross?' 'Did you *feel* sad?', etc. —it would be rank nonsense to ask whether one was *aware* of what one thus emphatically *felt*, such emphatic feelings being thereby shown to be none other than our own unmediated, but well-founded ideas and beliefs regarding our own emotional orientations. To *feel* cross is, in this use, not merely to *be* cross, but immediately to *know* or *perceive* that, and how, and with what, one is cross, and in what outward and inward ways one is showing this crossness. The central feature of a *feeling* (emphatic) may accordingly be held to be *cognitive*, even if it may also be many other things besides.

The features that distinguish 'feelings' from other cases of cognition, i.e. of idea and belief, are, however, manifold and important. They have all been noted in our previous treatment, but may be briefly resumed in the present context. Feelings have an intimacy and warmth not possessed by other forms of cognition in that they are the presentation to the conscious person of *his own* emotionally diffused trends, trends present in the central current of his thought and action which runs through his experienced world, rather than on its remote, variable periphery, and they are intimate and warm in so far as his awareness accompanies them *easily* and *familiarly*, and involves no strain of external compulsion. They are intimate and warm, further, because their diffusion is into the interior changes of *his own body*, the one constant inhabitant of the presented world, and because these changes seem to have the *detachment from objects and practice* which increases their *personal* character. This detachment is aided both by the *queer, fragmentary character of bodily sensation*, and also by the almost wholly *obscure, marginal character of the awareness* they mediate: were we clearly conscious of our own emotional orientation, and the sensations that symbolize it, we should cease to say that we *felt* it. Feelings are also intimate and warm inasmuch as they are *directly* produced by the same drifts that they present to awareness: there is nothing *derived, inferential, argumentative*, in their awareness of such trends. It is not by virtue of any observed feature of thought or behaviour that we know what sort of emotional seizure we are having, the object on which it seeks to discharge itself, and the precise sense

THE MODES OF ACTION AND ENDEAVOUR 175

of the gestures and pictures it makes use of. And feelings are further intimate and warm in so far as they are *sustained* by the very trends that they contemplate, which prevent them from vanishing like unserious trends whose sources lie in external stimuli or compulsions. Feelings are, in fact, so profoundly inwrought with the trends of which they take cognizance that they may be regarded as two sides of a single phenomenon: a trend pervading consciousness and behaviour which is one with an accompanying awareness of itself. We must, however, distinguish the two aspects, since to a large extent they vary independently. When an emotional trend consumes vast energy, as in the more noisy, spectacular emotions it must, understandably, be accompanied by shallow feelings. It is in the less energetic emotional disturbances that we must look for the deepest feelings. When we react most vigorously, our feelings are fleeting and evanescent, whereas in such non-energetic motions as blissful acquiescence or despondent self-abandonment the feeling overlay may seem solid enough to be 'cut with a knife'.

That the term feeling should be used to designate certain obscure, unmediated cognitions can be made more acceptable when we note that we so use it in the case of many other obscure, unmediated cognitions. Thus we say we have the feeling of an approaching storm, of a presence in a room, of our own approaching end, of a flaw in a piece of reasoning, etc. etc. And it explains too the remarkable fact that having emotions regularly enables us to see the things around us in various emotionally coloured lights or atmospheres, as terrifying, odious, sinister, attractive, mean, marvellous, etc. etc. These remarkable facts, to which Meinong gave the name of 'emotional presentation', would be strange indeed were emotional drifts not themselves apparent to mind. For how could the fear-, hate-, delight-, etc., arousing and discharging properties of objects be apparent to consciousness, and seemingly invest the object, if the corresponding fear, hate, delight, etc., were not? Plainly the two properties are correlative and logically interchangeable, and the conscious light in which the one is present readily swings over into the conscious light which presents the other.

All this does not involve, as one might imagine, that the simplest feeling involves a profound exercise of reflection: what a feeling involves, unacceptable as it may sound, is a direct intimation of causality, and of a causality neutral as between our conscious orientations and their objects. When we *feel* angered, we are directly aware, in an obscure, condensed manner, of a movement towards the demolition or pushing aside of X, perhaps also aware of X as *provocative* of this attitude—an awareness often misleading, since X may *not* be the real source of our anger, and may not even exist—and we can perceive this drift as as much attaching to the course of our actions as to the course of our conscious intentions. The life of feeling certainly involves a *sort* of reflection, in that it involves a person's awareness of his own activity or passivity, but it need not involve an awareness of the special properties of conscious clearness, etc., which differentiate conscious orientations from their objects. That the life of feeling should involve a direct awareness of causality may indeed appear shocking to many thinkers, to whom causality has become wrought up with the procedures of inductive science. But it need not commit us to a view of efficacy as some unique, directly intuited component. Hume established the truth, but failed to see the significance, of the fact that there can be no additional palpable element constitutive of causality. For were efficacy something additional to the reliable self-prolongation of pattern, we should still have to ask *why* the presence of this extra thing ensured such reliable self-prolongation. Obviously to ask for such a supposed extra thing is to ask for nothing, an attempt to turn a conditional expectation, with its ineliminable *modality*, into a fulfilled awareness of some qualitative matter of fact. We may perhaps hold, paradoxically, that, while in most other cases we must first have a fully illustrated idea of some relation, before being able to frame beliefs concerning it, in the case of causation we must first form beliefs as to what will or would happen in certain circumstances, before we can form the idea of it, and that, as this idea involves the boundless 'openness' or belief, it can never have an adequate illustration. Be this as it may, in what *will* or *would* come out of certain antecedents lies the whole content of causality, and a case of this, whatever its philosophical restatement, in what we may be held to 'know' in every case of feeling.

One casualty that has occurred in the present treatment may perhaps seem unwarranted: we have by implication rejected the notion of simple qualitative states of *being pleased* or *being unpleased* which has played such a vast role in traditional theory,

THE MODES OF ACTION AND ENDEAVOUR 177

and has seemed to some to explain why we do whatever we do. On our view the varying states of being pleased are all states of relatively unmixed acquiescence or basking dalliance in some activity or in the thought or sight of some object, and turned towards the satisfaction's, and its object's, continuance. *Feelings* of pleasure, on the other hand, are our immediate awareness of the deep *fit* between wants and circumstances, a consciousness expressible in such phrases as 'Let this be exactly as it is!', or 'This is exactly as it should be'. In much the same manner our varying states of unpleasure are all states of aversion inspired and sustained by some present or well-imagined object, and the corresponding *feeling* of unpleasure or unpleasantness is our immediate awareness of this aversion, and of the deep *misfit* between it and the circumstances, such as might be verbally expressed in such terms as 'Let this not continue a moment longer' or 'This is in every way as it should *not* be'. All this might appear intellectualized and peripheral, it might seem to have missed the heart of the matter, the glow or sweetness or bloom of pleasure, on the one hand, and the sick jars, squirming unease, and parched agonies of the unpleasant. (The metaphorical coverage of the unpleasant would seem less simple and well-established than that of the pleasant.) The glow or sweetness or bloom which seems the heart of the matter in our states of felt pleasure—we may presume corresponding things said in the case of unpleasure—can be none other than the condensing power of conscious experience, its ability to hold complex relationships in dissolved suspension, which we again and again encounter in the life of mind, and which here employs particular covering metaphors. To suppose otherwise would be to introduce an empirical surd into the very heart of conscious experience, in a place where it can on no account be. For were pleasure and unpleasure peculiar *qualities* of experience, as loud and sweet are peculiar qualities of what comes before us in sense-experience, it would be a gross, empirical accident that we uniformly sought the one and avoided the other, as it is a gross empirical accident in the case of the loud or the sweet, and this is of all suppositions the most incredible and absurd. Plainly it is in some sense almost trivially necessary that we should want pleasure (or *not* want unpleasure), if by 'pleasure' (or 'unpleasure') be meant either the satisfying (or dissatisfying) state towards which (or away from which) we move, rather than the object

178 VALUES AND INTENTIONS

consciously aimed at, or if, alternatively, by 'pleasure' (or 'unpleasure') be meant the pleasing or satisfying (or displeasing or dissatisfying) object itself, rather than the satisfaction (or dissatisfaction) we have in it. In both of these cases the notion of pleasure (or unpleasure) has the notion of a want practically built into it (whether 'analytically' or not, those who employ this term had better determine, since for us it represents a limiting rather than an applicable notion), and this could *not* be the case were it some simple empirical quality. But there is another sense in which there is an *a priori* connection between wants and pleasure which is remote from the tautological, the sense in which the vivid, believing thought of something as likely to please or satisfy almost inevitably generates a want for it, a want which is a consequence, rather than a presupposition, of its being thought pleasant. If pleasantness be practically a doublet of satisfied want, all this is intelligible, not so if it represents something simple and qualitative. There is a naturalness and logic in wanting a state of satisfied want, but no naturalness or logic in being *épris* with a particular quality.

The desire for pleasure is, as has often been held, a secondary want, but not less genuine on that account: it presupposes a basis of primary wants to whose satisfaction it in a general manner presses. Some of these wants may be the blind quasi-wants or 'needs' of the unconscious organism (which are 'wants' only by courtesy or analogy), the carrying out of which may generate conscious satisfactions, as in the delight felt in the sweet, or as in our obscure sense of total well-being. Such satisfactions, detached from a prior conscious want, readily generate secondary conscious wants, and provide the basis for a quasi-empirical exaggeration of a valid *a priori* principle: the exaggerated view of *all* wants as having pleasure as their supreme objective. It is in the complete abandonment of all merely qualitative modes of conceiving pleasure, or any other basic form of conscious life, that the removal of all such exaggerations, with their attendant problems, must be sought.

CHAPTER V

THE MODES OF WISH AND WILL

(I) THE NATURE OF WILLING

If our wants are capable of a 'development in warmth', leading to all the relaxed, diffused, emotional forms of wanting studied in the last section, they are capable too of a 'development in coolness', leading to the various forms of choice and will, which have been so much the central theme of moral philosophy. The 'development in coolness' is the development which led to the whole ancient Platonic, Aristotelian and Stoic view of the life of considered choice as a life directed by *reason*, as the life of primary wants and passions is not. In modern times, inspired by the other Aristotelian dictum that mere thought moves not at all, and by Hume's determined blurring of important distinctions, we have come to ignore or be forgetful of the profound gulf between what we may call a domination by urges and a direction by reasons, which, however much nurtured in the life of primary wants, need bear no sign of this lowly provenance. Not only is it not the case that a man needs to be goaded to action or decision by some hot-blooded urge: it is not even necessary that he should experience a breath of desire. What has effected some of the most momentous historic decision or displays of fortitude has often been no more than an overtly or secretly spoken *word*.

The 'development in coolness' is a development in which wanting loses all its crude, immediate strength, its power to dominate consciousness and behaviour, and to keep other directions of wanting from coming to the fore. In their place it acquires, by an understandable transformation, a somewhat different kind of strength, the strength to persist, to make itself manifest again and again, to channel thought and action in relatively sustained fashion. It is not merely an empirical accident that our various cool determinations leave what are called 'determining tendencies' behind them, which channel thought and action silently until countermanded by some other determination, and which make themselves known only when they

180 VALUES AND INTENTIONS

encounter problems and resistances, a kind of subtle persistence not normal in the case of warm-blooded wants. A cool determination to write in iambics or to walk to Chelsea will channel thought and behaviour in a manner alien to such 'primary' urges as hunger, thirst, rage, etc., and will even oppose formidable, though noiseless, resistances to the interferences of the latter. When fully set upon the least interesting, least important, task, we can become insensitive to the pricks of passion. Lust, anxiety, etc., can certainly channel behaviour with similar noiselessness, but their doing so involves an unnatural division and repression of spirit: their normal course is in the open, by no means subterranean. This quiet, but not resourceless inertia is the characteristic *facies* of wanting in coolness, just as mobile, diversified, highly transitory energies are the characteristic *facies* of wanting in warmth. That the life of endeavour, deprived of one sort of expression, should thus switch to another, and that it should find the particular other it does find, has something natural and understandable about it.

Wanting in warmth is not uninfluenced by what may be called 'cognitive factors', by the vivid picturing of something as X, by the fulfilled seeing of something as X, by the sure belief or knowledge that something is X. The various hateful passions of Achilles yielded to the sight of Priam suing for his son's body, and they might have yielded to the mere picture of, or mere belief in, such a petition. It is, however, evident that wanting in coolness is infinitely *more* sensitive to such 'cognitive factors', that to be cool is to have room for an awareness of what offers, and to be ready to be guided by it. Wanting in coolness may be made operative by the mere *realization* that something has (or would have) a certain property—of an overflow into 'stirrings' or felt 'impulsions' there need be not a rudiment—and our further methodical procedure in dealing with, or realizing, such an object may be all that shows that we want it. And such a want will be shaped throughout by the idea we form—not necessarily a fully believing idea, but at least not one involving suspense or rejection or belief—of the circumstances in which the object is set, of the circumstances that might naturally lead up to it, and of the circumstances that might naturally develop out of it and continue it. It will also be steered throughout by a regard for logic in the widest sense, by the insight that X 'analytically'

THE MODES OF WISH AND WILL 181

or less rigorously necessitates Y or is incompatible with Y, or is intrinsically, or by way of experience, favourable or unfavourable to Y. So close is the association of cool wanting with belief, knowledge and logic, or with mental poses having an affinity with these, that what we know, believe or logically seem to grasp naturally is made part of what we coolly want. A man coolly wanting X, wants it with such of the circumstances as seem to him to attend on it, and with such of the consequences as seem to him to flow from it, and he wants the means that seem to lead up to it for the sake of, and in a sense as part of, his end. It was the-freedom-of-Athens-compassed-by-the-death-of-Hippias-carried-out-by-themselves-in-a-given-manner that Harmodius and Aristogeiton coolly chose when they performed their historic tyrannicide, rather than the mere freedom or the mere slaughter. This 'logical' extensibility of the cool want is a property in which the warm want is notoriously lacking: it is characteristic of passion to want to eat its cake and have it, to disassociate itself from the means that it recklessly uses, to see what it wants in attractive aspects and to ignore others analytically equivalent, to be averse from the real consequences that it *knows* its chosen position must entail. It is possible to know of or to believe in certain precise circumstances or consequences of what one warmly wants without in the least wanting or accepting them *together* with what one thus wants: it is characteristic of cool wanting that we tend readily to this sort of extended acceptance, or that, not being ready to do this, we give up wanting what we want in such circumstances. These are truths of great obviousness, misrepresented as merely definitory, and not sufficiently considered by philosophers.

Not only is cool wanting thus sensitive to what we think and know: it may be held also to be sensitive to various attenuations of our wants in warmth, as well as to other present and past directions of cool wanting, and to be ready to effect an accommodation among these and with these. At the level of cool wanting we are, on the one hand, influenced by what may be called the relicts of our various wants in warmth: the seeing of objects in an attractive 'light', which in some manner survives the actual, full-blooded wanting—how this is so, will concern us later—the even more detached 'knowledge' that a thing is wanted, is to be wanted, is satisfactory, is of value or is good—all predications whose analysis will concern us later—and lastly the mere pinning to the thing of

182 VALUES AND INTENTIONS

the *verbal tickets* answering to such notions, which can affect our cool wanting without mediation of anything more urgent. We are also influenced by what may be called the relicts of our own previous wantings in coolness, which give notice of their presence as soon as something new comes up for determination. At the level of cool wanting, however, these correspond more to distinct possible directions of wanting than to distinct wants, since at this level wants lose their separateness, and it is rather the case that we want a single objective A and B and C and D and E, etc., than that we want A, want B, want C, want D, and want E. Singly orientated towards a number of distinct objectives, it is possible for us to defer the satisfaction of one to the other, to look for compromise solutions, in certain circumstances to sacrifice one direction of want to another.

The life of cool planning has accordingly a calculative rather than a balancing aspect: the columns of the accountant rather than the poise of the lever are its best analogon. To consider an obvious instance, a hostess planning for a picnic is motivated by various considerations of cost, beauty of site, social obligations to various individuals, mutual suitability of guests, appetite for various sorts of food, etc. etc., but she does so without activating any distinct wants or aversions. Her whole procedure is singularly dispassionate. She adds, subtracts, divides and multiplies the factors involved according to some applicable though perhaps not readily formulable arithmetic. There is nothing in her activity which suggests Caesar standing rent before the Rubicon, or St Anthony torn in twain by devout religion, on the one hand, and by manifold temptations, on the other. It is of all distinctively human properties the most amazing and most rich in consequence that we can plan meals without being hungry, can buy pictures without being aesthetically stirred, can marry suitably without being ruttish or on heat, and can consult our own good and that of our neighbours while stirred by neither fear nor love. The older philosophers recognized these facts in holding us to be ruled, in our calmer proceedings, by τὸ λογιστικόν or by some such rational principle as self-love. Modern philosophers, above all dreading the reproach of intellectualism or rationalism, have consistently brutalized the picture. Too many modern discussions of determinism operate with models of separate impulses mechanically acting on the person, and severally determining or not

THE MODES OF WISH AND WILL   183

determining the resultant direction of his choices. At the level of cool wanting, no such models can have application.

Cool wanting may be relatively superficial and short-term; it may also be long-term and deep-seated. The determination to find a rhyme to each word uttered by someone is an example of the former type: the determination to tell the truth on all occasions, to be reticent about one's feelings, to be loyal to X are examples of the latter. Such cool long-term orientations are for the most part operative in conscious experience without announcing their presence there, and they may be extended in *as-if* fashion in the preparatory work that sets the conscious scene—they may be thought of as, e.g., determining unconsciously what comes before consciousness and what does *not*: for long periods they may be thought of as purely latent, as being *ready* to sway the course of action and experience if occasion arises. Such long-term, channelling orientations would generally be said to form part of a man's *character* or characteristic habit of soul: character so interpreted *excludes* a man's primary and his warm-blooded wants, as well as his general proneness towards any of them. While a tendency to be compassionately overcome by suffering, and other similar sentiments, are in some sense part of a man's character, they are, in the present sense, no part of that character at all, whereas the cool wish or fixed determination to relieve suffering would be reckoned part of it. A man would be said to be of strong character, or simply to be of character, if cool, long-term principles prevailed over short-term wants, of weak character or of no character if the reverse obtained. Character as so used, covers not only a man's cool, long-term, positive directions of wanting, but also his corresponding aversions and preferences. And, owing to the general tendency of cool directions of wanting to achieve harmonious accommodations rather than frustrating conflicts, a man's character tends towards—though it need not of course reach—a relatively settled body of cool preferences, in which an A is regularly elected above a B, and a B above a C, and so on, in which a D is regularly avoided in preference to an E, etc. etc. The tendency of our conscious life towards relatively simple rather than unduly complex universality, since the former is, in an understandable sense, *more* universal than the latter, ensures that there will be limits to the fastidious specification of preference by circumstance, that there will be *broad lines* in the resultant

184 VALUES AND INTENTIONS

picture. And this broadly lined character will, if fully formed, act, as it were, monolithically: it will respond to the varying properties of things actual or thought of, and will do so differentially and preferentially, but in doing so it will rather be carrying out a total, built-in scheme, than giving way to distinct pulls and pressures. Such monolithic directedness will of course stand over against the separate skirmishing strength of distinct primary and emotional wants, to which it may at times yield, and by which it must be constantly influenced.

If our cool wanting tends, on the one hand to the wide generality of a fixed plan of preferences, it will tend also to the same sort of individualizing completeness that we found in the realm of idea and belief: the same basic properties of conscious experience are responsible in both cases. To want an A is to want an A completely fulfilled and realized, and this means an A fitted out with a complete set of determining properties, and directly presented as well as merely thought of, without gaps or conflicts in its constitution, and with a sufficiency of links giving it an incontestable place in the fabric of a continuous 'world'. To want an A must therefore tend to move from the mere vague wish for something that is A, that might remain at the level of thought and fantasy, to the wish for an A that shall be real and believable, and endowed with all the connections with compulsive experience that we have seen to be essential to knowledge and belief. And from the mere wish that the sort of thing wanted should be incorporated in *some* sort of completing 'real' order, which might occur merely in 'bracketed' fashion, as where we wish that something too admirable to survive had a world worthy of it, we must tend to pass to the wish that something should be carried out in *this* actual order, that is responsible for the compulsive experiences that we have had and are now having. And to the extent that our *actions* have relevance to realizing anything coolly wanted, we must necessarily tend to wish to have these carried out, and in the relevant situation actually to perform them. It may be said therefore to enter into the nature of cool wanting to press towards reality and towards practice; an emotional want, relatively insensitive to the claims of logic and belief, may remain happily on the plain of fantasy, but a cool, considered want can remain there only under the harsh duress of cirumstance. It is, of course, plain that the whole life of endeavour has its first actual expression in overt action in a

THE MODES OF WISH AND WILL 185

compelling environment, and that the possibility of expressing wants through fantasy is a relatively secondary development. This does not make it less important to stress that such a secondary development must by its nature tend back to its origins, that wanting is always implicitly realistic and practical, and that in cool wanting this character will be most manifest.

And the particular form assumed by cool wanting in pressing towards reality must further plainly consist in a 'carrying to the limit' of the systematic extendedness we noted above. Cool wanting must, as we saw, tend to cover in its acceptance the known conditions and the known consequences of what it strives for, or permit of its own supersession. What must now be added is that it must tend to cover in its acceptance all the *known or unknown* conditions, means and consequences of what it strives for, or else give up its endeavour. We see here the genesis of the property of voluntary *consent* which we previously assimilated to the *assent* of belief. When we assert something believingly, we are, as we saw, 'expectant' that future compulsions will continue to fit in with it, and will support it indefinitely, however far they may be prolonged, and the more fully the more they are prolonged. In the same way, in the phenomenon of consent, we include in our cool determination all the consequences and conditions and circumstances of what we determine: we accept them all *with* it. This is plainly what is felt to occur in acts of responsible choice: a man cannot know all that his choice entails, cannot even make plausible surmises regarding it, but in a sense he commits himself to *all* of it, like a man signing a document he has only partially read. The same phenomenon occurs less pointedly in cases of considered approval: in approving, in considered fashion, of X, we accept X with all its circumstances and consequences, and not merely in abstract detachment. Such acceptances may be wrong or mistaken—we may wish when we see certain consequences that they had not been made—but we have none the less made them, and it is *because* we have made them in this characteristically 'infinite' fashion that it has been possible for us to be wrong. This being wrong is, of course, not the same as our having been negligent or wicked, for this depends only on such definite implications of what we chose as seemed certain or likely, or would have seemed so had we given the matter some small attention.

Cool wants carried to the limit will permit of the same conflict

186 VALUES AND INTENTIONS

with similar wants that we have seen to be possible in the case of partial beliefs. There is not, at the cool level, a clash between crudely separate wants, but there still may be a clash between total policies, each carried to the limit, and to each of which, since there is such a clash, we may be said to be *partially minded*. We have here a situation parallel to that out of which the probability calculus takes its rise: were it more often the case that we hovered undecided among a number of alternatives, to each of which we were indiscernibly minded—as suitors have been among a number of equally lovely sisters—we might have an interest in talking of various cases of fractional-mindedness (half-mindedness, third-mindedness, three-quarter-mindedness, etc. etc.) whose manipulation might then describe or direct our further choices. Pleasantry apart, the analogy brings out the valuable notion of *whole-mindedness*, the state in which, while there may be many detached, dissident wants in the conscious person, there is yet only one cool policy adopted to the limit, all that it entails, whether known or unknown, having been accepted with it, and all that it excludes rejected. Such whole-mindedness is, in a sense, the complete *seriousness* of the cool style of wanting. As a serious emotional or primary want is not a derivative offshoot from some other direction of wanting, so a whole-minded cool determination tolerates no framework of encompassing policies that can deprive it of its complete grip on action and its consequent drift towards reality. It has often been held that we only seriously wish what we are prepared to act upon, a proposition acceptable if by acting upon one means acting upon with one's whole mind. All this involves nothing new and mysterious: it is a natural culmination of the tendencies present in cool wanting as such, and in the clear consciousness of fact and logic (in the widest sense) by which it is influenced.

The whole-minded state just considered may be *representative* of a man's whole character and personality, as an emotional or primary want seldom will be. Being an orientation open to the influence of fact and logic, and being open also, as we saw, to the influence of the quasi-cognitive residua, the 'reasons' left behind them by our various warm-blooded and cool-blooded determinations, it can assume a form that in some sense does justice to them all. That it will do so is ensured by the much emphasized process of deliberation, which some would see as an

THE MODES OF WISH AND WILL 187

essential prelude to whole-minded choice. In such deliberation relevant facts are discovered or rediscovered, consequences and probable consequences are explored, situations are envisaged with the greatest imaginative and sympathetic *approfondissement*, the distinct wants underlying our various cool policies are 'unfrozen' and allowed to resume separate existence, new wants are encouraged to show themselves and to upset old balances, principles are dragged out of their lairs and formulated afresh, and authorities, living or dead, are consulted. That such a possibility of *representative* self-determination exists, and that it is all-important for our practical life, goes without saying. What it must *not* be allowed to obscure is the relatively *loose* connection of whole-minded, realistic, practical self-commitments of the sort sketched above to the elaborate surveys and flesh-and-blood stagings involved in the deliberative process. It is as possible for a whole-minded, cool, practical orientation to *suspend* such proceedings as to encourage them, to *turn its back* on their outcome as to follow this meekly, to align itself with the most casual momentary impulse or stray suggestion as with the most weighty body of reasoned considerations, to act queerly and out of character as to act normally and in character. The detachment of our cool practical life from the pulls and pressures of primary wanting, and its ready response to such mere ghosts of the latter as are enshrined in our thoughts or our words, may make possible the reasoned taking account of *all* we know and want, but it will also make possible the comprehensive, unreasoned *dis*regard for this all: it will prepare the way, in short, for caprice, recklessness and perversity. That caprice, recklessness and perversity exist cannot be doubted: that they may be whole-minded in the sense set forth above, cannot be doubted either. We may align ourselves with a particular suggestion or impulse, perhaps entirely casual, in the full awareness that such alignment *has* weighty consequences, and perhaps in the clear awareness of *what* these are, and we may also *damn* all such consequences. 'Come weal or woe', we may accept our chosen objective with all it may entail. And having adopted a perverse position coolly, we may call into play the deep persistence of lines of action coolly adopted, as well as other secondary tendencies averse to inconstancy in action: deep-graven attitudes may be formed that will stand up to much rational and emotional pressure. In the end a perverse position casually adopted may

188 VALUES AND INTENTIONS

become part of one's settled character, and may require as much perversity to be evaded as it once required to establish.

All this need involve no concession to a libertarian picture of action. The perverse alignment, thought unrepresentative, may be as readily accounted for as a normal alignment: it may arise out of random associations, casual suggestions, immediate presentations, relatively slight impulses acting on an idle and unserious mind, etc. etc. Such an origin *may* coincide with an absence of whole-mindedness—as where we plead inadvertency or haste, that we acted on impulse without realizing what we were doing, that we were 'carried away' by a burst of emotion, etc. etc.—but often our alignment, though perverse, is felt to involve the fullest commitment to what consequences and implications there might be, and is therefore on our definition whole-minded. Older generations of moralists recognized the danger of levity, as a state well on the way towards perversity and corruption: we to whom 'earnestness' has become wholly absurd, are not less exposed to such danger. The mere fact that we repent of an act afterwards, that we find it unworthy and uncharacteristic, does not mean that it was not whole-mindedly done at the time: repentance, as opposed to regret, entails that our previous attitude *was* whole-minded.

All this does not mean that it is always a perfectly clear question whether we acted whole-mindedly or not: some people possibly *never* achieve such a state. It is not at all easy to say, when considering abbreviated, condensed, harried states of mind, whether we seriously accepted X with all it might entail, or were 'carried away', 'pushed along' or were merely impulsive. Sometimes acts that seemed to involve full commitment at the time are judged afterwards to have been done under some special 'spell' or influence, or to have involved 'diminished responsibility', etc. etc. Nor are inner, reflective criteria the only signs of whole-mindedness. The whole-minded alignment with a certain direction of action tends to show itself in a state of certainty as to what we shall do, and this is perhaps its most *signal* manifestation, but it shows itself also in resolute *persistence* in the line in question, and the mere fact that we *say* we are utterly resolved upon X, or even that we feel thus resolved, does not prove conclusively that we are so. Resolve is plainly a fact concerning the likely prolongation of our life of cool wanting, and is never identical with the feelings, acts, speeches, etc., which are indicative of it. There is further no

THE MODES OF WISH AND WILL 189

absolutely clear line between what we have called developments in warmth and developments in coolness: individualized primary wants channelled here and there by profound realizations of fact, need not operate in a wholly different manner from cool orientations steered by drily acknowledged considerations. We cannot say, therefore, exactly when we are being emotionally impelled, and when we are giving our calm, reasoned consent, especially since the two states need not differ in direction. Similar difficulties confront us in the field of belief: it is not always clear whether we *really* believe in someone's integrity, in a future life, etc. etc. The philosophy of mind must, here as elsewhere, frame notions of greater definiteness than are always exemplified, introducing latitude in its applications rather than in its actual conceptions, and so gaining the advantages of conceptual sharpness without sacrificing those of truth to experience.

Whole-minded alignment may assume the varied forms of the whole-minded *wish*, the whole-minded *approval* or *satisfaction*, the whole-minded practical *decision* and the whole-minded *action*. Though all whole-mindedness is essentially realistic and practical, it may be kept far from practice by untoward circumstance, or by our own total powerlessness in certain matters: in such cases it will express itself in a whole-minded wish or satisfaction. Whole-mindedness in the realm of wish and satisfaction is somewhat elusive, since it lacks urgency: we seldom trouble to commit ourselves completely in imaginary cases, nor is it easy to do so. It is difficult to nurture a full-fledged preparedness to realize X with all it involves, in situations where no such preparedness is called for, and what we feel or think we are prepared to act on or for in hypothetical circumstances, often differs from what we do act on or for when put to the test. Less intrinsically difficult is the preparatory resolve, the whole-minded commitment to realizing something through our acts which it seems will become possible in the near future. Preparatory resolves, though taken on the plane of fantasy, are often as serious in effect, and as productive of long-term channelling tendencies, as decisions manifest from the start in action. It is important to stress, lastly, that to engage whole-mindedly in action need not argue *prior* wishes, approvals or decisions: we may show our whole-mindedness immediately by the flow of our acts in a given direction, and by their long continuance in this, accompanied perhaps by the satisfied consciousness of

190   VALUES AND INTENTIONS

'nothing else being possible'. All states of whole-minded self-direction may be said, further, to involve *choice* or *preference*, inasmuch as the whole-minded commitment to anything involves accepting, among other implications of what is thus primarily accepted, the lack or sacrifice of countless things that are factually or logically incompatible with it. In fully deliberated approvals or decisions, the alternatives to X are fully presented and renounced: in reckless or blind decisions they are likewise renounced, without being fully presented. It is only a primary or an emotional want that can be without a hint of choice.

States of whole-minded self-direction may further obviously be negative as well as positive: we may withhold consent from, refuse to commit ourselves, refrain from endorsing some suggested policy, without opting for some other positive commitment, though such refusals or abstinences reveal themselves, by a change of perspective, much appealed to by moralists, as a higher-order mode of self-commitment, much as to accept something as probable, and to confide in it only in balance with other alternatives, becomes a higher-order manner of believing. They tend also, by an inherent logic, to pass over into embracing the corresponding negative policy, as accomplished unbelief swings over into the belief in what is contrary. We have here, however, room for a *refusal* to pass over towards the corresponding negation, which refusal, owing to its doubly negative aspect, readily turns into something wholly positive: we have the little studied mental pose of *permission*. It is not only possible to endorse a policy to the limit, or, negatively, to reject it in the sense of endorsing its *non*-realization, it is also possible to refuse to disallow the policy, or in other words to allow it. Such allowance may express itself in the same optative language as a positive wish or decision. 'Let X be done' may express positive self-commitment to realizing X, but it may also express non-commitment to avoiding or preventing this. Permission is of course normally given to other persons: it is *their* lines of action we refuse to hinder. It may, however, be extended to things— 'Let Rome in Tiber melt and the wide arch of the rang'd empire fall!'—and also to ourselves. Nothing is more frequent than to give permissive rein to one's own primary and emotional wants, which one none the less, in no positive fashion, cares to underwrite. Much of the ordinary morality—if not the morality of philosophers —is permissive rather than prescriptive, and the ends of life

THE MODES OF WISH AND WILL 191

certainly include much that we *may* choose or *may* avoid, as well as much that we really *should* choose or really *should* steer clear of.

What emerges from our whole examination of cool wanting is largely an endorsement of a traditional dualism, the dualism of the λογιστικόν and the ἄλογον, of the head and the heart, of Butler's various magisterial architectonic principles (self-love, benevolence, conscience) and his rabble of 'particular passions', of the Pauline 'law of the members warring against the spirit'. That models which transform the striving and desiring person into a parliament of distinct, warring principles, may be very misleading, goes without saying: to reject them, however, may go with an ignoring of profound gulfs among the forms of the spirit. A result, however, of the profound dualism we have been studying, is what might be called a certain natural dialectic which pushes us on from acknowledging the (in the ordinary sense) 'free' character of our cooler determinations—their freedom, i.e. from the duress of circumstance or of primary or emotional wants— to a much more radical sense of freedom, which tends to remove the last shade of external determination from our cool resolves. This dialectic must be briefly studied, since, whatever its validity or even significance if pushed to the limit, it certainly has its roots in important facts about our cooler, reasoned choices, and can be used to make these apparent.

(II) THE FREEDOM OF THE WILL

The notion of freedom, in the sense in which it interests the philosophy of mind, is essentially a *developing* notion. While, at the start, it covers a relatively clear-cut range of features of choice and action, which enable us to apply it unhesitatingly and without a trace of conflict, and while we can, by a deliberate policy or 'ordinariness', stay fixed indefinitely in such a blinkered state, it involves also a spreading penumbra of implications to which our thought cannot altogether help passing over, the force of which is to push the notion steadily in a given direction, in part to empty it of its content, and in part to bring it into conflict with itself and with other fundamental notions. The notion of freedom, like the kindred notions of the voluntary and the responsible, has, even in its first employment, a pointed use, which is more

192 VALUES AND INTENTIONS

than merely negative. To do something freely, is, in this use, not merely to do it without compulsion, not merely in doing it to do as one wants, not merely in doing it *not* to do what one does *not* want to do. To sit in my chair, to offer my cheek to my daughter's goodnight kiss, to turn the pages of magazines in a dentist's waiting-room, is certainly not to do anything I do not want, it is even in a sense positively to do what I want: it would, however, make little or no sense to say that I was sitting in my chair, offering my cheek or turning the pages *freely*, just as it would not make sense to say that I was doing these things *voluntarily*, or even that I was fully *responsible* for such actions. As Professor Austin has admirably shown, the involuntary is not the contradictory of the voluntary—since there are numbers of acts which are neither—and it is not even its true opposite, and the same holds regarding the compulsory and the free.

The qualification 'free' or 'freely', when applied pointedly, and not merely in a particular context of contrast, implies not merely that a line of action proceeds without hindrance or obstruction, but that it enjoys a peculiar *disengagement* from biasing influence, and a peculiar *openness* to alternatives. A line of action that is free in this special sense is one that, as it were, trembles on the verge of alternative developments, without anything obvious or palpable to channel or guide it. Its freedom is thought of like that of a mathematical variable, which can 'range' over a number of values without being 'bound down' to any one of them. Such openness to alternatives, if pushed to a philosophical limit, may be a notion difficult of illustration: there is, none the less, in its less extreme and perfectly worked out forms, nothing easier to illustrate. The whirling indicator on a roulette wheel, seen as it phenomenally gives itself out and not in some imposed, deterministic perspective, perfectly *fulfils* the notion of the openness in question, even if we should ultimately fail to fit the notion or its illustration into some unbracketed world-description. The openness in question is one that is thought of, further, as capable of developing without mystery into something determinate and definite. It is, we think, until philosophers have taught us otherwise, by no means mysterious that a precarious poise among several alternatives should come down on the side of one of them, that what is 'open' should become 'closed'. It would not really have been 'open' if it could not thus become closed. And though the 'open' becomes 'closed',

THE MODES OF WISH AND WILL 193

it remains 'open' in retrospect. It is still true that an activity *could* have been developed differently, even though it has now taken one actual course. The characteristic impediment to this sort of freedom is not therefore anything which blocks one line of activity: it is something that restricts or removes the broad openness of certain types of activity, that makes it impossible for them to develop in as many ways as previously, or perhaps only in one way.

It is important to stress that freedom, in the pointed sense indicated, need involve no limiting reference to the *conditions* or *circumstances* in which various alternatives might be realized. That there is an openness to alternatives in our special sense does not mean, for instance, that one will do A if one set of (unspecified) circumstances obtains, B if some other set obtains, C if a third set obtains, etc. etc. Much less does it imply that one only *could* have taken a course other than one did take, had the circumstances been appropriately different. The mere fact that it is physically *possible* for us to carry out several alternative performances—walk a mile in twenty minutes, in thirty, etc. etc., to modify one of Moore's famous examples—will not ensure that we carry out such a performance *freely*, in the special sense indicated. Even the fact that it is *psychologically* possible, in the right circumstances, for us to carry out several alternative performances, e.g. to break up a bar if intoxicated, or to see it as an expression of the Absolute if drugged with mescalin, etc. etc., will not entail that we do any of these things *freely*. One can indeed always say of a man free in the sense of being open to alternatives, that he can do A *if he chooses* to do A, B if he chooses to do B, etc. etc. Here, however, the 'power of alternatives' mentioned is *either* a mere case of the physically possible —in which case it is quite irrelevant—or the reference to 'choice' is wholly empty and redundant, since the 'doing' involved is no mere physical performance, but the carrying out of an act in a whole-minded, 'intentional' manner, and this sort of doing is not separate from choice, it is, in fact, choice realized and put into effect. The openness to alternatives in question is thus not merely something present *if* we choose: it is something built into and intrinsic to choice itself. There are, indeed, situations where we say that no choice but one remains open to us, but the closure involved here is *moral* rather than absolute: to choose anything

G

194 VALUES AND INTENTIONS

different would have been wildly unreasonable, madly perverse, etc. etc.

Of course it may be argued that one's notions of choice and freedom should be so developed as to include an essential reference to conditions, to have specific or unspecific provisos, whether factual, counterfactual or merely indeterminate, built into their content, that we should make no reference to what seems open to us, without making it subject to appropriate conditions, much as old-fashioned piety made no practical proposals without deferring in parenthesis to the will of God. Such a development of the notion of freedom is in fact attempted in the thought-contexts called 'deterministic'. What it is important to stress is not that such developments may not ultimately be forced on us, but that they are not present from the start. The notion of freedom as applied to our various acts of cool choice implies no thesis of obedience to the most weighty reason or to the most potent psychic pressure: it is in fact slightly weighted *against* their entry. As Professor Austin has shown, with amazing profundity and care, the 'sense' even of our most ordinary speech is more in harmony with the notion of powers liable to express themselves *differently*, and notably in the twin forms of doing or not doing something, without there needing to be something which *makes* them take one or the other. I may say, e.g., that I could have ruined you this morning (which I did not), and this may be a complete statement requiring no conditional supplement, e.g. if only I had had one more vote, and certainly *not* coincident in sense with a statement to the effect that I *would* have ruined you this morning, had certain conditions, specified or unspecified, obtained. He even goes farther in suggesting that 'determinism, whatever it may be, may yet be the case, but at least it appears *not consistent* [our italics] with what we ordinarily say and presumably think'.[1]

The notion of freedom as involving this conditionless—rather than *un*conditioned—openness applies best to our life of cool, voluntary determinations, and rests on a large number of its features. It rests, first of all, on a basic characteristic of that life, to be as it were *mediatorial*, to occupy, as it were, a position neutral and unbiased among particular wants, reasons, etc., to *side with them* or to *lend itself to them*, rather than to be intrinsically

[1] 'Ifs and Cans', *Proceedings of the British Academy*, Vol. XLIII, p. 131.

THE MODES OF WISH AND WILL

directed to an object, as is the case with a primary want. This characteristic remains a rudiment where there is a straight plunge into action, where the dismissal of *B*, *C*, *D*, etc., becomes as it were telescoped into one act with the embrace of *A*. It emerges clearly, however, where action follows upon decision, and decision u᷈ ᷈n long-drawn deliberation, for a man deciding is a man as yet undecided, and to that extent indeterminate, open to various possibilities. In such circumstances a man readily feels himself as something void of content, an essence freely floating, an obscure *source* of action rather than a clear cause of it, as was so regularly reported in the classical experiments on willing. The notion of a pure Ego, distinct from its definite poses, is no figment dreamt up by epistemologists: it is a natural attenuation of a man's preciser view of himself, inevitably begotten in the attrition of practice.

The pointed idea of freedom is applied, further, to the life of cool resolve, on account of the complex, largely concealed character of its aetiology, the sheer diversity of the factors out of which it grows. The simple picture of our cool resolves as automatic resultants of a number of wants pulling in different directions is wrong on many counts. Crude pulls of the sort intended only operate in transformed fashion at the level of cool resolve, they can at best give vitality and vividness to *reasons*, which do not move except as parts of a total field of reasons, both for and against, among which our resolve must be cast. There are, further, countless other determining factors besides crude pulls of this sort: the angles from which situations are viewed, the beliefs regarding their context and consequences, the imaginative force and detail with which their content is 'realized', the holding of things as more or less desirable or preferable, whether in normative or personal perspective—what such factors are will concern us later—the arousal of emotions and feelings which add depth to some ground of action, the long past resolves which now channel action invisibly, the humble pressure of association and rote-learning, the stimulus of what is now present to sense, the mere words which, unbacked by the smallest conscious dwelling on their import, can direct action in momentous fashion. All these factors, and many others, together with the structural arrangements, if any, which make us ready for one or the other, are among the items significant in the state out of which some

196 VALUES AND INTENTIONS

cool determination develops, and by means of which it can be understood. In an aetiology so diverse and complex, a large number of factors are wholly unmanifest, some disengage themselves only by reflection, while others, though often decisive, have nothing obviously dynamic about them. It is not therefore remarkable that we have the impression of our cool resolves as states largely cut loose from causes, and responsive more to their own intentionally inexistent household of reasons, to whose muted representations it seems possible for them also to turn a deaf ear.

A third ground for forming and seriously applying the idea of voluntary openness, lies in the many cases of the arbitrary, the gratuitous and the hard in action. It is possible to follow what may be called an order of reasons in our actions, pursuing what we assess drily as being of a more desirable character, whether personally or normatively, or pursuing what seems to offer us *more* of some desirable characteristic or some *more intense form* of it, or pursuing what seems to *lead more readily* to a state involving some desirable characteristic, etc. etc. All these types of reason, and many others, can obviously move us to various cool determinations. But it is plain, too, that our cool determinations need not, and often do not, defer to an established order of reasons, but are at times contemptuous of any, as in the case of the choices and decisions called 'arbitrary', and that they at times even run counter to reasons, as in the case of the choices and decisions called 'wanton' or 'perverse'. It may be held, of course, that where we are not obedient to reasons, we are impelled by factors of some other type: thus an arbitrary choice may be due largely to what we *chance* to see or remember, etc. etc. In the same way a wanton or perverse choice may spring from an urge to shine, to be singular, etc. etc., whose objectives do not masquerade as reasons. But the order of causes and the order of reasons are different, and influence choice and conduct differently. And it would seem that only some source of power not earmarked to either, and hence having no intrinsic direction, could be capable of mediating between them.

The seeming possibility of running counter to what may be called the order of causes would also seem to be illustrated, to the extent that such a thing *can* be illustrated, in the often cited phenomena of difficult decision and difficult execution of decision.

THE MODES OF WISH AND WILL 197

In both of these cases one often has the idea, endowed with all the urgency and authority of one's so-called 'practical knowledge', that the course chosen or persevered in is in some sense *not* the easiest or most natural continuation of the states it grows out of, that it is difficult, not merely in the sense of involving the overcoming of obstacles, but in the further sense of following a line of greater resistance, as involving the putting forth of an unearmarked power or virtue, a putting forth gratuitous in the sense that it might quite well not have happened, and that it would in fact *more readily* not have occurred. To have practical knowledge on such a complex matter might seem wholly mysterious and incredible, but it is merely an elaborate case of the knowledge involved in all cases of feeling, in all of which, as we saw, we are apprised directly of the drift of our mental and physical life in a given direction. And it need not be 'knowledge' in the sense of involving highly approvable belief-claims: it may be knowledge only in the sense of being a case of direct intimation, which to some extent tends to present things as they can be found to be by more trustworthy criteria. In the case in question the so-called practical knowledge may be wholly delusive. There may be ways of showing, by psycho-analysis or similar techniques, that the difficult course chosen is, like many physically difficult courses, the most ready, easy continuation of the situation on hand. The phenomena, however, are what they are, and what they lend support to is the conditionless openness we naïvely presume.

The notion of an absolute openness to alternatives rests, further, on what may be called the predicament of practical knowledge, that it makes no sense to forecast what one will do, before one has made up and practically knows one's own mind. A forecast, however well founded, necessarily contributes to the situation out of which our resolves grow, and may thus either help to make itself true, and be without a validating compulsion, or it may lead, in the fine poise of cool deliberation, to wide divergences which will falsify and frustrate it. The predicament of practical knowledge is deepened, too, by the necessary unpredictability of action passing on its course through the higher forms of personal experience, by the holding of detail together in condensed, dissolved unity, by the complete impossibility of a break-up into elements separately active, in other words, by the complete inapplicability of a mechanical model. When each new consideration enriches a total

198 VALUES AND INTENTIONS

state of mind in which crudely separate items play no part, and nothing acts as it might act in isolation, prediction can obviously have no satisfactory precedents to go upon.

The openness to alternatives suggested by so many facts of our cool, voluntary action, is an openness in which the possibility of a sufficient set of causal conditions is not thought of, rather than one in which such a sufficient set is thought of and *denied*. The atmosphere of the notion is not *favourable* to the transformation of its simple 'cans' into hypothetically conditioned 'woulds' and 'coulds', but this unfavourableness does not amount to a strict prohibition. We can be persuaded to think that we mean by freedom the mere fact that it is possible for us to move along certain courses, *if* certain conditions obtain: we can also be persuaded to assert our original idea more powerfully, by including in it a *denial* that any such set of antecedent conditions need be present in each case. Both developments of our original notion press it beyond the limits of experience, the former by its quite empty assertion of *something somewhere* to be found, and the latter by its quite empty denial that *anything* of this kind exists *anywhere*. Both developments arise in a thought-context involving the notion of causal determinism by the past, when this notion is developed in a philosophical manner.

The notion of causation is simply the notion of the *growing* of later stages of things *out* of earlier ones, a notion senseless if not involving recognizable continuance of pattern. It is, further, a notion so central to the interweaving of things in a common world, without which nothing could be conceived believingly, that all our beliefs suggest or imply it. There is something monstrous, *a priori* unlikely, in the thought of anything *not* born out of proper antecedents in regular fashion, a monstrousness which leads us to look for such antecedents even when no trace of them is apparent, and to accept only with the last reluctance anything that would block or end this search. This notion of causal determination requires, in its first rough form, only that whole phases should grow out of whole phases, not that every distinct feature of them, every distinct light in which they may be regarded, should have its own individual aetiology. But as the movement towards abstraction turns the aspects of things into things of a sort, the monstrousness of seeing something grow out of nothing becomes transferred to each abstract aspect, so that we become deeply

THE MODES OF WISH AND WILL 199

reluctant to think of the least feature of things without a complete causal permit of entry, however impossible, on account of multiplying infinities, it may be for us to fill this in. This reluctance then comes into a frontal clash with our pointed notion of freedom: we begin to feel that, if an *A* emerges out of the mere capacity for being *A or B*, it in a sense arises out of nothing. And with this feeling goes a threat to our whole cognitive security, the emergence of something which, if once admitted, may make it impossible to believe or affirm anything whatsoever. And this threat must be exorcised, either by modifying our original ideal of freedom so as to accord with our notion of exhaustive causal explanation, or by modifying our notion of causal explanation so as to accord with our notion of freedom. It may be held, as we saw, that we are free to act alternatively, though each alternative has its separate, sufficient causal explanation, or it may be held defiantly, that the mere fact that we *can* act in several alternative ways, sufficiently explains why we act in any one of them.

The notional developments leading to this old, interesting clash may be dismissed as belonging to the pathology of thought and diction. Obviously both developments press beyond the bounds of possible experience, since not only is the notion of a *complete* causal explanation incapable of empirical illustration, but even the simpler notion of a causal connection is in similar case. The notion of causation is in the singular position that, not only can it never be conclusively *known* to obtain in a given instance—since what appears causal may always prove casual—but that it cannot even be convincingly illustrated or imaginatively fulfilled. If we consider only the *use* and application of our notions, we can convincingly illustrate neither the causal nor the casual nor the free, since the very idea of each involves the open infinity which their verification plainly demands. The temptation is therefore to pare down the content of these conceptions to match their use, and to treat the infinity they imply as a mere play of reflections on the linguistic fly-bottle, an illusion from which we must be set free by a thorough course of linguistic 'therapy'. We shall, however, refuse to see these philosophical developments of our notions as mere products of illusion or misunderstanding. For a notion is nothing without the implications it carries with it, and the things demanded, though not always formally entailed, by its wholly satisfied application. And the way a notion develops when *deeply*

200 VALUES AND INTENTIONS

considered, is as much a feature of it as any detailed subtlety in its use. The fly-bottle, in short, is not anything that either can or should be escaped, and the reflections on it, with all their queer difficulty and meeting of extremes, are the inevitable 'appearances of the horizon', into which our ordinary speech and thought runs out and terminates. What we must do is to recognize the peculiar character and role of these appearances, and their complete difference from all 'notions of the middle distance'. A notion by which science is nourished is not necessarily a scientific notion, and a notion which nourishes practice need not necessarily be at all practical.

It is not fortunately our duty in this book, which is concerned primarily with practice and its ends, to plumb these difficulties to the bottom. Here we may only plead, as affording a better support for our treatment, for the approach which modifies our notion of causal determination to fit in with our notion of freedom, rather than for the approach which modifies our notion of freedom to fit in with our notion of causal determination. For the notion of freedom *can* be seen in such a perspective that the mere fact that something is thought of as capable of developing in alternative ways, is seen as *explaining* the fact that it does develop in one of them, rather than as leaving this unexplained. Freedom, if seen in this perspective, will not violate causality, but will be a species of it: it is the sort of causality, not felt as mysterious in ordinary contexts, which fixes its precise direction as it goes along. To see things in this manner accords best with the phenomenology of choice, and it accords best also with the nature of those higher experiences of deliberation and decision, with their 'nutshell' containment of detail, and the impossibility of breaking them up into distinct items separately active. Where mechanism and atomism obtain, as they do on the fringes of the mind's life, determinism can be significant and inspiring: where 'all things are together', it remains an inapplicable ideal. Nor has the freedom in question anything to do with chance, which is the random inter-weaving of distinct lines of causation.

To see things in the open way mentioned accords better, also, as we shall see, with the phenomena of moral approval and dis-approval, and with those of moral exhortation and suasion. All these can be squared with determinism, but the squaring remains disingenuous and intellectually uncomfortable. And we may note

THE MODES OF WISH AND WILL

further, in continuance of previous statements, that the notion of a range of openness continually closed by action and decision accords better with our ideas of time than does an image of sempiternal closure. For not only is it practically absurd that we should predict our own choices before we make them, such precise prediction seems even theoretically absurd, since it violates our sense of a profoundly different logic governing our talk about future and past, of the absence of logical equivalences in the one case which obtain necessarily in the other. This recognition of a differing logic runs through the long literature stemming from Aristotle's famous sea-fight, which, like the similar line stemming from Zeno's race-course, reveals by sheer persistance the presence of difficulties past trivial verbal cure. In the case of the past we can straightforwardly equate statements to the effect that someone was either in London or Paris yesterday with the verbally different statement that it either was the case that he was in London yesterday or that he was in Paris yesterday. In the case of the future, no such plain equivalence seems to hold. The statement that someone will be either in London or Paris tomorrow need not amount to the statement that either he will be in London tomorrow or he will be in Paris tomorrow, since the matter may be as yet 'undecided': one may make the former statement without making the latter. To affirm the futurity of a disjunction is not to affirm a disjunction among futurities. All this need involve no rejection of the Law of Excluded Middle, as it is sometimes held to do. 'X will not be in Paris tomorrow' need no more be taken to be the strict logical contradictory of 'X will be in Paris tomorrow', than 'X is said not to be in Paris now' is the strict logical contradictory of 'X is said to be in Paris now'. When the future has not been 'decided upon', I can only say that I shall be in Paris tomorrow or that it is not the case that I shall be there. But this second alternative does not entail that I shall not be in Paris tomorrow until the matter has been 'decided'. That it is not the case that I shall be in Paris tomorrow can, in fact, be understood as covering the two distinct possibilities (a) that I shall not be in Paris tomorrow, (b) that the matter is not yet decided. We shall leave on one side, as involving an undesirable and confusing convention, the manner of speech according to which what is not 'decided upon' now, becomes decided in retrospect, so that while it cannot now be said that I shall be in Paris tomorrow, since the matter is undecided, it becomes right to say

G*

202 VALUES AND INTENTIONS

the day after, when I *am* in Paris, that I was about to be in Paris the previous day. Such a usage injects the necessary determinism of the present into a future which is past, thereby creating many gratuitous problems.[1]

We seem prepared, then, in the case of the future, to deny at times that something will be so, without necessarily affirming that it will not be so, and this without more than a surface show of contradiction. We are not prepared to follow a parallel logic in our statements about the past. And this difference in logic ties in, not merely with various deep practical differences and difficulties, but with the theoretical absurdity of imagining that things should carry in themselves precise indications of their future, in the same way in which they often carry within themselves precise traces of their past. It is characteristic of the things in our world that they have in their structure nicks, dents, stains, etc., indicative of their former encounters: it is also characteristic of them that they have in their structure no such nicks, dents, stains, etc., indicative of their *future* encounters. What may be argued here is not that this obtains, but that it could not very well have been different: to anticipate, we perceive, goes against the grain of time, as to record does not. The queer exceptions to this rule show that it *is* a rule: their queerness and their exceptional character both seem quite necessary. If the future has an essential openness reflected in our talk about it, then we may expect this openness to be particularly manifest in the case of our cooler voluntary determinations. For these certainly condense in themselves, and hang poised among, indefinitely many influences, and are also able to respond largely to light pressures, all of which makes such openness more credible in their case than it would be in many others.

(III) THE FIRMAMENT OF VALUES AND DISVALUES

So far we have dealt with a development of the life of practice characterized by its mediatorial coolness and detachment, its capacity to ride loose from particular channelling and directive influences, and in the last resort, seemingly, from all influences whatever; we have also dealt with an aspect essentially individualizing and detailed, one that determines on a unique,

[1] See A. N. Prior, *Time and Modality*, for a precise symbolic statement.

THE MODES OF WISH AND WILL 203

concrete line of action in a situation likewise unique and concrete, and determines on it *together* with all its consequential and contextual entanglements, whether known or unknown. We have now to study the complement of this individualizing aspect of practice, in the shape of an aspect which, by smoothing, polishing and fitting together the goals set before us by our primary wants, constructs what may be called a personal firmament of values and disvalues, which latter, together with the fixed points of fact and probability presented by our beliefs, provides that total firmament of 'reasons' by which our cool choice may be guided, if it is willing to be guided by reasons at all. The cool life of the will is not, as we saw, pushed hither and thither by primary or warm-blooded urges: these can at best move by being remote conditions for the adoption of various fixed ends and counter-ends of endeavour, to which their presence lends additional animating and persuasive force. We have now to inquire into the agencies and forces leading to the rounding out of this 'firmament of reasons', especially as regards its axiological segments. We may hope that, along this line of inquiry, we shall find the origins of the narrower segment of *approvable* ends of action and endeavour, of things *rightly* to be pursued or avoided, or to be done or left undone, of the reasons, in short, that are *good* or *proper* reasons for conduct, or that *justify* effort in particular directions. Despite the high barriers naturally dividing the actual from the approvable, and their increased and justified heightening by philosophers, we may yet hold that there are ways round these oppositions at the 'limit', and that the same development which leads to the setting up of a system of reasons, leads ultimately to the setting up of reasons that may be styled 'approvable' and 'right'. This development will prove in a deep sense 'naturalistic', inasmuch as it depends on tendencies demonstrably inherent in and constitutive of conscious mind, but it will not be 'naturalistic' in depending on particular details of our contingent make-up, nor will it involve reducing the specific concepts and forms of discourse arising along this route, into others not belonging to this particular course of development.

There are many illuminating points of contrast between the development previously studied, that of the cool, whole-minded, voluntary orientation, and the development now to be studied, which may be called that of the rationalized want or valuation.

VALUES AND INTENTIONS

The previous development was towards disengagement, non-commitment, mediatorial poise among the objectives of distinct wants. The voluntary orientation 'sides' with one such want or another, precisely because it is intrinsically committed to none of them: its supreme manifestation is the *arbitrary*, the firm closure of an unsettled, open position on the slightest of impulsions. The rationalized want, on the other hand, has the same intrinsic directedness, the same *non-arbitrariness* in the fixing of its precise objective, as has the primary want: it is, as its chosen name indicates, a refined, or rationalized, want. What we coolly choose to do or pursue may vary immeasurably from moment to moment according as one or other slight reason moves us, or influence stirs us; not so what we definitely set store by or value, and regard as a reason for acting in a given manner. This store that we set on things, this rationalized desire directed upon them, is not anything we can acquire or lose except by a fairly slow process of training or untraining, and it persists even when undischarged in action. Our 'values' are the relatively fixed points of the compass by means of which our choices are guided: it makes no sense to speak of arbitrarily choosing them.

The same sort of deep contrast obtains between the development towards the individual and concrete, characteristic of our cool practical determinations, and the development towards the abstract and generic characteristic of our rationalized desires or valuations. In determining what we shall do, we progress gradually from highly general proposals to proposals incorporating more and more exactly the precise setting and consequences of what is at first proposed: in the end we accept this, if we do accept it, with all it may involve, even though much of this detail may be obscure or unknown. The practical decision operating at some distance in time, has the same *penchant* towards the concrete, and so has the whole-hearted supporting wish, unpractically operative on the side-lines. In making definite what we demand or value, the whole movement of mind runs in a contrary direction: we pass from the concrete goals and courses of action that recommend themselves to us, to the features that *make* them desirable, and which perhaps have never been considered separately, we cut such features off as far as possible from all that is extraneous, contextual or merely instrumental, we come by an attrition of cases to conceive of them more and more in pure

THE MODES OF WISH AND WILL 205

and abstract form, with all specifying and individualizing features stripped away, until in the end we have before us an extremely general set of 'motives' for acting: preservation of social position, success in business, avoidance of injustice or misrepresentation, the enjoyment of a good table, the greater flourishing of bull-fighting, etc. etc. The process by which these values come to be established in a general 'firmament' may be slow and unconscious, but it may be speeded up by semi-Socratic reflection on *why* we want or do not want certain things, or on the *ground* of their attraction and repulsion, etc. etc.

Being thus generic in spirit, our valuations necessarily have a more indirect and variable relation to practice than have our individualized voluntary determinations. These last, as we saw, cannot claim to be fully serious unless issuing in action in appropriate circumstances, and they involve an unbounded commitment to *all* circumstances and consequences that some project may involve. But valuations and rationalized desires, though turned towards practice, necessarily approach it in qualified fashion: we are *for* the realization of whatever is X, but only *to the extent* that it is X, and in so far as what we are *for* may have other features beside X, some of which we are much against, we are only *for* this case of X *prima facie*, and we may cease to be for it when our view of the matter develops. Not only such normative values as justice, but such purely personal values as a good marriage or business success have for us a purely *prima facie* status: our sincere fixation on them, and our due placing of them in our firmament, does not mean that we shall always be guided by them in practice.

Being thus at several stages removed from practice, our value-orientations will seldom rise to the whole-mindedness characteristic of our voluntary decisions. They will permit other conflicting orientations beside them, which they neither subordinate themselves to, nor subordinate to themselves. This is what is often expressed by employing the model of a society of persons: each of us, as we put it, has a number of 'selves', and as one or the other of them, we have quite different wishes or values. As *hommes moyens sensuels* we like X and prefer it to Y, but as art lovers we have the contrary preference: as religious persons we perhaps see both as mildly undesirable, and as members of a certain exclusive group we perhaps prefer the otherwise trivial Z

VALUES AND INTENTIONS

to either, etc. etc. Such a model no doubt leads to abuse, especially when the 'selves' are too neatly distinguished or too precisely numbered: it expresses, however, important facts about our 'values' which might else be forgotten. And it is important to stress that our 'moral selves', i.e. our selves *qua* wishing in a certain style of disinterested comprehensiveness, are only *one* among the consolidated wish-systems that affix stars to our value-firmament. And it is true of them, as of other similar 'selves', that they need not lose their characteristic integrity, merely because they become subordinated to other systems, or to chance arbitrariness, and are not carried out into action at all. There is doubtless a sense in which we lack sincerity in accepting a scale of values, if not prepared to act on it: if to be sincere is to be whole-minded, then we only accept values sincerely when we act on them in all relevant circumstances. A system of valuations may, however, have sincerity, as preserving its own characteristic standards and coherence, and not brooking alien intrusions and distortions.

Valuations, though no more than wishes, are certainly the most serious of human activities: the reputation of 'idleness' attached to all wishes by a too precipitate moral strenuousness, is in their case grossly undeserved. It is from many points of view more important that we should frame the correct aspirations, than that we should carry them out invariably, or conform to them precisely. The corruption of fundamentally 'wrong values' is arguably a worse corruption than an occasional, or even habitual, nonconformity to correct values duly acknowledged. Aspirations may no doubt be as frivolous as are many capricious acts: they are, however, also capable of a more thoroughgoing obedience to rational norms than can ever be achieved in action. The reason for this is plain: action, owing to human impotence, is but a fragmentary patchwork which must infinitely fall short of what can be approvably desired. It derives its whole significance from the system of aspirations surrounding it, of which it at best proves the seriousness. Wishes and valuations, on the other hand, form the total framework of which acts are merely the executed portion: they extend over the whole territory of the thinkable and the unthinkable, being as much of the imaginary as of the real, of the hypothetically entertained as of the concretely given, of the merely thought of as of the fully envisaged, of the quite

THE MODES OF WISH AND WILL 207

impracticable as of the readily practicable, of ultimate ends as of immediate means, of the non-voluntary as much as of the voluntary, of the remote as much as the near, and they certainly range over the whole of past and future time as they do over the present. If conformity to rational norms means matching their universality with a universality as open, then it is on the plane of aspiration and wish that such conformity becomes fully possible.

The contrast between the individualized voluntary, and the generic value-attitude is apparent also as regards the antithesis between the 'warm' and the 'cool'. If a voluntary, practical orientation has emotional warmth only adventitiously, as a sort of idle reinforcement of its own fact- and value-sensitive policy, a value-orientation, by contrast, shuttles back and forth between passion and dispassion, using the former to give force and firmness to the latter. It is constantly the case that we re-establish the hold of some valuation upon us by deliberately expanding it into an emotional overflow, a process aided by the concurrent activity of imaginative fulfilment. If listening to music is what I most highly set store by, and causing pain what I most ardently shun, I requicken my cherishing or repudiating attitude towards such objects, both by envisaging instances of them vividly, and by reviving the emotions and feelings which I normally discharge upon them. We may say, in fact, that just as we only fully know the content of our thoughts by fulfilling them imaginatively, so we only fully know what we value by fulfilling such valuations in emotion and feeling. Quite obviously, it is in the emotions called forth by, or discharged upon, anything that we are most fully conscious of its desirability or worthwhileness (or of the contrary).

But if the orientations called 'valuations' tend, in one direction, towards emotional richness, they tend also, in another direction, towards a coolness akin to that of pure cognition. For, as we have seen, our 'feelings' are in one aspect legitimately to be reckoned among cognitive phenomena, states in which the spontaneous drift of our minds in varying directions, not only exists, but is also sensibly illustrated and made plain to us, e.g. in feeling ourselves cross, we see ourselves tending explosively towards a goal of destruction. And, as we saw, such feelings permit of an outward-looking as well as of an inward-turned employment, and instead of seeing *ourselves* as being ready to react angrily

208   VALUES AND INTENTIONS

towards something, we may see *objects* as being irritating, provocative, galling, etc., as being in short appropriate discharge-points for anger. Through this extraspective inversion we rear as it were (to use Hume's phrase) a new creation. We surround the things we deal with with desirabilities and undesirabilities, with appeals and repugnances, with many points of goodness and badness. And the conscious lights in which things are thus viewed can survive the emotional experiences in which they were embedded: we can have unserious, factitious flickers of feeling which put as it were a halo of desirability round something not actually or at the moment desired. From this we may progress to the unfulfilled thought of something as valuable or desirable, which condenses desire into a mere atmosphere, and so on to the mere *verbal declaration* of it as valuable. (We refuse, in the above, to differentiate between the factual and the 'normative' sense of 'desirable', etc., since we hold, in harmony with ordinary language, that the one grows naturally out of the other.) It is further part of the strange magic of mental life, by which everything preserves in itself its origins and their virtues, that thoughts and words with this origin, can offer themselves as steering-points in a general firmament of values, and can determine the most immense consequences. Thus the mere notion of the dropping of an atom bomb as something duly ordered, as something to be acquiesced in and not resisted, perhaps the mere words of command audibly given, without further emotions or conative disturbances, sufficed to destroy Hiroshima.

The kind of generalized wishes responsible for fixing the firmament of our values may therefore be held to be complex mental 'realities', with distinct 'sides' held together by their mutual 'belongingness' and transformability, each of which deserves the name of a 'valuation' only in its connection with all the others. They have a 'side' turned towards practice, for what we wish for or value in a general manner we of necessity endeavour to realize with such means as we dispose of, even if this endeavour, though untainted and sincere, may be baulked of its access to practice by the press of other drifts or by the mere weight of inertia. They have a 'side' turned towards emotion and feeling: being detached from practice, they, by an understandable logic, overflow into surrogative gestures, including those staged in the penetralia of the body, and it is, moreover, by the ready arousability

THE MODES OF WISH AND WILL 209

of such gestures, that the strength, depth and genuineness of our valuation is attested. And they have, lastly, a 'side' turned towards appraisal and assessment, in so far as our emotional attitudes induce us to see objects in appropriate lights, as things duly provocative of certain attitudes, or as things on which such attitudes seek to discharge themselves.

It is, however, part of what we mean by a 'valuation' that it should have acquired a certain measure of fixity, and that it should have acquired this fixity by a process of careful trying out. The firmament of values cannot be peopled by passing meteors, whose place and brightness changes rapidly: its contents must be constant, and must have registered themselves *slowly* on an exposed sensitive plate. The 'trying out' by which this fixity is reached is not anything adventitious or conventional: it is merely a case of the development inevitable in whatever is held fast in the embrace of conscious mind. It involves, as we saw previously, a movement towards the abstract and generic: as we dwell upon various attractive or repulsive objects, we become increasingly aware of *that in virtue of which* we desire or abhor them. The nuclear 'reason' disengages itself from what is indifferently instrumental or circumstantial, from what is replaceably individual or specific, or from the confusing sidelights cast by other grounds of liking or dislike. This process is of course aided if we ask ourselves Socratic questions as to *what it is* renders certain sorts of things deserving of laudatory or pejorative appellation, or if we conduct Moorean experiments as to the desirability of this or that in imaginary existential isolation. These Socratic or Moorean experiments are not the abstract diversions of philosophers: the veriest typist conducts them, when she reflects on her preferences for garments or for 'pop-singers'. And it is no doubt true that the effect of such ponderings is not merely to discover our wants, but to stereotype them in forms fewer and more 'streamlined' than they previously were. Such stereotyping is a necessary adjunct of thought and speech, and it is its products, not shifting *aurorae*, which make up the firmament of our values. It is, further, not merely the selection of our main values and disvalues, but the placing of them in a fixed order of preference, which builds up our personal value-firmament, and this involves such things as repeated comparison, illustration by means of real or imaginary cases ('How would you like it if . . .', etc. etc.) as well

VALUES AND INTENTIONS

as by the repeated arousal of feelings and emotions which end by leaving lasting lustres on objects. None of the above processes comes unnaturally to conscious awareness: they are rather of its essence. To dwell consciously on anything is to see it in lights ever more varied, and also more abstract and generic, and to understand such abstraction and generality is to pass over constantly to a rich round of illustration and fulfilment. To have a liking or dislike for something, and to revolve on this liking or dislike in one's mind, is necessarily to try it out in the ways mentioned, and to end up, by a process of natural selection, with one's likes and dislikes more firmly fixed.

The fixation of values depends, however, supremely on the continued effort to communicate our wants to *others*, and to receive the impress of theirs. As conscious beings, we inevitably surround ourselves with a space of persons, and our wants inevitably overflow into this space: wanting X, we cannot but want others to want it also, we cannot but feel it natural that they *should* want it also, and we cannot but feel confirmed and strengthened in our wants by the fact that others apparently share them. (That this principle has important exceptions, is not to the case: no significant, *a priori* connection can be without them.) Contrariwise, we cannot but feel our wants chilled and reduced, by the failure of others to take on their infection. Since to want X is implicitly to want others to want X, the frustration of this extension of our want is in part the want's own frustration, and such frustration involves (again with significant exceptions) an understandable damping down of our want, a movement towards abandonment or extinction. The search for a sympathetic resonance, and the extinction of attitudes for want of such a resonance, is no mere accident of empirical psychology, but part of the inescapable, non-formal 'logic' of conscious experience. To like something is necessarily (in the absence of special reasons to the contrary) to like the liking of it, and to like this liking not only in ourselves but in others. By a logical transformation, the not-liking of something by others reacts unfavourably on our own liking for it. (Since I like X, you shall (will) like it; but you do not like it; therefore I shall (can) not like it any longer.) The result of this process is the elimination of a large number of wants with which no one has sympathy, and the retention among our personal values of those best surviving the sympathetic test.

THE MODES OF WISH AND WILL

To see things in a favourable light therefore moves in the direction of *judgement*, inasmuch as the person who so sees them cannot help seeking to spread this vision to others, has his vision intensified if he does so spread it, and dimmed if he is unable to do so, in so far as he *expects*, further, that they will see things as he does, and the more so the more they pay attention to the whole matter, envisage it thoroughly and from all sides, and allow their emotions unfettered play. 'Judgement' in this sphere certainly differs from 'judgement' in the sphere of theory, since the emotional light in which things appear to various people, has neither the uniformity nor the compulsive character conveyed to theory by the deliverances of sense. And in fact the wish to set a standard to others in the realms of value often founders on other people's simple refusal to see things in the light that we do: the whole field of personal taste, e.g. taste in food, drink, objects of sexual interest, etc., bear witness to this discrepancy. All this does not, however, preclude us from *trying* to make our valuations common or general, to make others feel as we do, and from expecting success in this venture, by means as unviolent as have led to our own likings. It is, in fact, part of the meanest valuation to seek to extend itself in this fashion.

By all the processes distinguished above, and by others yet to be considered, our wants must tend to build up a relatively fixed firmament of values which are our reasons for choice and action. There is no guarantee, however, that such a firmament will not contain as many blanks, and as many deep discrepancies, as did the maps sketched by the early geographers. And if we turn to the firmaments of different persons, even if belonging to the same society, mutual influence and persuasion may ensure some measure of agreement, but not one that is pervasive and over-riding: it will not be possible to see them all as projections mapping the same territory. Much less have we reason to think that the firmaments of individuals belonging to different communities will show many significant affinities. What we have now to argue, however, is that there are principles deeply rooted in conscious experience, which *must* lead to the segregation of a special region of an individual's value-firmament, and to its development in ways closely parallel to those obtaining in other value-firmaments, and that these principles have an interpersonal approvability of a sort no other principles can possess. We shall try, in short, to show

212 VALUES AND INTENTIONS

that the whole course of conscious experience, in beings subject to wants and urges, must be towards the consolidation of what may be called an *absolute* value-firmament, having many analogies to the orderly world of real objects consolidated through our beliefs.

(IV) THE APPROVABILITY OF VALUATIONS AND VALUES

Wants, wishes and valuations have been so far dealt with as *personal*, as arising and functioning purely within the individual person and his sphere of action, and as having no necessary application to other individuals, even within a given individual's sphere of acquaintance and influence, much less to all conceivable conscious individuals, however placed and situated. No sense has been given to any uniquely standard- or measure-setting class of valuations, and of the values they may be said to project, in relation to which personal valuations and values may be deemed approvable or the reverse. The desirable so far has been only the desired, and the desired by a particular person: we have built no bridge to a sense of 'desirability' in which it can be grossly at variance with what is desired. It is, of course, the case, by the non-formal logic previously studied, that, valuing X, we of necessity tend to value or approve the valuing of it, and to approve or value this approval, and so on *ad infinitum*: we shall in fact almost tautologically perform the transformations indicated, unless hampered by some extraneous consideration (e.g. self-depreciation). The situation is precisely parallel to that in which, having located X unhesitantly in the pattern of the real world, we as unhesitatingly approve of this location, and describe it as 'true', and approve further of this approval and so on, unless, as is frequent, doubts as to our own status and competence as judges make themselves heard. But it is plain that this trivial reindorsement of our own attitudes at ever higher levels is, by itself, powerless to validate them. If the foundations of the whole edifice are shaky, the higher storeys will not add to its stability.

It is further the case, by virtue of the same non-formal logic, that, valuing X, we of necessity tend to approve of the valuation of X by ourselves at all other times, and by all other inhabitants of our ambient 'space of persons'. It means also, by virtue of the deep association between desire and causality, to 'find it natural', and so in a sense to expect, that such an extension will take place.

THE MODES OF WISH AND WILL 213

The pushing of our valuations out into this space as into our ordinary space and time, seems characteristic of our most commonplace valuations, especially when expanded in emotional warmth, and unrestrained by good manners, personal deference or other inhibiting influences. To love even fishing enthusiastically is to demand that others should share this love, and to feel that only inexperience, prejudice or perversity can prevent them from doing so. To be measure-setting, magisterial is therefore a feature of *all* our valuations, and it is perhaps the main merit of Stevenson's *Ethics and Language* to have brought out this truth. But, being a feature of *all* our valuations, it cannot make any such standards unique, and yet that there are in some sense unique standards for valuation, is implied by our more careful and considered assessments. We set up a measure, for ourselves and others, not in enthusiasm, nor with our tongues in our cheeks, but with the deepest seriousness we can rise to.

There are here certain highly tempting but violent ways of solving our problem, which must be deprecated at the outset. These are ways, not clear in their import, and therefore not straightforwardly to be rejected, which regard the arrival at 'right' values, as being more or less like the compulsive encounters of sense, which end controversies, and which are thus describable as 'intuitions' or 'direct insights'. The 'rightness' of a valuation, or the intrinsic 'goodness', 'badness' or 'betterness' of what it sees in an appropriate light, are seen as 'properties' which affront us in the same direct manner as do the red and the loud, and which end controversy, since it is the implicit aim of our valuations to take note of their presence. That we should further make of the presence of such properties a reason for *endeavour*, that we should be *drawn* towards their realization or should *set store* by it, are then either simply confused with this taking account of their presence, and so left unexplained, or they are attached to this taking account by a mere connection of fact, or by a synthetic *a priori* necessity which, being no further explained, differs little from a purely factual connection. For it is clear that there can be no understandable bridge between a property simply acknowledged to be there, and capable of being so acknowledged without there having been practical impulses connected with it, or emotions discharged upon it, and the making of it a final reason for endeavour. If the nature of goodness or rightness can be

VALUES AND INTENTIONS

discerned perfectly in an atmosphere purged of emotion and impulse, then its relation to the latter can never be made understandable: an attitude towards it will necessarily be a mere fact of our nature, like our love of the sweet or our dislike of the over-bitter. And it will make no difference if we go on endorsing such a property at higher levels: if we say that it is *right* to value the property of goodness (or even that we *ought* to value it), and that it is *right* to be guided by this rightness, etc. etc. If the lowest-order goodness lacks a moving reason for endeavour, the same will be true of the superordinate 'rightnesses' piled upon it. On the other hand, it is not clear that these criticisms do not miss their target, since, despite disclaimers to the contrary, it would seem that the admission of *a priori* synthetic connections in effect denies the clear-cut isolability of notions that talk about 'properties' suggests, and that the added epithets 'non-natural', 'consequential', etc., in effect confess that we are not dealing with a *property* in an ordinary, straightforward sense, but with what may be called a 'place' in discourse, a notion which, like a point in space, has no content apart from the relations which fix its position. Value may indeed be said to be unique, simple, other than the relations which converge on it, etc. etc., but, if one tries to separate it from these converging relations, one finds oneself left with a surd on one's hands.

The one way to establish a 'measure-setting' in our valuations, which is not merely impersonal in some would-be, *soi-disant* fashion, would be to make this measure-setting spring from a specific urge to be impersonal, a wish, necessarily of higher order, to free oneself from whatever is peculiar, personal, merely contingent in one's first-order wishes, and to wish nothing but what could be wished by anyone *whatever* his first-order wishes, whether that 'anyone' be oneself in actual or imaginary situations, or any other person. This specific desire for impersonality, if it can be shown to exist, will of course be a personal desire in the sense of being one owned by particular persons: its impersonality will lie, not in its ownership, but in its intent, the peculiar *sort* of desire that it sets out to foster and become. To make any such measure-setting significant, what we may call the 'drift' towards impersonality must, further, have no origin in chance facts about the human person, not even in the profound need for co-operation and communication on which human society reposes. It must

THE MODES OF WISH AND WILL 215

spring from needs rooted in conscious experience as such, in our ability to set objects before us and make significant assertions about them, and in our ability to see both objects and ourselves in relation to that 'space of persons', that comprehensive, ambient 'We', that we may be said, in a manner of speaking, to carry about with us, whoever may occupy it. To make such impersonal measure-setting amount to anything, there must, further, be reliability in its emergence, some tendency for it to increase its hold, and an appreciable level for its final strength. A romantic, transcendental need that existed only in a few stray individuals in disintegrated periods of history, would have no relevance for our purpose. Most important of all, our supposed *nisus* towards impersonality must tend towards uniform results; it would be senseless to seek to derive unique standards from it, if it might be developed in quite different directions. It must not be something purely *formal* in which the most varied content could with like ease be accommodated: it must not, e.g., be quite as natural to be impersonally cruel as kind, impersonally to subordinate everything to the interests of John Jones, as to accord no special privileges to anyone, etc. etc. There must be something compulsively *sifting* about impersonality, which must lead, if sufficiently continued, to a fairly uniform set of results, whose difference in detail must not blind us to their broad, general affinities. There can be nothing in the sphere of valuation akin to the precise settlement due to the compulsions of sense, and it would be illusion to expect it: we must, however, be able to reduce differences within quite narrow limits.

Such systems of valuation as emerge out of the general quest of the impersonal, will be 'justified' only in the sense that they have hit the mark they have set themselves, that they have fulfilled their own aspirations. This characteristic they share with the least normative of the passions: anger and jealousy, too, have marks that they strive to hit, and may be said to be 'justified' when they hit this mark, 'unjustified' when they fail to do so. If I act or feel jealousy when the person I love does not love the person towards whom I feel jealousy, or if I show my jealousy in ways which are not such as to procure the diversion of love that I crave, then I am cherishing a groundless jealousy, and am showing it in an unreasonable manner. In the same manner, if my basic aim is to be 'impersonal', whatever this may involve, then I fail

216 VALUES AND INTENTIONS

of this aim, and act wrongly or amiss, when what I do is, in fact, done in a manner, and tends to a result, not squaring with the requirements of 'impersonality', though they may superficially seem to do so. The 'superiority' of the impersonal to the personal can, moreover, be a superiority only from its *own* point of view. It will in no sense be a superiority in power or in practical efficacy. One's impersonal valuations will not become less impersonal, and less truly in harmony with their own basic aspirations, merely because other forces and persuasive influences have usurped the channels of action. Nor will their sincerity be conclusively disproved by their practical inefficacy: it will be shown up, rather, by the use of a semblance of impersonality to cover personal aims. The 'higher' quality of the impersonal will consist, basically, in nothing more than its higher-order status, its presupposition of other primary wants from whose one-sided influence it seeks to be free. It will consist, secondly, in the fact that the difficult repudiation it involves must of necessity excite reluctant admiration and astonishment, the Kantian emotion of *Achtung*, in the personally interested side of our nature. If impersonality wears a crown, and occupies a throne, it must have conferred both on itself: true insight into the matter will consist in seeing that there is nothing damaging in this fact.

It will not be obscure, in the context of our argument, where these remarks have been tending. The craving for impersonality must not only emerge out of what we have sought to enumerate as the 'basic drifts' of consciousness, it must in some degree seek to make of these its ends or its values. Its ends must, in short, be the manners or modes of procedure characteristic of conscious experience as such, and evident in its pursuit of all finite, contingent purposes. The emergence of those ends must be their self-disengagement from the concrete wants with which they were entangled and blended, and without which they could have no content or existence at all. And their emergence will not be the suicidal removal of the finite wants out of which they grow, but merely a change of approach: the disinterested will be a new form of the interested, a form in which the former personal ends and values become demoted to mere means, and the rational ways of pursuing them become erected into a new set of absolute ends. 'Reason' must therefore rid itself of its initial servitude to the 'passions', to become the object of its own self-love: the

THE MODES OF WISH AND WILL   217

manoeuvres characteristic of consciousness, the filling in of gaps, the achievement of equitable balances, the self-extension over the space of persons, etc., which were merely instrumental in fulfilling other wants, will become the new points of orientation for this rational self-love, the procedures and constructs in which 'reason' may become pointedly and practically aware of itself. As we have said before, this new drift towards impersonality must preserve the old personal interests as its necessary material, but it will itself involve a new set of architectonic interests, whose goals lie in revising and organizing such personal interests and their objects. We have now to ask ourselves whether the facts of our conscious life necessarily point to just this emergent self-love of reason, on which 'absolute' values may be founded, and to an emergence with reliable frequency and appreciable strength.

We have previously sought to show that conscious experience must be the seat of various 'fundamental drifts', which all flow (though by no means analytically) from the mere fact that it *is* conscious experience, and is as such oriented towards 'objects'. There were drifts towards extension and completion of pattern, towards the following out of entailments and the elimination of inconsistency, towards appropriate types of fulfilment, towards deference to compulsive experience, towards reflection on one's own acts and procedures, and towards analogical extension to possible fellows, etc. etc. The 'family gathering' was vast and comprehensive, and it is not easy to keep track of all the names and faces. What is clear, however, is that all these drifts will not be less pervasive when the context is conative and practical, when the problem is one of satisfying one's wants or interests, or of determining one's values, and not merely of finding out how things stand, or what they are. There will be a steady movement towards a mutual accommodation and reshaping of interests and their objects, in the manners indicated above, and this movement must be of particular effect at what we have called the 'cool' level of interestedness, the level at which values are fixed in our firmament, and whole-minded decisions are made.

What it is important to stress is that these rational procedures must of necessity generate their own 'zest': they must, by the inevitable disengagement of what is common to a vast number of conscious manoeuvres, and by its necessary erection into something pointed and pure, become activities sought for their own

218   VALUES AND INTENTIONS

sake, for which our particular interests furnish only the material or the stimulus. There is here a 'value-movement' from means to ends, which is merely a case of the operation of a deep-rooted conscious tendency on the special stuff of desire and practice. And the tendency towards disengagement must be strong by virtue of the sheer universality of the rational drifts in question: wherever we plan, wherever we consider, wherever we give orders or receive them, wherever we debate things with others, we of necessity follow the drifts of extending pattern, equalizing cases, speaking for and with our fellows, etc. etc. Small wonder then that the form of such procedures 'works loose' from its infinitely varied material, that from being instrumental it becomes final, that the streams of endeavour it first fed become its humble tributaries. All this is a movement invariably witnessed as 'civilization', i.e. the operation of conscious reason, advances, though no doubt attended by many much advertised perversions and corruptions: what is important here is to recognize its necessity. The advance of civilization necessarily increases our awareness and our love of what may be called 'absolute values', even if it also increases untold hideous possibilities of defection and dissidence from them.

The drift towards the impersonal also has its roots in the detachment from particular interests, their transformation into 'values', that 'move' without urgency, that we have seen to be characteristic of the cool level of interestedness. It also has its roots in the judicial, quasi-mediatorial position of a man involved in practical deliberation and decision. As we saw before, a man determining how he shall act, or what he shall choose, is to that extent uncommitted and free: the 'self' involved in voluntary decision is of necessity an undetermined self, and philosophical doctrines of indeterminism build mainly on this undoubted fact of experience. But this non-commitment must, on the principles previously enunciated, generate its own zest: a man must come to *wish* to remain free from the particular pushes and pulls of his passions, and must, in this phase, feel them as troublesome masters, after the fashion of Cephalus in the *Republic*. This zest in freedom may carry him farther towards a desire for non-commitment in the face of the *values* he acknowledges, even of those recognized as normative: this is the foundation of the deep, necessary love of the arbitrary, of the *acte gratuit*, rightly

THE MODES OF WISH AND WILL 219

emphasized by Gide. Provided caprice is innocent, and offends against no approvable standard, it must itself (as we shall argue) come to be absolutely valued: it is absolutely good that we should not at all times be too strictly bound to what is absolutely good. But the freedom of caprice, divine and excellent as it is, must provoke interior conflict if it seeks to 'work loose' from the values representing the essential drifts of consciousness, and from the personal interests without which such drifts would have nothing to organize. The zest for freedom must therefore have a rational as well as a capricious form, and the former, with its richness of content and internal harmony, must necessarily prove a more satisfactory sort of freedom. A man as a free voluntary agent, therefore necessarily tends to make paramount those values, rooted in the nature of conscious experience as applied to practice, from which he cannot divest himself: the German idealist equation between the will absolutely free, and the will moved by laws and values it prescribes for itself, must therefore, with qualification, be accepted. It is acceptable, as this is the form on which the zest for freedom must finally fix, not acceptable, in so far as this form necessarily evolves out of forms having greater *prima facie* eligibility, and never losing their subsidiary fascination.

The drift towards impersonality has its source, further, in one major empirical contingency, an incomparable kindness of nature, the existence of *actual occupants* of that theatre of persons into which consciousness emptily extends, persons who make their presence known compulsively through strange accents, intrusive wishes and unforeseeable opinions. While the *possibility* of such disjoined personal standpoints is as readily intelligible as the possibility of objects round corners or behind barriers, and deserves to be called *a priori* if anything deserves the name, there is the same difference between actually *encountering* what fulfils this possibility, and being ready for it, that there is between the empty thought of the other side of the moon and seeing its picture in *The Times*. And while all faculties for what may be called the higher life of practice, exist perfect in us, through the mere fact of being conscious, it is as idle to suppose that we should ever have exercised these without the pressure and help of others, as it is idle to suppose that we might have risen to rational science, without the aid of that other great kindness, the irruptions of matter on our senses, giving rise to the precious possibility of

220 VALUES AND INTENTIONS

believing and explaining something. If compulsive experience peoples our auditorium with persons, it provides the necessary parallax for the formation of abstractions resting on widely disparate instances, for the reaching of beliefs confirmed by widely differing types of evidence, all things which individual experience could not provide on a comparable scale, however little it may be true that it has *no* power to see things from varied angles, and to weigh one view against another. Above all, by providing a new dimension, into which the drifts of consciousness may spread, and by ranging obstacles along its course, it creates an instrumental urge towards the making and receiving of communications, which must necessarily engender its own zest. It is to this urge, among others, that we owe the existence of speech, without which we should possess no conceptual tools that had sharp edges, lasting employment, freedom from the immediate occasion and subtle relations to application, without which we should enjoy no continued interior discourse, and no power to characterize our inner life by analogies borrowed from external things. It is to this urge also that we owe the settled system of common beliefs which compose our picture of reality, since it is through communication with others that this picture comes to be worked out. To treat all this as contingent is, in fact, a somewhat artificial perspective, which has value only as placing something on the horizon of thought and discourse: it describes nothing that we could encounter in the middle distances.

Obviously, too, the urge towards communication must spread over into our emotions, our valuations and our practice: we desire to communicate such forms of interest to others and to take the impress of theirs. This process of sympathetic influence, and submission to sympathetic influence, must engender its own zest. We must come to love, pursue and abide in the attitude or interest that is communicable, and to preserve the attitude that is personal or idiosyncratic only to the extent that it can be harmonized with this. This craving for the communicable underlies tribalism, conventionalism and the closed society, but it is responsible too, if carried far enough, and allowed to exercise its essential impartiality on the enlarged privacy of the group, to those widest exercises of *Fernstenliebe* and liberal benevolence met with in all highly civilized, stable societies, and in none more conspicuously than upper-class England in the last century. It is not our task

THE MODES OF WISH AND WILL 221

here to trace psychological or social processes in detail, but to stress, what should be obvious, that a craving towards impersonality emerges necessarily out of the basic drifts of consciousness, when fertilized by intercourse among persons, and by understanding of their interests. Adam Smith has shown how the processes of sympathetic influence among persons, lead to the planting of an 'impartial spectator' in each bosom: he was wrong only in making its origin so casual, and its final product so amiable, and so lacking in authority. Could we combine with his doctrine the frightening transcendence of a Butlerian conscience, and the necessary development of the Hegelian dialectic, we should have a truer picture of the whole matter. If it is asked 'Should we be disinterested?' or 'Why should we be disinterested?', the answer must be that we inevitably are so, at least in an indefeasible segment of our nature, and that the very fact that we frame this question proves it. For, by the very fact of speech about what we shall do or pursue, we have left the paths of animal absorption behind us: we are demanding *reasons* for acting, and reasons that can be given to others as much as to ourselves. Though the possibility of giving egoistic answers may not be excluded, such egoism will itself have a strange touch of impersonality. The leaven of the impersonal is at work, and while it may lead to much that is imperfectly 'risen', it can be seen also to tend towards a completely rounded, fully 'risen' pattern.

We have shown, then, that the very nature of conscious experience is such as to push it steadily in the direction of the 'impersonal'. That the aspiration to be impersonal in one's practical endeavours and actions tends to pass, by a natural 'logic', to the pursuit of impersonality in forms other than those of practical endeavour, and in relation to persons and things other than ourselves, will, we hope, become evident: we shall see impersonality throwing an explanatory light on the whole assemblage and system of the ends of living. What is here our concern is not, however, this detailed working out, but to consider the forms necessarily taken by this aspiration towards the impersonal, in so far as these concern our practical endeavours. We may maintain here, that the most charateristic expressions of the aspiration towards the impersonal in the region of practice, are a set of orientations whose impersonality proclaims itself in *language*, and in language which, however much it may have close relations to

222 VALUES AND INTENTIONS

speech-forms of an optative, imperative or ejaculatory cast, prefers to avoid suggestions of personal idiosyncrasy and arbitrariness, and suggests the ineluctable character of what must be impersonally pursued, by employing forms of utterance akin to the declarative speech-forms of belief. The characteristic expressions of the aspiration towards the impersonal in the region of practice are, in short, what are usually called 'value-judgements', whether these involve the use of the mainly appreciative, eulogistic (or dyslogistic) expressions 'good', 'bad', 'better', or 'right', or their synonyms or superaltern expressions, or more urgent, moving expressions such as 'ought' and 'should'. The words in question are, of course, not always used in an impersonal spirit, and their use is not then, in our present sense, the expression of a value-judgement. But they may be used in the characteristic impersonal spirit, in which case they involve an endeavour to speak from no special personal standpoint, but only from a standpoint (if standpoint it may be called) which is necessarily sharable by all. We may say also that they involve a *claim* to speak for everyone, since to endeavour to speak for all is, in default of frustrating evidences of failure, to claim to speak for all. Implicitly they may be said to declare—of course they do not explicitly do so, since they are not about themselves—that this is how the impersonally minded will desire and feel and do, and it is this implicit declaration which makes it not misleading to rank them beside the judgements of theory, though in other respects they depart far from such judgements. For they do not defer in anticipation, as regards their central value-expressions, to the compulsive deliverances of sense, or to any confrontation having the same looseness of relation to practice characteristic of these deliverances. Though there may be said to be such a thing as direct insight into values and their relations, it is but another name for a swift, well-founded value-judgement, not anything which settles what we shall judge. And while all attributions of value involve the possibility of seeing objects in certain lights, as desirable, admirable, etc., these lights merely reflect emotion and feeling in ourselves, and have, in themselves, no intersubjective standing. If our impersonal valuations defer to anything, they defer to the emotions and feelings aroused by an appropriate contemplation of certain things and characters, for it is by such emotions and feelings, among other things, that our impersonal valuations are tested, it being senseless to say that we

THE MODES OF WISH AND WILL 223

value anything, whether personally or impersonally, that we never feel about at all. But the test by feeling and emotion holds no such central and decisive place in the confirmation of impersonal valuations, as do compulsive sense-experiences in the testing of beliefs.

What we may stress, however, is that an impersonal value-judgement, like a judgement of theory, does go with a wide array of testing procedures, by means of which it can be brought nearer to validation, and without which it would not make sense to speak of it as a judgement. While the word 'true', carrying with it a suggestion of deference to the compulsively given, is more or less pre-empted to the judgements of theory, and is not naturally applicable to value-judgements, the words 'correct', 'sound', 'valid', 'right', 'justifiable' and 'justified' have the same application here as in theory. Our impersonal valuations look forward, as it were, to appropriate tests, and may be said to claim implicitly that they will survive these. The 'expectation' and the 'claim' alike enter into the meaning of impersonality, as does the nature of the tests for which survival is claimed.

As to the precise nature of these tests, it is not necessary, for our present purposes, to do more than indicate them. Plainly if our aim is to react to interests and their objects in a detached impersonal manner, it will first be necessary to see those interests and their objects in the most vivid and complete manner, with all circumstances relevant to what we are assessing, and with no circumstances extraneous and irrelevant. Views lacking in vividness and completeness can be so in vastly different ways, as can views which incorporate the irrelevant, or which neglect the relevant. Only complete, wholly relevant, maximally vivid views can be uniform among persons, and it is only on such uniformities of idea and belief that we can hope to rear uniformities of valuation. This requirement will dictate the use of such techniques as widespread conceptual experiment, the consideration of cases in which A is present *without B* or C, as well as of cases in which A is present *with* them. It will involve following out the consequences, or possible consequences, of varied assemblages of characters and conditions on varying backgrounds of circumstance or dispensations of nature. The would-be impersonal judge, will, further, have to rise to the maximally vivid view of his object by employing every kind of imaginative or perceptual

224 VALUES AND INTENTIONS

fulfilment. He will have to find out what to think worth while, not merely by manipulating counters in thought, however legitimate this may be once values are established, but by imagining situations in the most vivid manner, filling in their possible or actual settings in some detail, etc. etc. And where spontaneous imagination fails, he will have to have recourse either to actually being in certain situations, or to hearing or reading of them in some detail. The fulfilments necessary will, further, have to be of the emotions, feelings and other experiences had, or possibly had, by the persons studied, and it is here that the techniques of sympathetic self-extension will be of supreme importance. Sympathy for the axiologist is a technique as indispensable as are observation and experiment for the scientist, and as little involving ultimate partiality or sentiment. For to the sympathy that immerses itself in the peculiar standpoint and interests of a given person, must be added the sympathy which immerses itself in the standpoint and interests of all other parties to the same transaction, or of all other onlookers and judges, some actual, some merely imaginary, and especially of all those who are attempting to be thus comprehensively sympathetic, who hope to find a reaction that will sum up and give a lead to all these reactions, much as a man of science makes a statement that he hopes will sum up for, and give a lead to, the whole observing and experimenting community.

Our standard-setting impersonal reactions—how we feel that the detached, impartial, but also deeply sympathetic and understanding, person would feel—must also be affected by the tendencies native to the consciousness of objects which were set forth in an earlier chapter. For, being less attached to the directions of interest peculiar to individuals, one must of necessity become more attached to the directions of interest common to all thinkable persons, which are also the directions of interest common to them as *thinking* persons. One will tend, in particular, towards the regular extension of pattern, towards the filling in of gaps and the levelling of anomalies. The profound grasp of remote analogy from which spring most of the bridging hypotheses of science, will be no less significant in the realm of values: we shall be constantly finding that this case is not 'fundamentally different' from that, that X is no more than a peculiar case of Y, that it is absurd to treat A in this manner while treating B quite

THE MODES OF WISH AND WILL   225

differently, etc. etc. Formally there may be little cogency in such reasonings, since there is no good formal expression of profundity of likeness: they will have enough cogency, however, to level the unevennesses and to relax the stiffnesses of the most firmly established social systems. Men will tend, further, by virtue of other basic drifts of consciousness, towards more and more open universality of attitude, and towards the elimination of arbitrary bias, whether in the preference for considerations, for interests, for kinds of interest, for specific persons or classes of person, etc. etc. While it is barely possible to find a formal expression for the impartial—the most biased attitude being capable of a description which makes it seem impartial—it remains plain that we can successfully grade attitudes according to the depth of their impartiality.

It is clear, lastly, that a good test of the impersonal, as of the scientifically real, will be its repeatable character, whether for ourselves on varied occasions, or for others as well as ourselves. Hence the all-importance of repeated consideration of the same feature or matter, to see whether the reactions it arouses are not due to some biasing want in temporary dominance. (Such repeated consideration no more proves the merely empirical character of our impersonal valuations, than the fact that we test our additions by repeatedly adding up the same column of figures proves the empirical character of mathematics.) The approvably good, like the approvably assertible in theory, is what will accumulate more and more reactions in its favour, and fewer and fewer proportionately against it, the longer it is considered, and to value it impersonally is, among other things, to make an open claim to this effect. The assent of judicial approval has, therefore, the same essential infinity as the assent of ordinary judgement, or the consent of the will. This appeal to, and this faith in, unending confirmation, extends, however, not only to our judicial life in time, but to the whole jury of persons perpetually surrounding us, a privileged segment of the space of persons consisting of those, and those only, who seek to be disinterested, to see themselves and all others 'in an equal light'. In this reasonable company we of necessity live, whether we encounter its actual members or not. If we do not meet any, we appeal to posterity, to the *sapientiores*, to the Buddhas who have preceded us on the path. Fortunately, however, most of us know actual members of the fellowship: hence

H

226 VALUES AND INTENTIONS

the endless discussion and consultation characteristic of all value-inquests, a process as essential in shaping our impersonal valuations, as are the conferences, the exchanges and the publicly conducted experiments of men of science.

The processes we have listed all consist fundamentally in seeing, in different ways, whether valuations and values will survive projection into the most widely differing personal positions, whether these be our own in the present or past, those of actual other persons, or those of persons wholly imaginary. So much is plainly part of what we mean by being impersonal. That a valuation and its projected value will survive the treatment we have indicated, and be strengthened by its repetition, must, further, be no empirical accident: if it were, it could have no interest for the present inquiry. The survival must in some sense 'flow' from the nature of impersonality, and must permit a 'deduction' from this, even if this deduction may not in all its points follow lines of purely formal entailment. Such a deduction it will be the whole aim of the remaining part of this book to provide, and to provide in some detail. On the success of this venture the significance of what we have so far said must depend, just as the sense and nature of Kant's transcendental deduction of the categories is determined only by the use it is put to in other parts of the system. We must expect nothing crystalline: where the compulsions of sense have no relevance, the vague workings of the emotions, even if guided by rational aspirations, cannot hope to achieve sharp edges. But though nebulous in their contours, it would be wrong to suppose that our final values have no shapes or boundaries. Like the clouds of heaven, they have limits fixed by firmamental temperatures and pressures, which in their case are the linked, ordered requirements gathered together under the name of 'impersonality'. This notion, and these requirements, we must now seek to elucidate.

CHAPTER VI

THE VALUES OF WELFARE

(I) THE VALUES OF SATISFACTION AND DISSATISFACTION

We have so far shown it to be inevitable that conscious life, if sufficiently enriched and prolonged, should develop aspirations towards what we have called the 'impersonal', and that with this tendency should go a reinforcement of the tendencies essential to consciousness as such, and a reshaping of all interests merely personal and peculiar, so as to make them fit into the general framework provided by 'the impersonal', and to constitute its content. Conscious endeavour, in its less obsessive forms, must acquire a 'set' towards forms necessarily capable of being shared by anyone, however they may be inclined or placed, and, as tending in such directions, must necessarily be endorsed and approved, not merely idly, in a spiritual segment of the individual to which they belong, but also in corresponding spiritual segments belonging to other conscious individuals. And its reshapement of peculiar, personal interests will have general validity according as it flows, most naturally and logically, from the general set towards impersonality, a flowing of which we can become extraneously and deductively conscious, as in a meta-ethical work like the present, but of which we can also become aware in the concrete work of ethical deliberation and discussion, as irrelevancies drop away, plausible steps show themselves up as misguided, and different people's impersonal reactions converge towards uniformity. Were there no such convergence, we should have the position that the form of the impersonal was without selective or sifting force, a position in which many formalists have believed, but which we have held not to obtain. That it does not obtain can be shown, however, only in detailed working out, and this we shall begin in the present chapter.

Our ensuing chapters will not, however, deal with the desirability of highly concrete acts and projects, but only with the *main heads* of desirability, the supreme sorts of reason in virtue of which things are judged to be intrinsically desirable and

228 VALUES AND INTENTIONS

choiceworthy or the contrary. These heads are, by an over-whelming tradition, comparatively few, and we shall find no reason to augment them vastly, since they rest on the comparatively few directions in which our mental life defines and differentiates itself. We may here, by anticipation, distinguish: (*a*) values or disvalues attaching to states of satisfaction (or pleasedness), and their objects *qua* satisfactory, or to states of dissatisfaction (or displeasedness), and to their objects *qua* dissatisfying, as well as to the various emotions and feelings connected with all these—we may speak somewhat generalizingly of *hedonic* values and disvalues; (*b*) values and disvalues attaching to states of successful or seemingly successful apprehension and contemplation, and their objects, considered as such, and to states of frustrated and defective (or seemingly frustrated and defective) apprehension and contemplation, and their objects considered as such, as well as to the various emotions and feelings relevant to all these—we may here speak of *contemplative* and *aesthetic* values, the latter being a sub-species of the former, though the most important as regards interest; (*c*) values and disvalues attaching to states of successful, or seemingly successful, cognitive penetration, together with all attendant emotions and feelings; also values and disvalues attaching to states of frustrated or defective penetration of the same sort, and to the corresponding objects, considered as such, and to corresponding emotions and feelings—we may here speak of *epistemic* and, in some contexts, of *logical* values; (*d*) values and disvalues attaching to various types of successful or frustrated (or to seemingly successful or frustrated) penetrations into the life lived at other points in the space of persons—we may here speak of values of *understanding* or *fellowship*. The four heads (*a*) (*b*), (*c*) and (*d*) may be grouped together as values of *welfare* or *well-being* (or disvalues of a contrary 'ill-fare' or 'unwell-being'), since they may all be regarded as cases of advantage or disadvantage, profit and counterprofit, necessarily belonging to given individuals, and 'enjoyed' by them alone. To these may be added, with less clearness that they should count as 'welfare', (*e*) values and disvalues pertaining to the possession and exercise of powers and freedoms of various sorts, or to the corresponding impotences and unfreedoms, and to the various feelings and emotions connected with all these—these may be comprehensively referred to as values of *power* and *freedom*. To these may be added (*f*) the all-important

THE VALUES OF WELFARE 229

disvalues which are not primarily disadvantageous to individuals, but pertain rather to maldistributions of welfare among such individuals, though they have necessary connections with individual disadvantage. To these may be opposed a class of somewhat bloodless values, whose whole goodness depends on the absence of countervailing ills. We may speak comprehensively of the values and disvalues of *justice* or *fairness,* and these will be dealt with in our next chapter. Finally we shall deal with (*g*), the values and disvalues attaching to conscious causality directed to values and disvalues of the various kinds distinguished above, or to what are believed to be such values: we shall speak comprehensively of *moral* values and disvalues. The present section of the present chapter will accordingly deal with (*a*), the values classed above as 'hedonic'.

We may here revert to a point previously stressed: that were pleasedness and unpleasedness (pleasure-pain) the simple modalities of experience they are sometimes supposed to be, it would merely be an odd, empirical fact that we were moved to active endeavour by the thought or actual presence of one of these qualities, and to destruction and retreat by the other. The philosophical traditions that made the pursuit and avoidance of these things inevitable, on the one hand, or rational, on the other, would be alike mistaken: it would be quite conceivable, and in no sense irrational, that a reverse preference should obtain. The traditions, however, though marred by absurd confusions, and by a constant shuttling between assertions true by definition and assertions genuine and substantial, have obviously seized upon something irrefragable. That something is thought likely to please ourselves or someone else, is inexpugnably a *good reason* for directing our practical endeavours towards it (and so also, *mutatis mutandis,* if something is thought likely *not* to please), though not by any means the only reason for such a direction, nor one tautologically implicit in the notion of desire, wanting or practical endeavour. The more, however, a connection departs from the analytic, the more essential is it that we understand it, and assure ourselves of such understanding, of our capacity to *see* how one notion has a built-in relevance to another, and is not empirically found, nor dogmatically asserted, to go with it. We draw nearer to such understanding when we learn to see in all pleasingness and pleasedness the presence of a want satisfied, whether this want

230 VALUES AND INTENTIONS

existed *before* the satisfying fulfilment, or was aroused by the very circumstance that satisfied it, and whether it was a want that put its object before consciousness or merely operated in the *as-if* fashion understandable in contexts which include the completing possibility of consciousness. For something to please, it must be as some drift within us would make it be, and for something to be *felt* as pleasant or agreeable (in the emphatic sense of 'felt' discussed above) it must be 'seen' as falling in with, as happily carrying out, or as agreeing with such a drift. The notion of a coincidence, a non-necessary accord, is part and parcel of the notion of the agreeable, as the very name expresses. We provided, in a previous chapter, enough argument to show why such a 'cognitive' analysis of agreeable feeling is not really inadequate: obviously there are cases, there sufficiently explained, where one might look on something as fulfilling one's drift, *without* therefore finding it pleasant. And what we have held of course also demands an elaborate rewriting for the case of the disagreeable and the painful, which we shall not here attempt. We have, however, come to a view of the pleasing as being, roughly, what is both wanted and also encountered or believed actual, the greeting of which normally involves an emotional discharge, often slight, which announces its presence to feeling: being-pleased is the subjective correlative of the same phenomenon. Being unpleasing and unpleased will have, then, a parallel relation to frustrated wanting, and to attendant developments of emotion and feeling. What we have now to ask is *why* the satisfaction, or the satisfying object of a wholly personal want, when presented directly in feeling, should itself become the object of a higher-order, *impersonal* satisfaction, why we should impersonally like the personal liking of anything, and what is liked in so far as it is personally liked? In the same way, we may ask why we should impersonally dislike what is personally disliked, together with the personal dislike itself. There is nothing tautological about the matter. It is formally possible that A should have the strongest of tastes or distastes for B, without having the smallest taste or distaste for his taste or distaste, let alone a taste or distaste that he wishes and expects all other persons to share.

It is plain that, whatever is liked and wanted by someone, will have, in virtue of the characteristics which appeal to that person, no impersonal call on the liking and wanting of himself and

THE VALUES OF WELFARE

others. The qualities which recommend food or drink, or a male or female companion, or a manner of occupying leisure time *to you*, have, as the qualities they are, absolutely no hold or purchase *on me*, as a detached and impersonal, though imaginative and sympathetic judge: in so far as I put myself in your skin, they become things that I find it *possible* to like or love, and are accordingly to be ranked, so far as no further consideration arises, as things that one may impersonally be *allowed* or *permitted* to like or love. This impersonal legitimation cannot, however, be raised to something inescapable and mandatory, for the mere reason that it stands opposed to countless contrary legitimations. For in so far as I put myself into the shoes of other parties, I can very well understand how such qualities should *not* recommend themselves to them, and nothing but an entirely arbitrary decision—which is as such abhorrent to the detached judge, swayed only by the tendencies intrinsic to consciousness—could deny the legitimation to the one taste which it extends to the other. The contingent objects of our likes and dislikes enter therefore into our impersonal valuations only as things that we *may* like or dislike: contingency and possibility ground only a permissibility. But in so far as we progress from considering *what* qualities are liked or disliked, to considering the circumstance that they *are* liked or disliked, the situation alters. Though we cannot impersonally endorse a liking for A, without further conditions, merely because A is liked by someone, we can endorse a liking for A, *in so far* as A is liked by someone, without further conditions whatsoever. In other words, we find we must approve impersonally of the liked as such, though not necessarily of its associated content, and that our approval extends as naturally to the actual state of liking.

The logic of the situation is somewhat perplexing. For with the symbolism of intentional discourse in its present undevelopment, we have no satisfactory symbolism for expressing the commonplace situation where we like A for its feature X, and dislike it for its feature Y. And the connection of the impersonal liking for A *qua* liked with the personal liking for A, is plainly not one of logical entailment: it can in fact be evaded. But that it is hard to evade it, if we apply the tests constitutive of impersonality, can be readily seen by considering *what else* we might do beyond impersonally endorsing the liking of X *qua* liked. Should we, in

232   VALUES AND INTENTIONS

so far as we detach ourselves from the situation, be *indifferent* to *X* in so far as it is liked? Should the fact that here something is as someone wants it to be, be a matter of profound indifference to us? Should we even go farther, and regard *X* with aversion in so far as someone likes it, and be sorry that someone is finding something to his liking? Obviously such suggestions are monstrous, and we understand that it can only be through perversity, i.e. through a wanton and difficult flouting of what naturally suggests itself, or through the presence of special factors, e.g. personal resentment, rightly regarded as prejudicing or biasing, that any such line could be followed. We understand this, as we understand that it would be wanton to expect *A*'s never to be *B*'s in the future, merely because they were always *B*'s in the past, or as we understand that something like *A* is more likely to emerge out of *A* than something not like *A* at all.

There might even, we may note, be a sort of profound conflict in attempting impersonally to dislike, or to be indifferent to, things *qua* liked, in so far as this would not only involve our disliking (impersonally) whatever we liked (personally), but perhaps also, if we elected to make being disliked a ground for impersonal liking, a higher impersonal liking founded upon this, and a higher impersonal dislike founded on this liking, and so on. This situation, by its very possibility, would be more uncomfortable than attempting to nourish a formal contradiction. The same discomfort further extends to any *arbitrariness* in liking the liked *qua* liked: there could, one would say, be 'no rational basis' for liking a thing *qua* liked by *certain* other persons or sorts of person, and not liking them *qua* liked by certain other persons or sorts of persons. That there is nothing formally defective in such a 'universality' only shows how contemptible an instrument is 'logical form' in representing distinctions of thought. Nothing but the influence of a preference not necessarily shared by all, and so not capable of being impersonally cherished, could make such an attitude possible. Many quasi-impersonal attitudes involving an element of the arbitrary and contingent are indeed possible and lamentably real, but the only one involving no injection of this sort would be one involving the liking of *everything qua* liked, the one, in short, that desires that *everyone* should have what happens to please him, to which may be added the implied correlative, that no one should be made to suffer anything that does

THE VALUES OF WELFARE   233

not please him, or that gives him pain. The immense provisos to which this rational norm is subject—provisos concerning the conflict of wants and satisfactions, the instrumental value of sufferings, and the impersonal undesirability of wanting certain things, etc. etc.—do not affect its fundamental compelling force. It is part of what Plato called the divine freedom from envy to desire that everything should be as good, i.e., in this limited context, as satisfactory as possible.

The 'values' we have deduced are in a sense 'formal' in so far as requiring a content or filling dependent on actual wants or satisfactions. They have not, however, the worse than formal character of traditional hedonism, in which the one quality, pleasure, is relentlessly pursued, whatever acts or experiences it may attach to, and the one quality, pain, relentlessly avoided, no matter what its context or its origin. In traditional hedonism, things found pleasant or painful are *sources* of pleasure and pain respectively, not things which, in virtue of their own character, please or displease us. For such hedonism there can be nothing impersonally to be approved in what would for most of us be the 'good things of life': a good table, a good mate, good friends, a good appearance, a congenial occupation, firm religious or other ideological supports, etc. etc. Only the drops of agreeable feeling painfully distilled from such sources have for it the smallest value, and for such value it is unimportant whence they may have been derived, or by whom enjoyed. Such hedonism was no doctrine fit for pigs: it was one of the most ascetic formalisms ever conceived, so ascetic as to sacrifice everything to the barest of abstractions, and so formal as to swing over into a higher type of materialism, there being nothing for its form to inform. With the abandonment of a psychology framed in terms of qualified and related existents, we are delivered from these false abstractions. We may impersonally approve satisfactory tables, mates, friends, occupations, appearances, ideological supports, etc., as being so inseparable from the satisfactions they yield, as rightly themselves to be called 'satisfactions'. (Such things are also so inseparable from the *impersonal* satisfactions they yield, as rightly themselves to be called 'values', not, in the insufferable modern fashion, 'bearers' or 'grounds' of value.) The impersonal approval of the satisfaction a man takes in such objects is an approval of the same matter, but differently slanted or emphasized. The only

H*

234 VALUES AND INTENTIONS

weakness in the hold of tables, mates, etc., on impersonal valuation, lies in the (at least partially) empirical character of their satisfactoriness: while the satisfactory must have *some* content, it might have had a content different from this. The nature of angels is not thought to be such as to replenish itself at tables, nor to marry or be given in marriage, and the mere fact that such beings are conceivable removes tables and marriage beds from the inescapable framework, and relegates them to the permissive filling, of the absolutely good.

We may go farther and hold that, in so far as certain things satisfy us in an essentially *different* manner, which is none the less essentially related to our satisfaction, these differences themselves may be impersonally significant: satisfactions cannot be ordered in a single lineal order of greater and less. There are, it is plain, satisfactions which are 'deep', in so far as springing from wants radical and architectonic; there are satisfactions termed 'broad', inasmuch as fulfilling a large range of interlinked wants; there are satisfactions classed as 'lofty', in so far as springing from wants of a gratuitous, disinterested, admiration-evoking sort, and there are satisfactions 'deeply felt', the 'deeply felt' differing from the 'deep' in its reflectively evident character: there are, finally, satisfactions classed as 'exquisite', in so far as springing from some rare, little exercised or seldom adequately satisfied side of our nature. None of these differences are differences in anything other than our satisfactions, nor are any of them irrelevant to an impersonal assessment: a satisfaction may be *more* satisfactory along any of these distinct dimensions, nor is one of them a plainly prior ground of preference to another. On these points Mill would appear to have reasoned more justly than his predecessors or his critics. We may here note how, traditionally, the whole question of the place of a satisfaction along a scale of degrees, generally travestied into the notion of 'amount' or 'quantity', was itself confused with the quite different question of its value or preferability. That a satisfaction is *more* of a satisfaction in one or other respect may be a ground for esteeming it above some other satisfaction. If the respects vary, it cannot, however, be the sole ground, and there must be ways of accommodating such differing measures with each other, and with other measures extrinsic to satisfaction.

We may now skirt, without entering profoundly into them, the

THE VALUES OF WELFARE   235

traditional problems regarding 'sums of pleasures', where the distinct issues of the value of satisfactions extending over many contributory satisfactions, and the value of mere classes or distributions of satisfactions are maladroitly confused. We may deal with the former first. There is a sense in which the satisfactions and dissatisfactions extending over a whole period of action and experience sum themselves up in a satisfaction or dissatisfaction which covers the phase as a whole, which takes account of the passing satisfactions and dissatisfactions which occur in it, but is not reached by an elaborate application of Benthamite arithmetic. Thus I can assess the satisfaction derived from a three weeks' stay in Italy as regards intensity, breadth, depth and any other hedonic dimension: this assessment takes account of the partial satisfactions and dissatisfactions of visits to monuments, confinements to bed with dysentery, etc. etc., but in no sense sums them up externally, or merely arithmetically. The total satisfaction or dissatisfaction of a whole period or phase of activity is in a sense experienced over the whole period, and not only at the end: we know whether we are enjoying our Italian visit *throughout* the visit, and the later phases but 'confirm' or 'refute' this pervasive 'knowledge'. Nothing is plainer than the basically cognitive character of such assessments, even if they express themselves in unreflecting, instant pronouncements, unbacked by a long survey of what we have been through. What is singular, however, is their extraordinary asymmetry as regards time: disasters occurring at the beginning of our stay may be quite blotted out by subsequent enjoyments, whereas the same disasters occurring at the end of the stay taint its whole satisfaction. What is plain, too, is the quite different role played by pleasure and pain: many painful experiences of perhaps quite limited duration so cloud the whole picture that no satisfactions countervail against them. Interesting, too, is the comparative unimportance of length of periods of time monotonously filled with the same sort of satisfaction, except where this mediates a sense of 'eternity': a few days exquisitely filled, and involving this sense, need not differ in satisfaction from thrice as many days filled in the same fashion. Plainly this sort of comprehensive hedonic or eudaemonistic summing-up can be carried out over the whole of one's life, and can sometimes be done surrogatively by the sympathetic bystander, and perhaps more readily than by the man himself. The sort of summing-up we

236   VALUES AND INTENTIONS

are considering, whether performed by a man or his neighbours, differs widely from assessments bridging assemblages of satisfactions and dissatisfactions which have never been in a single self-conscious purview, and perhaps could not be so, because separated by periods of nescience, or by the profound gulfs constitutive of the space of persons. In this latter type of case, we can speak of totals of satisfactions, but not of total satisfactions; one such total can be more satisfactory than another, only in the extraneous sense of being preferable from the point of view of an external assessor.

We have now to ask ourselves how all this stands from the point of view of impersonal assessment. Will an impersonal assessor accept such judgements of total satisfactoriness or unsatisfactoriness over whole periods, and base his valuations on these, or will he prefer to use piecemeal Benthamite techniques, disregarding temporal asymmetry, considering pains on a level with pleasures, having a strict regard to duration, and employing the same quasi-arithmetical approaches in the case of the dispersed satisfactions and dissatisfactions of a single person, that are inevitable in the case of experiences separated by nescience or by the disjunction of persons? The answer to be given to this question would appear to be that summings-up of satisfactions which are impersonally acceptable, and a basis for impersonal valuation, cannot differ fundamentally from those pronounced by the individual experient, but can at best seek to better these by reflection. For, if one rejects a man's sense of his total satisfaction over a period, why should one accept his sense of the briefest satisfaction or dissatisfaction? Our conscious life is continuous in time, and there is no fundamental difference between the deliverances of what may be called 'hedonic knowledge' over a longer and a shorter period. What Benthamite reflection can do is, by bringing all the partial satisfactions and dissatisfactions of the period into vivid review, to do justice to all of them, a justice plainly implicit in the notion of impersonality. Thus, while not altering our fundamental judgements of total satisfaction, it may at least make them more stable, and less liable to be shaken by recollection. We may now briefly summarize some of the Benthamite and non-Benthamite principles that we propose to endorse, with some justification in each case.

First of all, we endorse the view that the satisfactoriness or

THE VALUES OF WELFARE 237

unsatisfactoriness of a continuous phase of life is not found merely by considering separate satisfactions and dissatisfactions, and then performing a quasi-arithmetical summing-up on them: plainly our experience and activity over a period have endeavours which pervade and unify them, and may in some sense be held to have a satisfactoriness or unsatisfactoriness characterizing them as a whole. The summings-up we perform to determine the value or choiceworthiness of totals of satisfaction dispersed among many individuals is, of course, not strictly arithmetical either, but it is much more nearly so: it resembles a rough sum performed upon roughly estimated numbers. None the less, even the most 'organic' summing-up of satisfaction must take profound account of component satisfactions or dissatisfactions: it must in some sense emerge or result from them all.

In the second place, we may impersonally endorse the somewhat strange attitudes to time adopted in our ordinary summings-up. Time is a side of experience where anomaly is so essential, differently placed items necessarily obeying quite different 'logics', that we may expect anomalies even in our impersonal assessments of satisfaction or dissatisfaction. Ends, adding the crowning touches to total experiences, whose character is previously somewhat problematic, are obviously more important, *pro tanto*, than beginnings or middles: hence the supreme importance of happy endings, and the ruinous character of deeply miserable ones. It is, for this reason, one of the great tragedies of existence that most of us die so pitiably. Past satisfactions have, in a sense, no existence except as summed up in later ones, and future satisfactions only in so far as confidently anticipated: in both cases we may accept the Benthamite principle that remoteness and uncertainty reduce the contribution to total satisfaction. Here too we may endorse the unsatisfactoriness, rightly stressed by the hedonistic poets, of the prospect of death, or rather of the absence of prospect involved in the dominant idea of death. Even the most satisfactory of lives, when ended, can be satisfactory only in the sense of being thought to have been such, and, as so thought of, of giving satisfaction to others. An undying, historically-minded posterity would, therefore, seem to be a minimum postulate both for a hedonistic, and for any axiology. We may endorse, further, the 'telescoping' character of monotony: satisfactions prolonged monotonously up to a

238 VALUES AND INTENTIONS

certain point are rightly felt to be more satisfactory, because more sensibly extensive: beyond this, we must have something like a flattening out to a fixed level, and possibly even a decline. It is the prospect (not necessarily believed in) of eternal continuance that is important for satisfaction and dissatisfaction, rather than any actual eternity.

In the third place, we may impersonally endorse the asymmetrical attitudes unreflectively taken up towards satisfaction and dissatisfaction, or towards pleasure and pain. Dissatisfaction and pain involve in some sense the 'demoralization' of the active self, its retreat or collapse into itself, and this must lead after a finite number of steps to a position where no positive endeavours, and consequently no satisfactions, are possible. Such a position in a sense counts as infinity over against any number of countervailing satisfactions. How it counts will, however, be determined by its position in the experiential sequence: dark Gethsemanes and Golgothas of the spirit can be cancelled by *later* renaissances and resurrections, whereas the contrary arrangement would absorb almost any amount of happiness in final misery. It is not, however, possible to be scholastically precise in these regions, where philosophers have mainly purveyed simplifying nonsense, and only poets and saints have had anything sensible to say. What it is important to underwrite is the compassionate principle —recognized in all deeply sensitive moralities—that no augmentation of mere happiness, however intense, or widespread, or prolonged, will suffice to nullify certain profound pains.

We may now turn to the somewhat different, more difficult, question as to the *values* and *disvalues* impersonally to be attached to total satisfactions and dissatisfactions, as to dispersed aggregates of satisfactions and dissatisfactions. In raising such questions, we are trying to achieve impersonally valid satisfactions which *concern* primary satisfactions and dissatisfactions, not merely establishing the *degree* of satisfaction or dissatisfaction in the latter. At this level, a plurality of dimensions is inadmissible, for, while one satisfaction can exceed another in intensity, breadth, depth and other dimensions, it does not make sense to say that one satisfaction (or its object *qua* satisfactory) is in various distinct manners more or less valuable. As to the principles here to be followed, we can only hazard a few suggestions, as points for reflection rather than as dogmas. We may, first of all, adhere

THE VALUES OF WELFARE 239

to the obvious view that total satisfactions, if of the same sort, or satisfactory in the same manner, should be valued, *pro tanto*, according to the degree of their total satisfaction: the principles for assessing total satisfaction prevent this from having any unacceptably simple meaning. This principle must, however, be limited by one which asserts the rights of the parts against the whole. Time may be self-unifying and self-summarizing, but it is so only out of prior incompleteness and disunity, and it would ignore its character entirely to preach limitless subordination of the contributions of earlier phases to an emergent total. The best arrangement of satisfactions over a period will not necessarily be one which involves most satisfaction in the final summing-up, but which also distributes the satisfaction over the period with the nearest approach to equity, so that each phase, in its greyer or more brilliant manner, reflects the satisfaction of the whole. We should wish, e.g., immaturity to have its own exquisite satisfactions mingled with anticipations of those of maturity, while mature life should have both its peculiar satisfactions as well as reliving those of immaturity. The dispersal involved in temporal existence creates something like a profound injustice if long years, wherever placed in one's history, are spent in dreariness or in agony.

We may further sponsor the principle that satisfactions of precisely the same sort decline in value if added steadily to satisfactions of the same type, whether this addition be of an organic or of a quasi-arithmetical type. The impersonal attitude is essentially concerned with the universal, and with the particular as embodying the universal, and it has absolutely no interest in, and is even positively offended by, the multiplication of like satisfactions *ad infinitum*. Up to a point multiplication mediates a change from the small to the great, a positive and therefore valuable transformation: beyond this, it mediates only the trivialization of all greatness, however prodigious. There is no proposition more self-evidently absurd that we should seek to multiply satisfaction *ad infinitum*. This is not, of course, to say that, should someone's satisfaction be endless and monotonous, like the μέθη αἰώνιος of the Olympian gods, we should seek to abridge this, nor yet that, if the world's population consisted of infinitely many monotonously pleased persons, we should relegate some to the gas chambers. It is only to say that the existence of

240

VALUES AND INTENTIONS

such beings is, from an impersonal point of view, not edifying, and even positively affronting. (Though, once existent, they have rights.) Much the same, with like provisos, applies to dissatisfaction and pain: indefinitely many wholly miserable beings are perhaps not much worse than a few. Monotony being reductive of value, it seems plain that variety and rarity increase it. Satisfactions are more precious, and pains more atrocious, if spread over many dimensions, and concerned with many objects, than only a few. And a rare sort of satisfaction connected with a rare object is *pro tanto* more valuable than an otherwise like satisfaction of a common sort. Similar principles have recommended themselves to rational economists: it is not clear why rational moralists should have ignored them.

The estimate of hedonic values, is, however, to a large extent senseless, since it is often only by a false abstraction that the value of some state, as involving satisfaction or dissatisfaction, can be held apart from its value or disvalue on other counts. In the case of satisfactions distributed over disjoined consciousnesses, it is perhaps possible to distinguish the values or disvalues of these satisfactions as such from the values or disvalues in their manner of distribution. It is not, however, possible to keep apart the value or disvalue of an activity or an experience, as satisfactory or the reverse, from its value or disvalue as being the sort of activity or experience it is, and as concerning the object it does concern. To seek to judge such aspects separately would be to pass nugatory judgements, because concerned with nothing that is there. Thus a satisfaction arising out of an evil activity, or intent upon an evil object, does not become less evil by being a satisfaction: it becomes, by universal insight, more so. Cruel actions and spectacles are, e.g., rationally to be regarded as rendered more evil by the pleasure they afford, since a respect in which they would otherwise be good is here corrupted by something from which it is impossible to disengage it, and which it powerfully underlines. And the pleasure is more an appanage of the cruelty, and hence corrupted by it, than the cruelty a source of the pleasure, and so bettered by it. Values of satisfaction and dissatisfaction, in their pure form, can be realized only in a narrow range of cases, where there is absolutely no other reason for impersonally setting store by something (or the reverse) beyond the fact that it is satisfactory (or the reverse) to someone.

THE VALUES OF WELFARE 241

Even in these simplest cases, the criteria listed above will not suffice to reach absolutely uniform results, but they will powerfully limit the field of argument.

(II) THE VALUES OF APPREHENSION AND CONTEMPLATION

Having established the values of satisfaction and dissatisfaction, which constitute, as it were, our *mere welfare*, or the material side of the good life, we pass to consider what may be called our *higher welfare*, whose presence adds an element of desirable form to the unorganized mass of mere welfare. The sorts of welfare considered in the last chapter were impersonally valued, but they had themselves nothing impersonal about them; they included satisfactions and dissatisfactions derived from the most brutish instinct or the most idiosyncratic taste. We now pass to consider forms of welfare which have themselves a touch of the impersonal, and which are impersonally valued because the impersonal segment of our nature sees in them a reflection or specified form of itself. We may expect to find the fronds of the higher welfare springing from the distinct nodes of our conscious experience: the nodes of apprehension and idea, of belief and knowledge, of desire and will, of social experience, etc. etc. The first alone concerns us in the present section. We shall investigate the values that may be impersonally attached to the clear and the obscure, the fulfilled and the 'empty' cognition, the various types of 'conscious light', as well as the values connected with such fundamental 'drifts' as the *nisus* to continue pattern, to point abstractions, to reintegrate these in objective syntheses, etc. etc. Actually the whole field to be covered will reveal itself as more simple and unified than the above account suggests: it will show itself all as not unfitted for the general label 'aesthetic'. It will not be our aim, however, to consider the scope of this or any other name, but to delimit and explore a peculiar territory of value.

The ideal of impersonality, as applied to the unbelieving 'idea', will plainly tend towards detachment from cognitive interests biased towards particular, contingent objects, and, in particular, such cognitive interests as are parasitic upon other non-cognitive interests, e.g. the desire to see or imagine things edible, or things sexually titillating, etc. etc. Plainly, in so far as one's wish is to care for nothing except as anyone else might care for it, one will,

242 VALUES AND INTENTIONS

within the bounds of the attitude in question, deprecate cognitive interests that dwell one-sidedly and fixedly on what is not as such interesting to *any* cognizing person, or which would be interesting only as exemplifying a special type or pattern. Cognitive interests parasitic upon one-sided, contingent, purely personal interests, are not, of course, necessarily to be *rejected* at the impersonal level; they may be *permitted*, like the individualized satisfactions and objects of satisfaction at the hedonic level, in so far as they can be subordinated to other unbiased cognitive interests, and used to give content and life to the latter. Thus it is agreed, e.g., that an interest like sex may deepen our cognitive interest in certain bodily forms, modes of behaviour, etc. etc., without thereby making such interest subservient to itself, and so destroying its 'disinterested', higher-level character. And in so far as impersonality applies itself as an ideal to the mere idea or thought-reference, it must tend also to lend special endorsement to the tendencies we listed in an earlier chapter as 'fundamental drifts' of consciousness, and to such things and features of things as are in special accord with such tendencies. Some objects, it is plain, are more naturally and more readily imaginable and thinkable than others; they more readily become objects for us, their pattern is better adjusted to our cognitive powers—points emphasized with admirable clearness by Kant in the *Critique of Judgement*, but perhaps requiring a more transcendental, more *a priori* treatment than he contrives to give. It requires, e.g., no special appeal to human idiosyncrasy to show that things seen on a background that contrasts strongly with some character they possess are more readily apprehensible as having this character than things which tone meltingly into their background. (Many principles appealed to by Gestalt psychologists have, we may note, a purely *a priori* status, and are in no sense part of an empirical psychology.)

The impersonality which applies itself to the mere idea may, however, go farther: it may *refuse* to develop the idea in a direction where it passes over into belief or disbelief. It may, that is, not merely *fail* to develop its notion of an object to a point where is involves ineluctable regularity, incorporation into a unique, indefinitely expanding, continuous fabric, and control by compulsive experience: it may *actively stop short* of this step. This active stopping short amounts to the positive *not caring* whether

THE VALUES OF WELFARE 243

what one is thinking of *is real or not*, or in caring about its reality merely as an 'idea', i.e. as the mere *possibility* of attaching one's object to a unique, indefinitely expanding fabric, fitted on to compulsive experience, *without actually so attaching it*. There is nothing unnatural in such an active stopping short: it represents *one* way of satisfying the intrinsic *nisūs* of consciousness. For the compulsions of sense constantly import an element of the unforeseen and unpredictable (and must do so to be compulsions); they frustrate the smooth fitting on of part to part or the development of them natural to conscious experience. They push us into a much 'longer circuit', a discovery of modes of linkage not at first obvious, in order to bring the new datum within the grasp of belief. Faced with such difficulties, there is a natural alternative of escape and evasion, which will satisfy *some* of our conscious drifts, and do so better than do extraneous deliverances, even if it does not satisfy *all* of them. Objects conceived *without* intrusive compulsions can obviously achieve a better rounding out, even if a more artificially limited one, than objects given in and through such compulsions. This route of evasion must, in the last instance, be impersonally unsatisfactory, as Plato and others have felt, but it may none the less win complete impersonal acceptability when associated with, and completed by, other types of approach. And it is impersonally satisfactory, further, as involving liberation from the particular compulsions of *one* contingent world, from which other thinkable beings might be free.

We arrive, therefore, at a form of interest whose impersonal character *must* render it impersonally approvable, which is at once indifferent to, or impartial between, particular non-cognitive interests and their objects, and which is also indifferent to the various compulsive deliverances so essential to a believable reality (though not to a believability untrammelled by *actual* compulsions). This kind of interest will, further, by virtue of its withdrawal from, and subordination of, the merely personal, involve an implicit aspiration, and an implicit claim, to 'speak for all', an aspiration and a claim which prescribe a peculiar process of testing, involving attempted communication, use of persuasion and mustering of reasons, consideration of counter-reasons, etc. etc. It seems plain that we have reached the kind of interest describable in a wide sense as 'aesthetic', the interest

244 VALUES AND INTENTIONS

which presses toward a certain kind of 'vision' of things, and is communicable by virtue of its detachment from the reality of what is thus envisaged, and also by its detachment from the variable, non-'visionary' wants things may happen to satisfy. This kind of interest and its objects are necessarily an object of impersonal satisfaction, and if such a satisfaction can be endorsed from a higher level, as having been true or loyal to its own requirements, of a satisfaction that is justifiable, right, reasonable, valid, etc. etc. Many of the objects of such an interest will not, however, be such as are usually called 'beautiful', and it will extend to much that has nothing to do with art.

Impersonality exercised in this region will both approve or disapprove of (i.e. be satisfied or dissatisfied by) certain satisfactions or dissatisfactions, and will also *endorse* these satisfactions, i.e. reinforce them, by approving indirectly of their *objects*. The first kind of approval is a straightforward case of *valuation*, since it is concerned with the *existence* of its object. We are glad that someone *really* delights in the look or thought of something in a disinterested manner. The latter, however, is not a straightforward case of valuation, since we may be indifferent to the object's actual existence, or to its existence as it is thought of, or as it seems to be, and may be *averse* from its realization on other, non-aesthetic grounds. It is the presence of something *to consciousness* that is important for this sort of satisfaction, not its incorporation into the fabric of reality through countless strands of binding circumstance, most of which are not there for consciousness at all. Often, too, the object, in whose consideration we delight, is not one of which existence could be predicated: it might, e.g., be a mathematical relationship. Beauty, or excellence for contemplation, or whatever else we may care to call it, is not therefore a case of value, though it is intimately connected with value. It can be predicated of that of which the contemplation is valuable, and it may also entail value in its possessor: that what is excellent for contemplation should exist, and is in this respect valuable, is, however, a synthetic, not an analytic, truth. It will, however, be convenient to speak of objects, satisfaction with which is valued, as themselves valued, and the impersonal endorsement of a purely contemplative satisfaction, as itself a case of impersonal valuation.

The basic requirements for the impersonal endorsement of the

THE VALUES OF WELFARE 245

satisfactions and objects in this region can be further seen to be threefold. We may hold, (*a*), that to be impersonally endorsed, what is contemplated must fit in with one or other of the basic drifts of consciousness, e.g. unbroken continuity, pointing up of character, etc. etc., must, in short, have the character of a possible *object* of consciousness, and not be a mere heap of disjoined elements, which either do not constitute an object or do so only in an exceedingly poor fashion. Obviously no consciousness, and no object of consciousness, can be impersonally approved, which has, owing to the defective bringing of its beams to a single focus, only imperfectly become the consciousness of anything, or the object of such a consciousness. It is plain, further, (*b*), that to be impersonally approved, what is contemplated must have its object-making characters *perspicuously*: they must be *plain* to the observer or contemplator. Much in the world is aesthetically unsatisfactory, not good for contemplation, since its constitution and character are not plainly brought out: they lie smothered in irrelevances, hidden behind obstacles, full of gaps that mar their coherence, etc. etc. If the structure of things, to be aesthetically approved, need only be *apparent*, in the negative sense of requiring no full backing of reality, it must also be *apparent* in the positive sense of being fully revealed to consciousness. Since our valuation is of a state of consciousness, and of an object only *qua* object of consciousness, it must obviously rate things more highly in proportion as consciousness is greater, in proportion, that is, as something is clearly, and not turbidly or confusedly, brought out. And this leads on naturally to a third requirement for an approvable contemplative consciousness: that what it contemplates should have its object-making features *pregnantly* or *poignantly*, not in some muted, worn-down, undistinguished fashion. What shows itself as built up in a certain manner, or as possessing a certain character, must not show this with too facile an obviousness, else it will not make us alive to itself. It must employ all devices of emphasis, contrast, variation, novelty, etc. etc., to be for us impressively what it may be in itself. Plainly, if the focus of approbation is on what promotes conscious aliveness, it must see in the merely obvious the last abysm of failure. We may now briefly consider the implications of these three fundamental requirements.

We may deal with perspicuity first. This must involve, first

246 VALUES AND INTENTIONS

of all, the *clearness of attention*, and that with some naturalness. An aesthetically approvable object must, in other words, be *arresting*, a requirement that paves the way for pregnancy and poignancy, but is not identical with the latter. It must involve, further, some progress towards *fulfilment*, for the consciousness of the make-up and character of an object becomes more perspicuous in proportion as it approximates to direct presence, i.e. to fulfilment. Obviously, all that *spring* involves is brought home to us most perspicuously when spring is there, or when it is illustrated or described with some vividness, not when our reference to it is drily analytic or symbolic. Here there is a tendency to lay stress on the fulfilments of *sense* and *fantasy*: to some, these enter by definition into the notion of aesthetic satisfaction. What is aesthetically enjoyed must, on this view, be somehow attached to sensuous deliverances, and must even stand in some relation of 'intimate fusion' with them. It is possible to define ideas in this manner, but to do so is not to conform to accepted usage, nor to the broad affinities which take us outside of the sphere of sense. For it is clear that there are ways of deploying the content of complex thought-references which involve no carrying-out in sensory or fantastic material, or only such as are irrelevant or symbolic, and yet give us an intimate sense of what those concepts cover, which must count as their 'fulfilment' quite as much as do the fulfilments of sense. And when such a fulfilment satisfies certain fundamental 'drifts' of consciousness, e.g. the drift towards smooth continuance, it may be as proper to call the resultant object 'beautiful', as when it is sensuously fulfilled. Thus certain stories are rightly said to have a beautiful construction, certain theorems follow beautifully (in no metaphorical sense) from their premisses, etc. etc. The kinds of satisfaction are so very much the same that it is arbitrary, and covertly materialistic, to classify them under different heads.

We are here brought up against the exceedingly dreary, confused disputes of traditional aesthetics, as to whether all objects of aesthetic approbation have 'meaning', and as to the extent to which such 'meaning' conditions their aesthetic worth, it being alternatively suggested that 'meaning' is merely an aesthetic drug, that merit attaches only to properties of 'sensory surface', etc. etc. Such disputes are confused, since, if 'sensory surface' means the mere raw stuff of our changing conscious references, that which

THE VALUES OF WELFARE 247

stays constant when the 'look' of things varies, it is not anything of which we can be separately conscious, and since, even if we could be conscious of it, it could not, in its brute, empirical contingency, offer points of attachment for impersonal valuation. What is contemplatively prized is necessarily an object of consciousness, and an object of consciousness is necessarily seen *as* something or other; it must show itself in this or that 'light', it must be looked at in one way or another. It is only because an object can be thus regarded, and because it provides special facilities for being so regarded, facilities which are there for everyone because springing from the very nature of conscious awareness, that it can be aesthetically approved or found beautiful. The distinction, therefore, between contemplative satisfactions which 'bring in meaning', and those which confine themselves to 'sensory surface', is by no means fundamental. It is the distinction between a fulfilled awareness which ranges *far*, perhaps dangerously far, beyond its fulfilling base, and one which is tethered *close*, perhaps timidly and trivially close, to that base. All beauty is necessarily abstract, one-sided, perspectival: it is odd that the cases in which it is least so should have been classed as 'abstract'.

The distinction between an aesthetic satisfaction which brings in 'meaning', and one which stays close to sense, has been confused, further, by the linguistic connections of the word 'meaning'. A way in which it is good to see a pattern of coloured forms, or a composed array of tones, is certainly not a 'meaning', if by a 'meaning' is meant the precise scope of reference of some well-established *word*: notoriously there are no words equal to bringing out the subtle nexus of characters brought out by a visual design or by a piece of music, and the attempt to find them results in much that is horrible and grotesque. The language of appreciation lags far behind the resources of creative expression. If, however, a 'meaning' means the scope of a particular way of looking at things, and of referring to them emptily when absent, then there is meaning even in the least representative of art-products or natural situations. The problem of 'what the flowers say' is, as Wittgenstein holds, in one sense unanswerable and delusive: there is no analogue of unspoken words behind their brilliant, scented show. In another sense, however, what they say is not doubtful: it is what, with their

248 VALUES AND INTENTIONS

endearing subtlety and richness, far exceeding our verbal discriminations, they make us feel that they are.

From the requirements of perspicuity we pass on to that of *poignancy*. Here it is all-important to stress, as mentioned previously, the deteriorating force of the obvious. It is not merely *we* who blunt our aesthetic sensibilities by hackneying nature and art: objects themselves lose their power to evoke a poignant consciousness in anyone, and with this power, their beauty. It will be long, e.g., before the Egyptian monuments suffer themselves to be enjoyed 'by moonlight', after late Victorian and Edwardian decades of vulgarizing visits: it is realistic, and not snobbish, to recognize that the same is now being done to the coach-haunted cities of Europe. The laws of fatigue and satiety hold sway in the impersonal as in the personal sphere, and they do so of right: it is absurd to deny that multiplication cheapens values, above all the refined values of contemplative appraisal. From these truths follows a *nemesis* for art: to live hag-ridden by the furies of perpetual innovation, or to sink moribund on a flowered, classical couch. If the latter course has its obvious disadvantages, the former is not without its difficulties. From the genuine discovery of new territories of experience or new presentative techniques, it must tend to pass to the mere disintegration of this or that established rule, rightly finding a new harmony and accord in the apt expression of primary disharmony and discord. That it is possible to reach valuable new experience and expression along this *via negativa* need not be doubted, but, like the flagellant's whip, it soon achieves steadily diminishing returns. The same applies to the aesthetic *approfondissement* which exploits the element of shock and pain consequent on conscious enlargement. The enhanced consciousness of an object's make-up which counts as aesthetic, cannot by its nature be wholly agreeable; it must, like the sacrifices of science and morality, entail discomfort for the natural man, its impersonal satisfactions must be blended with personal pain. It is not, therefore, mere snobbery which leads people to tread the difficult path of 'culture', and to subject themselves to the discipline of the art-gallery, or the austerities of the concert-chamber. If their state of mind is perhaps too anguished to be good, it is preferable to those who expect merely to *enjoy* works of art. The exploitation of shock is, however, only valuable if it leads to comfort at higher levels:

THE VALUES OF WELFARE   249

it cannot profitably be reiterated *ad infinitum*, nor for its own sake. Perhaps the happiest of aesthetic situations would be that of a culture strong in academic traditions, but permitting also of internal revolutions, and which exploited an experience so various as to need few innovations of mere form. European art-experience prior to 1914 was possibly in this position: we have now entered the flagellating age. It is arguable that the fallowness of mere classicism would be preferable to our present state.

Apart from being perspicuous and poignant, the objects of impersonally approved contemplative satisfactions must match one or other of those fundamental drifts of consciousness which we enumerated previously. An aesthetic object is not a special sort of object: it is merely an object that is poignantly and perspicuously what it happens to be, that announces its make-up and character notably to consciousness. Any of the features that make something, in one or other of its characters, *more* of an object for consciousness, are features relevant to aesthetic appraisal. As we are not here writing a treatise on aesthetics, it is not our task to pursue these far. Suffice it to say that aesthetic worth may be sought in a variety of directions, all equally relevant, with suitable modifications, both to science and morality: in the disengagement and pointing up of abstractions; in their redintegration into solidly unified objects; in the carrying further of pattern and theme; in the pursuit, at least, of an *appearance* of clear-cut completeness; in the profound deference to the atmosphere and character of certain wide territories of experience; in the avoidance of anomaly and inconsistency; in the suggestion of an infinitely detailed, coherent working-out characteristic of the believably real; in the avoidance of warped emphases due to powerful, non-contemplative interests; in the expression of what is universally and communicably human, etc. etc. What is distinctive of the aesthetic approach to these 'values' is the neglect of them in all situations where their presence is neither poignant nor perspicuous, and in the acquiescence in their sufficient indication rather than their complete presence. What is distinctive, too, is the willingness to pursue them separately, and even to see a merit in such separateness. There is a legitimate *vocational* emphasis even in the spheres of science and virtue, but it is always to some extent suspect, since it runs the risk of

250   VALUES AND INTENTIONS

ignoring the mutual support and requirement of the things we impersonally value. Where all that we are concerned with is the perspicuous, poignant presence of features to consciousness, quite regardless of their backing in reality, we can afford to be one-sided, rather suggesting the mutual supplementation of various aspects of the real than bringing them together in a focus which will disturb the clearness of them severally.

To what extent, and in what sense, do our views entail acceptance of 'absolute' aesthetic values, beauties which can be said to have some sort of 'objective' status over and above anyone's actual enjoyment of them? They entail not at all the existence of properties 'out there', in the sense in which weight and size are 'out there', having the extremely precise values determined by compulsive experience. In the case of the aesthetically fine, such out-thereness is doubly absurd, since the object to which it is attributed need not be actual at all, or not in the respects in which it is judged beautiful, nor need its actual realization be an object of concern. If, however, the acceptance of absolute beauties means that we may expect both ourselves and others increasingly to endorse and approve the approbation of certain objects of contemplation, and the more firmly the more closely and repeatedly we consider them in certain lights and contexts, and the more we attempt to ride clear of contemplative entanglements and of the concern with reality or unreality, and the more, lastly, we accommodate ourselves, in aesthetic argument and persuasion, to the angles from which others view objects, and to the grounds of appeal which especially count with them—then there is sense in speaking of such beauties. For the particular proceedings described are precisely those which define (though by no means trivially) attitudes which are impersonal, disinterested and purely contemplative, and the grounds of appeal to which such proceedings open our minds are all, as it were, the reverses or projections of such proceedings, while the manner in which we subordinate or co-ordinate such grounds must reflect either the manner in which such proceedings are parts of more inclusive proceedings, or lie side by side as mutually irreplaceable and different. It would only be wrong to allow such an acceptance of 'absolute beauties' to suggest a precise limiting outcome not permitted by the vague, broad tracks that lead to it. How things are to be ranked in respect of their beauty, or, what is the same,

THE VALUES OF WELFARE 251

the nature of the beauty manifest in cases so different and so differently linked, is rather to be conceived as a regulative Kantian idea of reason, or with the inspired nebulousness of the Platonic *Symposium*, than in any too definite form. The order of things arranged according to the style and degree of their beauty is something towards which, in aesthetic persuasion and argument, we increasingly draw near, but only in the sense that we inevitably lessen our differences. It would be a mistake, too, if such an acceptance of 'absolute beauties' were to make us forget the essential relevance of the best authenticated beauties to contexts and conscious lights. For it is obviously not an object as thus and thus actual, qualified or related, but an object as *thought of* or *seen* in a certain light or manner, e.g. as a characteristically Renaissance echo of the architectural forms of antiquity, that is the subject of various contemplative assessments, and the same object may, without impugning 'absoluteness', deserve the most varied assessments if seen in *different* lights or manners. Thus a wholly banal statement of fact may chance also to be a pregnantly satirical expression of banality. Important too it is to see the context of an appreciation, since (as we have seen) triteness or rarity enter into the very texture of contemplative assessments, and may, once more without impugning 'absoluteness', differ widely in different contexts. An experience or mode of presentation rare, and for that reason precious, in a Renaissance context, or to us as reliving Renaissance experience, may be banal or worthless in a contemporary frame.

To speak of 'absolute beauties' may mean, finally, that we have some obligation to realize, or seek to realize, beautiful objects without considering who, if anyone, will actually enjoy them. It is arguable that we have some obligation in this direction, even if this cannot be wholly divorced from a connection with *possible* observers or contemplators. The fine disinterestedness of constructing something that *would*, if rightly approached, afford disinterested joy to *possible* contemplators, even if, in the sad state of things, no such contemplators are in prospect, has a strain of formal nobility so exalted as to be necessarily approvable from an impersonal point of view, even if its extreme quixotism, and its appeal to egoism, may place it at the end of a long procession of more binding obligations. All this needs to be argued in more detail than is possible here.

252   VALUES AND INTENTIONS

We may also take up a stand in regard to certain 'metaphysical' views of the beautiful, to views which hold that aesthetic contemplation somehow affords us a 'deeper glimpse' into the nature of 'reality' than do science or practical life. These views are readily dismissed as confused, but we have a deep sense that, though confused, they are less superficial than their dismissal. We may contend, in fact, that, since the aesthetic attitude moves towards the *perspicuous*, there is no frame of mind other than the aesthetic in which anything can be adequately understood and enjoyed. It is in aesthetic accounts or pictures of objects that objectivity is itself perspicuous: no other approach mediates the actual sense, and actual working out, of the unity of the thing. Science abounds in claims and formulae, applicable to variously styled 'objects', most of which are neither 'cashed' nor capable of a complete 'cashing': ordinary thought, likewise, deals in objects whose detailed make-up is largely unknown. It is in aesthetic contemplation, perhaps employed on imaginary, simplified material, that we can alone fully understand what we talk about or refer to. In the same manner, it is in the aesthetic coherence of a developing theme that we have our best insight into the nature of causality: in ordinary thought and science too much remains intractably dark. And it is a commonplace that aesthetic 'reality' and 'probability' often surpass 'real' reality and probability in their carrying out of the purport of such notions: in aesthetic 'reality' no test asked for in the context is withheld, and aesthetic probabilities rest more on understandable affinities than on brute regularities of happening. To be guided by 'pictures' in science and philosophy is in many respects rightly to be deprecated, since pictures only do justice to a small range of features of what we conceive and know. It is important to realize that it is only within that range that understanding can be fully consummated, and that it is by their nearness to, or farness from, a pictorial ideal that other cases of understanding are to be reckoned such.

Our treatment calls for a final touching on the aesthetically bad or detrimental, which may be ranged under the two heads of the aesthetically feeble and the aesthetically debased. Under the former we may enumerate such weaknesses as lack of perspicuous or poignant presentation, cancellation of one presentation by another, lack of pointing or purity, loose and vague unity, etc. etc. The aesthetically feeble is not greatly to be deprecated. In its own

THE VALUES OF WELFARE 253

place and season it is essential and necessary, on principles previously argued for, if the truly poignant is not to be cheapened. Otherwise we might have to live in a world as nauseously cloying as is the prose of Walter Pater or D. H. Lawrence. It is only at the great curtains or climaxes that the aesthetically feeble is misplaced.

As opposed to the aesthetically feeble, the aesthetically debased will exhibit such faults as the pretence of poignancy attached to the commonplace or the obvious, an exaggerated unity and continuity which cheapens and sickens, a gross lack of fairness or balance in presentation, the marring of the purity of a presentation by gross irrelevances, gratification of non-contemplative interests under the guise of contemplative ones, the search for new experience through a mere violation of canons, etc. etc. The aesthetically debased is also not to be too greatly deprecated. By its contrast with the aesthetically excellent, its place in the formation and maintenance of our sensibilities must be indefeasible. It is not its presence but its multiplication that appals. If rendered aseptic by the neutral, and dominated by the fine and pure, it may be innocuous, and even amusing. It is when whole countries and epochs come under its sway, and when that sway is fixed by immense acquisitive or propagandist concerns, e.g. the Counter-Reformation, that its menace becomes alarming. At its worst, however, it is hardly one of the great evils. The love of beauty, being one of the highest and purest of goods, is also one of the most indispensable and gratuitous: its very character repels obligation. The love of the aesthetically debased barely exists as such at all, being in most cases merely an undeveloped or distorted love of the beautiful. It is *sub ratione pulchri* that the most hideous objects are fabricated and multiplied. In condemning their badness, as not in the long run successfully mediating a consciousness of the well-formed, and that not accidentally, we must remember that they do mediate it: oleographs have possibly mediated more experiences of this sort than have the paintings of Fra Angelico. It is the keeping of the way open to a better taste that is to be striven for, not the tormenting or baffling of a poor one. We must remember, too, that deep aesthetic sensibility, with its high-level evasion of practice and reality, has a more natural alliance with certain forms of high-level moral depravity than a debased taste can readily compass. This is not, however, the place

254 VALUES AND INTENTIONS

to condemn a dalliance in Tahiti or with La Guiccioli. The ground for the comparative unimportance of a misplaced aesthetic taste lies in the essentially surrogative character of the aesthetically satisfactory: the aesthetically fine, with its indifference to actual existence, is in some respects a mere hieroglyph of the absolutely good, for which existence is all-important. In beauty we see a shadow of the absolutely good but not its substance. That substance must lie, it seems clear, in the solid stuff of human consciousness and performance, not in the lines, shapes, arrangements and suggestions of variously interpreted external realities.

(III) THE VALUES OF BELIEF AND KNOWLEDGE

We now turn to a series of values standing in close relation to the various features conditioning the approvability of beliefs, which we dealt with in our third chapter. The mind *qua* believing has various consummations towards which it tends, and various paths along which it pursues these: its object is treated as fitting into a fabric indefinitely extensible, from which it will not in future extensions be extruded, but with which it will become more and more closely knitted; it is treated as having endlessly numerous, discoverable strings binding it to compulsive experience; it is not 'bracketed' in some more inclusive picture; it is placed at the end of many long vistas of continuity which we look down impartially; it is thought of as ready to be applauded and recognized by a whole host of fellow-witnesses, etc. etc. The believing mind does not, however, make of these features its values, nor need it be at all conscious of them: its interest is centred on the content to which they lead it, which lies at the *end* of the labyrinthine ways for which they furnish the winding clues. In other words, the believing mind has no primary interest in the rightness or sureness of its full beliefs, but in the *truth* they seem to mediate: it is *what is the case* that it is after, not the state of being secure about the latter. In the same manner, the believing mind, in so far as its beliefs are partial, does not make its conscious end the achievement of a nice poise among various more or less well-based inclinations: in a sense, as we saw, it projects the whole issue 'outwards'; it treats the matters which are for it basic as 'requiring', with more or less insistence, a number of alternative completions, which latter are in con-

THE VALUES OF WELFARE

sequence seen in a more or less 'likely' or 'probable' light. What the mind is after in such situations is *das Wahrscheinliche* or what looks like the truth, and it is after it in the sole hope that, if seized upon and held fast, until further evidences and experiences accumulate, it will indeed prove to *be* the truth.

The true, and its somewhat poor substitute, the likely or seemingly true, are not, however, in any sense 'values' for the believing mind: they are not things in whose *existence* it has, *qua* believing, an interest, which it seeks to produce, preserve or multiply as a man might do in the case of money, friends, power or anything else that he valued. One might indeed seek to *make* truths or make things true by altering objects in appropriate ways, but this procedure would be dogged by the countervailing disadvantage of making as many contradictories false. (One may be pardoned if, in an essentially nonsensical context, one avoids dealing with those who maintain truth to be 'timeless', and so incapable of being made or unmade.) It is plain, however, that no such proceedings would be undertaken or encouraged by those who love truth, and that the only respect we can show truth is to discover what it independently is, not to aid it to be one thing or another. Exactly the same considerations apply in the case of the likely: while there are acts by which something could be rendered more or less probable, we have *qua* seekers after the probable, no *special* interest in probabilities manufactured in this fashion.

The true and probable have in many ways a close analogy with the well-formed or beautiful, and both have, further, an analogous relation to what may be strictly called the 'valuable'. A thing whose existence or realization is wanted at the level of primary wanting, and whose conceived existence can furnish a *reason* for realizing or enjoying that existence at the 'cool' level of wanting—a reason having its source in primary wants and being ready to develop into the latter, but not necessarily involving such wants when it coolly 'determines' us—may be said to have 'value' for us, and impersonal value if it has undergone the sifting definitory of an impersonal attitude. The feature in virtue of which it has value, has been said by us, in a perhaps loose but intelligible phrase, to be *a* value. A feature of things to whose existence or non-existence we are indifferent, or which we would as lief see supplanted by its contrary, cannot be said to be a value for us, even if it happens to be the object of a deep interest, perhaps even an object fitting the requirements of a deep-set *impersonal* interest. Now the interest in the things that we call well-formed or beautiful is an interest *in* looking at them or *in* contemplating them, whether they exist or not, and whether or not they have the properties that they seem to have. The peculiar appeal such objects have for us, and may, on occasion, even be 'seen' to have—the beautiful, like the valuable, may contribute to what appears 'out there'—is not therefore rightly denominated a 'value', though its connections with interest may be said to make it 'value-like'. At the same time, it presupposes a genuine value in the appreciative experiences in which we enjoy it—we must, we saw, care about the existence of these if we love the well-formed—though the experiences which have value cannot themselves be said to have a jot of beauty. In much the same manner, an object or state of affairs, fitted by our belief into the seamless fabric of reality, has an appeal *like* that of the valuable, though not rightly classified as such, since the interest which corresponds to it is indifferent to the precise character of what is thus fitted into reality, and as readily satisfied by its contradictory or its contrary. It is an interest in the authentically real as such, and only contingently connected with what happens to be real. This peculiar appeal or interest may also, on occasion, present itself to feeling as a 'dignity' out there in the object—the precise character of this dignity is felt when we dwell on the *authenticity*, the complete *genuineness*, of the real and true, and the approach to a similar authenticity in the probable. The words 'real' and 'true' have, therefore, an approbative as well as an epistemological force: they not only serve to 'place' a content in a certain infinitely expanding, compulsively shaped setting, and perhaps to express the consciousness of it as so placed—'true' and 'probable' can be used performatively or recordingly—but they also express our satisfaction, and sometimes our felt satisfaction, in doing so. The dignity-aspect of the real, true and probable is not then properly classed as a value, but only as a sort of reflection or simulacrum of the valuable, since it lacks an essential relation to 'existence-concern'. Its being such a reflection or simulacrum leads, however, logically, though not indeed formally, to the discovery of value in another quarter, in the various states of mind in which some-

THE VALUES OF WELFARE 257

thing reveals itself, or seems to reveal itself, as real, true or probable. The man who loves the authentically real or true, and whose love extends even to its plausible shadow, is driven inescapably to set store by states of mind in which the true or probable *declares* itself, or appears to declare itself to some person. And this 'setting store' is a genuine case of valuation, since he must want such declarations to *be*, and to be more abundantly, and he must also want to *make them be*.

If we now ask why values attaching to mental communion with the true or probable should be *impersonally* approvable, the answer, or rather array of reason-giving answers, does not lie far. The pursuit of the true involves, as we have seen, an anticipatory deference to future compulsions, and such deference necessarily involves, at least as far as its scope extends, the abnegation of all other particular interests: we must judge as true or factual *whatever* compelling experience forces us to judge, and not what we should like, though such judgement may of course be the immediate prelude to realizing what we like. Even if the deference to compulsive experience had no intrinsic impersonal appeal, but were solely an instrumental need (as it undoubtedly in part is), or a fanatical urge no more worthy of impersonal regard than the love of a particular person or cause, there would still be something impersonally admirable in the thoroughgoing subordination of all other interests to this. It would at least have loosened the hold of 'particular passions', even if only in service to a ruling passion of the same sort. The deference to compulsive experience springs, however, from something more than a particular ruling passion, since it exists not alone, but only in close conjunction with a number of other completing endeavours, which *together* make up what may be called our interest in reality.

For compulsive experience is, for belief and knowledge, not merely a harsh intrusion into the smooth continuum of our life, but an element to be wrought into an indefinitely extended continuum in which we and our thoughts will occupy only an infinitesimally little place. Compulsive experience is, for belief and knowledge, the point at which we touch those infinite elements of reality which lie outside us and the narrow range of *our* causality, where we experience *their* causality. And not only is the system of objects which compulsive experience is taken as revealing, thought of as infinitely more *extensive* than the range

I

258   VALUES AND INTENTIONS

of our own bodily and mental action, it is also thought of as infinitely richer in characters, patterns and virtues. It is only by constant contact with the whole system in which our narrow being is set that that being can hope to be expanded, refreshed and fructified. From the impersonal point of view, it would be grossly biased to prefer the small range of qualities, forms and virtues that are narrowly our own, to the indefinite range of qualities, forms and virtues that are thought of as present in the real world, to which compulsive experiences with their shock of novelty are thought to be the door. And in the continuously constructed picture of reality, other persons play the same sort of insignificant role as ourselves: for them, too, it would be absurd to prefer the narrow range of being within them, to the incalculable wealth of being 'beyond their doors'. The compulsions out of which the vision of reality grows are thought, moreover, to involve analogous compulsions for others as for ourselves, so that fundamentally the same vision emerges out of the compulsive experiences of all persons. The deference to compulsive experience is therefore a deference to what is *common*, and this yields an additional reason for finding such deference impersonally satisfactory. But where compulsive experience is *not* thought of as mediating access to a systematic totality infinitely more extensive, powerful and rich in character than our own, or than anyone's, conscious existence, there is little impersonal approvability in deferring to it. It is unimportant to devote much time to penetrating insignificant corners of reality which give small indication of patterns dominating large segments of the whole.

And if we turn from the true to the probable, it is clear why the mental following of the probable should be impersonally approved. For the probable has its roots in compulsive experience, and has the same openness to unbounded, ambient reality that we saw in the last paragraph to be impersonally commendable. And the probable extends thought along the lines of the analogous and the continuous, and diverges as little as possible from the affinities which declare themselves most plainly to thought: in this it, like the beautiful, presents consciousness with the most readily comprehensible of objects, only comprehensible in a manner satisfactory to thought, and not necessarily displaying itself perspicuously in unbacked surface-show. That the consciousness of an object so unified should satisfy impersonally

THE VALUES OF WELFARE 259

goes without saying, since, like the enjoyment of beauty, it represents a satisfaction necessarily shared by all capable of being conscious at all. The probable also, as we saw, follows lines of impartiality and equity. One piece of evidence, equally assured, is not to be preferred to another like piece of evidence, one alternative covering a certain range of realizable difference or frequency of realization is not to be preferred to another alternative spanning a like range of difference or frequency of realization, etc. etc. This sort of equity is not only approved as representing a basic tendency of the believing consciousness: it recommends itself to our impersonal judgement in an even more direct manner. For nothing but some personal interest irrelevant to belief or disbelief, or an exercise of arbitrary choice, or some other accidental factor, could move us to treat differentially evidences and alternatives having such precise equivalence as regards the measurable aspects of what they cover.

The general pursuit of the true and the probable having been thus shown to be impersonally approvable, we may canvas in more detail the various typical values that it covers. These lie along the three directions of conformity to the real, as guaranteed by the compulsively given, preservation of continuity or 'synechism', and strict observance of equity and impartiality in believing. It will be our task to consider each of these in turn.

As regards the first, we may recall the fact that there are testing compulsions which do not stem from the deliverances of sense, but from other quite different types of experience. Not only our observational contacts compel us to frame our beliefs in a certain mould, but also activities having nearer or remoter analogies with such contacts. Thus the addressing of appropriate questions to ourselves and others often suffices to elicit those expressions of practical and emotional knowledge considered in previous chapters, in which we are able to tell without investigation just what we want, or how we are emotionally inclined. These displays of practical and emotional knowledge are not merely usefully informative and directive, whether to ourselves or others: they also have value as directly revealing drifts which, though shaping a man's thought and behaviour, are yet far from making their presence evident. In the same manner there is a form of compulsion deeply and uniquely valuable on account both of its difficulty and its rarity, which we encounter whenever

260 VALUES AND INTENTIONS

we reflect upon, and endeavour to characterize, our immediately past experiences, and this not merely in categories ready to hand and familiar (then I thought of X, and made up my mind to do Y, etc. etc.), but by way of novel affinities and analogies, generally with objects and processes in the public world—'the slow, dead heave of the will', etc. etc.—which not only link the impalpable with the palpable, but bring the otherwise private into the sphere of the public. Finally, there is a form of compulsion that may be called 'notional', which occurs where one's packed understanding of something is felt to *require*, i.e. to compel, a certain analysis or definition, or a certain working out of wider implications—a cube, e.g., compels us to assign to it only twelve edges—and is also felt to reject certain other circumscriptions or implications as unacceptable or inadequate. This form of compulsion has at all times practically compelled philosophers to describe it in terms of *intuition*: though the condensed understanding of some notion may not be like a direct acquaintance of sense, both incline our further acts of analysis and detailed characterization in a closely similar manner. All these types of compulsion represent for belief and knowledge 'windows opening on a wider world', and have accordingly a high impersonal value, as opposed to remaining within the narrow bounds of one's established ideas or judgements.

It is clear, further, that we must find in the sphere of ideas and beliefs a kind of value akin to that of the *poignant* in the sphere of aesthetic appreciation. A compulsive encounter must impersonally be valued, not in so far as it merely accords with, or repeats what we should confidently have expected, but in so far as, without shattering the established mould of our reasoned confidence, it yet offers us something which no established category or concept or law readily fits, or which even forces us to modify or develop established categories or concepts or laws. The discovery of the Western hemisphere and the Pacific, the Michelson–Morley experiment, the Würzburg discovery of imageless thought, the mathematical discovery of irrationals or transfinite numbers, the philosophical changes of perspective associated with Descartes, Berkeley, Kant or Wittgenstein: all these are examples of cognitive encounters to which the highest impersonal value attaches on account of the revolutionary widenings they involve. Obviously the merely novel involves a

THE VALUES OF WELFARE 261

less serious widening than the profoundly revisionary: Captain Cook is not to be compared with Darwin.

The value of a cognitive encounter, though absolute and impersonal, is yet obviously contextual: what represents a revolution at one moment of time may be a mere commonplace at another, what is for one man a momentous step may be a routine development for another, etc. etc. We may stress, too, that the importance of a cognitive step does not depend on its ultimate acceptability or its absolute truth: while we may approve less of an insight which ultimately breaks down and proves unreliable, than of another which maintains itself longer, yet we may also, in virtue of a vast *apparent* step forward, prefer the former to the latter. The thought-revolutions initiated by Freud and Marx and many others represented vastly valuable cognitive steps, even if, for hindsight, they may seem to have darkened many issues. Contact with the real is important mainly because it is *stretching*: where a stretch depends on an error, that error too becomes impersonally valuable. We may stress lastly the value of the element of hardship, even of discomfort and pain, not only in widened insight, but in the whole process of pursuing it. The endless difficulties involved in all genuine research, the constant sacrifice of personal preconceptions, the resigned acceptance of theoretic collapses: all these are to be admired in virtue of their very impersonality, their subordination of goals attractive to the natural man to ends that attract only at a disengaged level.

From the values attendant on cognitive contact, or seeming contact, with the enlarging irruptions of an infinite, ambient world, we turn to the values attendant on the mind's successful subordination of such irruptions to its own reductive simplicity, its success in making any part of what it cognizes depart as little as possible from the pattern of the rest, and particularly from what borders upon it, so as everywhere to have the least suddenness and least sharpness in such transitions as obtain. These endeavours have been traditionally gathered together under the general aim of the 'coherent', though this term has varied in sense from the mere absence of formal contradiction at one end of the scale to the most rigorous pattern of all-ways entailment at the other. We in our usage have extended it to cover all the lines of non-rigorous and plausible continuation that our thought inventively follows, and through which it can be said to be intent on a

262 VALUES AND INTENTIONS

theme or object. Impersonally we value all such endeavours, and we value their success and its attendant satisfaction, in so far as they represent the defining *métier* or function of the conscious mind, a thing that must be wholly constant whoever we are, and whatever we may busy ourselves with, the side of our life impersonally sharable *par excellence*.

It is clear, however, that this synechistic side of our mind and its value stands diametrically opposed to the deferential side we have just been studying. Where the latter seeks the extraneously irruptive, the former seeks to explain and minimize it: where the one craves the unexpected, the other searches for the expected, etc. etc. On reflection, it is plain that we have here a case of a tension of opposites working towards a harmonious result. For if, as we saw in the last paragraph, an irruption is valuable for its stretching, enlarging function, this really means the exchange of a narrower for a much farther-going synechism, and just so synechism is sought after for its explanatory, simplifying power, its ability to resolve what appeared as irruptive surds into disguised illustrations of some subtler order. We have once more something analogous to aesthetic poignancy: if an irruptive fact is worth knowing in so far as it *largely* supplements or *largely* disturbs some existing balance of thought and belief, so an exercise of reductive synechism is to be esteemed in so far as it effectively masters a large supplementation, or achieves equilibrium, as by some inwardly regulating mechanism, after a large cognitive disturbance. There is nothing astonishing in all this. Obviously we must *realize* the presence of continuity in the most profound manner, not when it shows itself in the affinity of the obviously like to like, but rather when it leaps forth among things apparently alien, disparate and discrepant. We have most of a coherent object, and most accordingly of the consciousness of an object, when what threatened to be least one has triumphantly 'weathered' this threat.

It is not necessary that we should here enumerate all the differing types of synechism, nor compare their resultant values. It is enough to say that there are values accruing to the loose coherence of descriptive and historical truth, which increase according as material is marshalled to yield answers to definite questions, or subsumed under a limiting number of guiding points of view, and according as various seeming alternatives can

THE VALUES OF WELFARE 263

be seen to be ruled out or rendered difficult of entertainment. It is seen at the opposite pole in the tightly entailed coherence of a system which, remaining rigidly within the space defined by its meagre base of notions and axioms, none the less contrives to pirouette marvellously on the spot, quite disguising its cramped limits by the variety of the feats it does within them. And it is seen lastly in the relaxed, yet not chattily relaxed, coherence of a philosophical work like the present, where the unifying principles and points of view are never simple reformulations of an identical content, and yet shade into one another, and introduce one another like members of the same family, and whose value is at a maximum where a small step precipitates a considerable dialectical turnover or change of perspective. If it be asked which of these modes of synechism is the best, the answer must be that their difference defines different types of inquiry, and that each is the best 'in its own particular way'. And the best policy in regard to all of them would be one of considered fairness, which did not allow the charms of a certain but immobile coherence to prejudice it against coherence of a 'woollier', more genuinely inferential type, nor to value the bringing together of contents that are 'really different' above the perpetual transformation of a content that remains 'really the same'.

The mention of 'fairness' leads on to the third class of cognitive values whose impersonal sanction is peculiarly obvious, those attaching to unprejudiced, unbiased or impartial thinking. Such a requirement assumes a host of specific forms: we must not arbitrarily prefer one sensory channel to another or one personal observer to another—preferences must be based on such things as the range of differences revealed, tallying with other sources, etc. etc.; we must not arbitrarily prefer one type of explanation and its supporting evidences to another; we must not arbitrarily prefer one deductive base of definitions and axioms to another; we must not arbitrarily emphasize one line of philosophically relevant affinity at the expense of all others, etc. etc. Here as elsewhere there may be a relaxation of the requirements of justice for what may be called 'vocational' reasons. If you represent one one-sided emphasis or exaggeration, for whose exposition you have some aptitude, I may balance it by another one-sided exaggeration which comes natural to me, etc. etc., so that the

264   VALUES AND INTENTIONS

final result as disseminated abroad will be impartial and equitable. All this justifies a certain amount of theoretical *parti pris* with one's tongue in one's cheek. The requirement of fairness merges into that of paying preponderant heed to what is acknowledged in one's contemporary and perhaps local *orbis terrarum*, while not ignoring that which only seems credible to a few. This last is a pressing obligation, since logical, scientific, historical and philosophical heresies often hold in themselves the germs of revolutionary world views, able and fit to form new communions of belief.

From the consideration of the values of belief and knowledge, we pass on to glance briefly at the opposing disvalues and evils: these we may list hastily as ignorance, error, confusion, vagueness, incoherence, blind belief, internal contradiction, irrelevance, prejudice, etc. etc. Intuitively we at once doubt whether any of these is to be reckoned among the *great* evils. Instrumentally it may be disastrous to be ignorant or mistaken in matters connected with one's interests or welfare, and it may be exceedingly unjust to be denied knowledge freely available to others, etc. etc., but all this does not make an ignorant or mistaken or muddled or self-contradictory view of things an evil comparable either to pain, moral badness or the doing or suffering of injustice. Especially is this the case when a view liable shortly to break down in the face of new facts rejoices for the time in its own limited coherence, and provides an explanatory framework into which all things may be intelligibly fitted. The states of mind it engenders may be judged superior to those involving too many injections of unassimilable truth. The Aristotelian-Catholic world view, the encyclopaedic 'enlightenment' of the eighteenth century, even the unstable synthesis of the British nineteenth century, were perhaps preferable to the 'truer' knowledge of our own age, where no one makes sense of more than a fragment, where intuitions are systematically flouted without inducing the comforts of higher-level understanding, and where large segments of our beliefs, especially on scientific matters, are completely blind. We would seem here to have another case of the asymmetry of the good and the bad. The penetration of knowledge and belief being amongst the highest of conceivable goods, on account of the immense widening which they alone can give, are not balanced by great countervailing evil. To be ignorant of much is to suffer

THE VALUES OF WELFARE   265

no injurious limitation, and error and muddle are far from being
signally bad, since they are mainly frustrated attempts to achieve
truth. Only when we consider epistemic evils from the standpoint
of *justice* is their evil salient: only the meagrest good can be
achieved, and great evils will be necessarily incurred, if I remain
ignorant or misguided on matters essential to my fleshly or my
spiritual welfare. It is one of the most unforgivable of injustices
wantonly to deprive men of knowledge freely available to others,
or to keep them misinformed on matters that they may, for their
own vital purposes, claim to know. Such aspects of epistemic
evil will, however, concern us later.

(IV) THE VALUES OF PERSONAL TRANSCENDENCE

Having dealt with the values of satisfaction and dissatisfaction,
of the contemplation of the well- or ill-formed, of the encounters
with and circumscription of the real, we now pass to a fourth
class of values whose impersonal standing is particularly clear:
those pertaining to states and activities of mind which *transcend
the division among persons*, which in one way or another become
joined or mixed with the satisfactions and endeavours of other
persons. Such joining or mixing may go no farther than knowing
about or understanding the mental positions and attitudes of
others, it may go farther into various forms of participation or
entering into such states, or it may consist in having various sorts
of endeavours connected with the inner life and inner attitudes
of others, those, e.g., expressive of respect, love or benevolence,
which constitute the minimization of personal division rather
than an aggravation of it. When such division is deepened, we
shall expect to find the *dis*values peculiar to the sphere we are
considering.

The foundation of all these values and disvalues is not at all
obscure. Values, as we saw, have an impersonally approved status
when they are such as necessarily to keep and strengthen their
hold on a man in proportion as he seeks to rise above the contingencies of his personal position, to cherish only such things
as *must* tend to be cherished by everyone. Now everyone who
endeavours to rise above the contingencies of personal position
must of necessity admire the performances which are, from at
least *some* points of view, cases of rising above the contingencies

I*

266 VALUES AND INTENTIONS

of personal position, which involve a difficult entry into wholly novel territories of experience, and these not merely imaginary, and so involving the mere extension and reduplication of self, but *real ones*, involving extraneous and compulsive enlargements of spirit. That such transcendence of the personal merely exchanges one case of contingency for another, that its altruism is no more than a shifted selfishness, is of course evident: plainly the only genuine transcendence of the personal would be one that transcended *all* contingencies of personal position, which retained them only in permissive form, which had achieved the untrammelled openness of a free variable. Not all points of value would, however, accrue to the credit of such an open transcendence, as opposed to one that exchanged the narrowness of self for some other, merely different narrowness. For an unbounded transcendence, a pure 'selflessness', being merely abstract and notional, must always have something empty and easy about it: it must multiply and extend the self. It will seldom achieve the difficult enlargement of the *amitié particulière*, attained best when the positions to which a shift is made are extremely alien. It can be deeply valuable only when representing a sort of free fringe added to this last, an exercise in general selflessness given serious meaning by the more difficult real substitutions of which it represents the extension. From an impersonal standpoint, it is plain that values of personal transcendence will be high in proportion to the completeness with which the division among persons is bridged, and according to the difficulty of such bridging. These factors will to some extent weigh against each other, and there will be cases where an easy bridging will be preferable to one difficult and painful, in virtue of its sheer completeness, while there will be cases where an exceedingly incomplete bridging of personal gulfs will be precious on account of its extreme hardship. Here, as elsewhere, an element of the ascetic, of the embrace of pain and difficulty for the sake of the effort and activity it evokes, enters into the constitution of our impersonal values.

The first sort of value of personal transcendence may be held to attach to the mere knowledge of (i.e. approvable and not to be refuted belief in) the existence of other minds. Our knowledge that there are other conscious beings about us, active, not only in ways manifest to us, but in ways involving such things as

THE VALUES OF WELFARE 267

conscious clearness or obscurity, fulfilment or non-fulfilment of idea, etc. etc., which are necessarily unmanifest to the outside observer, has a value obviously higher than that of any other kind of knowledge, because it involves the overcoming of a profounder predicament. Our beliefs concerning the way things look or feel to others involve an exercise in extrapolation, as do most of our other beliefs: we *fit on* to what can be distinguished as physical, and displays itself to our senses, other matters, not naturally classed as bodily, nor open to observation, which are felt to *assort well* with such physical matters, and to continue their pattern, whether such assortment refers back to our own experience in the past, or presents itself as a not previously experienced case of appropriateness or affinity. What is peculiar about the kind of extrapolation involved is that it is, by its nature, incapable of complete fulfilment. We may reliably hold that other people's conscious orientations (in their full inwardness) exist, we may reliably determine *what* they are, but we cannot be said to reflect on, or take note of, or advert to, those conscious orientations *themselves*, all of which phrases connote neither more nor less than a necessary defect in fulfilment. The extrapolation involved is not wholly unlike the extrapolation to the remote in time and space, or to the minute in physical theory, for there too fulfilment is denied us. The remote and the minute are, however, continuous with what is present to sense, and it is not absurd to suppose ourselves tricked out with extended faculties which might bare them to our gaze. The difficulty in reflecting upon, or in taking note of, or in adverting to, the conscious orientation of another is that it seems that this would involve bringing it into the charmed circle of our own conscious orientations, in making it not another's, but *our own*. For though it is not the same thing to be consciously intent upon X, and to advert reflexly to this intention, yet the second intention in some sense builds upon the first: it is like the same diagram seen in a more complex perspective. It is well known that these difficulties created the labyrinth in which the genius of Wittgenstein strayed bemused for untold years, sometimes inclining to a solipsism so absolute as to swing over into a pure realism, sometimes inclining to a publicity so stringent as to threaten all talk of private experience.

The predicament which creates the labyrinth is, however, both trivial and profound. It is trivial because it exploits the mere

268 VALUES AND INTENTIONS

force of a negation, the thought of the complete *absence* of the 'togetherness' present in all conscious experience, and manifest only through its variability. All things in one experience have a discoverable bearing on one another, and form a 'whole' of some sort, if only a class or assemblage: the subjective correlate of this 'whole' is a unitary awareness or act of consciousness. To form the idea of something in *another's* experience is then merely to form the idea of something *not* having any degree of this 'togetherness' with *these* things of which there is now *this* consciousness, and which are all more or less closely assembled together in this single field. The thought of this negation is, however, not one formed by any slow psychological process, but is present in our recognition of the *variably close* assembling of all we are aware of. In being aware of this, we have also the thought of a *limit* where all such assembling fades out altogether, where the consciousness of things falls completely *apart*. This thought involves, however, with little more than a change of emphasis, the complete impossibility of *fulfilling* its own content, for it is self-contradictory to have *disjoined* objects or states of consciousness held *together* in one surveying or enjoying regard.

The difficulty of the thought is increased when one reflects that everything *but* the disjunction of persons can be fulfilled: whatever I think of 'someone else' as experiencing, i.e. as *disjoined* from this experience, I can *ipso facto* think of *myself* as experiencing, i.e. as *not* so disjoined, only *not* the disjunction which separates another person's experiences from these ones. I always therefore seem to be on the verge of understanding something, and yet infinitely removed from it. The difficulty is further increased by the thought of the possibly *lasting character* of the division, its essential *parallelism*: *these* experiences are now disjoined from some *others*, which may be continuous among each other, just as *these* are, but however far they are extended in either direction, the disjunction may be thought of as obtaining. Hence it is not as if what is cut off from *these* objects and *these* experiences is something transitory and paltry: it is a whole possible *world* of experience, infinite in its range of objects and possible duration, and to think, as we do think, of many such minds, is to think of many such worlds. There is, however, nothing to prevent us from thinking of these separate lines of experience as *converging*, or as *intersecting* at this point or that,

THE VALUES OF WELFARE

or as *debouching* in some common stream, and these possibilities show the triviality of the whole difficulty. Such confluences will, however, altogether fail to resolve our predicament, since the confluent experiences cease to be disjoined, and so fail to fulfil the notion of disjunction. Brahman, at the close of a world-period, may remember together all he previously felt and thought in separate creatures: what he will not, however, recapture is the previous separateness of these experiences. Turn it as we may, the predicament remains trivial, however, since the unfulfillable character of a reference to conscious disjunction rests on the content of what it intends, and since it would be a bad begging of the question to reject a notion indispensable and intelligible for not satisfying a test that it itself excludes.

But though thus trivial, as resting on no more than a negation, the thought of another's experience involves a profound step, since it is a thought which, though formed by everyone, and necessary to the developed consciousness of self and the world, yet represents what even the humblest consciousness feels to be a difficult extension, a gnostic leap, a venture of meaning into an interior where eyes and feet cannot follow. It is philosophers, not ordinary people, who see *nothing* strange and difficult in our undoubted knowledge of other minds. And as being thus hard to know, the knowledge that there are or may be other minds around us, in a sense that need not and cannot be fully illustrated or exhibited, represents something profoundly valuable from an impersonal point of view. It is an immensely significant, because not inescapable achievement, on which the *full* development of our impersonal references and performances depends. That it is a considerable exercise of our conscious life, though rooted in our essential conscious nature, becomes plain when we reflect on the many schizoid and psychopathic personalities who perhaps never really rise to it, and on the fact that a major philosopher like Wittgenstein, whose whole thought revolved around the difficulties of self-transcendence, perhaps did not make it.[1]

From the value which attaches generally to the recognition of other minds, we pass to the values attaching to particular cases of such knowledge. It is not hard to see that value will increase with the difficulty and novelty of our knowledge of others: the

[1] This remark is based, not merely on inferences from Wittgenstein's writings, but on elusive personal impressions.

270 VALUES AND INTENTIONS

harder and stranger it is to know someone, the more such knowledge overleaps interpersonal barriers, and the greater the consequent value. In general, it is true that the more *unlike* the contents and workings of some mind to our own, the greater the task it sets our understanding, and the more impersonally satisfactory, i.e. the more absolutely valuable, must the achieved understanding prove. But there will be value, too, in the discovery of profound likeness transcending personal differences, especially in circumstances where such likenesses are not to be expected, or provide relief from pervasive unlikenesses that frustrate rather than stimulate. There is only a superficial contradiction in all this: as Aristotle says, in discussing whether nourishment is by the like or the unlike, it is the unlike that nourishes us, but it must become like to do so. If this entails the declining worth of an understanding that has become too facile, this also is in accord with our ordinary judgements.

The value of knowing the mind of others will depend further on the degree of penetration of that knowledge. The knowledge that is mainly of the behaviour in which mind shows itself, though pointing naturally to the orientations which complete it and are not really separate from it—as we saw, the inner state 'condenses' what external behaviour 'expands'—yet penetrates less far into another's mind than a knowledge that also seizes the way things look from the other's viewpoint, which apprehends them in *his* personal, not a neutral perspective. In the same way, a knowledge that is merely 'knowledge that', remote, discursive application of concepts to things not even present in surrogate, yields place in penetration to what may be called 'knowledge how', the imaginative and sympathetic grasp of the way things seem to the other person. I penetrate far into your 'inner life' if I realize, not only that you saw through my deception, but that there seemed to you to be a mocking undertone in my voice, that my eyes seemed to swivel in a calculating manner, etc. etc., and if I not only experience the condensed significance of such words, but can also expand it into suitable actions, pictures, gestures, emotions, etc., and contract them back into ever-richer concentrations. The words 'realize' in varying combinations—'realize what it is to do . . .', 'realize what it is to be . . .', 'realize what it is for it to be the case that . . .', etc. etc.—are the best verbal expression of this perpetual oscillation between expansion and contraction. We

THE VALUES OF WELFARE 271

may here note that the values of personal penetration are not confined to cases where the life penetrated is actual, nor even to cases where it is believed to be actual. There may be wonderful extensions of consciousness to types of life not really enjoyed by other conscious beings, and representing no more than the inspired stretchings of a man's own mind. We may 'commune' with multiplied Messianic and Bodhisattvic figures, with deities having the awful 'otherness' of the Thugs' Kali or of Kierkegaard's Jehovah, etc. etc. There are likewise valuable 'communions' with characters of fiction, whose surprising but logical conduct may stretch us more than the behaviour of those among whom we move.

The values of personal transcendence spill over, further, into the values of all such things, real or imaginary, as enjoy the enlivening regard of a great multitude of persons: in busying ourselves with them, we as it were enter upon a shared life with others. This is the rational basis of the often debased store set upon the historic, the well-known, the contemporary, the fashionable, etc., which we all recognize in practice: even the Ideas had the additional distinction for Plato of being πολυθρυλητὰ, much talked about. If there is something paltry and shamefaced about these values, this depends mainly on the petty and dissolving character of the groups on which they depend, and which we forget when we feel them. Being creatures of time and place, we should perhaps not seek entirely to disown our predicament. We may here mention, too, the values set on objects of other than purely cognitive concern by great 'publics' of various sorts: what is admired, wished for, practically pursued, etc., by many, becomes *pro tanto* of *some* impersonal consequence. That this consequence wilts before the greater consequence of what must appeal to the greatest of 'publics', i.e. those who have truly abnegated 'self', will not destroy the impersonal status of even the humblest of 'publicity values' in their own time and place. Honourable fame may not be an exalted value, but to love it is no infirmity of noble mind.

If there is value, from an impersonal standpoint, in ideas, belief and knowledge which concern other minds, there will be still more value attaching to various emotional and practical attitudes to other minds, which embody something of the spirit of impersonality. Such attitudes will not be negative or hostile ones,

272 VALUES AND INTENTIONS

e.g. attitudes of malevolence, envy, contempt, anger, cruelty, etc., for all such attitudes are in essence partial: they mete out to the other something unwelcome which is not meted out to the self. There are of course attitudes of so-called self-hatred, self-contempt, self-torment, etc. etc., and there may be moments at which they form part of an attitude of disgusted malevolence towards persons at large. There remains, however, an inherent anomaly and absurdity in such self-enmity; it is only *as if*, or from one point of view, that we are thus self-hostile and self-divided, and it is not this divided attitude we mete out to those whom we authentically hate. It is clear that hostile attitudes among persons both feed upon and produce disagreements, even if this may become obscure in distorted and marginal cases. It is because you like what I do not like, do what I do not do, or at least seem to tolerate what I cannot tolerate, e.g. your appearance or manner, that I hate you, and this hatred blossoms into a wide range of further differences, e.g. stopping you from doing what you intend to, doing to you what you do not like, etc. etc. Impersonality is, however, an attitude intent upon agreement, and upon agreement that can, moreover, only with difficulty and wilfully be withstood. If its whole trend is towards sweeping aside contingent agreements, it will be much more towards sweeping aside and submerging contingent disagreements. Sympathy, as Adam Smith logically put it (though the logic is not formal), is inherently sympathetic to sympathy, and antipathetic to antipathy, and impartiality or impersonality is merely the grown-up child of sympathy. Inimical or anti-attitudes to others, whether based on knowledge or not, are therefore in principle such as impersonality must discourage or exclude. Their enmity perverts to greater division the bridging knowledge they contain. Non-inimical or pro-attitudes, *per contra*, are correspondingly such as impersonality, all else being equal, must approve, since they involve no conflict either in their application to a man's own self or to others. It is the varieties of personal pro-attitude that must next be considered. We may distinguish Respect, Benevolence and Love.

In the respect for persons we have a largely negative deference before what is realized to be a complete other world, one with its own sun, stars, etc., all personally stressed and interpreted, with drifts and trends peculiar to itself, with its own possibilities of nullity and anguish, and with the mysteriousness attaching to its

THE VALUES OF WELFARE 273

essential inaccessibility and facultative infinity. Another person, as conceived by those capable both of thinking and surmounting the gulf between *these* experiences (of mine) and those (which can never be mine) is essentially an awful and mysterious object, one which exacts from us, even in its most commonplace expressions, the sort of half-comprehending reverence that religion accords to its God. It is the sort of reverence that is merely absurd on naturalistic or behaviouristic or solipsistic suppositions: there is simply no reason why one finite part of the one world, or of the one experience, should be infinitely respectful of another. The true consequences of eccentric philosophical doctrines concerning other persons is not to be found in the personal kindness of those who profess these, but in determined totalitarian ruthlessness. The respect for persons rests and must rest on thoroughly metaphysical foundations, on the acceptance of a ghostly society each of whose members is always a noumenon for the other. Wittgenstein somewhere said that men might be as considerate of other men, whether they were realists, solipsists, idealists or whatever, suggesting thereby the nullity of such philosophical distinctions. By this dictum he really only showed the impervious amiability of his own character.

The characteristic policy followed by respect is, as we said, one of deference: its line is to *inhibit* or *lame* the endeavours of the conscious person, so as not to impede the expression of the endeavours of *others* in a common world. Respect shows itself too in a *delimitation* of activity, so that the activities of others may, within similar limits, enjoy free play. From pedestrians who avoid jostling each other in the street, to conscientious persons who avoid unduly influencing each other's minds, we have differing forms of the same fundamental attitude, impersonally approvable because itself moving towards impersonality, and constituting a sort of subjective rudiment of what will afterwards concern us as justice. At present we are not considering the value of the actual delimitation of spheres of rights, but the value of the respect that inspires it, and its value not for the individuals who profit by the respect, but for the individual who has it, and who in having it transcends the limits of his narrow standpoint and interests. The value of such respect will of course increase according to the variety of ways in which it is manifest, whether as a practically operative trend, a trend enriched by emotionality and feeling, a

274   VALUES AND INTENTIONS

trend which has left a value-deposit behind it with power to move to decision, etc. etc. And it will, of course, be increased in value to the extent that it is free from contingent narrowness, from a limitation, e.g. to human as opposed to animal conscious beings, males as opposed to females, members of certain castes or classes as opposed to 'lesser breeds', etc. etc., and if, while deferring to the infinite and noumenal in each conscious person, it none the less performs *additional* obeisances to such approvable qualities as wisdom, aesthetic taste and the moral qualities that will concern us later. It is the respect for personal otherness which is, however, most fundamental, and this, while not vitiated by limitations of a casual, transient character such as ignorance, lack of imagination, religious dogma, etc., will be gravely vitiated if limited in a fully aware manner, certain sorts of conscious beings being deeply respected and others not at all. Such a corruption will occur even if respect is limited to cases of approvable qualities such as knowledge, benevolence, etc. Respect for the 'whole world' concentrated in each conscious person is *presupposed* by the respect for various excellent qualities, and not *vice versa*, and beside the immensity that this 'world' encompasses, and the ready possibility of frustrating *all* that it aspires to, the special claims of knowledge, virtue, etc., can seem nothing but petty. The various holy persons of history who have gone farthest in their other-regardingness, have been least willing to confine their regard to the worthy.

From respect we pass on to positive benevolence, a 'bridging' attitude, or range of bridging attitudes, manifest in the endeavour to give other people what they want and what will satisfy them, and also in the endeavour to promote in others what are taken to be approvable qualities, e.g. knowledge, aesthetic cultivation, etc. We are again considering such benevolence only as an attitude which represents something valuable, because self-transcending, in the life of the benevolent individual, and not on account of any benefits accruing through it to others. Such benevolence will obviously have increased value on a large number of distinct counts, all expressive of its impersonality. It will have value according to its practical efficacy and its energy, which is connected, on the one hand, with the greatness of the advantages it achieves, or is prepared to achieve, and also with the personal pains, losses and hardships it undergoes, or is prepared to

THE VALUES OF WELFARE 275

undergo to achieve its benevolent purpose. There is the peculiar case of personal sacrifice, where a satisfaction or other advantage for self is given up on account of a satisfaction or other advantage for some other. It is of course the case that there is some proportion to be observed between alien benefits and personal sacrifices, but within those limits sacrifice, by virtue of its transcendence of the merely personal, must be approved. There will be value too, on another count, in the degree to which there is really an endeavour to achieve what the *other* person finds satisfactory, to adjust oneself to the strange demands prevailing in his alien world, and not merely to extend to it demands which dominate one's own life, or the life of most persons. Obviously there is a lack of respect in extending *our* schemes of happiness to others, except through ignorance or unimaginativeness or thoughtlessness, and there is a similar lack of respect in extending to others our own demands for approvable goods, without regard to *their* capacities, *their* preferences, *their* insights and *their* independently taken decisions. There will likewise be a lessening of value on account of arbitrary and contingent limitations, though here we must of course distinguish between limitations which are wanton and needless, and those set by our impotence or our weariness. What seriously vitiates benevolence is not the mere failure to extend it further, but the deliberate stopping of it at certain points where extension would be easy. Plainly, too, we must count as having the value of benevolence efforts which fail of their benevolent purpose, or which are even fundamentally misguided as to what will satisfy others or what will be approvably good for them. The 'counts' we have enumerated are nothing new—they figure in the most common assessments of well-wishing and well-doing—and we may be forgiven for rounding them off with a comprehensive *etcetera*.

From benevolence we pass to love, which will here, in view of the thoroughgoing ambiguity of the word, be conceived as a drift of soul of the 'pathological' rather than the coolly directed type, which 'grips' consciousness and behaviour, and which makes it revolve, as it were, in satellite fashion round some person distinct from itself. We are not here concerned with 'narcissistic' love, probably always a secondary product, which revolves about the person himself, nor with such loves as revolve about objects, institutions, places, abstractions, etc. etc. Love in

276 VALUES AND INTENTIONS

our sense is a case of 'valuing': it involves (with significant and explicable exceptions) the positive interest in the being and continuance of what is loved. It involves, however, much more than this: what may be called its fascinated circling makes of it a contemplative demand, one that finds satisfaction in thinking about, dwelling upon, picturing, seeing, savouring and otherwise achieving cognitive contact with the object loved, though such contemplation is not its conscious object. Love, as distinct from mere benevolence, may be said to have an element of implicit selfishness, in that it moves towards a position where the person *himself* can dwell upon, enjoy, contemplate, etc., the person loved, though this need not be in the conscious forefront, and in fact seldom is in the essentially other-absorbed, etymologically ecstatic, access of love. It may also be said to have an element of implicit selfishness in proportion to the narrowness of the personal segment upon which fascination fastens and feeds. This may merely be the segment that impinges saliently on the person himself, and may embrace the loved person exclusively in certain details of his or her physical appearance—the fact that appearance is physical does not divorce it from the conscious person, of which it is seen *as* an appearance—or in his or her behaviour in certain circumstances or moods and in certain circumstances and moods of the fascinated 'lover'. What makes 'love', in the sense outlined, impersonally valuable, lies in its ecstatic, other-absorbed character, the thoroughness with which, within characteristic limits, it dwells upon and lives in the alien personal life. It is something which, as ourselves rising above absorption in merely personal interest, we must find admirable and astonishing. And it must recommend itself impersonally to the extent that the segment found fascinating is *not* narrow and superficial, but extends far into the alien person's life, to the extent that it approaches the *whole* of the alien person, with all its quirks, dimnesses and oddities and other indices of individuality. To the extent that 'love' loses segmental restrictions, and extends itself to the total alien personality, it loses its quality of selfishness: what the self pursues and finds fascinating is not some segment specially impinging on itself, but the alien person itself.

That 'love' should be narrow and contingent in its range of objects is only abstractly regrettable, since it is part of its committed, 'pathological' character. Could we direct our love, like

THE VALUES OF WELFARE 277

Gotama the Buddha, to the four quarters of the universe, with undiminished redemptive passion, and embrace in its scope all gods and all men, there would be a defect in restrictive partiality, but where, as with ourselves, such cosmic directedness could yield only a sentimental effusion, there can be no defect in loving only where we must. Love will further obviously have value in proportion to the differences and distances that it bridges, and the difficulty overcome in bridging these, for these measure its approach to impersonality. And it will plainly have value according to the fixity of its hold, the energy of its practical manifestations, the warmth and depth of its emotionality and its feeling, the degree to which it successfully exacts the undergoing of hardship and suffering, etc. etc. It will have value, too, we must remember, even if the object loved is not real: there is as much precious love directed to the various mythically kind and pure figures of certain religions as to the historical persons who propagated those faiths.

It is here perhaps the place to insert a brief, obligatory paragraph on sex. Sex obviously involves a vast number of unphilosophical contingencies, but it has features which explain the impersonal approvability of many of its forms. It involves, in the normal case, the bridging of profound differences, and, even in less normal cases, the overcoming of many strange difficulties and hindrances. It exploits an interest in organic detail, which is by nature excessive and therefore embarrassing, to reach an intimacy of contact with another personality, which organic details represent something important for the person, and something as it were symbolic of what is most central and secret in himself. The possibility of using sex in this symbolic, sometimes called 'sacramental', fashion depends on many personal and social conditions, but plainly it is in chaste, more or less repressed individuals or societies that the sacramental symbolism of sex reaches its highest development. It is not an accident that works such as *Tristan und Isolde*, like the remarkable sex-life they romanticize, should have flourished in the heavily-draped, secretive nineteenth century.

Since nature has chosen to supplement a simple external bifurcation with a bewildering internal interplay of sex characters, so that it is scarcely possible to perform a sexual act without seeing it, as it were, from the other side as well, there are

278 VALUES AND INTENTIONS

obviously many deviant possibilities of using the symbolism of sex to express personal intimacy, possibilities covering some of the forms of behaviour classed as 'abnormal' as well as those classed as 'normal'. The 'abnormal' sides of sex may perhaps be thought of as the as yet untamed territories, where an acceptable set of limiting repressions has not yet been found, and where all remains clothed by a primitive growth of guilt, shame and fear. It would appear reasonable, but perhaps Utopian, to expect that—with possible increase in security and abundance, and mastery of the problems of population—these deviant forms of sexuality will develop their own regulative chastity, and cluster, like other deviant forms of universals, around their central, normal paradigm, through which alone they achieve value and sense.

From the various values of personal transcendence we pass to the corresponding disvalues or evils. Here we have the conditions that imply the defect or the frustration or the complete reversal of the forms of positive other-relatedness considered above. There will first be the various forms of defect of knowledge of the existence of other minds as displayed by the schizoid or the psychopath, and the more limited defect in knowledge of the blither vivisectionists: these forms of ignorance are evil in their consequences, but they are also evil in essence. There is also the philosophical ignorance of, or unbelief in, or non-understanding of, the existence of other minds: that this ignorance is an evil comes out in the sterile evasiveness of the thought, and even of the conduct, it produces. Less evil than the complete failure to realize that other minds exist, in a sense *not* covered by showable phenomena, is the inability to realize *how* other people feel, as displayed by the hidebound, the hard, the unimaginative, the insensitive and the unsympathetic. Obviously the very possibility of all but a mechanical, imitative impersonality is removed, if men are unable to put themselves into other men's shoes.

Immensely more evil than any cognitive defect in the approach to other persons, must, however, obviously be the substitution for positive, bridging attitudes towards such persons, of attitudes of a contrary kind, which deepen personal divisions, and which exalt the personal at the expense of the impersonal. Antithetical to the respect for other persons which is the subjective foundation of justice, will be the disrespect and contempt for other persons which is the subjective foundation of injustice. Impersonally we

THE VALUES OF WELFARE 279

cannot but disapprove what runs crassly counter to the attempt to be impersonal. Antithetical to benevolent attitudes to other persons will be attitudes that are in various ways malevolent, that aim, without looking for excuses, at reducing their welfare, whether hedonic or 'higher', and at increasing their hedonic and higher ills. And here almost the greatest of conceivable evils is achieved when profound sympathy and understanding, which should provide a basis for thoroughgoing benevolence, are made a basis for systematic and wholly wanton malevolence, as in the various forms of sadism and cruelty. The brief period of Nazi rule in Europe was at least instructive in showing us that forms of evil, which one might have regarded merely as cautionary limits, can be concretely exemplified in huge organizations of systematically perverted human beings. Infinitely less evil than malevolence of the Nazi or the ordinary kind, will of course be mere indifference or hardness to others, especially when benevolence would not be difficult.

Antithetical to the various forms of love will be forms of fascinated hatred, like love having a pathological rather than a cool adherence to their objects, and luxuriating in various ugly forms of destruction, hurt and harm. The evil is here in the positive satisfaction found in frustrating the satisfactions of others, or in otherwise doing what is disadvantageous for them, than which nothing can be more diametrically opposed to an impersonal spirit. Only where such fascinated hatred confines itself to attitudes like itself, can it have any impersonal justification, and even here it does not require the genius of a Scheler to detect the element of *personal* resentment in most cases of the moralistic hatred for injustice and other evils. All this is not to say that a certain amount of such personal resentment is not to be tolerated on account of its irremovable, pathological character, on account of its provision of the necessary difficulties that augment the value of benevolence, respect, etc., and also on account of its assistance to the extirpation of evil. Less evil than luxuriating hatred will be the negative attitude of aversion from certain persons and classes of persons, the simple refusal to keep them in mind or consider their interests, and still less evil, mere indifference. It is not necessary for us to comment on the degradations which are antithetical to the higher uses of sex. While the latter subordinate the instruments and procedures of sex to

280 VALUES AND INTENTIONS

intimacies transcending the division of persons, the former exploit the transcendent aspects of persons in order to add piquancy to various personally degrading procedures. This is not to say that some mild excursions into the degrading, possibly such as are comic, may not serve to point up, and to give relief to, too oppressive a sacramentalism.

We have now completed our quick glance at the varied ways in which value attaches to the overflowing of personal barriers, barriers which are at once the conditions and the impediments of the highest along every avenue of value. One cannot be impersonal, except in relatively abstract, empty fashion, in spheres where there are no actual persons, with large differences of interest and outlook, that can be taken up into suprapersonal unities. The values we have been concerned with have been specially connected with the constitution of that space of persons which all other values presuppose. That value is to be found in the direction of overflowing personal barriers, does not, of course, mean that it is not *also* to be found in the enrichment and deepening of what lies within those barriers, which often in fact raises those barriers to greater heights. Personal overflowing presupposes the presence of locks, dams and sluices: only high ones permit large overflows. Here as elsewhere some asceticism enters into the constitution of the highest values.

(v) THE VALUES OF POWER AND FREEDOM

Yet one important form of welfare remains to be considered: the welfare that consists in the possession, the exercise and the effective exercise of power, capacity, and in a wide sense 'virtue', and the various 'feelings' which amount to the direct awareness of such a possession, exercise or effective exercise. To this must be added the *disvalues* accruing to a countervailing *lack* of power or feebleness or impotence. Quite plainly we not only set store by satisfactions and the objects of satisfactions, or by the activities, objects and satisfactions of admiring the well-formed, knowing the actual or likely, respecting, benefiting and loving others, etc. etc.: we also set store by the more or less lasting *powers* evinced in such exercises, the might or virtue that brings them into being or which maintains them in being, and which can do so against weighty resistances. There is a transition naturally, and

THE VALUES OF WELFARE 281

it would seem approvably taken, from setting store by certain outcomes or results, to setting store by the capacity for these things, or by that which has this capacity; and there is also a transition, it would seem approvably taken, from valuing such capacities *instrumentally*, as things to be valued *for* their outcomes, to valuing them *regardless* of the magnitude and multitude of these outcomes. Thus we set store by the 'poetic gift' of Gérard de Nerval, regardless of his restricted poetic output: in valuing each piece we pass beyond it to a style or way of writing that *might* have been most variously expressed, and that even derives a *cachet*, not snobbish but somehow rational, from the fact that its expressions are so few. In the same way economic power is valued, not for overt proliferation in display, but for its occasional expansion into astonishing smoothings and facilitations, into remarkable magnificences and generosities, etc. etc. And the sacred partiality that Gotama expended on Ananda, and Jesus on John, would not, we feel, have been made more precious by being more lavishly extended. There seems, in fact, something valuable about the reserved, unmanifest character of power, that what *could* be, is not, or is not always. And we tend to invert what seems the natural order of valuation, and to value, not power for its manifestations, but the manifestations for the power. And we set store by power, not only when its manifestation is satisfactory, but also in a reserved, 'aspectual' fashion, when its expression is indifferent or even evil: despite moralistic denigration, power seems one of the approvably precious features of personal existence, as shown by its attribution to the 'Almighty'. It is even valued in 'as-if', aesthetic manner, in its attribution to unconscious objects, as brought out in Kant's treatment of the sublime.

The valuation of power is connected, even if not always clearly and directly, with the notion of wanting and satisfaction: power is valued because connected in thought with a conscious want, which is *able* to make itself actual, or which is satisfied by what is actual. (To enjoy a 'facility' provided by some outside agency is in a sense to enjoy a 'power'.) As so connected, the approvable basis of such a valuation is in part clear: if we are approvably satisfied by what a man wants or would find satisfactory, *just in so far* as he wants it or finds it satisfactory, we must also be impersonally satisfied, even if only instrumentally, by the power or ability he disposes of, which enables him to have what satisfies

282 VALUES AND INTENTIONS

him. The power to produce what is unwanted or definitely *not* wanted, e.g. universal embarrassment, is not, considered as such, valuable: it is often counted the greatest of misfortunes. Evil power is admired, in the qualified manner in which we do admire it, as achieving what is wanted, despite powerful resistances, and the natural power of tornadoes, earthquakes, etc., is admired only because it is *as if* they were carrying out what they wanted.

It is easy to say, accordingly, why power should be valued instrumentally, but not why we should hold it to be intrinsically valuable, a difficulty increased by the fact that powers seem, at a certain level of philosophizing, to be 'just nothing at all', a mere projection of 'inference-tickets' or licences which correspond to nothing 'objective'. We may, however, deprecate a conception of the objective which excludes from it all but what may be called realities of lowest order, and which is so impressed by the non-actuality of certain items as not to see that a clear recognition of this non-actuality, is in fact tantamount to the recognition of a higher sort of actuality, which indisputably involves such a non-actual object. Walls such as those which guarded Babylon may be 'nothing at all', but this makes it all the more obligatory to recognize that their *absence*, their *pastness*, and their *presence to thought* are most importantly something, and something essential to a thinking account of the present occasion. The same obviously applies to the *power* or real possibility of rearing such walls again. The character of what we are understandingly aware of, even through the senses, is, in fact, as much made up by the possibilities *of* various alternatives—not of course by the possible alternatives themselves—as by the grosser core to which we attach them: we have but to think of the 'forcefulness' which is part of many happenings and experiences, and the 'flexibility' which is part and parcel of others, to be clear that this is so. If it is possible, in some reductive, philosophical perspective, to remove powers from the thinking description of what is, or to replace them by merely existent elements, this is not the perspective at which our ordinary, or even our impersonal, valuations operate. For we value whatever we value in respect of the categories in which we actually think of it, and this means that the nerve of value may at times lie, not in some unthinkably isolated existential core, but in absences, references, pastnesses, futurities, etc., and particularly in powers. And once the higher-order

THE VALUES OF WELFARE

objectivity of powers has been conceded, we have no ground for refusing to value them impersonally. It would be absurd to rate something capable of many desired or desirable outcomes, on the same level as one capable of only a few, merely because, promise apart, their actual outcomes were of equal value.

If the power to have what one wants is then, *qua* power, approvably valued, it is not hard to enumerate the main counts on which such value will depend. It will depend, first of all, on the mere degree of the power, as measured, in one manner, by the absence of hindrances, in another by the presence of hindrances overcome, in one way by temporary dominance, in another way by long-term persistence, in one way by speed, and another by output, etc. It will depend, secondly, on the variety of its expressions: a power or powers credited with a wide variety of expressions represents something with more reasons to recommend it impersonally than a power or powers credited with but a few. It will depend, thirdly, on the impersonal value of the expressions or outcomes, for though power, *qua* power, has a value distinct from that of what it produces, it is not really separable from the latter: it is only in a consciously one-sided sense, e.g., that a power for evil can be approved as good. Fourthly, it will depend on the degree to which we feel or are conscious of our powers, for the *sense* of power is as important as the possession or exercise of it, and it is arguable whether it would not be better to feel powerful without being it or to be powerful without feeling it. And, lastly, it seems reasonably plain that the successful exercise of power is to be valued above the mere possession of it, and that an unsuccessful exertion of power is probably to be ranked beneath either. The questions, however, bring us to the unclear, and even contradictory, fringes of the concept of power—should we, e.g., speak or not speak of ineffective powers— and our valuations are infected with a parallel obscurity. As to the varieties of power which perhaps specify its value as well as its notion, we may list skills, aptitudes, sensitivenesses, responsivenesses, charms, tastes, perceptivenesses, tendernesses, firmnesses, persuasivenesses, etc. etc., and also in a final column moral virtues, e.g. courage, love of truth, etc., which are admitted, of course, to be more than merely strengths of soul pertaining to separate individuals and to be numbered among *their* assets. We may note, further, that a power may be ours in the sense of

284 VALUES AND INTENTIONS

contributing to *our* welfare even if it is not, narrowly taken, *our* power. We dispose of, in the sense of relying on or using, the warming and illuminating power of the sun, the co-operative goodwill of our neighbours, the facilities offered by various public institutions, the redemptive power of holy persons, etc. It is not merely the results of these powers that can be said to benefit us, but the actual powers or facilities themselves. We may here also mention the 'powers' conferred on persons by a constitution or legal system, which are in fact freedoms from certain sorts of hindrances and provision of certain facilities which the constitution or legal system guarantees. The notional field here is complex and confusedly mapped: it is not the business of a work on value-theory to clarify it.

Beside the values of power we may set the obvious disvalues of impotence or weakness. For the inability to achieve what one wants or to see it achieved by agencies external to oneself, there is nothing impersonally to be said. The same sort of reasoning which shows it to be difficult to the verge of impossibility to be impersonally satisfied with what dissatisfies another, shows it likewise to be difficult to be impersonally satisfied with what removes want-satisfying facilities or powers from another, just *because* it removes these. There is an inner repugnancy between the proceeding known as putting oneself in another man's shoes and the attitude of wanting his powers and facilities to be cut down. The cases where we apparently value weakness and impotence, and do so in seemingly impersonal fashion, are all cases where weakness is instrumental to some subtler power, or where powers might be employed for evil purposes, etc. etc. Thus one might impersonally value the infirmity of purpose which prevented one from becoming a Thug or an S.S. man, or the brokenness of will which opened one's heart to Divine Grace. Tao is praised for being weak as water, but also for having water's all-penetrative power; the meek are praised for not pressing their claims, but through such backwardness they inherit the earth, etc. etc. Since impotences and weaknesses receive names mainly in cases where there is a definite want for something, and the ability to realize it is in principle possessed, such names come to carry with them a suggestion of the untoward, which masks, rather than brings out, the independent connection of weakness with untowardness.

From the values and disvalues of power and impotence, we

THE VALUES OF WELFARE

pass to the related values and disvalues of freedom and unfreedom. The notions of power and freedom are closely allied, and can be pressed so as to coincide completely, every deficiency in power being regarded as a curb on freedom, and every curb on freedom as a deprivation of power. The emphasis of the notions is, however, different, one stressing the exercise of our proper causality, the other the absence of impeding (initially outward, but finally also inward) factors. It is best, therefore, to keep them apart, if one is not to get into trouble with language, and to let them be bound by complex bonds of *presupposition.* The effective exercise of power presupposes, we may say, the freedom from counteracting hindrances, but there may be freedoms to exercise unexercised powers, as there may be frustrated exercises of power involving unfreedom. In the same way, freedoms may be held to presuppose powers, as we should not say that we were free to do something if we had not the power to do it.

Freedoms obviously have the same relation to wanting as have powers: we are free or unfree only in directions where we want, or could conceivably be made to want, something. This means that it is only metaphorically that unconscious things can be called either 'free' or 'unfree', since wanting is without application to them, and that there is likewise practically no limit to the unfreedom of highly imaginative and reflective beings, who can want anything whether possible or impossible. The freedom or unfreedom of such beings may likewise be the mere freedom from hindrance in satisfying its primary wants, but it may come to be the higher freedom from such wants themselves, a freedom comprehensively achieved when we are moved exclusively by considerations of fact and value, the latter having no longer a trace of the primary wants that engendered them. And it may come to be a freedom from all but the impersonal segment of those values, the values which survive and thrive in the process of putting oneself into one's neighbour's shoes. And it may come, finally, to be a freedom or partial freedom, from any sort of determination or determining consideration, the pure arbitrariness or gratuitousness of self-determining spontaneity, which whether actual or not, still seems to represent an 'idea of reason', a limit towards which much in the life of choice seems to be tending.

If we now inquire into the values impersonally to be assigned to these various levels of freedom, it is plain that we must imper-

286 VALUES AND INTENTIONS

sonally value the freedom which enables anyone to have or do what he wants, if only for the sake of the satisfaction which, it has been shown, we must impersonally approve. And we can defend the shift from an instrumental to an intrinsic valuation by arguments similar to those used in the case of power. Obviously, too, we must impersonally value the freedom from primary wants, and their replacement by values or reasons, since the whole shift to a judicial, surveying pose is a step in the direction of impersonality, which must in all things value what resembles itself. And more obviously still, the shift to a freedom from all but the moving force of the impersonal segment of those values, must approve itself to an impersonal assessment. To pass from this to the ideal of pure spontaneity or self-determining causality, might seem, however, to involve a declension from the impersonal, and towards unbounded whim and caprice, a view held by all those deterministic moralists who see in a *non posse peccare*, rather than a *posse non peccare*, the *maxima libertas*. We may, however, here defend a contrary assessment, emphasizing that the impersonal lives and thrives only in the organization and control of personal wants, and that the highest value must therefore be assigned to an autonomy which adheres spontaneously to standards which represent its own impersonal development, while being able and free and even feeling an urge to do otherwise. *Posse peccare sed non peccare* must, in short, be the *maxima libertas*, and the one that distinguished Michael from Lucifer. The notion of pure self-determination (sometimes wrongly confused with chance or with the absence of causality, as explained in an earlier chapter) is, however, one lying on the horizons of rational discourse, and is as little capable of complete elucidation as it admits of convincing illustration: it is clear, however, that it inhabits a peculiarly radiant segment of that horizon, and that this radiance compensates for its poor outline. We need not burden our chapter by going at length into the disvalues of unfreedom, except to say, generally, that these disvalues depend on the presence of relevant wants, and can be often removed by removing or disciplining such wants, but that where unfreedom frustrates wants that are irremovable and basic, or wants expressive of man's impersonal nature, and where such unfreedom is arbitrarily and violently imposed, it represents a great evil, which will concern us more fully in our treatment of injustice.

CHAPTER VII

INJUSTICE AND ITS DISVALUES

(I) THE JUST AND THE UNJUST IN GENERAL

We have, in the previous chapter, sketched the main varieties of welfare (or its opposite), the features in which human activity and experience must yield satisfaction (or dissatisfaction) to all who seek to surmount the contingencies of personal position and direction, and who, in this particular segment of their life, consider only that to be desired (or not desired) whose attraction (or the reverse) is reinforced by a translation into anyone's and everyone's shoes. That there is a content dictated by this purely formal aspiration has disclosed itself in our treatment: to disinterest oneself in what may be called the particularity of human desire, its direction to radios, girl friends, race meetings, etc., is also, by a non-rigorous but still logically guided step, to become interested in the interesting *as such* and in interest *in general*, and in the power to achieve whatever happens to interest 'one', i.e. in all satisfactory and unsatisfactory things *qua* satisfactory or unsatisfactory, and in the satisfactions, dissatisfactions, powers and impotences and freedoms connected with such things. It is also to interest oneself especially in such interests and objects of interest as emerge out of just such a withdrawal from exclusive absorption in self, and just such a determined projection of self into anyone's or everyone's personal standpoint. It is to interest oneself in matters aesthetic, *qua* aesthetic, in matters scientific, *qua* scientific, and in matters communal and social, in so far as such. In all these cases we have watched the normative growing out of the actual, not descending unintelligibly from a machine. Impersonal desire, which judges and reshapes what we personally desire, is itself the inevitable conscious development of personal desire, and derives its lure and impetus from the latter, while the higher assessments which endorse and criticize our original judgements and criticisms are merely more careful, self-revisionary exercises of the same impersonality, and hence ultimately of personal desire. Mill was not wrong in connecting

288 VALUES AND INTENTIONS

desirability with desire: the desirable is merely an ideal limit for self-revising desire.

Now, however, our inquiry must turn in a wholly new direction. We must cease to consider the values and disvalues realizable in separate conscious persons, which are in some sense their property and which make up their 'welfare', and must concern ourselves with the values and disvalues attaching to the connections *among* such conscious beings, values and disvalues which belong to none of them individually but only as interrelated. Such values and disvalues will in fact reflect what we mean by 'impersonality' better than any others. For if impersonality emerges out of the simultaneous self-projection in countless possible personal positions, its characteristic contributions will be found rather in the *interstices* of persons and their interests than in separate personal cells.

It is plain that the interstitial values and disvalues here to be examined will be those mainly covered by the names of 'justice' and 'injustice'. We shall have to consider what are traditionally called the Justice of Distribution and the Justice of Retribution, though the latter leads far beyond simple questions of welfare and its distribution into deep questions of imputability and guilt. We shall also have to deal with what may be called the justice of instituting and keeping what may be called 'understandings', and the injustice of violating the same, a heading under which fall most of the duties recognized in ordinary codes of ethics. But we shall also have to find a place for a set of values wrongly introduced under the banner of justice, but not less important and interesting in their own right: the values covered by such terms as 'same-mindedness', 'solidarity', 'co-operation', etc. etc., values which Plato misguidedly treated as forms of justice, and to some extent used to corrupt the latter, but which others have just as misguidedly linked with ugly totalitarian distortions. We shall show that the values of what may be called Platonic justice are not the replacement, but the natural complement of the values of justice properly so-called, much as, in the sphere of theory, the values attaching to explanatory unity complement those governing the calculus of chances. The tension and mutual requirement of the two 'justices' are in fact almost exactly analogous to those binding the two 'probabilities'.

In the region of justice, our concern is not with the *moral*

INJUSTICE AND ITS DISVALUES

virtue which goes by that name, nor with the contrary fault or point of moral badness, but with the conditions, good or bad, which these virtues and faults serve severally to produce, and which their own goodness or badness presupposes. The justices and injustices, fairnesses or unfairnesses we are about to discuss are such as may have been produced by a conscious and voluntary agent, but they are also such as might have arisen through unconscious and non-voluntary agencies, and are not less good or bad on that account. There are, it is plain, unfair dispensations of gifts and capacities to persons equally desirous and deserving, which it is agreeable to think are products of chance or unconscious nature and not of unjust design; there are likewise just and purifying 'retributions' which do not seem due to any design, and one of the major religions believes all wrongs to be punished in this manner. If our concepts of the just and unjust were undoubtedly forged to fit situations involving only the mutual dealings of men, and there is something queerly 'personifying' in making men receive justice at the hands of things, there is also logical advantage in framing the latter concept. It separates off two kinds of goodness and badness plainly independent and distinct, one of which logically presupposes the other. Plainly the malign and biased will is an evil different from the maldistribution it normally effects, and is bad, in part, *because* it intends such maldistribution.

We may note next that, in the sphere of the just and unjust, evil plays the predominant role, and the goodness of justice (when not treated as a moral virtue) is parasitic upon the evil of injustice. Obviously we think that injustices can become indefinitely more considerable, and that, with such an indefinite increase, goes an indefinite increase in their badness. Their progressive removal is thought of, however, as tending to a definite limit, the perfectly just or fair arrangement, and this, while it may be an object of congratulation, is so mainly in circumstances where it supervenes on the removal, perhaps prolonged and strenuous, of injustices. If no such injustices exist or have existed, the just arrangement is not normally regarded with enthusiasm: we express this by making such deprecatory statements as 'It is no more than proper', 'It is simply his due', 'It is what he had every right to expect', etc. etc. And whatever value one may attach to the just arrangement, this value does not seem capable of indefinite

K

290 VALUES AND INTENTIONS

increase, except when we look to the special difficulties of achieving or maintaining it, in which case we are concerned rather with the virtue or serviceableness of what *produces* the just arrangement than with the just arrangement itself. The just arrangement seems in fact to be the almost indifferent limit of a long series of states ordered according to diminished undesirability: when no special circumstances attend upon it, we do not set particular store by it. No one feels called on warmly to applaud the fact that he has the same eyes, ears, etc., as other men, and that he is not the innocent subject of an atrocious form of discrimination.

Nothing in the peculiar testing procedures implied in being impersonal entails any revision of this ordinary attitude; only an artificial passion for symmetry could seek to reverse it. There is nothing in putting oneself into everyone's shoes, which requires that one should be enthusiastic about the mere vacuum which corresponds to something appalling, or that one should have the *same* attitude to the mere absence of something, and that an evil, that one has to the positive presence of something, and to its possession of countless excellent properties. Such a requirement would, moreover, reduce all our impersonal valuations to nonsense, since in *all* situations there are an infinite number of desirable and undesirable things absent, and of things desirable or undesirable in every conceivable degree, so that, if absences of evil counted as balancing goods and *vice versa*, the value of all things whatsoever would be wholly unassessable. The mere fact that the removal of an evil sets a term to practical endeavour in the same manner as does the realization of a good, should not be allowed to confuse us. The absence of the evil is really a *goal* of endeavour in quite a different sense from the presence of a good, and in the sense in which a good thing is the goal of our endeavours, our efforts to remove evil have really no goal at all. They may be said, with some illumination, to be efforts *away* from a certain situation rather than efforts *towards* its absence or towards anything else. To the extent that there is a toward movement to something else, or to an absence, its direction is as such indifferent, it is merely instrumental to the movement away from what is undesired. We are saying, in short, that aversion, or mental activity away-from, is the attitude through which evil is presented, and in terms of which it must be basically

INJUSTICE AND ITS DISVALUES 291

understood. This attitude is irreducible to activity-towards, however much, in the context of immediate practice, the two may be indistinguishable. Mental activity towards may have unimportant beginnings, but it has an important end, about which it circles feelingly; mental activity away from may be said to have an important beginning, from which it moves feelingly towards an unimportant end. This is not, of course to deny that the demolition and evasion of evils may not develop its own zest—it can and must do so—we must only maintain the derived character of that zest. We have no reason, therefore, to reverse our intuitive assessment on impersonal grounds. Just arrangements are, as such, poor things, which derive their importance from the immense ills of which they are the negation.

Since the values of justice stem from the disvalues of injustice, we can understand why the passions connected with the just should be of so overwhelmingly negative a character, why they should be forms of horror, disgust or sick aversion shading over into the more dynamic forms of anger and destructiveness. To love justice (when this is not a virtue of individuals) is to sicken at the sight of the martyr tied to his stake, or the political prisoner meaninglessly maltreated, and perhaps even, in vigilant hatred, to go out of one's way to meet occasions of such sickness: it is also to call for weapons, and to engage in struggles which seem uncalled for, vulgar and insensate to the well-situated or socially satisfied. To have the passion is, further, to be prone to sundry exaggerations and transferences, to see injustice even when it is not present, and to extend one's hatred to persons and institutions who are perhaps only distantly responsible for the injustice in question, also to mix with the hatred of injustice, resentment, envy, fear and other unamiable emotions. The lover of justice is, in fact, unless exercising careful self-criticism, always on the verge of deserving the accusations of hypocrisy, trouble-making, etc., which the complacent readily lavish on him. If injustice, however, be an important evil, and if evils are seldom abolished in default of passion, then the dangers of hypocrisy, envy, resentment and other evils chargeable to the love of justice are a small price to pay for the corrective work that he does, often in situations where his remoteness from the scene of injustice gives his acts an energy and a valuable irresponsibility that they could not have if done 'on the spot'. The

292　VALUES AND INTENTIONS

various liberal and left-wing busybodies of England and other advanced countries may often have fallen for hollow causes and scanty information, but they have provided the emotional fuel without which the just would not have been valued or preserved.

The notion of the unjust has close connections with various concepts associated with the English word 'wrong', and in some languages no separate existence or verbal expression (e.g. *Unrecht*, ἀδικόν), as the just has a similar association with the concepts connected with the word 'right'. What it is held *wrong* to do, e.g. deceive, steal, generally involves inflicting *a wrong* on someone, and this wrong either is or involves an injustice, and an injustice that might, by a stretch of language, have come about by unconscious agency, e.g. a flood may 'rob' me of my property and my livelihood. In much the same way, there is a close tie-up between the various senses of the word 'right' and the notion of justice. For a man to have justice, is for him to have his rights, to have what it is right for him to have, to be allowed to do what it is right for him to do, etc. 'Right' and 'wrong' are, of course, further applied, not merely to situations which involve justice or injustice to someone, but also to the acts or decisions which produce such outcomes, and it is here that the notions begin to have their intimate tie-up with the notions expressed by 'ought' and 'ought not', which is much less close in the case of the just and the unjust. The meanings of 'right' and 'wrong', of course, extend in other directions. Acts which achieve *any* evil are denominated wrong, even if that evil cannot be classified under the specific heading of injustice, e.g. encouragement of low interests in oneself which militate against higher development. The word 'right' is similarly applied, not merely to acts productive of no injustice, but also to acts unproductive of *any* evil, including other evils beside injustice. Puritanical exaggerations have further tended to alter the meaning of 'right' so as to make it coincide with the *obligatory*, that which involves a bond towards someone, whose breach would certainly involve a wrong and the creation of an evil. These exaggerations seem to stem from the need to see evil in as many directions as possible, and, if not in all, then in all but one. It is not here our task to clear up the unmeasured confusions caused by these overlapping, shifting usages: 'right', 'wrong', 'ought', 'obliged', etc. etc., will concern us in our next chapter. Here we need only remark that the sort

INJUSTICE AND ITS DISVALUES   293

of ethics in which the words 'right' and 'wrong' are prominent is in most cases an ethics of injustice. Stealing, killing, deceiving, breaking faith, etc., which are the preferred instances of 'wrongness', are all readily brought under the heading of injustice, while the obligations to which the word 'right' is then pre-empted are those involving abstinence from such injustice. Ethical theory has been much vexed by the puzzling relations of the 'right' and the 'good', the former having the peculiar property of having no natural comparative 'righter' as the latter has the comparative 'better'. What is not seen is that the right has this odd property merely because it is a basically negative notion, because it amounts to the non-evil, generally the not-unjust, which is necessarily a limit to lessening stages of evil: it is either the non-evil which has several other non-evil alternatives (the permitted), or the non-evil which has *no* non-evil alternatives (which generally coincides with the obligatory). Moral systems of the right are mainly concerned with the avoidance of evil and particularly of injustice, whereas moral systems of the good have been concerned with quite different tasks. It is not remarkable that these two types of system have, except by confusion and trespass, found so few meeting-points.

The values and disvalues of justice and injustice may be held to be fruits of the *disjunction of persons*, much as the probabilities and improbabilities of the calculus of chances are products of the disjunction, the mutual exclusiveness, of *alternatives*. The same sort of rational impartiality which, when it fully and simultaneously enters into two disjoined, incompatible possibilities, feels unwilling *arbitrarily* to extend a credence to the one that it does not extend to the other, nor to base its credence in one on a feature, e.g. frequency of realization, which it does not bow to in the case of the other, may be held also, when it enters fully and simultaneously into two disjoined states of mind, to feel unwilling *arbitrarily* to consent to a treatment of the interests of the one which is not extended to the other, nor to base its consent on some feature of one, e.g. superior capacity or virtue, which it is not willing to consider in the case of the other. There is absolutely no 'objectivity' or clearness of application which obtains in the case of the probable, which does not obtain also in the case of the just: both resemble fog-bound coasts with some rockily resistant promontories.

294 VALUES AND INTENTIONS

That the values and disvalues of justice and injustice *are* connected with the exclusiveness of persons, appears too in the way in which they steadily lose application as this exclusiveness is mitigated, according as men consent to co-operate, enter sympathetically into each other's enjoyments and sorrows, and become benevolent and loving towards one another. Where profound love and understanding exists among persons, it no longer matters that *A* should have very different functions, privileges, insights, enjoyments from *B*. Each in a sense enters into and enjoys the activities and experiences of the others, and it does not, from this point of view, signify who does what or experiences what. However this may all be, it is clear that the high walls disjoining persons—which are merely the *non*-togetherness of their conscious states—are only *in a sense* removed by sympathy, co-operation, co-ordination, etc., and that the acts which do away with the justice they entail, do so only by ignoring their presence and not by demolishing them. (Demolition would involve the 'confluence' of disjoined streams of experience, which is not self-contradictory unless one is determined to make it so: such 'confluence' would remove justice because it would remove personal disjunction.) And the values of justice obtain because the immense otherness of conscious persons means that they each constitute, as it were, a complete monadic world, extending *in posse* indefinitely into the past and future, and comprising what may be called a private sun, sky, sea, earth, etc., inasmuch as these objects can as rightly be considered in the context of a man's expectations, pictures, values, needs, etc., as in the abstraction from these which makes them public and single. To move in sympathy away from the common centre of public objectivity, along ever more divergent lines of private subjectivity, and to hold these divergent radii together in an ever harder exercise of imaginative self-extension, is to become more and more revulsed by proposals to tamper with the direction of any one such line, and to twist it round and subordinate it to some other. And it is because conscious experience radiates out in this manner that so much of what would otherwise be senseless duplication becomes indispensable and obligatory, e.g. the wide diffusion of opportunities for aesthetic experience, knowledge, etc., as opposed to their confinement to a few. And wherever privacy is minimized in thought, justice incontinently vanishes: there can be no reason

INJUSTICE AND ITS DISVALUES 295

whatever why the overall good should not be furthered by any desired liquidation or penalization or subordination of individuals. If an individual is stripped of his immense separateness and boundlessness, his destruction must count as a trivial matter: it becomes, as Hegel says of the multiplied executions during the French Revolution, like the cutting off of a head of cabbage or a draught of water.

It seems plain, in the next place, that the values of justice and injustice presuppose wanting or interest. In regions where there are no wants, the unjust, and consequently the just, are without application. The impersonal attitude from which justice springs is one co-ordinating innumerable wants or interests: where these do not exist, there is nothing to co-ordinate, and hence no injustice. The only exception to this rule is that justice or injustice may exist where there is a genuine *capacity* for a want or interest, and where some coaxing or even pushing may be justified, because a person not interested in something may by such means acquire a deep interest in that thing, and may hold retrospectively that he would have been *deprived* of something, perhaps widely enjoyed or used by others, had he not been thus coaxed and pushed. It is in this manner that we seek to justify the wide variety of educational compulsions that we impose on children, compulsions to eat certain foods, to play certain games, to acquire linguistic, mathematical and musical skills, to become socially accomplished, etc. etc. In all these cases we assume that certain wants will arise in the persons thus compelled, and that they will become capable of satisfactions, to be deprived of which would involve an unfairness in comparison with others who enjoy such satisfactions. And we disapprove strongly of cases where persons are deprived, through a lack of suitably applied, timely compulsions, of the exercise of certain impersonally approved powers, e.g. those of an aesthetic or scientific sort, and of the 'higher satisfactions' which attend on their use. It is far from clear, however, whether we should call it *more* unfair for a person arbitrarily to be deprived of the possibility of such higher satisfactions than of ordinary personal ones. What *is* clear, however, is that if someone cannot, by any manner of means, be made to want something or have a taste for it, then, whether this thing be ideally valuable or not, we should not apply the term 'injustice' to his deprivation of it, unless in some extremely

296 VALUES AND INTENTIONS

abstract frame of mind he might come to feel a want for wants that he had never actually experienced. If certain refinements of aesthetic sensibility, scientific insight or interpersonal responsiveness are definitely 'beyond me', and I acquiesce in this 'beyondness', it is arguable that there can be no trace of the specific evil called 'injustice' in my deprivation of such unwanted satisfactions, insights, etc., no matter how this compares with the situation of others. In the same manner, to consider ill-fare instead of welfare, i.e. the fact that I exemplify a state of mind, which, from an impersonal point of view, is one of ill-fare, e.g. one of intellectual confusion, aesthetic debasement, etc., there can in such a situation be nothing deserving the name of 'injustice' as long as I remain invincibly content with my position. The alternative to this view is the view that, not to have some satisfying or impersonally valuable kind of experience, or to experience what would, in an impersonal perspective, be undesirable, is to exemplify an injustice, in which case the creatures with the fewest wants and aversions would be most unjustly circumstanced. Not only Diogenes in his tub, but a primitive organism of acquiescent, pliant habit and elementary conscious life, would be a supreme instance of injustice. Obviously we do not use the word 'injustice' in this manner, and this is to say that the sort of ill, or wide-spreading family of ills, that the word picks out, is one which centres in frustrated want or interest, and is with unnaturalness pushed beyond it.

What emerges from our discussion is the necessary connection of justice or injustice with welfare and ill-fare. What is just or unjust must be an allocation to persons of what represents welfare for them or its opposite, even if this welfare be only the lower welfare of engaging in the activities they want to engage in, and realizing the goals they personally want to achieve. There can be nothing just or unjust in a certain person's being in a certain state if this state has no conceivable value or disvalue from an impersonal point of view: it will be remembered that to do what one wants, or have what one finds satisfactory is, as such, impersonally valuable. At the same time, what is just or unjust must involve an allocation to conscious persons of what *they* regard as their welfare or ill-fare, or can be readily brought to do so. We may say, in fact, that the just and unjust attach themselves to those elements of impersonal welfare which are also elements of

INJUSTICE AND ITS DISVALUES 297

personal welfare: it is just or unjust to have good or bad things, or be deprived of them, according as these are also what one wants or does not want.

The nature of our higher, impersonal interests is, however, such that every man must have the germs of them in him. There is, therefore, always some justifiability in a situation which forces a man some way in their direction, since he cannot be wholly incapable of forming them. It is clear, however, that the mere enjoyment of conscious life and the basic traits of prolongation of pattern, projection into other persons, etc. etc., out of which all our impersonal interests grow, does not mean that such growth is inevitable, or even possible, in certain actual conscious forms in certain situations, any more than the fact that all the natural numbers and their properties are in a sense implicit in the procedure shaping the first few natural numbers, means that all the properties of all numbers will be illustrated in these. The conscious life of the different types of animals, and of variously developed and educated men, differ basically in their properties, and there is sense, therefore, in saying that certain forms of welfare, e.g. profound philosophical insight, are beyond the scope of some, and that their absence represents nothing inequitable. We may note, further, that the forceful educational invasion of the conscious person which results in the development of many higher interests, is in itself an evil, because involving the subordination of one 'boundless monadic world' to another, and an evil of the family of injustice, which becomes graver the more forceful the educational methods used, and the more highly developed the conscious life involved. It is therefore plain why the more invasive forms of education should be limited to children and childlike personalities.

It would appear, too, that we see a close connection between the evil of injustice and those higher forms of welfare dealt with under the headings of 'power' and 'freedom'. If the just and unjust are connected with welfare and ill-fare, it is clear why they should be closely connected with power and freedom: power and freedom in the higher conscious beings are necessary to the achievement of most forms of welfare. Hence the stress in discussions of justice on 'opportunity': it is not *things* that it is just or unjust to allocate to persons, but various lower and higher satisfactions, and since the possibility of these can be best

K*

298 VALUES AND INTENTIONS

discerned and pursued, in the case of beings of some conscious complexity, by those beings themselves, what it is just or unjust to allocate are the *powers* or *facilities* or *opportunities* to achieve a wide range of results, and the *freedom* to use these powers. Quite apart from this, there would appear to be a profound invasion of the conscious person in all arbitrary, external restrictions of power and freedom. If the kernel of injustice lies precisely in this sort of external invasion, this finitization and physicalization of what should be infinite and separate, then it is clear why it should be so evil that persons should be shorn of their powers and freedoms, especially when their use is guided by an orderly firmament of facts and values. We feel, in fact, that the highest form of voluntary freedom so concentrates in itself all that is unique in the conscious person that it can in a sense transform welfare into ill-fare, and *vice versa*; certainly we credit it with the power to turn an injustice into justice. An invasion of myself which would in itself be a grave case of injury, ceases to be so if I completely consent to it: *volenti non fit iniuria*. What I undergo may be evil, and the wills which inflict it malign, but I cannot complain of the specific evil called 'injustice'. Whereas if my power and freedom be invaded, the very source of justice and injustice is in a sense invaded, and such invasion cannot be anything but unjust.

(II) THE JUSTICE OF DISTRIBUTIONS AND UNDERSTANDINGS

So far we have largely been pursuing the just and unjust through a medium of verbal usage. We have been concerned to delimit, at least in certain directions, the general sphere of evils to which we should allot the name 'injustice', when this word is used to cover the bringing about of a wrong, whether by human hands or the hands of nature, and not so much the moral badness of the person who does the wrong, or the wretchedness of the person who suffers it. Possibly we have forced usage in giving so wide a meaning to the term 'injustice': our concern, however, has not been to explore the intricate working of language-bound concepts, but to bring into sight a range of peculiar interpersonal disvalues, distinct from the disvalues of welfare previously considered. Circumscription must now yield place to 'deduction', in

INJUSTICE AND ITS DISVALUES

the sense in which this means the natural filling out and rounding off of a notion, not the statement of what it analytically contains. Of the notion of the 'impersonal' we have, in fact, given no precise definition, and our reasonings largely establish what it *is* to mean, as we go on and on, rather than what some pre-existent sense entails. But because we shift our ground continually, our procedure is not, therefore, illogical. It continues the course we had previously taken, even if it does not achieve, or aim at, the feat of hovering motionless over one spot, after the fashion of formal demonstration.

The simplest and most abstract form of justice is that traditionally known as the distributive. It represents the negation of the various ills involved in the *maldistribution* of welfare (or ill-fare) among conscious persons, without regard to complicating clashes of personal interest, the fact that one man's advantage may in some cases mean another's detriment, and without regard to the degree to which different conscious persons themselves consciously adhere to what is right and just, and so have the *virtue* of justice or *vice* of injustice. This form of justice may be considered in relation to the distinct levels of welfare: that of the purely conative or hedonic, that of the 'higher' mental activities, and that of power and freedom. The spirit of distributive justice plainly works in the direction of some sort of *equality*: so much is involved in the very notion of impersonality, which presupposes nothing if not an *unbiased* self-immersion in everyone's activity and experience, and which would be violated were we arbitrarily to dwell more fully and favourably on *one* person's activities and experiences. And this plainly means an equal concern with everyone's welfare, which may at present be taken in its lowest form of having what one wants or what one finds satisfactory, and it would appear therefore to tend in the direction of some sort of equality of satisfaction and freedom from dissatisfaction. This tendency is reinforced by what we previously said about the 'monadic separateness' of persons: the satisfaction achieved in one conscious person is, in default of special appropriation, nothing at all to another, and hence demands a reduplication in the other world by a satisfaction equally great. When one attempts, however, to go farther, one is faced by a large horde of intricate questions, some so seldom considered that it is hard to confide in initial plausibilities.

300 VALUES AND INTENTIONS

It is plain, first of all, that distributive impartiality *presupposes* the existence of a body of conscious persons among whom welfare is to be distributed, and that this existence is not itself a matter of justice or injustice. We do not here, as in the forms of impartiality through which welfare and its values were established, consider *possible* individuals and their satisfactions as well as actual ones. The body of persons among whom questions of just distribution arise may be an imaginary body, but the existence of this body must be hypothetically presupposed when we consider distributions of welfare among them. We do not, in other words, in a given frame of reference, mix questions regarding beings *not* supposed to exist with questions regarding beings who *are* so supposed: a frame of reference confines us to beings supposed *antecedently* to be there. The non-existent, in short, have no rights, unless it is certain or probable that they will exist, in which case they do merit consideration. The question as to whether there should or should not exist beings who do not now exist, is a very important one, but it is not a question of justice or injustice: we do no wrong to someone by not bringing him into existence. What we have said is of course utterly obvious, but by no means philosophically empty, since in many fields it *is* important to treat the sentiments of possible persons with as much respect as those of actual ones, and in this field this is not the case.

If we now try to render precise the notion of equality, we find it changing its shape as we consider it, but this does not mean that there is not a definite direction in this change of shape. We start by conceiving crudely egalitarian divisions of *commodities* or material assets; e.g. a peasant holding might be cut up into equal shares for the peasant's sons. Such divisions have the merit of stopping further argument, since, like decisions based on tossing coins, they ignore the *grounds* on which decisions in this sphere could appropriately be made. Plainly it is not equality in the having of things, but in the having of satisfaction and dissatisfaction that is relevant. There would obviously be inequity if equal distributions of things resulted in grossly unequal satisfactions and dissatisfactions, and it is only the extreme difficulty of establishing such equality to everyone's satisfaction—a difficulty by no means beyond the reach of judgement in *all* cases—that makes us acquiesce in more materialistic forms of egalitarianism. But once the notion of

INJUSTICE AND ITS DISVALUES

equality of satisfactions and dissatisfactions has been mooted, it too begins to transform and develop itself. If equal regard for conscious *persons* is to be our basis of estimate, then it would seem that the satisfactions and dissatisfactions of a conscious life *rich* in its wants, should *not* be preferred to those of a conscious life simple and restricted in its wants, and *vice versa*, which means, paradoxically, but not, on reflection, absurdly, that it is *not* a case of iniquitous privilege that beings endowed with rich and varied wants should be enabled to satisfy them—clashes of interest and anti-social interests apart—while those with few wants and aversions should have an equal opportunity of enjoying their simple life. And if conditions of scarcity, difficulty of division, etc. etc., render this impossible, then equality of well-being means that each person should have, as nearly as possible, the *same proportion* of his total wants satisfied, and the same amount of necessary frustration and pain. (The qualification 'necessary' must be added, as it would involve grave disrespect to the person to inflict on it *unnecessary* ills in the mere interest of greater equality. *Schadenfreude* is rationally judged to be an impersonal-seeming form of personal malice.) Justice in the sphere of satisfactions demands, therefore, that those with multifarious (but innocent) wants should be considered on a level with those with exiguous (and likewise innocent) wants, and that there is an *equal* departure from equity if *A* is deprived of the refinements, comforts, amenities that he needs, as if *B* is deprived of his much simpler amenities. We all realize this, in comparing the lot of distressed gentlewomen with that of distressed charwomen, however little we may approve of the social arrangements which have led to their differentiation. The fairness of providence—and of Karl Marx—if either is appropriate to a discussion like the present—provides for all the differing needs of different sorts of creatures, no matter how different they may be, and it is in such a direction that the notion of equality in the distribution of satisfactions must develop. Of course there will have to be distinctions between wants deeply rooted and ineliminable, and wants shallowly planted and factitious, the former being less equitably frustrated than the latter, otherwise we shall be giving *carte blanche* to a multiplication of what Plato calls 'unnecessary appetites'. We shall also have to differentiate between wants which really agree with the capacities of the

302 VALUES AND INTENTIONS

individual and the realities of the situation, and wants which do not. While it represents an inequity that one should lack capacities for satisfactions of which one has enough to form the appetite, it represents no added inequity not to be assisted in futile attempts to achieve such satisfactions. We shall not endeavour to pursue the dialectic of 'equality' further, nor suggest that we have done more than loosen (without untying) some of its knots. But it seems plain that, in its ideal form, it involves much that would seem, on a first view, to be grossly inegalitarian. We have, in the rough justice of political arrangement, to follow gross rather than highly refined patterns of equality, if only because this prevents embittered, almost metaphysical controversy, and a sense of injustice in those of grosser tastes and perceptions. Where people know each other well, as in a family or a spiritual fellowship, it is plain that considerable inequality of surface distribution may succeed in hitting the target of true equality. We ignore, as inspired by the false lure of the instrumentally measurable, objections resting on the incomparable character of different people's satisfactions. Such comparisons are frequently made and within limits agreed upon, and they exceed in importance comparisons leading to less dispute.

To have justice is, as we have said, in default of the special difficulties it involves, or the virtues it calls forth, *no great thing*. But departures from the equality of justice—in the difficult sense of the equal adumbrated above—are all incapable of satisfying us in so far as we enter impersonally into everyone's satisfactions, and are therefore in an absolute sense evil, and the more so the more they depart from such equality. Despite the obfuscations cast about this near-tautology by envy, resentment or political simplification, so much seems irrefragable and clear. And, as we have said previously, such departures are evil whether they come about by conscious intention or by a fortuitous atomic concourse. It is unfair, evil, that I, who wish so much to take part in certain sports, in which others like myself excel, and who would derive immense satisfaction from doing so, should spend my days in a cripple's chair, to give but one grossly obvious instance. Such an evil may of course be compensated for by the virtues it calls forth, or by the benefits it may have conferred on others: its unfairness may also be removed in so far as it is for such reasons *accepted* by the disabled person. Considered in itself, however,

INJUSTICE AND ITS DISVALUES 303

it should not be whitewashed, and the name that best fits it is a 'wrong', or an 'unfairness', or an 'injustice'. It is plain, further, that an inequality becomes more of an injustice the more clearly men are conscious of it, or have to live side by side with it. That our frustrated dreams may be fulfilled realities for the Martians is no great matter: that our neighbours, colleagues, contemporaries, etc., should enjoy privileges arbitrarily denied to us is the height of injustice. Obviously if arbitrary inequalities are an evil, it is still more evil that they should flaunt themselves in the eyes of their victims. It is important, however, that we should here remember the entirely different role played in all value estimations, and hence in all considerations of injustice, by satisfaction and *dis*satisfaction, pleasure and *pain*. As pointed out previously, pain or dissatisfaction carried beyond certain limits lames, sears and ultimately disables the conscious person, and must by its nature do so: there is no sense in which it can be compensated by countervailing satisfactions, however intense. There is therefore an infinitely greater evil in departing far from equality in the distribution of unavoidable pains, than in departing far from equality in the distribution of satisfaction. If the latter distribution involves no pain at all, not even the pain of invidious comparison, it would certainly not involve a serious evil. More monstrous than arbitrary inequalities of sufferings, would be sufferings undergone for the mere satisfaction of others, and not for their relief from pains. That an enslaved class should suffer merely in order that a dominant class should *enjoy* itself, however intensely, goes against the very grain of justice, and even its voluntary acceptance could not be impersonally sanctioned. On the other hand, it is plain that the voluntary sacrifice of satisfactions, and the acceptance of great pains, for the *relief* of others from still greater pains, may be in the highest degree justifiable and admirable.

We now pass from considering injustice in the distribution of satisfactions and dissatisfactions, to considering injustice in the distribution of the higher welfare of aesthetic cultivation, scientific penetration, etc. etc.: here we shall be faced by similar transformations. Superficially it may appear unfair that people should have differing capacities for achieving these goods, and particularly so if they themselves chafe at their want of taste, of mathematical grasp, etc. etc. Since, however, the germs of

304   VALUES AND INTENTIONS

these capacities are present in all conscious beings, even in animals, the injustice is confined to their being at a certain stage in the development of such capacities, and not capable of going as far as others. To the extent that we are clearly conscious of such disabilities, and desirous of passing beyond them, there is plainly injustice in such inequality, and one which certain religions have sought to mitigate by allotting to all conscious beings an indefinite span of conscious existence, in the course of which all such capacities may be fully realized. In so far, however, as there is complete ignorance of certain developments, or no developed need to achieve them, or a wise acceptance of the barriers set by existence and circumstance—tolerable because no one has intended them or planned them—this injustice is progressively mitigated, and in many cases removed altogether. If there is no injustice in the absence of unwanted mental developments among animals and primitive peoples, there is also, at the other end of the scale, no real injustice to the man who has sized up his physical and spiritual limitations, seen what goods can be best cultivated by him in the circumstances and time in which he lives, and has made of these limitations a spring-board for more important personal and social virtues. Avoidable deprivation of higher goods for which there is a developed demand and capacity will, however, for obvious reasons, be a much worse evil than similar deprivation of satisfactions. In so far, further, as the distribution of higher goods becomes a practical political and not an ideal matter, it will resolve itself into a programme of creating, not the higher developments themselves—for these depend on want or interest in persons—but the *opportunities* and *facilities* for such developments, and, in the early stages, the educative *compulsions* and *suasions*, and not to be neglected *techniques* and *drills*, without which such higher developments would rarely become open. Such political elaborations cannot be pursued here.

We saw previously that freedom in various senses occupied a high place among the forms of non-hedonic value. At a lower level we have the freedom which consists in the absence of external hindrances, and the presence of powers, facilities and opportunities which enable a man to realize his wants; at a higher level we have, not only the absence of external hindrances, but also the absence of internal hindrances in the shape of excessive

INJUSTICE AND ITS DISVALUES 305

biasing passions, and the presence of facilitating factors such as full information, a well-developed firmament of values, which enable a man to act rationally in accordance with, or perversely against, his guiding facts and values, and in either case to exercise the highest freedom. Quite plainly unequal distribution of these two kinds of freedom constitutes a grave injustice. It is unjust to have hampering restrictions put on the fulfilments of one's wants that are not put on those of others, and it is unfair that one should, through no choice of one's own, have stronger passions and less opportunity to develop knowledge, and a well-integrated system of values, than others. These latter injustices seem largely those of nature, though they may be strengthened by the enslaving education or influence of others: deprivations of the simpler sorts of freedom occur both as natural and social injustices. The injustices which restrict the exercise of our cool, voluntary determinations, arise only to the extent that there is developed capacity for such determinations: animals or children suffer no injustice by lacking opportunities for exercising a faculty they do not possess. It is in virtue of the grave injustice of depriving those capable of cool self-determination of the opportunity to exercise it and carry it out, that it is proper that people should be allowed to make their own mistakes and failures, persist in their errors, within limits persist in courses that are impersonally to be adjudged evil (though not so judged by themselves), even to persist in courses that they themselves judge evil, and follow *because* they judge them so. On the lower levels of freedom considerable 'nagging' and moulding of the conscious person constitutes little injustice: children, e.g., may be inadequately or even falsely informed, cajoled by the attraction of the moment and not permitted to form overall, long-term views, have their major decisions made for them, be deprived of opportunities and facilities, and compelled to do much that irks them. To the extent, however, that conscious beings become capable of the higher type of freedom, its exercise must be conceded them—of course with provisos concerning conflict and misuse: equality of freedom is here the basic equality, taking precedence over equality in respect of satisfaction, aesthetic experience, etc. It is more important, we intuitively hold, that men should be free to choose for or against their own system of impersonal values, and that inequalities should arise in the distribution of satisfaction,

306 VALUES AND INTENTIONS

aesthetic experience, etc., than that all should enjoy an *enforced* equality in respect of these valuable qualities. The ground would appear to be that the detachment basic to impersonality and all its values is the same detachment also present in the higher form of freedom, though this latter may also be perverse and value-resistant: the pure autonomy responsible for our impersonal values is bound up with the possibility of perversity. To violate freedom, even if this be employed perversely, is, therefore, in some sense to violate the *source* of all values and all justice in a person, and no claim to be egalitarian can take precedence over this. All this may be highly platitudinous at commonplace levels of sermonizing, yet it presents great interest and difficulty for philosophy.

From the abstract justice of distribution we proceed to the more complex justice of mutual understandings and 'spheres of rights'. We must here do the unfashionable thing of discerning a 'natural', i.e. impersonally unavoidable, framework of laws and rights, of which positive laws and rights represent the specification or the distortion. The 'space of persons' in which impersonality is exercised is not merely an imaginary space, like the 'heavens' of speculative mysticism, in which we may locate what beings we choose: it is a space tied down to 'reality' and compulsive experience at countless points, and not capable even of an imaginary use without this. For though, in our view, the notion of the non-togetherness or disjunction of experiences which generates the space of persons is not borne in upon us by or derived from anything in compulsive experience, and is in this sense *a priori*, it would never be developed or applied did we not encounter those sensorily compulsive, spatially located phenomena which are such as to have a natural completion in conscious orientations of some sort, but which do not naturally continue the pattern of those which by contrast make up the 'home team', i.e. our own personal experiences. The effective use of the categories of the space of persons may be said, therefore, to entail an initial *clash* or *disharmony* between behavioural drifts attached to different bodies in space, of some of which we have direct 'practical knowledge' and call our own, and attach closely to experiences reflectively given which also complete them, while other drifts are attributed to other persons, to whom we also attribute experiences *not* together with those we call our own. (It is often convenient

INJUSTICE AND ITS DISVALUES 307

to speak as if the distinction of 'our own' and 'other people's' experiences preceded the distinction between certain experiences reflectively given, and others, which are thought of as *not* together with these: actually, however, the distinction is *constituted* by the non-togetherness in question.) A clash or disharmony of behavioural trends is, however, in conscious beings a clash of interests, and it is accordingly in an initial clash of interests that the republic of persons takes its rise, an insight distorted in the various 'states of nature' of Hobbes, Locke, etc., but given a deeper interpretation by Hegel. (See, e.g., the 'Life-and-Death Struggle' in the *Phenomenology*.) What we have said inverts what we usually say. Usually we say that, where there are *in fact* many distinct persons, all penned together in a common environment, and having interests which converge on the same objects, there are likely to be many conflicts among their interests, and in the exercise of their free choices, and many struggles in carrying such interests and choices to fulfilment. We, however, have based the real distinction of persons upon the reality of this struggle. The categories constitutive of the space of persons only have application where living beings sometimes surprise, thwart, resist and attack us, evincing trends which merit a conscious completion, but not *this* conscious completion which by contrast is 'our own'.

From an impersonal standpoint, however, which projects itself equally into the needs of *all* struggling persons, a demand must necessarily arise for the fixing of definite, agreed 'spheres of right', within which each person's wants can be satisfied, and his freedoms exercised, for so only can all achieve as much of what they want as is possible, and with the least departure from inequality. The precise fixing of these 'spheres' must of necessity be arbitrary and contingent, and must rest on the growth of various 'understandings', whether dramatically and consciously arrived at, or quietly fallen into, and whether embodied silently in action or declared in speech, the foundation of all philosophical stories of 'social contract'. It is not our task to study the psychological origins of such 'understandings', nor to pursue their development into the extremely complex understandings which govern social and political life. What it is important to stress is that an 'understanding' is, as its name suggests, an exercise in impersonality, albeit limited, the rise to an arrangement among persons based on a mutual entry into each other's interests and

308 VALUES AND INTENTIONS

wishes, and involving no mere overriding of one person's interests and wishes in favour of another's. Being thus exercises in impersonality, the existence of understandings must, as such, be impersonally approved, and this approval reindorsed at ever higher levels in a fashion which renders them 'absolute'. Such understandings will, however, fall into very different classes, some of them being necessary and indispensable, in the sense that, without them, grave dissatisfactions, frustrations and denials of freedom will be inevitable, while others will be merely impersonally *desirable*, in that, while their non-formation will not give rise to the grave frustrations just mentioned, their existence will promote greater positive satisfaction, and greater facilities and opportunities for achieving what is wanted. Obviously there is no clear line to be drawn between such 'necessary' and such merely 'desirable' understandings. Understandings will, further, differ in their definiteness or vagueness, and in their genuine or merely presumed mutuality. What we take to be understandings may prove in part to be misunderstandings. Understandings will also obviously differ in their wide or narrow spread, the widest understandings applying to men in general, while the narrowest extend to but a few persons. A narrowly spread, but profound understanding is not, as such, of less value impersonally than a widely diffused but vaguer understanding. What is important, impersonally, however, is that narrower understandings should accord with, and be themselves made the subject of the widest possible understandings, as when there is communal approval of private contracts, marriages, special commitments, etc. etc. Understandings may, further, depart more or less from equality in the more deep-going senses of that notion—in some societies they crystallize inequalities and unfreedoms as in others they buttress liberties and equalities—and will obviously be more or less impersonally approvable on that count. And they may be directed to the promotion of what, impersonally, must be judged 'ill-fare' for some or all, e.g. the Nuremberg laws, or to what involves a lessening of someone's positive welfare, in which cases they may be judged doubly evil for their abuse of what is impersonally to be approved.

In all these possible cases of 'understandings' there will be an 'injury', an 'injustice', or at least what is abstractly to be considered an 'injury' or an 'injustice', in the violation of the

INJUSTICE AND ITS DISVALUES 309

understanding, however little there may be of equality or inequality in the whole matter. The understanding, as it were, crystallizes and defines equality, so that, in one sense, for persons to be treated equally, is for them to be able to exercise their 'understood', their agreed rights and liberties. If to walk alone in a garden enters into my agreed sphere of action, then to be denied access to that garden, or to have others thrust there alongside of me, is for me to be treated invasively, unequally, to suffer an abatement of my sphere which for others represents an extension, and so to undergo an injustice. I undergo this injustice even if the delimitation of spheres which allows me to walk alone in the garden is itself so unequal as to constitute an injustice, which those who keep me out, or who thrust themselves beside me, intend to remedy. In the latter case, injustice quarrels with injustice, and a conservative with a rectifying justice, and which is to be approved can be decided only in the full context of circumstances, consequences, understandings and interests. That a just rectification of inequalities may constitute an unjust infraction of understood spheres is shown by the *compensation* used to make such rectification acceptable.

Among the injustices involving infractions of agreed spheres of activity and enjoyment are most of the wrongs recognized in current moral codes, even if such codes may seem more intent on viewing these wrongs from the point of view of an agent, as things to be abstained from or punished, than in the much more fundamental perspective of the patient, without the evil of whose invaded 'world' there could be no active wrong or infringement at all. How ordinary morality revolves about the maintenance of necessary and desirable understandings, and the avoidance or prevention of their violation, need not be established in vast detail. To spread error and falsehood, or to deny access to useful knowledge, is to be responsible for evils that can be shown to be impersonally disvaluable, but the evil of deceit presupposes also the evil of violating an all-pervasive understanding, impersonally approvable if any can be called such, that men shall be eyes and ears, and generally informants to one another. In the same manner, for a man to be deprived of an object he undisputedly uses and disposes of, is an abatement of power constituting a natural injustice, but for others to take from him what it is agreed should stand to him in this relation, constitutes the injustice of

310 VALUES AND INTENTIONS

undergoing a theft which underlies the wrong of performing one. In the same way, for a man to lack the instruments, the appliances, the assistance, the defences, etc., that will save him from various great distresses is itself a great ill, but the injustice or wrong suffered in being unhelped by others in such predicaments, lies in the shocking violation of a deep-laid understanding of mutual aid, which shows itself by the shock readily awakened even in the violator, to have been written into each man's sphere of rights. It is not necessary for us to dwell long on those verbally created, circumstantially limited understandings known as promises and contracts, whose violation constitutes an evil proportional to their definiteness, nor on the vague special understandings between friends, lovers, allies, parents and children, etc. etc., as to what each party may expect the other party to perform. Difficulty and paradox enter when we consider that last violation of a man's agreed sphere of action which arises when he suffers death at the hands of others, a violation which would seem superficially to liquidate itself with the liquidation of the person violated. That we cannot accept this liquidation implies that we treat a conscious person, like a line in geometry, as something extending infinitely into past and future time, though only a small segment of that line represents actual conscious life. So great is the awe awakened by another man's otherness, that it extends even into the period when that other man is not. Hence too the fulfilment of promises made to the dead, etc. etc. Paradoxical, too, are the rights un-questioningly extended to animals, which seem to depend on a unilateral understanding. The wrongs suffered by innocent or faithful horses, consigned in old age to buffetings on the Irish Sea or in French trains, are not less the violation of a sphere which should be uninfringed, because such creatures have no under-standings with us. If we are to understand such paradoxical things, we must not flinch from embracing views which are daringly idealistic: we must (as in the parallel case of unconscious purpose) insist on understanding certain restricted forms of con-scious life are approximating towards, or as completing themselves in, forms of conscious life that are *in fact* beyond them. No man who has loved an animal can doubt that it merits a loyalty and a respect that it only inadequately reciprocates, and which extends beyond the limits of this present life. We cannot hope to sketch the ground-plan of the Kingdom of Ends without finding it spread

INJUSTICE AND ITS DISVALUES 311

into regions that are 'not of this world'. What must be kept in mind, however, in the labyrinthine windings of basic morality, is the necessary division of legitimated power or right into arbitrarily defined spheres or territories, in relation to which injury will acquire a more precise content and measure. The necessity that there should be such a division (i.e. the evil of its absence), rooted as it is in the mutual otherness of conscious persons, which in its turn is implied by the existence of any consciousness at all, should not blind us to its necessary arbitrariness in detail, though most moral theories have tended to forget one side or the other.

Delimitations of spheres or territories of right cannot be made in a wholly *ad hoc*, particular fashion, which fixes the boundaries within which a man's activity must remain, for each separate case or occasion. Such a delimitation would not only constitute an infinite, and therefore futile, task; it would also not be one on which many persons could *agree*, or on which they could *rely*. Not being agreed or relied on, it could not in effect delimit the spheres or territories of different people's activities at all. It is plain, therefore, that any delimitation of territories must be in some measure *general*, that there must be *rules*, not necessarily formulated or formulable, determining *when* a man's pursuit of his interests or exercise of his freedom are *within* his own sphere of activity, and therefore free from evil, and when they entrench on the sphere of someone else's permitted activity and experience. The understandings, therefore, which give persons their reliable scope must all be general: this is even so if they apply only to certain individuals or groups, or for limited regions and seasons. We comprehend, accordingly, the great stress on rules in the common morality: without rules no man could have his due, since it would not be clear what his due was. What should also be stressed, and is in fact stressed in countless criticisms of formalism or legalism, is the entirely auxiliary character of rules: they are needed to give concreteness and existence to the just and the unjust, they are as it were a bounding wall which contains the latter, and prevents them from becoming quite nebulous, but their value depends on *what* they contain, and will reverse its sign if this is profoundly altered. In other words, without any worthwhile activities to set bounds to, and without any general directive away from arbitrary inequality, there could be no point

VALUES AND INTENTIONS

to rules: they might give firm contours or reliability to the indifferent or the bad. If in a concentration camp everyone knew what torments to expect and at what times, this could only in travesty be the reception of one's due. It is only when a system of rules gives definite shape to the desirable and the equal that it can have any claim to be valued, let alone to be impersonally valued. And where the bounds of the desirable and the equal *can* be decided step by step in the concrete, as they are by travelling companions, etc., who 'get on well' with one another, the need for rules largely vanishes. Attempts, therefore, to make possible erection into rule the defining character of the moral, must be held gravely superficial. To see the right and just in situations where similar cases receive similar treatment, is to consider merely the shell of justice and morality, whose content might be totally rotten. To be in any way acceptable as a principle of the right and just, erection into rule must be given a powerful negative meaning, which will give it a connection with equality. It must mean a *rejection of difference* in the treatment of different persons as regards their participation in welfare, except in the case of such differences as are *internally* related to such welfare, differences, e.g., in the capacity or wish of individuals to participate in certain forms of welfare, differences in their willingness to forward welfare in themselves and others, etc. etc. Universality must accordingly have the meaning of *overriding* all but a set of differences relevant to one's special material, for each of which a case, and an *a priori* case, must be made out; if it is geared to any and every trivial difference, it becomes the empty universality of formal logic. It is plain that Kant, in applying his first formulation of his Categorical Imperative, meant the universality of what is willed by his pure will to be of the former kind: it has regard to the maintenance of conscious life, to the development of its higher potentialities, to the fabric of mutual trust and aid necessary for this higher development, etc. It is neither too indiscriminate in its generality, nor too narrowly discriminating, but may be said to discriminate against anything that tends towards the arbitrary and the contingent, and to discriminate *in favour of* of whatever favours *its own* existence and perpetuation. It is not, however, our aim to enter into the difficult minutiae of Kantian criticism, beyond saying that, though superficially formal, his moral theory shows all the readiness to develop into a highly

INJUSTICE AND ITS DISVALUES 313

specified teleology that has been the inspiration of the present work.

(III) CORRECTIVE JUSTICE

From the justice of distribution and mutual understandings we pass on to the justice traditionally called 'corrective', which plainly belongs to the same family. This is the justice that 'puts right' injustices in distribution or violations of spheres of right, and may be reckoned with the other forms of justice, both because it is concerned with the distributions and spheres just mentioned, and also because it is concerned with a kind of equality: the correction must measure up, must be equal to the disturbance of justice, so that the original equilibrium is after a manner restored. The basic case of this justice is the *redistributive*, where an unjust departure from equality, or an unjust encroachment on a sphere of rights, is corrected (if it can be simply corrected) by a countering change in the distribution of welfare or its contrary, until a just arrangement is come to. To this may be added the more complex form of punitive and rewarding correction, in both of which the departure from equality, or the encroachment on spheres of rights, is attributed to a conscious, and in most cases to a fully voluntary, agent, who is normally advantaged or disadvantaged by the unjust state of things. In punitive correction a conscious, and in most cases, voluntary disadvantaging of, or encroachment upon, unconsenting others, is met by a balancing disadvantage to the injurious person. In rewarding correction, it is rather a voluntary self-disadvantaging for the benefit of others, whose outcome is of the nature of a transformed (because accepted) injustice, which is met by some countervailing advantage. The notions of such punitive and rewarding correction may be extended to cover all cases where something impersonally judged good or evil is voluntarily compassed, whether this good or evil be concerned with the relations of welfare among persons or not: we may approve of a correction undergone by someone who did some evil to himself alone, or who created an evil, e.g. ugliness, mental confusion, in many people's experience, but not more so in others than in himself. This extended use, however, covers the liquidation of evils that can only by a stretch be called injustices—a man acting within his rights, and necessarily consenting to what he himself does,

314   VALUES AND INTENTIONS

cannot be said to suffer injustice at his own hands, nor can the creation of ugliness or confusion rightly be ranked under injustice —and so cannot itself count as a case of justice.

Corrective justice has a relatively clear countenance, but its features have been blurred by the bringing in of features pertaining to that other justice which is a *virtue* in men's minds and behaviour, and which normally issues in arrangements that are just. Corrective justice is used, and is by its nature fitly used, to turn persons lacking in the virtue of justice into persons possessed of that virtue, or to maintain those who possess it in their possession, but the possibility of making an unjust man just by correction, or of keeping a just man just, presupposes that such men recognize and fully accept the justice of what they undergo. This means that there must be a justice in correction, independent of and logically prior to the justice it induces or strengthens. It is not, however, in virtue of this 'justifying' (in an old sense) power that the correction of an injustice is just, which is not to say that the making just of persons may not be a reason, and perhaps the strongest reason, for punitive and rewarding correction. We may also recur to the point that we are at present concerned with, correction from the point of view of the corrected person and his victim, and not from that of the correcting agent. Punitive and rewarding correction, if suitably 'appropriated' by the persons concerned, may be administered by a fortuitous or by a mechanical agency. I may, e.g., be rewarded for my thankless tutorship of some pupil by his brilliant performance in an examination, which is not at all done to reward me, and I may 'meet my deserts' for neglecting another pupil by his lamentable breakdown, by being myself neglected by my intellectual superiors, etc. etc. A connection or appropriation in my own mind is of course necessary to make a piece of misfortune into a requital—I am not punished for neglecting a pupil by failing to win in the pools, but it need not be a connection in the mind of some punishing authority.

Our judgements of corrective justice, like our judgements of justice generally, have a great deal of initial clearness: here if anywhere we seem to *know* what is disvaluable or the reverse, and even the extent to which this is so. In no field, however, do our judgements so readily transform themselves, so that what emerges is often neither corrective nor deserving of the name of 'justice'. It will be our task to develop and apply impersonality

INJUSTICE AND ITS DISVALUES 315

in this field, trying to keep a place for our deep sense of the importance of the ἀντιπεπονθός, of refined impersonal requittal, in achieving adjustments among persons.

In the case of what we have called redistributive justice, it is not hard to see how it can be impersonally justified. If a distribution of welfare is impersonally frowned on, as departing too far from equality, or as involving encroachments on understood spheres of right, there can be nothing but right reason in having the matter put straight, whether by an 'act of God' or the hands of men. As regards inequitable distributions, the best way in which unequal shares in the good could be levelled, would be by a levelling *up* all round, just as the best way in which unequal shares in the bad would be levelled would be by a general levelling *down*. To prefer reduction in the positively good, or increase in the positively evil, merely because it secured greater equity in distribution, would, however, involve a profound misjudgement: the misjudgement of treating justice as a value, and injustice as a disvalue, independent of, and superior to, the well-being or ill of which it represents the ordering distribution, and to which it at best contributes a perfecting form. Obviously without the various forms of welfare, there could be nothing to be impersonal or equitable about, and hence only an unreasonable and purely personal interest in the empty form of justice.

It follows that where there is scarcity of the means to produce welfare, or difficulty in transferring those means, it is preferable that *great* inequalities of welfare should exist rather than that satisfaction or other forms of well-being should be lessened, or that pain, ignorance, etc., should be augmented. This is the standing justification of the brilliant, unequal societies of the past, which will presumably not hold in the more abundant, more 'liquid' future. It is plain, too, that since the working shape of justice is nothing without some arbitrary delimitation of rights, to abrogate or remould that system necessarily involves injustice, sometimes justifiable, sometimes not. In the case, further, of all violations of spheres of rights—considered apart from moral badness in their perpetrators—there must likewise obviously be not merely restitution of values foregone and surcease of evils suffered: there must also be 'damages' for values foregone and evils suffered in the past, compensations as like in form to the values and evils in question as circumstances allow, including

316   VALUES AND INTENTIONS

among circumstances not only the availability of various sources of satisfaction, but also the changing tastes and wills of the persons concerned. All this, with its indefinite plastic arbitrariness surrounding an unmalleable matrix, is the basic stuff of law and jurisprudence, into whose detail we cannot enter. We may only stress that it has an application quite apart from law and the human agency which law directs. I might, e.g., be compensated for the breach of your promise by fortuitous circumstances which gave me what you had promised: unless it is all-important to me that the service or facility promised should be provided by *you*, my compensation is full, even if it does not remove *your* moral badness for letting me down. When compensation cannot be exact, it must be more or less arbitrary or 'token': the wronged person must accept it *as* compensation, *as* satisfaction in place of desires foregone, evils endured, etc. Objectivity in these matters is not separable from the agreement of all concerned.

From the justice of redistribution and restitution it is but a step to a sort of justice which presses on beyond unfair distributions and encroachments, to the personal wants and dispositions from which these spring. To disapprove of the former is plainly to disapprove of the latter. So far we are not considering any pure love of the disposition of which just arrangements are the issue, nor any pure abhorrence of the dispositions issuing in outcomes which are unjust: we are considering an attitude wholly derived and instrumental, one which draws its strength wholly from the love of the just, and detestation of the unjust *outcome*, and which proportions itself wholly to the latter. It is plain that we do not here have a peculiar sphere of justice, but of quasi-justice parasitic upon genuine justice. It is at a second remove just that such activities should be bounded or restrained or deterred as are likely to lead to outcomes which are in the primary sense unjust, and to leave undisturbed, or positively encourage, activities which are likely to lead to outcomes in the primary sense just. That power should be so allocated that persons likely to subvert justice should be scant of it (the irresponsible, the criminal classes, etc.), while those likely to respect justice should have more of it (the responsible citizenship), is a rudimentary maxim of statesmanship, having a sound, if humdrum, *a priori* justification. So too have the institution of various purely preventive or deterrent, or encouraging or cajoling measures, whether applied to a man's

INJUSTICE AND ITS DISVALUES 317

immediate and animal, or emergent and rational nature, and regardless whether just or unjust outcomes are actual or merely in prospect. The deterrent and preventive justification of punitive measures is no refining gloss on primitive retaliation: obviously it has at all times played a part in our moral logic. And it is plain that there is no limit to the interior depth into which the merely instrumental treatment of personal dispositions may not press: any sort of spiritual machinery that will reliably produce just outcomes will be impersonally approved. We may even justify in this manner the differential treatment accorded to the free, voluntary choice of an unjust outcome over the impulsive, passionate pursuit of the same: admonition and punishment have stronger effect on the former than they can hope to have on the latter. It is thus that certain modern philosophers have justified the more or less exclusive ascription of responsibility to fully voluntary determinations, and the praise, blame, reward and punishment that go with it: we ascribe and praise, etc., where such a course is likely to be influential in shaping conduct in the direction of justice.

To value men's attitudes or characters for the just or unjust outcomes which issue from them is impersonally to be approved: it does not, however, lead to any *new* notion of the just or unjust, but transfers the approval accorded to an outcome to its productive instrument. If there is to be a new form of corrective justice, in which the movement towards 'inwardness' will be essential and not accidental, then it must be one in which that inwardness is respectfully left to itself, and neither harried nor moulded. Yet this is precisely the note lacking in the forms of instrumental 'justice' we have been examining. Such new forms will leave intact a man's sphere of intimate, personal decision, and avoid all encroachment upon it, yet it is precisely such encroachment that is practised when we seek to deter men from decisions productive of unjust outcomes, even before they have made them, when no distinction is drawn between wrongs done and wrongs merely possible to be done, nor between wrongs having their source in unrationalized wants in the conscious person, and wrongs springing from whole-minded determinations having regard to a total firmament of facts and values. Procedures which encroach on something so central, which by its detachment from defined wants is so intimately related to our impersonal valuations, cannot

318 VALUES AND INTENTIONS

be impersonally approved: they must have a savour which ranks them among the subtler forms of injustice. If it is an injustice, an invasion of my personality, that I should be deprived of my expected, in aspiration equal share of well-being, it is an injustice, likewise, that I should be pushed hither and yon in order that unjust outcomes should not flow from my actions, that I should be remoulded *ab extra* so as not to produce these. All this is what we deeply feel, in our horror at various forms of intrusive personal and social betterment, and which can be seen to have the profoundest justification. For it is of the essence of our higher conscious causality that its alignment or non-alignment, even with its own firmament of values, should have an element of purely self-determining gratuitousness, and to seek to give it any antecedent definiteness and reliability, other than that which it gives itself in action and decision, is to seek to demote it to the lower levels of primary wanting, to seek, that is, to expunge it altogether. And justice must certainly set aside a space for the exercise of this higher conscious causality, as it sets this aside for the lower, and especially since the detachment of conscious causality from primary wants is the source of all impersonal value. None of this, we may note, makes sense if the self-closing 'openness' of our higher voluntary causality is denied, an argument for taking such 'openness' very seriously. This is not to say, of course, that the injustice of invading someone's sphere of 'free-will' may not at times have its justification, the invasion of a possibly injurious man's personality being preferred to his invasion of other people's welfare and personal liberty. All of which leads us to a corrective justice which respects, rather than overrides, the corrected person's sphere of self-determining choice, and which is a justice of *repayment* or *requital,* one which in a sense gives a man exactly what *he* has asked for by his actions, and so realizes a novel pattern of justice.

If I have wilfully (not ignorantly nor on some hot impulse) overridden the well-demarcated boundaries of spheres of right, in which the abstract ideal of the equal achieves concrete embodiment, then it seems just that, in addition to restitution or compensation, *my* sphere of right should be invaded to what is, from the point of view of *my* lower or higher welfare, an equal extent, that I should suffer an ill equal in my sphere to the ill inflicted by me on others, and that for me *not* to suffer such an ill is itself an evil, an injustice. It is unsatisfactory that I, having voluntarily produced an injustice, should not suffer at the hands of others, or by the dispensation of fate, or through my own agency, what would in itself have constituted an injustice, or at least an evil, had it not occurred in this context. I must, for depriving others of what they personally find satisfactory, or what satisfies also some impersonal segment of their nature, suffer as nearly like a diminution in what I myself find satisfactory, or in what satisfies the higher side of my nature. I must, for giving pain, be made to endure pain; for deceiving or betraying, myself be deceived or betrayed; for turning back friendship have my own friendship turned back, etc. etc. And for such requital to be perfect, I must myself connect it with my own voluntary transgression; I must see in it, as it were, my own wrong come back upon me, and in some mysterious manner restoring equilibrium through such return. This somewhat grim picture is balanced by a more endearing one when we consider the requital of unsolicited acts of generosity, benevolence, love, etc. Here it is just that the generous or gracious person should receive an unsolicited kindness or act of grace, perhaps at the hands of some wholly unconnected person, perhaps even through natural workings, and there is injustice in its total absence, even if not a grave case of injustice. And for such requital to be perfect, the man rewarded must himself consciously connect the reward with the action—he need not, however, see any causal connection between them, but only one of justice or fitness. In all this we without thought approve almost exact equations, both in quality and quantity, which it is not often possible should be achieved in fact, and for which there must be a great deal of taking the will for the deed, imaginative turning of near-likenesses into exact ones, and, in general, 'token' or symbolic substitution. But despite the often comic difficulty of 'making the punishment fit the crime' (or the reward the benefit), we still feel it to be an ideal to which sense can be attributed, and whose token-achievement must afford impersonal satisfaction.

The feeling in question is, however, subject to reverses, and that not merely as regards the absurd pressure towards a mechanical, mathematical exactness, which can mean nothing once the vast inward differences of persons are reflected on, but also as regards its basic principle. For while the requital of good by good

320 VALUES AND INTENTIONS

is at least an innocent augmentation of good, the requital of evil by evil seems to involve an augmentation of evil by evil, which it is hard to see could be approvable under any colour. Can it really be a just state of affairs that such evils as betrayals, sufferings of cruelties, subjections to deep deceits, loss of freedoms, etc. etc., should be balanced by more or less exact counter-evils, and can it be that for them not to be so balanced is a state unjust and therefore evil? Is there not something heartless in Professor Moore's well-known appeal to a 'Principle of Organic Wholes', which makes it true that two evils put together in one miscreant, the evil of wrongdoing and the evil of pain, should make a *positive* contribution to the betterment of things? There are at least Socratic, Buddhist and Christian protests against such returning of evil for evil, with a strange effect of being 'higher' and more authoritative than the cruder equity they seek to displace. These protests have had the effect of shifting the justice of repayment into instrumental channels: repayment is justified only by its deterrent or by its educative power. The deep sense of a peculiar fitness and unfitness, at once original and yet having affinities with various members of the family of the just and the unjust, is not, however, so lightly to be exorcised. We must search, therefore, for its impersonal foundation.

There are two directions in which we may hope to find the impersonal foundation in question. We may see it, on the one hand, on a carrying over of an injurious personal wish on to the plane of impersonal justice, thereby providing a sort of *reductio ad absurdum* of such a wish: we may see it also in a carrying over of the demand for justice on to the plane of personal satisfaction and dissatisfaction, thereby creating a sort of personal *symbol* for the former. We may now attempt to give clearness to these two suggestions.

The impersonal attitude which inspires the desire for an equal, reliable justice among persons, must of necessity seek to *attune* personal wants and wishes to itself, to make of them the materials through which it can be made manifest. Being thus directed, it must even work towards the impossible goal of harmonizing injurious personal wishes with itself, of endowing them with the equal respect for all conscious persons in which they are so characteristically lacking. It must, to use the language of Kant, seek to make of the maxims of an unjust wish a universal (i.e.

INJUSTICE AND ITS DISVALUES 321

impartial and equal) law. But to raise the injurious wish to the impersonal level is to wish, in addition, that whoever inflicts the injury should be willing to suffer it at the hands of others, and it is this transformed wish that can alone have a standing at the impersonal level, and that must persist there as long as the injurious personal wish persists. As beings capable of rising to impersonal wishes and decisions, we must, then, of necessity wish that the latter should be requited by injuries exactly balancing those that they seek to compass. This wish necessarily involves a conflict, since the injurious wish is itself inimical to an impersonal cast of mind, but it is a conflict reduced to a stalemate, and so the nearest approach to the impersonally satisfactory in the circumstances. If wrongs are to be perpetrated at all, then it is least evil, that those who do them, and who experience only their advantageous side, should experience their other side as well, that the full impersonal development of a wrong should be achieved for them. The fitness of the whole strange balance is not unlike that of a *reductio ad absurdum* argument. Having accepted an absurd premiss, we must, by reason bound, accept an absurd conclusion, and we must continue to embrace the latter as long as we refuse to rescind the former. Only by retracing our steps altogether, and abandoning both conclusion and premiss, can we be freed from this embarrassment. It is not absurd to compare punishments to arguments: has it not often been said that 'he who will not hear must feel'?

Alternatively, we may look on requital as a transference of the impersonal dissatisfaction directed to an injury to the personal level, where it is, after a fashion, *represented* by a personal dissatisfaction. Injuries, *qua* injuries, i.e. as infractions of equality and of duly appointed spheres of right, are not necessarily looked on with aversion by either patient or agent. To the former they may appear only as something unwanted, i.e. personally disadvantageous, and to the latter they may appear only as personally advantageous. But being impersonally opposed to injuries and injurious wishes, we impersonally wish that our opposition should penetrate to the personal level, that it should not be by-passed or ignored by a man absorbed in his own wants. To desire, however, that it should penetrate to the personal level is to desire that something should *represent* it there, something which, though not the same as impersonal disgust or displeasure, should in some

L

322 VALUES AND INTENTIONS

fashion naturally serve to rouse or introduce the latter, should in some manner *symbolize* values which have an impersonal status. Our impersonal attitude to injustices and unjust acts is, however, one of rejection, displeasure, disvaluation, and the light in which it makes us see objects one of disvalue. What more intrinsically suitable symbol, therefore, for such disvalue than the personal disvalue which reflects our own personal frustrations and dissatisfactions, which is for us, as particular individuals, precisely what the absolute disvalues of injustice are for us as impartial judges? There will therefore be an intrinsic fitness or justness in bringing the injustice of outcomes, and, in a different sense, of wishes, *home* to the injurious individual, by way of a symbolism intrinsically fitted to do this, and this means by a symbolism of personal frustration and pain. For such justice to be consummated, it is of course necessary that the person whose injustice is being requited should be himself clear what his pains or frustrations symbolize or are meant to bring home: otherwise we should be merely piling evil on evil. Hence, too, the obvious difficulty of punishing animals or very young children, and especially after a lapse of time: they cannot pass from a pain to the infraction it penalizes, nor succeed thereby in seeing the latter as an infraction. On this particular way of regarding the matter, punishment is to be assimilated, not to an argument, but to the intimation of a single value-assertion or judgement. The evil of an injustice, which may not touch an individual nearly, is brought home to him in a symbolism of personal pain and frustration that he is unable to ignore and cannot but understand. Normally, of course, this 'bringing home' is effected by other conscious individuals, often by the individuals wronged, but there is no reason why, if the 'bringing home' is effective, it should not come about by unconscious agency. Thus I may be punished for my selfishness in refusing to have the bother of bringing up children, by the absence in my old age of children who will bother about me. Even if the condemnation symbolized by my present abandonment is neither entertained nor intimated to me by others, it may still be entertained by, and expressively symbolized for me: the parallel with speech is therefore sustained. This parallel also shows itself in the way in which admonition regularly passes over into punishment. Here, as in our previous interpretation, we may endorse the slogan: He who will not hear must feel.

INJUSTICE AND ITS DISVALUES 323

The two justifications of the deeply felt justice of requital are, of course, not the only ones that could be given, nor are they necessarily the clearest or the most direct. There must be many other routes of non-rigorous proof leading from truths involving basic notions like that of impersonality to the peculiar positions in question. Every knot in the impersonally attested web of values is the meeting-point of countless threads of connection, more or less subtle or strong, which give the knot its place in the whole fabric, and which communicate approvability from part to part. As in a system of symbolic logic, practically any proposition could be made an axiom, and could permit the deduction of many other propositions, so in the system of values there are innumerable lines of support leading from one notion or principle to another. That particular lines may be perhaps thin and prone to snap when examined does not affect their overall strength, which seems, despite all sorts of rational tensions, to hold requital firmly in its place. Requital, we may say, has a *residual* approvability over which countless considerations of benevolence, love of good, desire to reform, etc., properly take precedence, for reasons to be discussed more fully later. This approvability is subject to fewer tensions in the parallel case of reward, which we have not discussed in detail, for there is no piling on of evil if the generous man finds his bread cast upon waters returning to him after an interval, or if the value to be accorded to his generosity is brought home to him in the love and gratitude of his fellows. That such reward may corrupt the generosity it rewards is undoubted, but, unlike punitive requital, it involves only a probable, not a certain production of evil.

Our justification also explains why requital, in the full and proper sense, attaches only to coolly taken decisions and determinations, to those involving the 'consent' of the will, or parallel considered forms of acceptance, and not to primary wants and impulses, which do not pursue what they pursue in the full light of an organized firmament of facts and values. We may *penalize* immature beings for impulsive acts involving unjust outcomes (and may in the same way encourage them to acts having just outcomes), but such penalization and encouragement are merely a propaedeutic which it is hoped will lead to the attachment of an impersonal bad or good 'mark' to certain outcomes or wishes. Only when this training has been completed can we begin to

VALUES AND INTENTIONS

speak of requital, i.e. of a penalization which is also fully just. The *rationale* which limits requital to what is freely and voluntarily chosen is therefore evident: in our impersonal aspect our pronouncements are cool and fully reasoned, in that they accept what they accept in its full setting of facts and values, and we can therefore only 'speak' to and reason with an attitude that has something of the same organized, systematic, well-weighed character. A man who coolly determines that 'for him' the gratification of sexual or acquisitive interests shall override considerations of justice, higher cultivation, etc., is making the same sort of whole-minded, to-be-carried-through-in-all-circumstances sort of determination—though not of course *exactly* the same sort—as a man (the same or another) who, in his impersonal capacity, rates the fulfilment of justice above such gratifications. What we choose voluntarily, or accept in some other whole-minded fashion, we in a sense accept with a whole 'philosophy' attaching to our acceptance: our attitude is not like that of primitive personal wants which race hot-foot to their immediate objectives without being committed to anything beyond these. A 'philosophy' that attempts to be impersonal can parley with other 'philosophies' that have something of its own thorough-going, well-weighed character, and can attempt to lift them to its own plane: it can have no argument, only disciplinary relations, with mere impulses that do not expand into such a comprehensive 'philosophy'. Since requital is an exceedingly drastic form of moral exhortation or reproof it can by its definition only be applied where it can be *understood*, i.e. to beings capable of whole-minded, fully consequential determination both of an impersonally acceptable or not acceptable sort. The Hegelian insight which makes all punishment in a sense self-inflicted, the reaction of one's own fully developed, rational will to its more undeveloped, immediate forms, can therefore be very fully sustained.

Our justification further explains why punitive and rewarding requital are not satisfactory, when merely proportioned to the disvalues of injustice (or uncovenanted well-being) achieved, but must also be proportioned to the degree of *wittingness* and whole-minded determination underlying such achievement. Obviously to the extent that our determination to effect an injustice reaches the whole-minded level, and we commit ourselves to the injustice in the full light of its infinitely numerous

INJUSTICE AND ITS DISVALUES

consequences, *to that extent* are we capable of being reasoned with or requited. To the extent, however, that our determination springs from relatively blind, one-track impulsive forces, to that extent do reasoning and requital alike become out of place. Requital will also obviously be justly proportioned to the degree of force manifest at the level of cool, whole-minded endeavour and the degree of force manifest at the impulsive level. If I am being hurried towards injustice by relatively blind impulses of various sorts, which would make a cool decision in the opposite direction difficult, I am only to a small extent open to requital, since the unjust outcome largely springs from sources not to be reasoned with, while those that *can* be reasoned with have perhaps exerted themselves in vain. If, however, an unjust outcome has been chosen without difficulty, or perhaps even in the face of difficulty, its source is one justly to be reasoned with, and this, in the extreme case, through the drastic method of requital. What we are now touching upon ties up, however, with the various complex values and disvalues of moral goodness and badness, of the degree of dedicated self-committal to the production of good or bad respectively. Obviously it is moral goodness or virtue, not merely good results, that is justly rewarded, and it is moral badness, and not merely bad or unjust results, that is justly punished. The treatment of moral goodness and badness cannot, however, be attempted by the way, but will concern us fully in the next chapter, where we shall also attempt the 'mopping up' of some remaining questions regarding reward and punishment.

Our justifications will also have made clear the necessary connection of reward and punishment with betterment and reform. To have had one's unjust attitude developed for one, in impartial, systematic fashion, so that the injustice one has been willing to inflict on another now recoils on oneself, is not necessarily to suffer a translation of mood to the impersonal plane, nor to abandon injustice to be quit of this recoil. But, in much the same manner, to follow a *reductio ad absurdum* argument to its conclusion, and to find one's favourite premiss entailing something unacceptable, is not necessarily to abandon that premiss. One may adhere to it, and reject the sort of reasoning involved, or not make *any* consistent decision. There is, however, something difficult and uncomfortable in adhering to a premiss which lead one on, along a seemingly unobjectionable route, to an outcome

326 VALUES AND INTENTIONS

one cannot believe in. There is a necessity or near-necessity, neither formal nor belonging to the merely natural order, which forces one back along one's path, and, if one cannot find fault with its steps or other premises, ultimately compels abandonment of a given premiss. In much the same manner, it is a near-necessity, in beings capable of putting themselves in their neighbour's shoes and thinking impersonally, that the recoil of injustice upon themselves should force them back upon the injustice which led to the recoil, and should end by eroding and destroying the latter. That this is a near-necessity, of course, sets no precise limit to the period in which it may be resisted. In the same manner, if the pains of requital naturally and understandably symbolize the injustice of certain transgressions, there is reason to expect that they will transfer part of the dislike felt for what painfully requites us to the injustice it symbolizes: to be punishable at all is to be capable of this sort of transference. That penal fires purify is therefore neither a superstition nor an empirical fact; it has, as we always obscurely know it to have, a considerable tincture of the *a priori*.

The justice of requital is, in some ways, one of the most impressive expressions of impersonality, and is in fact usually recognized as such. The impartiality of punitive justice, which overcomes even our shrinking from what must be impersonally accounted evil, and which achieves the highest good of the transgressor only by resolutely ignoring it, is obviously among the loftiest of impartialities. It is plain, however, that, like the justice of distribution, it has point only as containing and stabilizing the welfare of conscious persons, and that it loses all sense if maintained to the destruction of persons and their possible welfare and moral advance. Though the removal of the discomforts flowing from injustice, and the purification of the unjust individual, are not *all* that gives it its importance, it could have no importance *apart* from their possibility. All this means that punitive justice lives very much on sufferance, and that circumstances are always mitigating or abrogating its claims. If an unjust orientation can be cured by methods other than those of punitive justice, and without its admixture of evil, e.g. by various forms of mild and kind treatment, then the whole mechanism of such justice loses its justification, and becomes even inappropriate and evil. There are also injustices of such

INJUSTICE AND ITS DISVALUES 327

atrocity that their strict requital would be predominantly evil. Himmler may have borrowed the horrors of his concentration camps from Hieronymus Bosch's notions of the concentration camps of the Almighty, but the Almighty, we may be sure, will not visit on Himmler anything like the horrors he compassed, but only others more decent, more subtle and in the long run more profoundly erosive. In traditional words, it is clear that punitive justice always demands either a seasoning of, or a super-session by mercy: it cannot be divorced from concern for the person punished and his possible return to virtue. When requital becomes an end separated from the other ends which merit impersonal approval, it becomes the expression mainly of egoism, resentment, hatred and other odious passions. To crude sensibili-ties its claims may seem paramount and overwhelming, but moral reflection always drives it into a rather narrow corner, where it has strength only in conjunction with values less equivocal.

(IV) PLATONIC JUSTICE

Our account of justice demands completion by a treatment of a simulacrum of justice which resembled the original sufficiently to have been confused with it by a great philosopher. This is the justice which does not so much strive to apportion welfare equally, as to distribute it in widely differing, mutually complementary ways, which does not seek to build up rigorously delimited spheres of right, but rather co-ordinates persons and their activities in a complex, co-operative, highly variable plan or enterprise, which does not reward excellence and punish transgression so much as shape a person's whole character continually by a thousand subtle influences, aesthetic, intellectual, ethical, etc. etc. Both Plato and Hegel have sketched the profile of this semblance of justice, and have written into it features vaguely disruptive of the outline sketched above: the use of political deceits, the fixation and limitation of opinion, the somewhat arbitrary division of persons into classes having unequal shares in responsibility and experience, the value set upon military regimentation and the discipline of war, etc. etc. Hegel has, in fact, done this infinitely less than Plato, since for him the highly integrated state-life *presupposes* the basic respect for persons and the system of spheres of right, etc., characteristic of ordinary justice: it is superimposed

328 VALUES AND INTENTIONS

on, and does not override the latter. Most of the hostility to Hegel's ideal of integrated social life is in fact quite ignorant and prejudiced, based only on some of his more ebullient statements, and on vague associations with Prussianism, Nazism, etc. It is, however, plain that the notion of a justice in some ways diametrically opposed to what may be called 'classical justice', has had a heady effect on many, and has led in our time to the worst atrocities perpetrated in history. We shall not see around or through these, however, nor direct to them anything more fruitful than invective, unless we become clear as to the deep values which this notion corrupts and twists, which, though they may not perhaps have title to the name of 'justice', have none the less their own indefeasible, impersonal warrant.

Our treatment of values of 'personal transcendence' in the last chapter has made it plain that there is an impersonal warrant for all states in which personal barriers are reduced, in which there comes to be a profound *sharing* of the ideas, sentiments and enterprises of other persons. We were then concerned with such self-transcendence merely as something of great moment to the individual person, as a unique enlargement of his welfare. It requires only a small shift of standpoint to perceive a cognate value in profound communion and sharing *among* persons, a value, like justice, attaching to the way persons stand to one another, rather than to what they experience and do by themselves. Plato's description of a profoundly unified society, where the whole, as it were, suffers and rejoices *in* each member, and is not made up of disjoined persons battling for their own rights, is obviously a glorious rainbow on the horizon of our values, even if not readily realizable in the middle distances. It is the same ideal which arouses our necessary enthusiasm when we read of the still, white rose composed of blessed spirits in harmony with which Dante ends his *Paradiso*. It is also what Hegel describes in many of the most beautiful passages in the *Phenomenology*. What is very plain is that, as men come to share in common rational enterprises of various sorts, the whole rigorous separation of the *meum* and *tuum* loses its *raison d'être*, and classical justice becomes, not so much superseded, as inapplicable. And it is plain that such a sharing—if not pushed to a limit where there are no differences or barriers to transcend, and sharing is consequently no achievement—must itself be an approvable object of endeavour.

INJUSTICE AND ITS DISVALUES 329

It is evident, first of all, that likeness and equality, the cornerstones of justice, have only recommended themselves on account of the schism and parallelism among persons, because one person's satisfactions, developments and freedoms might be nothing to another, and because each person was, in a sense, an infinite world of experience capable of production in every direction without intersection with others, and outweighing by its simple infinity every difference of intelligence, sensitivity, practical capacity, etc. etc. In themselves, however, likeness and equality represent only the readiest, most obvious, and therefore least precious form of continuity and unity. There is in them no element of the difficult which makes the creation or imposition of unity and continuity an achievement worthy of remark. And reduplication of the like and equal plainly becomes more facile and empty the farther it goes: its effect must be to *cheapen* the value of what is so multiplied. Nothing, e.g., can be more cheerless to contemplate than an endless increase of the conscious population of the world, without increase in the diversity of their gifts, enjoyments, insights, etc. If it were unavoidable, it might exert a reluctant pressure on our sense of justice, but it could give satisfaction only to Benthamite greed, insensitive to every value beyond an increase in satisfaction. It follows that, to the extent that conscious persons do not merely live unto themselves, but enter deeply into each other's achievements, experiences, etc., and to the extent that they *consent* to departures from equality, we really reach a situation where it is possible to speak of the 'fruitful inequality' with which Fascist ideology made so much play. Obviously in all relations of deep love and understanding it is a blessed thing that the parties are diverse and unequal, that the one soars where the other crawls, that the one is all warmth and colour, while the other is austere, silvern order, etc. etc. The wonderful fringe experiences, where it is permitted to each to stray among the strange fruit, foliage and climate of an alien, but graciously welcoming world, would be impossible without it. The incredible delights of conversation presuppose disparities which, if not accepted, would constitute injustices. It goes without saying that in relations of deep love and understanding the boundaries of spheres of right become blurred: it does not matter that something is done by A's effort and not B's, that A explores this new territory and not B, etc. etc. And all forms of exact

L*

330 VALUES AND INTENTIONS

requital, whether rewarding or punitive, will become odious; they will introduce a formalism into relations in which even impulsive injustice would be more acceptable. Obviously, in lesser degree, all these things will be true in a well-knit, organic community, which, while preserving a firm framework of classical justice, supplements this with all sorts of unconvenanted kindnesses, flexibilities, mutual adjustments, etc. etc., the sort of cohesive spirit which informs whole segments of certain societies and makes it a joy to live in them.

In what then shall we see the fault of those totalitarian-minded theories which have corrupted what is so much the flower of human existence into an image so loathsome? Their error plainly consists in forgetting that it *is* the flower, something that can be coaxed, not forced into blossom, the very heart of whose sensitive being abhors all obligation. And their error has lain in trying to make it *take the place* of the classical justice, to which obligation is essential, which must impose a system of equal rights and requite their violation forcibly. Plainly injustice, whether in the patient's form of having one's share diminished or one's sphere invaded, or the agent's form of performing such diminution or invasion, or in the agent-patient's form of doing so unrequited, are things gravely evil, which merit the strongest measures of prevention, resistance and abolition, in which classical justice, in its essentially negative character, will automatically make its appearance. But Platonic justice, unlike classical justice, is essentially positively good, something which adds a grace to existence; it is something to be striven after, encouraged, carefully nurtured, but whose absence is regretfully to be tolerated. It is not therefore something to be maintained in being by beatings, brainwashings, continuous propaganda or terrors, not even by anything mildly threatening and compulsive. To this may be added that Platonic justice only can superimpose its inequalities and disparities on the equalities of pure justice through the mediation of sympathy and consent: these must be largely lacking in a system bolstered by force. Totalitarian corruptions of Platonic justice have further erred in two respects: by imposing artificial uniformities on conscious persons in directions where true Platonic justice would foster diversities, and by producing artificial diversities under which conscious persons are arbitrarily divided up. The *Gleichschaltung* of the Nazis illustrates the former

INJUSTICE AND ITS DISVALUES 331

corruption, the classes of Plato's *Republic* the latter. These classes would be admirable if they corresponded to genuine diversities of human endowment, as would the domination of various sorts of 'master races' over 'lesser breeds'. Since they have in fact a basis largely in upbringing and instilled prejudice, and can be wholly changed in a generation, organic systems which stereotype them do not go far in exploring the true possibilities of Platonic justice. And totalitarian distortions of this justice have normally combined cohesion within the group with injustice and cruelty beyond it. All of which horrors do not make it improper that men should live in a number of circles of lessening intimacy, passing from a central group in which classical justice is dispensed with, and Platonic justice reigns supreme, to wider and wider groups in which there is less and less of Platonic, and more and more of classical justice, until in the outermost zones only the latter remains. Fraternity is obviously best maintained if its sphere does not coincide with those of liberty and equality: there is as much a place for the closed tribe as for the 'open society'.

What we have sought to do in this section is not to decide the various vexed questions as to the due place of our two 'justices' in practical situations, but to claim for both a definite place in the same firmament of 'absolute values'. As remarked previously, the relation between the two 'justices' rather resembles the relation between the two 'probabilities': one, the classical, being disjunctive and egalitarian, formalistic and tychistic, the other (that of theoretical science) being implicative and preferential, synechistic and ampliative. The former flourishes in a field of ignorance and mutual irrelevance of factors, as does classical justice in a world of mutually disregarding persons: the latter flourishes where there is deep immersion in the peculiarities of one's material, as Platonic justice flourishes where the mutual understanding of persons leads to new forms of diversified co-operation. These resemblances are by no means superficial or fanciful: they point to the basic unity of what is impersonal or rational despite surface differences of medium and direction.

CHAPTER VIII

DUTY AND MORAL VALUE

(I) THE NOTION OF 'OUGHT': HORTATORY AND MINATORY IMPERATIVES

We have so far sought to enumerate and deduce the various separate ends (and counter-ends) which, as interpersonally and suprapersonally attuned, we must tend to move towards (or away from): we have distinguished a number of ends constitutive of the common and the 'higher' welfare, a number of evils constitutive of what may be called 'classical injustice', and of values constitutive of its somewhat colourless contrary, classical justice, as well as the very colourful positive end called by us 'Platonic justice'. These ends may all very well be said to be limbs of the same body, or members of the same family, all expressive in different ways of the same basic *nisus* towards the impersonal. But if they are limbs of a body, or members of a family, we have not yet shown how they fit and function together, and on what principles, in the detail of practice, one of them is to take precedence over another. What is here the desideratum is a value-concept or set of value-concepts which is at once connective, contextual and preferential, which will somehow superimpose itself upon, and bring together in one outcome, a number of distinct points of value and disvalue, all attaching to some single, well worked out project, which will do so in an actual context which extends some way beyond the project judged, and which will do so in a context of other hypothetical projections, which might have been preferred to it, or to which it might have been preferred. The kind of concept we are seeking is the kind covered by such phrases as 'the worthwhile thing on the whole, in the concrete case', 'the best thing that could happen in the circumstances', 'the right choice in the circumstances', 'what ought to be or be done in the circumstances', etc. etc. It is because our valuations permit a drawing together to this sort of outcome, that they form an organized 'body' at all, a body being a structure in all which all parts work together to produce a single result, as when heart, lungs, legs, eyes, etc., help us to jump over an obstacle, scale a height, etc. etc.

DUTY AND MORAL VALUE 333

We have a great temptation to think that the coming together of separate strands of valuation in an overall result can be like the putting together of premises in some formal argument, that there can be a number of definite *principles* which will enable us to *infer* an approvable outcome from certain starting-points, and this temptation readily takes the further form of believing this inference can be cast in the form of a straightforward *calculation*, once precise relative measures have been assigned to various types of value. Determine what satisfactions precisely outweigh what pains, determine further how much of a higher form of welfare like knowledge weighs against a certain amount of pleasure or pain, determine the badness of various types of injustice in relation to satisfactions, higher welfare or ill-fare, etc. etc., and one will be in a position, by a simple manipulation of grading marks, to answer haunting questions as to what should on the whole be, or be done, questions presenting difficulty only owing to their extreme complexity, or to the vagueness with which they are formulated. Whether or not concrete value-problems permit such a relegation, after due doctoring, to mechanical computation, may be left undecided. It is clear, however, that there is *some* way of answering the question 'What is the worth-while thing on the whole in the circumstances?' or 'What ought to be the case here?' and that what emerges has the same sort of impersonal sanction as the points of value and disvalue that go into it. And it is the nature of this sort of question, and its answer, that now concerns us. Though frequently figuring at the opening of works of ethics, it arises for us only at the end of our treatment.

In the consideration of the partial ends to be integrated in this overall 'worth-whileness' or 'ought' there is one notable omission: we have neglected one of the most salient points of value that must be brought together with others in such a final outcome. This point of value (or rather constellation of points) is that of *virtue* or *moral goodness*, or its various specifications the virtues, while the contrasted points of disvalue are those of *moral badness*, *vice* or *wickedness* or *baseness*. The values or disvalues in question are those, in the main, of our various 'whole-minded' orientations towards objectives, projects and states of affairs, of which our fully voluntary choices and decisions are the most salient examples. We postpone the consideration of virtue, the virtues and moral value (and of the various forms of baseness) till after the

334 VALUES AND INTENTIONS

consideration of what ought to be achieved in the concrete, since the former to such a degree presupposes the latter, one of the highest forms of moral goodness being that of a man who endeavours whole-mindedly to realize what ought to be, or what ought to be done by him in the circumstances, for the sole reason that it ought so to be, or to be done. Issues or virtue or baseness may very well enter into our various concrete determinations of what is worth while on the whole, or what should or ought to be or be done, but there is at least a lowest level at which they cannot without nonsense be made to enter. There must be a 'worth-while on the whole' or an 'ought to be' or 'ought to be done' which is independent of issues of virtue or baseness, for such issues to be relevant to another overall worth-whileness or ought-to-beness or ought-to-be-doneness at some higher remove. It is this more basic practical worth-whileness or ought-to-be-doneness which is our concern at the present juncture.

The auxiliary verb 'ought' which we have temporarily tended to prefer in carrying the theme of our inquiry, is one of a large family of value-words, all used in a confusing variety of ways, and each carrying its own biasing load of suggestions. To say what one wants to say in this field is to treat all these words without ceremony, and to abandon one for the other at the slightest call. (This is not to say that there may not be important philosophical studies of ordinary speech in which this is precisely what we do not allow ourselves to do.) The functioning of the words 'ought' ('should', 'to be . . .') overlaps teasingly with that of the words 'right', 'good' and 'bad', as well as with that of the more solemn locutions 'duty' and 'obligation'. In its least specialized use it merely gives verbal expression (without talking about what it expresses) to the *urgent* mood of our unappeased wants, as opposed to the tranquil appeased mood of our satisfactions. When we are striving to realize some objective, or are wishing for it to be realized, we may say, without necessarily reflecting on our endeavour, that that thing *ought* to be. ('There ought to be a cupboard in that corner', etc.) The word may also be used to give expression to a 'light' in which a situation is viewed by us, though not in full seriousness, as in some sense calling for, requiring a feature that is absent, being itself 'moved' towards a certain goal or outcome as we are moved in certain circumstances. Whenever our striving is appeased, this situation

DUTY AND MORAL VALUE   335

may be given verbal expression by the use of the word 'good', which is here used in preference to some phrase involving 'ought' or 'should' ('This is as it should be') and this word may also express a 'light' in which the situation is 'seen', as being itself brought to appeasement, as having had its requirements met. Similar accounts may be given, *mutatis mutandis*, of the use of the expressions 'ought not' and 'bad'.

It is plain, further, that the expressions 'ought' and 'ought not' may be used in an impersonal as well as a personal manner, in which former case they may be said to give voice to an attempt, sometimes achieving success (but not *commenting* on the attempt or on the success) to wish or choose *for* all possible persons, yielding only to such attractions or aversions as are invariant and inescapable for all, however much they may imagine themselves and the situation varied. And they may at times, also, give expression to a 'light' in which certain objectives are viewed, as having precisely this sort of unfading crown or halo, the invariant, inescapable attraction or repulsiveness which the parallax of personal approaches leaves unaltered: we may, in short, *be aware of* the invariant, inescapable moving power of certain objectives, instead of being merely *moved* by those objectives and in this manner. And we may here add that, however little we may *believingly* adopt teleological approaches in our interpretation of unconscious things, such approaches undoubtedly enter into the *phenomenology* of the situation whenever we in all seriousness hold that something *ought* to be. Just as we in our conscious life, in addition to the causal pressure of existent realities, experience the *moving power* of various ideal objectives which do not as yet exist, so in holding seriously that certain things *should* be, we conceive of the things in the world as being in some analogous manner subject to the moving power of certain ideal objectives. Such a mode of conception may not, as we have said, be incorporated into our beliefs, but its believing use would not be at all absurd: if there is sense and value (as we argued there was) in interpreting certain forms of unconscious causality by their analogy with conscious causality, then it is not absurd to suppose that unconscious things may act *as if* moved by the ideal ends which emerge as invariant among persons, e.g. in their simplicity, their beauty, their strange obedience to 'models' of different sorts, etc. etc. However this may be, it is, as we have said, part of the full

336 VALUES AND INTENTIONS

description of the situation obtaining when the words 'ought' and 'should' are seriously and impersonally used that all persons and all things should seem ready to be moved (or as-it-were moved) by certain objectives. And it is, further, not merely to *conceive* or to *conceive believingly* of something as being thus categorically and invariantly motive, but also to be oneself actually moved by it or to be ready to be so moved, and in an appropriately detached manner. A judgement of impersonal 'oughtness' may be said accordingly to involve 'existential' as well as merely notional moments, and its verbal statement may be said both to *evince* and *express* a peculiar motive power, active in the speaker himself, and to refer to and recognize its inescapable presence in and for all. Ethical theory has over the last decades drawn sharp distinctions between utterances regarded as *evincing* or *expressing* peculiar attitudes in the speaker, and utterances regarded as *referring to* or *talking about* the latter. It would suppose, e.g., that these two ways of regarding the use of a word like 'ought' should exclude one another, or that it was at least dangerously confusing to combine them. We by contrast maintain that the two ways of regarding the use of a word like 'ought' are intrinsically complementary, and that a profoundly thoughtful, responsible use of the word will permit them both. It is by being *ourselves* drawn, in detachment from personal lures, towards certain objectives, that we are put in a position to say that they absolutely ought to be the case, and our judgement also *declares* them to have such a universal motive power.

To judge impersonally of something that it ought to be is therefore to conceive and experience it as universally motive and categorically attractive without regard to the contingent make-up of particular conscious beings or unconscious things. It is in fact merely a dynamic way of conceiving and experiencing what, in an appeased frame of reference, is thought of categorically satisfactory or impersonally valuable. In this way all our impersonal valuations may be said to generate their peculiar 'oughts' or imperatives. (We may use the word 'imperative' as conveniently covering the content of an impersonal judgement of what ought to be, since statements as to what ought to be or what should be replace imperatives in many oblique contexts, e.g. 'He said I should do—should have done—X', etc., and since straightforward commands uttered in a peculiar solemn manner, e.g.

DUTY AND MORAL VALUE 337

'Love one another', 'Do not steal', etc., *may* be used to express the ineluctable attraction or repulsion of certain objectives.) Among such imperatives are, accordingly, the imperative that everyone ought to be satisfied, and that we ought to pursue satisfaction for everyone and for this one, that knowledge should 'grow from more to more' and that we should make it grow from more to more both in general and in this particular case, that injustices should be avoided or prevented and that we should endeavour to do so and in this case, that our judgements of what ought to be done should be impartial and that we should strive to make them so, etc. etc. Most of the 'oughts' or imperatives that are thus generated will, however, not be *full* 'oughts' or imperatives which hold regardless of circumstances, but rather imperfect 'oughts' holding only *under the proviso* that no similar provisional 'oughts' can be cited against them. They will not so much correspond to the hypothetical imperatives of Kant, since the latter are interested as these are disinterested, but they will correspond rather to the *prima facie* duties and 'rightnesses' of Sir David Ross, which suspend themselves, at least in their first unquestioned form, when other similar *prima facie* claims oppose them. These imperfect 'oughts' are not in the least degree ethically or philosophically unimportant, nor will it prove convenient to refuse to talk of 'imperatives', 'duties', 'obligations', etc., in connection with them. They require, however, to be brought together with other imperfect 'oughts' in a framework of circumstances representing the whole actual or likely setting and development of some concrete situation, before they can generate an 'ought' or an imperative which holds *without provisos*, such an 'ought' being 'categorical' or unconditional in a sense similar to but not quite the same as the famous sense of Kant. Such a categorical 'ought' will hold without provisos only because it takes account of *all* relevant features in the factual and value-landscape, and, having such a comprehensive reference, it will also prescribe the form and content of a cool, whole-minded determination that might arise in just those circumstances, and, in particular, that of a practical voluntary determination or act of will. The sort of overriding 'ought' that binds the ends and counter-ends of living together, in a concrete situation, is accordingly the sort of 'ought' that also represents the expression of a pure and impersonal will, and of its legislation for an actual, often distorted or capricious

338 VALUES AND INTENTIONS

will. So much we may take over, with a certain amount of contemporary patching and touching up, from the basic treatments of Kant.

We shall, in what follows, largely move on the line of least resistance, concerning ourselves mainly with those 'oughts' which concern the *actions* of given individuals, which are what someone ought *to do*. This is harmless, provided we remember that such 'oughts' are necessarily somewhat lamed and purblind 'oughts', tied down to what actually is, to what a given individual can compass, and, if we apply the notion reasonably, to what he could do with some endeavour come to know. What ought to be done by a given person on a given occasion, must necessarily leave out all the desirabilities that are not immediate practicabilities, and practicabilities for him, and it is a senseless notion if it does not operate within a fairly narrow horizon, perhaps going a few steps beyond what the person actually does forecast or surmise, but certainly not extending itself, in a barren and silly manner, to all that *may* eventuate in an indefinite future, and in all possible complexions of circumstance and voluntary choice. (It may be questioned whether such a quite horizonless 'totality of circumstances and consequences' is in any case a meaningful conception.) But beside this restricted and somewhat uninteresting sort of 'ought', one has the 'ought' which expresses the realistic and logical, but not practical attitude of the man on the side-lines, who is not restricted in his whole-minded wishes by what actually is, by the powers anyone possesses, or by the precise horizon of anyone's knowledge. Such a man can make valuable determinations of what 'ought to be' in circumstances of varying sort and with horizons of varying (though not infinite) width. It is possible to regard these side-line activities as mere substitutes for fully practical ones, as being 'what we would do if we had the power', and this mode of regard is perhaps the correct genetic perspective. In the axiological perspective, however, the unpractical 'ought' takes precedence over the narrowly practical one: what ought to be, what, if realized, would afford the fullest impersonal satisfaction, is more pivotal, more explanatory than what anyone ought to do.

The word 'right' overlaps in its use with the word 'ought', but is in some respects more satisfactory, as expressing the mood of acquiescent satisfaction as much as that of urgent striving. It

DUTY AND MORAL VALUE

has the advantage, too, of stressing the *contextual* character of our meaning more than the word 'ought'. It suffers, however, from disastrous ambiguities: while the 'rightness' of something may mean that it ought to be, or that it ought to be done, it may mean merely that it is not the case that it ought not to be, or not the case that it ought not to be done. It is used, that is, to cover both the permissible and the genuinely binding or pressing.

We cannot, however, proceed far with what is covered by the words 'ought' and 'right', without noting and giving verbal recognition to an extraordinary ambiguity that both cover, and that has produced the most unfortunate confusions. There are, we may say, two quite different 'oughts', one *hortatory* and one *minatory*. The former is a case of being impersonally moved *towards* an objective—and of course desiring and expecting that others will be similarly moved; it may be said positively to urge us to do or to realize this or that, while not necessarily urging us *not* to omit this desideratum, i.e. not urging us *away* from such an omission. The latter, on the other hand, is a case of impersonally urging us *away* from something, which may be an omission, without necessarily urging us *towards* the contrary commission or omission. The minatory element is clear in the case of such utterances as 'Never tell lies', 'You should never tell lies', etc. etc., but it is not so clear in the case of such utterances as 'Always tell the truth'; the import of both these utterances *may*, however, be precisely the same, both seeking to warn us *off* from lying or urging us *away* from it, and neither using positive suasion to urge us *towards* truth-telling. Whereas utterances like 'You ought really to cultivate your mind, not to be so boorish', etc., are plainly hortatory in their tendency, and do *not* warn us off from remaining uncultivated. Hortatory 'oughts', we may say, present certain objectives in a *winning* or *enticing* light, whether those objectives be affirmative or negative in their content: minatory 'oughts', on the other hand, present objectives in menacing or repugnant light, whether these objectives be positive conditions or freedoms, and positive acts or omissions. In many cases it is of course clear that a verbally expressed 'ought' combines both characters, perhaps in varying proportions. Thus it is a predominantly minatory 'ought' that adjures us not to break faith with our neighbours, i.e. its form is '*Don't* break faith' rather than '*Do* not break faith', while it is a

340 VALUES AND INTENTIONS

predominantly hortatory 'ought' that urges us to take a positive interest in them, i.e. its form is '*Do* take an interest', not '*Don't* fail-to-take-an-interest'. There are, however, 'oughts' of almost purely hortatory, and 'oughts' of almost purely minatory type. Those that urge us to increase beauty are plainly of the former type, and would be corrupted by a Ruskinian or other minatory infusion, whereas those forbidding us to impose great and gratuitous sufferings fall entirely in the latter category. In general, the *value* of an *objective* corresponds to a *hortatory* imperative to realize it, whereas the *disvalue* of an objective, which may be a freedom or an omission, corresponds to a *minatory* imperative to 'keep off' it. (There are significant exceptions to this ruling, since action has its *own* values and disvalues, distinct from those of its 'objective'.) There is, as argued on a previous occasion in a similar context, no reason why an impersonal assessment should overturn all this. It is mainly failure to distinguish between two roles of the word 'not', one as expressing the character of our attitude, and one as indicating something in its objective, which is responsible for the confusion. There must be things which ought to be, or which ought to be done, predominantly in the sense that their omission achieves or constitutes a disvalue, whereas there are things that ought to be, or that ought to be done, in the quite different sense that their performance achieves or constitutes a value.

The word 'right', we may now note, in addition to the ambiguities formerly noted, reflects *these* ambiguities of the word 'ought'. It may be applied both to the positively desired in conduct, and to that whose omission is to be deplored. It is in the latter use that it behaves so queerly in relation to the words 'good' and 'bad', having no comparative 'righter' to set beside *their* comparatives 'better' and 'worse'. If the distinction between the hortatory and the minatory is observed, these linguistic anomalies will be cleared up. 'Right' as expressing a hortatory attitude merely behaves eccentrically in not having more and enthusiastically accorded grades of rightness to set beside it—sometimes we say 'You were so right, so very right, in what you did', etc.—whereas 'right' as expressing the mere absence of a minatory attitude *cannot* have these grades, since there are not many degrees of not-threatening or not-warning-off. The word 'wrong', the typical expression of a minatory attitude, is plainly capable of

DUTY AND MORAL VALUE 341

use with comparatives and adverbs such as 'more', 'much more', 'very', etc. We may perhaps clear up the obscurities of the relation of the right to the good in conduct, by saying that an action which fulfils a hortatory imperative is to that extent positively good, even if only instrumentally, and that there is one use of 'right' which expresses just this, whereas an action violating a minatory imperative is *pro tanto* bad, and its omission *pro tanto* indifferent, and that the use of 'wrong' in the case of the commission, and of 'right' in the case of the omission, expresses just this. The values and disvalues which attach thus to *action* are, however, largely superficial: only when we begin to assess factors determining the *moral* virtue or *moral* badness of actions, will our treatment become profound and penetrating.

It is therefore plain that what in a wide sense a man ought to do falls into two quite different segments: a fairly restricted focus consisting of what he is warned off from omitting and therefore ought, in a minatory sense, to do, and a much wider penumbra consisting of the things from whose omission he is not thus warned off, but which he ought, in a hortatory sense, to do. We shall find it convenient to use the word 'duty' to cover both segments of what we ought to do, since both are noble and serious. If we do so, however, not all duty will be 'stern', nor demanding punishment if violated. There will be duties that wear a purely winning aspect, and which will smile, perhaps a trifle wistfully, over a case of omission. Gratuitousness is of the essence of many of our noblest activities, but the term 'hortatory duty', while it acknowledges this gratuitousness, also stresses the nobility. And it will be a noble task to attempt to lay down our hortatory duties, as it is to lay down our minatory ones. We shall speak then of hortatory and minatory duties, and of hortatory and minatory imperatives, and in both cases we shall apply the distinction (sometimes leaving it tacit) between duties or imperatives which hold *provisionally*, becoming *full* if they are the *only* provisional duties and imperatives relevant to the situation, and duties and imperatives which hold categorically and fully, because they have taken account of *all* relevant facts and provisional imperatives in the situation.

In the nucleus of a man's minatory duties we may now recognize a narrower nucleolus: the relatively small class of what, properly speaking, he is *obliged* to do (or not to do). The word

342 VALUES AND INTENTIONS

'obligation' may of course be used so widely as to cover all that it is in any way desirable for a man to do: in this sense it becomes coincident in coverage with 'ought' or with 'duty' as defined by us. But there can be no doubt that the tendency of the word is 'restrictive', not ampliative: when we ask what is our duty, we are for the most part asking what we are *not* obliged to do. And its connection with evil, rather than good, is obvious. This is plain even in non-moral uses, as where we say that we were obliged to take a longer route to avoid obstacles or hazards, the attempt to cope with which would involve frustration or many other forms of evil. But it seems plain that its predominant connection is with *other persons*, to whom we are in various ways *bound*. Even more strongly than the word 'duty', the word 'obliged' demands completion by words telling us *to whom* we are obliged, *to whom* our obligation is *owed* or *due*. If given this stress, which seems its natural and distinctive one, our obligations will all fall within the segment of justice called by us the justice of *understandings*. Wherever there is an understanding between ourselves and other persons, whether verbally stated or silently sanctified by usage, we have an obligation to act in the sense of that understanding, and we commit an injustice, we violate faith, we break our bond, if we fail to do so. The meaning of an obligation is therefore that of an action that we have, perhaps obscurely, undertaken to perform, that others regard us as having so undertaken, and whose non-performance *therefore* constitutes an evil (though it, and its effects, may also be evils in their own right).

The plainest cases of obligation are accordingly those created by freely made promises or engagements (whether one-sided or two-sided): in these we voluntarily delimit the boundaries between another man's sphere of power and our own, and we concede to him a reliance on certain actions or abstentions from ourselves, in return perhaps for similar concessions on his part. Having thus given a concrete form to justice, we cannot alter our determination without mutual consent or overriding circumstance: we are *obliged* by our undertaking, and have this obligation *towards* those with whom we have undertaken it. And the violation of this obligation is an evil of a quite specific kind, it constitutes the rending of a bond between persons, which is quite different from such an evil as the creation of pain, which might as much be

DUTY AND MORAL VALUE 343

inflicted on oneself as on someone else. But obligation applies not only to cases of voluntary delimitation of spheres of right, but to the more fundamental unspoken delimitations and mutual concessions on which social life depends: the understandings which involve mutual respect for life, mutual avoidance of gratuitously given pain, mutual assistance in circumstances of need, mutual courtesy and graciousness going beyond the bounds of need, mutual provision of reliable information, etc. etc. In all these respects we are, without needing to say so, bound to our neighbours and they to us. And obligation will apply to cases where there is a special unspoken relation of trust between ourselves and some others, e.g. between close friends.

The whole field of actions that affect the ill-fare of other persons, and some part of the field that affects their positive welfare, comes therefore within the sphere of obligation, and it is by an understandable exaggeration that everything that is worth while in life is thought to be covered by some obligation or other. Clarity is not, however, best served by such an exaggeration, and it is best to restrict obligation to cases where there can be said to be something like a mutual understanding among persons. Below this level there can be evils inflicted by one person on another, but not as yet violations of obligation. Thus children can inflict evils on others, or can fail to confer benefits normally expected, but can scarcely be said to act contrary to their obligations in so doing. Wholly asocial or anti-social beings, who neither in word nor deed confess genuine, abiding respect for others, nor concede to them a fixed sphere of rights, may similarly be said voluntarily to have contracted out of obligations, rather than to have violated them. This does not make what they inflict on others less evil, nor less evil their very refusal to form understandings or to contract obligations with others. It is clear, further, that, as we have defined the concept, we cannot have obligations exclusively towards ourselves, though our actions towards ourselves may be governed by many hortatory and by few minatory imperatives. We can have no such obligations, since these involve agreed allotments of powers and freedoms among persons, and we can make no agreements with ourselves, however solemn, that we cannot as solemnly and at once revoke. It, in fact, has none but a derived and imperfect sense to speak of agreements and revocations, in the case of ourselves, as single conscious persons.

344 VALUES AND INTENTIONS

It is of course clear that we can have many obligations that *involve* ourselves and involve ourselves principally, the obligation, e.g., to be clean, to be cheerful, reasonably well-informed, personable, etc. etc., but these are all obligations that we owe *to* others, as we exact similar obligations from them. And it is clear, of course, as said previously, that we can treat ourselves as we ought not, both in a minatory and a hortatory sense. In a minatory sense, we ought not to sit on spikes, since this causes pain, no approvable object of satisfaction, but we violate no obligation in so sitting, and in a hortatory sense we should seek to deepen our knowledge of many matters, since such knowledge is an object of approvable satisfaction, but even less do we violate obligation in omitting this.

The extension of obligation to cover *all* minatory and all hortatory 'oughts' is, in part, due to the prevalence of theistic forms of religion. If all our activity falls under deep religious understandings with a Creator external to ourselves, which it is in some manner impossible for us to disown, we shall at all times be either respecting or infringing the boundless rights of God. And if God is conceived as legislating on every possible topic, and as issuing only minatory and not hortatory imperatives, such obligations will spread their web over the whole of human conduct, till nothing remains outside: men will, in relation to God, have no effective sphere of rights whatsoever. It is to the great credit of the theologians of the Society of Jesus that, while acknowledging a God capable of such universal minatoriness, even in matters, e.g. baptism, indifferent in a non-religious perspective, they have at least conceived of this God as voluntarily limiting His minatory authority in certain directions, and as leaving to men a sphere within which only hortatory counsels are appropriate. In a non-theistic perspective obligations of course cease where there are no natural persons to be obliged to, though what we do may still be, in an impersonal perspective, something to be either done or not done. Remaining within such a natural perspective, we may therefore divide a man's duties into three classes, to some extent overlapping: some are hortatory, their fulfilments being good, and their non-fulfilments, *as such*, indifferent, some are minatory without being obligatory, their non-fulfilments being bad, and their fulfilments *as such* indifferent, and some, finally, are obligatory, these being minatory duties depending upon profound understandings among persons.

DUTY AND MORAL VALUE 345

But most of our commoner duties will, for varying reasons, have a tinge of all these three aspects.

(II) THE DETAILED DETERMINATION OF DUTY: GENERALITIES

The notion of duty in all its forms would, however, be wholly empty were there not ways of determining its contents unambiguously, of deciding among differing judgements as to what a man in given circumstances ought to do. For, like the partial valuations on which it reposes, it is nothing if not an inevitable outflow of impersonality, of an attitude which puts itself in the place of everyone and speaks on behalf of all. It would not, however, appear that impersonality in an attitude either demands or produces anything like a series of norms for determining *which* of the various values and disvalues it generates will take precedence over another, much less any general procedure for rendering them commensurable, so that decision as to the practically best will become a matter of calculation. Once one is clear as to the *wholly different character* of the various values steaming from impersonality, and the *very different manner* in which each expresses this impersonality, and once one reflects on the profound difference between sternly minatory and winningly hortatory imperatives, it becomes absurd to imagine *rules* that might subordinate one to the other, much less procedures presupposing measurement in terms of some common unit. Obviously the value of the satisfactory as such, which is based on an *abstraction* from whatever is individual in each man's objects of satisfaction, or the value of satisfaction, which is based on a *transition* into the reflexive mode, has quite a different foundation from the values of cognitive penetration and the higher forms of welfare, which all rest on the *affinity* of the attitude involved in such experiences with the attitude underlying our impersonal valuations. It would therefore be absurd to seek general rulings as to when to prefer the merely satisfactory to the cognitively penetrating, etc. etc. And equally the very different deductions given of each style of the higher welfare, would forbid us to look for simple principles of substitutability and convertibility there: it would be absurd, e.g., to try to determine when cognitive penetration is to be preferred to freedom,

346 VALUES AND INTENTIONS

or to contemplation of the well-formed, etc. etc. The disvalues of injustice, lying essentially in the submerged regions of evil, can likewise not be compared simply with any positive values of well-being: there is something absurd in asking *generally* what degree of satisfaction, cognitive penetration, etc., for some, will justify us in betraying the interests of others, or in overriding their individual claims. And it seems plain, further, that, where the notion of the impersonal or the disinterested does not suffice to grade or rank values and disvalues in a general manner, nothing *else* will suffice. We cannot, with Aristotle, say ἐν τῇ αἰσθήσει ἡ κρίσις and appeal to any sort of direct intuition, For this would be to bring something quasi-factual, externally compulsive, into a sphere where no step is justified that is not wholly *a priori*.

It is here that one might be tempted to follow a modern tendency, and to substitute 'decisions' for 'intuitions', to hold, in fact, that ἐν τῇ προαιρέσει ἡ κρίσις. Each man's duty, we might argue, involves his own personal choice in giving weight to one sort of reason over another, in preferring, e.g., the claims of truth to any other high-sounding consideration, or to seeing the avoidance of someone's pain as the ruling consideration in certain circumstances. Such a solution would, however, *by itself*, be no solution at all. The arbitrariness of personal decision is as powerless to bring this sort of dispute to settlement as is the arbitrariness of intuitive compulsion: both are contingencies of precisely the same sort. An approach to the reasonable can, however, be found in seeing the fact that someone in fact prefers one impersonal ground of action to another, as constituting a *good* reason, i.e. an impersonally valid reason, why *he* should act in one way, as producing what must be impersonally judged a duty *for him*, if not a duty for everyone. That we do in fact judge in this manner cannot be doubted. If *A* experiences an invincible repugnance to subordinating the claims of truth-telling to other claims in some situation, this deep repugnance is itself a factor that deserves impersonal consideration. And we do in fact hold that it would be wrong to override such a profound repugnance. Our whole concept of conscience, the individual's sense of what *he* ought or ought not to do, is in fact that of something which is not necessarily uniform among persons, but which tends to speak differently to different individuals. Certainly among non-philosophical men to refer something to conscience

DUTY AND MORAL VALUE 347

is to expect disagreement—*vide* the tribunals for conscientious *objectors*—but it is also to accord equal respect to all such disagreeing deliverances. The justification for this is plain, and is not to be found by a reference to aberrant but sincere moral judgements. Just as we impersonally find satisfactory whatever personally satisfies some conscious person, not in its particularity, but only *in so far* as it so satisfies someone, just so we impersonally find satisfactory whatever choice among the impersonal grounds for doing something represents someone's paramount reaction, his considered, whole-minded response to the impersonal firmament beaming down upon him, and his *own* way of making it concrete. The determination of duty which emerges may *apply* only to the man in question—it is what is right *for him* or obligatory *for him*—but its sanction is universal and impersonal. Everyone who realizes the determination to be in fact the man's paramount attempt to bring together the various strands of value into a single overall reaction must recognize its complete rightness for him. Conscience, so characterized, has the majestic self-sufficiency, the power to bind and loose, attributed to it by Hegel in a famous passage in the *Phenomenology*, which is distinguished from almost all other treatments of conscience by its full recognition of its variability from person to person.

We have, then, a personal preference as to the course to be steered among various impersonal landmarks, which becomes transformed into an impersonal determination, or judgement of what is best on the whole, or of what ought to be done, by the person's own act. Prior to a man's personal decision there is no general way of determining how he should act: once his decision has been made, such a determination emerges. The situation is in every way analogous to what confronts us in works of art. A work of art at a given point of its creation may have several possible continuations, none of which would seriously lower the aesthetic value of the work. There may be no principles obliging the creator to choose one continuation rather than another in many cases. The artist's own aesthetic individuality, however, guides the work into peculiar channels which both please and surprise, and for such an artist, and for his peculiar individuality, such a continuation then becomes 'right'. In all art there rightly comes to be something sacrosanct and universally valid in what were at first the mere likings, preferences, fancies and mannerisms of

348 VALUES AND INTENTIONS

the individual artist, e.g. Giotto, Bernini, Wagner, Picasso, etc. Familiarity with an artist's work rightly gives us the key in terms of which it may be judged, but the ensuing judgement is no *mere* expression of familiarity.

All this must not, however, be carried to the point where it cannot be said that a man has determined his own duty wrongly. Obviously there are not one but a number of ways in which an aberrant determination of duty is possible, to each of which will correspond ways in which such a determination may be right, and consequently a number of senses, some more and some less abstract, of a man's duty itself. A determination of duty may be defective in that it omits many of the values which have a necessary place in an impersonal value-firmament, or recognizes them only in limited classes of case, e.g. we may discount the disvalue of the ugly, or of pain when suffered by animals. It may be defective in so far as it adds to its firmament values and disvalues for which no impersonal justification is possible, which do not even represent a personal choice among various strands of impersonal value, e.g. the superstitious values and disvalues of certain religions and customary codes. It may also apply principles having an impersonal status in an extremely eccentric and unwarranted manner, e.g. the principles of equality in the field of distributive justice. It may also go astray in its defective grasp of the facts, or in its failure to extend the horizon of the facts as far as it reasonably can. And, even in the case of those peculiar determinations in which a man's own individuality plays a decisive role, it is still possible that a man may make hasty and capricious determinations, in which his own moral individuality is not felt to come to full expression. And, corresponding to all these possibilities of error, there will be a whole spectrum of senses in which a determination of duty may be right, extending from the pole of the most 'objectively right' on the one hand, where we take into account all the values and disvalues affecting a certain choice or action, and make our factual horizon both accurate and wide —it cannot significantly be made *infinitely* wide—to the pole of the most 'subjectively right' on the other, where we consider only what *seem* to be impersonally justified values and disvalues, what *seem* to be incontrovertible facts or well-grounded probabilities, and what *feel* to be the profound stirring of our own moral individuality. Only at the very end of this spectrum will

DUTY AND MORAL VALUE 349

we reach the point at which whatever a man thinks his duty will also be so, and the possibility of being right loses all significance with the vanishing of the possibility of being wrong. Before this point, there will be many good senses even of being subjectively right in one's determination of duty: thus I may be subjectively right, despite my defective pattern of values, and my limited and distorted horizon of facts, in thinking X to be my duty, since the choice of X would in fact result from my defective firmament of fact and value, and from my stunted moral individuality, if I gave either sufficient time to exert their full influence, and since I can in fact be in error as to the outcome.

We may note here, in view of much modern confusion, that a man's determination of his own duty, is not the same as his decision to act on this determination, nor need such a determination be insincere because a man fails to act on it. A determination of his own duty is a man's reaction to himself from an impersonal angle, in which he is to himself as another, and speaks to himself as he might speak to another. A similar determination can in fact be made upon another in all situations where we have sufficient insight into the situation as it appears to the man in question, and into his own moral individuality. Such a determination is quite different from a man's actual decision, though both are, in the sense given by us to the word, whole-minded attitudes which accept some line of action with all it may involve. That they are both whole-minded is, in fact, their quarrel; the impersonal, conscientious determination seeks to dominate action as completely as does the personal decision, but in practice is worsted. 'Had it strength as it hath right, it would absolutely govern the world.' Its sincerity is not shown by its translation into action— by no means a complete test of the sincere—but by its dominance on its own plane. It is in a man's impersonal remorse or guilt over his own conduct, rather than in this conduct itself, or in his strictures on the conduct of others, that a man's sense of his own duty is most effectively shown. The factors that militate against carrying such determinations into action are many: in the sphere of the hortatory, e.g., we may become slothful and weary of well-doing, whereas, in the sphere of the minatory, we may be more afraid of palpable, personal discomforts than of a subtler unease felt only in a narrow, not necessarily dominant, segment of the soul.

350 VALUES AND INTENTIONS

We have now reached a point where we may hazard a few vague, tentative generalizations as to the content of human duty, as to the things which a man ought (whether in the hortatory or minatory sense) to do or leave undone. Though there may be no absolutely clear principles of preference among our various impersonal values and disvalues, much less any possibility of subjecting them to some solvent technique of measurement, there are none the less principles, largely negative, governing their relations for which an impersonal sanction can be obtained. It can be seen, e.g., that the more urgent minatory imperatives must take precedence over the more rarefied hortatory ones. It will be far from clear in our discussions just how far such discussions may in right go, and where the last limiting generalities require supplementation by the reactions of a man's own moral individuality, where ethics, the *a priori* science, passes over into ethics, the personal art or skill. The non-rigorous character of all ethical arguments makes this transition intrinsically obscure: it is not clear when a dispassionate judgement is becoming a case of persuasion or personal pleading. Such unclarities can only be odious to those who, neglectful of Aristotle's warning, have a misplaced passion for ἀκρίβεια.

(III) BLUE-PRINT FOR PRACTICE

We may begin our laying down of principles of duty, by considering the relation of duty to *quantity*, to the *more* and the *less* in every field. Though we have rejected as non-significant any notion of measuring values and disvalues in terms of some common unit, so as to make the process of determining what is best, or least bad, in the circumstances a simple matter of calculation, and though this rejection involves rejecting the notion of *sums* of good and evil, if understood in a straightforward sense, yet it does not involve denying a meaning to agglomerates or constellated unities of goods and evils, and to a goodness or badness attaching to such agglomerates or constellated unities. Thus we obviously have to determine what is the worth or unworth *on the whole* of some complex spread-out pattern of existence covering many distinct times and persons, and we obviously often have to determine the worth or unworth of many possible contributions to this pattern. Many of our duties, likewise, must be expressed

DUTY AND MORAL VALUE 351

in terms of increase or decrease: we are exhorted, e.g., not merely to produce states of cognitive penetration *in vacuo*, but to *deepen, widen, extend* the cognitive penetration that actually exists. In the same way we are warned off from *increasing* pain, mental confusion, hatred and other evils. Duty seems, as it were, to lie mainly along the advancing frontier of enterprises already undertaken, and to extend, not so much to the production of totally new goods, or to the prevention of unheard of evils, as to the steady enrichment or attrition of what is already there. The more and less therefore enters into duty at every point, and we are concerned, as it were, with an interest on capital, rather than with sheer capital accumulations, as the story of the talents was perhaps designed to show. That the value of having more or less of this or that is, further, no simple function of the value of each item of what one has more or less of, is part of what is expressed by Professor G. E. Moore's *Principle of Organic Wholes*, which may be taken as saying that the value of a sum-total of elements is not to be construed as a sum of the values of the separate elements. To this might have been added a Principle of Context, that the value or disvalue of this or that contribution to some particular sum-total of elements, varies with the character of the sum-total in question, and is no function of its value in isolation.

In determining what a man ought to do, we must, as said previously, make our determination within a more or less limited horizon of actual circumstances, though there is no single horizon within which such a determination must be made. There must obviously be a term, a horizon set to the *non*-subjective circumstances and consequences relevant to the determination of a man's duty, a horizon usually covered by such phrases as 'the amount of information then available' or 'what the man could reasonably be expected to know', etc. etc. Such a horizon may be extended to afford prescriptions for beings more penetrating and more prescient than men, but it cannot be extended indefinitely, since action, choice and therefore duty plainly presuppose the unforeseen and the unforeseeable. As matters lie nearer to the chosen objective horizon, they will swim more and more in a haze of uncertainty, and with this duty too will speak in a more hesitant voice. This particular kind of horizon is not, however, the only one in which personal duty can be determined: we may proceed, not farther outwards, to take in more and more of the

352 VALUES AND INTENTIONS

objective circumstances, but farther inwards, to take in more and more of a man's conscious approaches, his defective picture of the facts, his more or less imperfectly developed pattern of values, the peculiar slant of his interests, his personal capacities and powers. There is, e.g., a determination of what a man should do, thinking things to be what he does think them, but on values sounder than his own: there is likewise a determination of what a man should do, thinking things to be what he thinks them, and on the values he actually acknowledges. There are also determinations of what a man should do, taking into account, or not taking into account, these mentioned factors, but further taking into account his own personal interests and capacities, which, on the one hand, may give him a vocation for doing X, or which make it supremely, perhaps fatally easy, for him to do it, while, on the other hand, we have the incapacities and disinclinations which make the doing of X more and more hard for the man, until at length the doing passes over into the impossible. Duty, being relevant to the individual person, must obviously limit its demands to what a man can do, and it must obviously vary those demands, and speak with a more or less urgent voice, according as a performance lies near to, or far away from, what is personally impossible. Determinations of duty which take in what a man believes, what a man values, and what a man finds personally interesting and can readily do, are necessarily limited in their horizon, and there is no temptation to extend them indefinitely, as there is in the case of more objective determinations. We must, however, resist the temptation of for that reason looking upon them as narrower and more restricted than so-called objective determinations: in a sense they take in more. For to ignore a man's actual beliefs, values, interests and powers is to have only an abstract, if useful, concept of his duty, whereas to take in all these personal circumstances is to find out what the man's *full* duty, in the concrete circumstances, actually will be. We shall not here, however, attempt too subjective a treatment of a man's duty, since the duties which arise in a context involving aberrant beliefs and values will be best understood as regular distortions of the duties which arise in a context involving more correct beliefs and values, and since the personal factors of interest and capacity have a relatively simple modifying force, which can be best treated *after* the effect of other factors has been fully

DUTY AND MORAL VALUE

examined. To know what a man should do if the situation both really involves certain impersonally justified values and is also thought to do so, is to know what a man should do if he only *thinks* that the situation involves such values, and to know what a man should do if certain things are all equally easy and interesting, is to know what he should do if such interest and ease become unequal. These at least are the assumptions we normally work upon, and which will guide the comparatively abstract treatment of personal duty which follows.

We shall attempt, then, to state a few detailed principles of personal duty and their relation of precedence to one another. And here we may first consider the relation of duty to positive welfare, whether this takes the form of *mere* welfare or satisfaction, or one or other of the forms of 'higher' welfare, i.e. appreciation of beauty, cognitive penetration, interpersonal understanding, power and freedom. (Pain and other forms of ill-fare are for the time being excluded from consideration.) We are plainly subject, we may hold, to a *hortatory* imperative or duty (naturally provisional or *prima facie*) to increase well-being in any form, in so far as this lies within our power, and provided that no claim stemming from some other quarter of the value-firmament affects such a determination. Impersonally we must desire ourselves to move in a direction in which the impersonally approved values lie. And plainly such an imperative will become more stringent, more near in note to the minatory, the *less* personal difficulty there is involved in creating such welfare, and the more we are personally inclined to create it. To omit an increment in welfare that would be easy to create, and that we in fact have an impulse to create, would almost merit condemnation. The reason for such an increase in stringency is obvious, as indicated before: the voice of duty speaks not at all, when something *cannot* be done or avoided by us, and it therefore speaks less and less urgently, the more difficulties come near to making something impossible for us, while its voice becomes more urgent the easier a task is for us and the more attractive. (On the other hand, the voice of duty will become more winning, more purely hortatory, the greater the personal difficulty in making some increment of welfare, and it is to this greater winningness, as we shall see later, that praise and merit are apportioned.) Ease or difficulty remaining equal, the voice of duty will obviously exhort us more urgently to create *more*

M

354 VALUES AND INTENTIONS

increments of welfare and *larger* ones, than to create *few* and *small* increments: were we in a position to create untold bliss by crooking our fingers, it would almost be obligatory to do so. In fact, however, the creation of many and large increments of welfare generally occasions more and more personal difficulty, and at length becomes wholly impossible. For this reason we are more urgently exhorted to produce a few, small increments of welfare, which are easy and lie close at hand, than to create many large increments, though we might be counselled winningly to aim at the latter, and might secure greater merit by doing so.

It may be asked whether we have no *minatory* duty connected with increase in welfare. Must we not *warn* ourselves and others off with deep disapproval from *failing* to increase welfare when we can do so? Many moral philosophers have held that we must do so, and that it is in fact our absolutely stringent duty to increase well-being to the greatest extent within our power. It may, however, be argued that such theses stem from intellectual confusions and moral rigorisms alien to our actual judgements, for which no jot of rational justification can be provided. For the absence of welfare is on no ground necessarily ill-fare, and we cannot therefore be forbidden to achieve the wholly indifferent. In actual fact, however, it is very often the case that the absence of welfare entails ill-fare: in situations, e.g., where welfare has been expected, or is seen to be enjoyed by others. Wherever this is the case, we shall obviously have a duty which warns us off from failing to create an increment of welfare, if this lies within our power. And from the point of view of personal virtue, there is something of a mean and grudging spirit in refusing to increase welfare when we can do so without immoderate cost to ourselves, and it is in connection with *this* that we are warned off from such a refusal. But no minatory imperative warns us off from failing to increase mere welfare at great personal cost. It is not, e.g., wrong to refuse to make personal sacrifices to amuse millions of school children. We may repudiate, further, the doctrine that we have any duty, whether minatory or hortatory, to increase welfare *ad infinitum*, or to the maximum degree possible, to pile delights on delights, insights on insights, exercises of power on exercises of power, etc. etc., and to multiply persons to increase such excesses. Such Faustian exaggerations ignore a principle of the most profound approvability: that the multiplication of anything

DUTY AND MORAL VALUE

without accompanying variation leads to declining values with each new supplement, until we reach a state which remains constant in value, or even declines. This is so because what we value is essentially something universal, a kind or type, which requires adequate, but not more than adequate, illustration. In mere multiplication, sheer numbers submerge the kind. (This does not of course mean that, should the world unhappily contain too many persons, we have not a duty to increase welfare for such as exist.) The increase in welfare demanded of us at each moment is really no more than a case of maintenance or perpetuation, for welfare is nothing if not continuously recreated.

If we now, finally, raise the issue of self and others, it would appear, contrary to what is usually held, that we are more urgently to be exhorted to pursue *our own* welfare, and that of those *near* to us, than the welfare of remote persons, if only because we more strongly *wish* to do the former, and are more likely to *succeed* in increasing welfare by this course than by any other. This principle, on which we largely and legitimately act is, however, masked by several others: by the fact that others are so much more numerous that we are often called on to prefer their welfare to our own, and because our preference for ourselves is so inveterate and obsessive, so much an obstacle to the impersonal in conduct, that it must be counteracted by systematically slanting our conduct in an opposed direction. It is also masked by the great value of love, which we are inclined to forget in assessing welfare. Nothing we have said implies that we have an *obligation* to pursue our own welfare: we are dealing solely with hortatory imperatives, which carry no penalty for non-fulfilment, and which do not by themselves involve a *bond* that can be broken. And we do not deny that *Fernstenliebe*, the promotion of the welfare of remote persons, has something wonderfully winning about it: in the rare cases where we can do as much for such remote persons as we usually can for ourselves or our neighbours, a preference for their lower or higher interests is itself rarely admirable.

From imperatives which concern welfare in general, we pass on to imperatives concerned with the differentiation among types of welfare, and above all with the differentiation between *mere* welfare, i.e. satisfaction and pleasure, and the *higher* welfare of cognitive penetration, aesthetic absorption, etc. etc. Here we may first reassert and reapply the principle of cheapening stated for

356   VALUES AND INTENTIONS

welfare in general: that a form of welfare progressively declines in value the more it is monotonously multiplied, and that the accent on duty then shifts to other more uncommon types of welfare. (If persons are monotonously multiplied, some such monotonous multiplication of types of welfare may, however, be a duty on grounds of fairness.) The various forms of welfare are justified by quite different deductions, and therefore evince impersonality in quite different ways: one can no more be blindly substituted for another than multiplied eyes can take the place of legs, or a series of livers replace a heart. Unbalanced overgrowth in one or other of the types of welfare will, however, necessarily demand supplementation by other types of welfare both in the individual and society. A man or society too much given to intellectual sophistication or aesthetic refinement will do well to cultivate the affections or the basic animal pleasures, and *vice versa*: in all such cases the voice of duty calls in the direction of the undercultivated and the rare. This voice would appear to be mainly hortatory, not minatory, and it becomes more purely hortatory the rarer and harder the sort of welfare it encourages: it would appear, however, to come close to using minatory tones in the case of a certain amount of *basic happiness*, whether this carries a savour of the higher aspirations or not. What we call basic happiness plainly comes first in urgency, if only because its alternative is no abstract possibility of indifference—which seems barely a real alternative for beings consciously alive—but a peculiarly laming type of frustration and misery, and because no higher type of welfare can be erected except on such a basis. Beyond this level, however, it becomes urgent to increase the higher types of welfare at the cost of basic happiness, both on grounds of variety, and by virtue of their impersonal savour. As to the preferability of various types of higher welfare among each other, no principles will be hazarded: these would appear to be as pointless as the childish preferences for one colour over another. To the extent that such preferences exist, however, they create vocations for particular people, and with such vocations peculiar duties. If I am both by inclination and capacity an artist, it becomes almost in a minatory sense my duty to enrich the world artistically: popular romanticism often makes such duties *override* genuine obligations, as in the admiration for careers like that of Gauguin, Rimbaud, etc. On the other hand it

DUTY AND MORAL VALUE

can be only in a purely hortatory sense that I am bidden to strain myself to make contributions to forms of welfare that come difficult: where such efforts are magnificently successful, as in the case of Flaubert, the achievement seems doubly admirable. It should be stressed, however, that, while coaxing, encouraging, honouring and rewarding are quite appropriate reactions to the fulfilment of a man's artistic, scientific or other vocation, and the natural expressions of hortatory imperatives, compulsion, branding, dishonouring and penalizing, which are the forms naturally taken by minatory imperatives, and widely applied in modern dictatorships, are not. The note of the gratuitous and freely gracious remains indispensable to all higher contributions to welfare.

We now turn from the consideration of the lower and the higher welfare, to the readily neglected issue of ill-being or ill-fare. Here the characters to be considered are characters to be regarded with hate, aversion and disgust, and the imperatives which concern them are accordingly *minatory*. We are *warned off*, that is, in the absence of special excuses, from increasing pain, ignorance, error, confusion, the contemplation and creation of the ugly, hatred and non-rapport among persons, impotence and unfreedom, and other like evils. And since the imperative is minatory, its voice will be urgent and stringent and will carry repudiation and many penalties in reserve. And since the whole of communal life rests at least on a minimum understanding to abstain from gratuitous harm to one another, the imperative will carry with it a bond of obligation, at least in all cases where other persons are concerned. The more strongly minatory imperatives, moreover, by their very nature take precedence over even the most strongly hortatory imperatives, partly because urgency and precedency have been *framed* as minatory notions, that 'coming first' or being most urgent whose non-fulfilment represents the greatest threat, but more fundamentally in that the 'great evils', e.g. intense pain, gloating lust, hatred, despair, etc., are so not only intrinsically but also because of their immense disabling, transfixing and disruptive power. A great evil shakes the foundation and possibility of all good, and that not accidentally: it not only overwhelms the whole ground floor of existence, but must preclude the rearing of any fairer, serener storeys upon it. All evil is near to a lower limit of *total spiritual ruin* as good has

358   VALUES AND INTENTIONS

no natural upper limit. This being so, the claims of the hortatory only make themselves felt, and only deserve to do so, when the claims of the more basically minatory have been met: we have, accordingly, a stringent obligation to abstain from all serious hurt and harm to others, for which no accumulations of positive well-being can be held to compensate. And while it does not make sense to speak of an obligation to oneself, the fact that something is an object of just aversion carries with it the requirement not to produce it even in one's own case. One may justly be rebuked for abusing one's gifts, darkening one's mind, and even for enduring unnecessary pains and cares.

The situation must not, however, be sketched with too simplifying a brush: obviously what we have said demands great qualification. Extreme pain, as remarked previously, is of so disruptive a character as to be fenced round with a minatory imperative of the most stringent character, which takes precedence over practically all hortatory considerations: the production of practically no good, however noble or enduring, could atone for the infliction of certain major agonies, even upon an animal. This is not to say that such evils might not deserve to be borne to *save* beings from greater evils of various kinds. But the pain that can with some difficulty be borne could, we feel, readily be compensated for by producing positive goods of some sort. And it is further the case that the various forms of higher welfare, cognitive penetration, personal love, aesthetic understanding, etc. etc., all involve the overcoming of difficulties raised by external circumstance and the natural man, and it is in this that their impersonal character is most strongly evident. Difficulty and resistance, however, necessarily entail frustration and pain, which is therefore an essential element in the highest forms of good. This last proposition may be said to be the most important discovery of the Christian religion, and its unique contribution to the appeasement and betterment of men. Pain also has, as argued before, a cathartic role in all forms of moral debasement, and no man who has flouted imperatives which, in his impersonal capacity, he recognizes as authoritative, can fail to wish the impersonally odious character of his transgression to be borne in on him in the truly appropriate symbolism of what is *personally* odious, i.e. great personal pain. It would appear then that there are many contexts in which pain, though evil, subserves, and becomes integrally part of, the

DUTY AND MORAL VALUE 359

higher welfare of those who suffer it, and that in all such situations the imperative which warns us off from inflicting it will be suspended in its application. There are even situations where we are warned off from *not* inflicting it, as in a punishment for ill-will, or in the education of the immature. The infliction of profound pain on another represents, however, so extreme a distortion of the impersonal—which has its basic task in the organization of *satisfactions*, not frustrations—and so perilous an intrusion into another's sphere of freedoms, as to be justified much less often than our natural vindictiveness makes us fancy. If profound pain is to exercise its cathartic and stimulating power, its endurance is best undertaken in complete voluntariness by those who undergo it, and not imposed from without.

If we now turn to consider the higher forms of deprivation and 'faring ill', it would appear that the strongest of minatory imperatives concern states which destroy the possibility of all higher welfare, and these are *not* states of being exposed to the ugly, of being plunged in mental confusion, of being surrounded by those to whom one can only have relations of indifference, incomprehension or positive ill-will, or of being deprived of all opportunities and facilities for carrying out one's wishes, etc. etc. The latter are all obviously evils, but not necessarily ruinous evils, and we can think of circumstances in which, like the less severe forms of pain, they might be cathartic or stimulating. Thus it might be a good punishment, or even a good stimulus, for one who had failed to cultivate his artistic talents, to inhabit certain London suburbs. But the antithesis of the higher welfare is to be found rather in certain obsessive, paralysed or gloating states, states ruinous from the point of view of the higher welfare because they forbid all higher co-ordinations and interests from arising. Among such ruinous conditions are those dominated by inertia, despair, greed, anxiety, lubricity, sadistic cruelty, and, briefly, all addictions, infatuations and paralyses of soul. The content of some of these obsessions is indifferent, e.g. food, sex, that of others merits impersonal horror, e.g. sadistic cruelty, but this content is not here in question. What makes such states ruinous to the higher welfare is their obsessive, disorganizing power: lubricity, e.g., can keep us tethered for hours within the narrowest range of contemplation and performance. And this disorganizing, narrowing character is not merely external to these states: it is felt in

360   VALUES AND INTENTIONS

them and makes them inwardly troubled. Against any production or encouragement of such states there must be minatory imperatives of a stringency coming close to that of those warning us off from the infliction of profound pain. And they differ from these latter in that the very character of the states in question precludes their having any cathartic or stimulating power, except possibly for others, and to encourage them for this latter reason would be a most heinous and abominable case of injustice. One could not purify or stimulate a man by allowing him to become an addict: addiction would rather render all purification and stimulus impossible. Of course, to the extent that obsession was less extreme, its overcoming or systematic expression might contribute valuably to aesthetic, scientific or ethical experience. Much great art, great mathematics, great philosophy and great personal saintliness has, e.g., been almost clinically schizoid. But the narrowing and mechanization of soul represented by what is obsessive certainly also represents the *great evil* standing over against the higher forms of welfare, from whose increase we should most urgently abstain.

We have so far only considered our duty to abstain from creating or augmenting the lower or higher evils: we have not considered the further-going duty of not permitting the existence of such evils, or, in other words, of *preventing* or *removing* them. Here we intuitively feel the case to be somewhat different, though it is not easy to show why this should be so. The duty to remove or prevent evils with whose origin we have nothing to do, is much less plain than our duty to abstain from *creating* similar evils, and it by no means always countervails against our largely hortatory duty to produce good things of various sorts, and would therefore seem itself to be mainly hortatory. We do not think well of those who, neglecting to make the positive contributions they very well might, devote themselves to rectifying abuses in Cathay. This last sentence, however, provides, in part, the key to what is anomalous in this deontological situation: the ease or difficulty of fulfilling a given imperative. To uproot or prevent evils with whose origin we have nothing to do, and which are perhaps remote from our usual 'beat', is, in general, a hard undertaking, sometimes a well-nigh impossible one: the voice of duty, which cannot significantly command the impossible, must become less clamant as the impossible is approached, and must assume an

DUTY AND MORAL VALUE

almost hortatory tone. To this may be added the near-certainty that, in uprooting evils of whose source we have but a faint understanding, we are liable to uproot much that is good, and ourselves to create much evil and injustice. Whereas to produce the good things for which we have a vocation, and which others perhaps expect of us, is, on account of its comparative ease and freedom from adventitious evil, almost a minatory, not a hortatory 'ought', for which reason it will take precedence over the duty to expunge remote evils. Were it a sure and easy thing for us to expunge remote evils as it is for us to contribute our own poor quota of immediate good, such prevention or removal of evil would at once become 'our own affair', and pressing at that: we should not feel free to neglect it as something which did not concern us closely. As things are, the difficult duty of expunging remote evils is minatory and stringent only for those to whom it represents an invincible vocation, the true reformers whose zeal adds sweetness to the universe: for most of us it is happily hortatory. And it would appear too that, even to the principle giving deontological precedence to the avoidance of evil over the creation of good, there must come ultimate limits: quite apart from the issue of difficulty, in a world abounding in evils, and consequent opportunities for reform, it might more behove us to provide some refreshment of beauty, kindness, etc., in the waste, rather than to labour exclusively on lessening the mountain of ill. Our discussion has, however, more than the usual artificiality and unreality inseparable from *too general* a treatment of moral issues.

Unreality also assails us when we turn to consider the various imperatives connected with justice—those concerned with distribution, with spheres of right and with requital—and their relations with the other imperatives we have listed. We shall stress again, what has been several times argued, that justice is not as such very positively valuable, but that injustice is in varying degrees evil. This means, from the point of view of the practical agent, that he has a *minatory* duty warning him off from the commission of injustice, and that, since injustice always violates bonds of understanding, whether explicit or tacit, he has an *obligation* to avoid injustice. Wherever an injustice that might result from his action *can* also readily be avoided, he is stringently obliged *not* to produce it. This obligation becomes less and less stringent the more *difficult* it is for the person to avoid producing

M*

362 VALUES AND INTENTIONS

it—whether owing to external circumstances or his own proclivities—until at length it becomes purely hortatory. A man's relation to injustices for which he is not himself responsible will follow much the same lines as does his relation to other evils. In general, it is hard to remedy alien injustices, and to do so unblunderingly, and this is more the case the more remote they are. In view of this difficulty and this risk of grave blunders, it is only to a small extent a duty for us to remove remote injustices, and then mainly a hortatory duty, to which other hortatory duties, e.g. that of pursuing art, may take precedence. The avoidance of injustice is, however, integral, and men are obliged positively to resist injustice with more force than they put into their other duties and obligations. And since blunders in remedying injustices are often least, and an assisting readiness to fight them greatest, when the injustices are *one's own*, a man is (contrary to many injunctions) most stringently obliged—not to himself but the society of persons—to resist injustices *to himself*. Parliamentary legislators often do well by not starting to remove injustices till those suffering under them have begun to clamour. There are, however, a valuable class of persons, pejoratively known as 'agitators', whose vocation it is to make articulate injustices actually but dumbly felt by wide bodies of persons: for fulfilling this function, they deserve praise rather than abuse.

As to the differing forms of injustice, our obligations to each are quite different. Where a system of spheres of right, though unequal, is not monstrously so, and where it lays down reliable frontiers among persons, guaranteed by stable customs and laws, our obligation not to violate such a system, as long as it obtains, is far more stringent than any obligation to work towards an ideal, but as yet abstract equality. This is the case, since an equal disposition of facilities, powers, opportunities, etc., must necessarily be a *disposition*, i.e. a relatively fixed framework of things done and expected, and since it is possible to work from a moderately unequal framework to one more equal, but not readily from a shapeless ideal nebula to a definite social framework. Respect for existing law and usage is essentially the more minatory demand, while pressure towards greater equalization is essentially more hortatory. Of course there are some social stabilizations so monstrous in their inequality, those, e.g., of Calvinist *apartheid* in Africa, that it may be obligatory to smash them at any cost.

DUTY AND MORAL VALUE 363

Among the most stringently minatory of our obligations, all resting on deep-laid understandings, are the obligation to keep faith, to provide true information, to abstain from injury to life and limb, to afford reasonable co-operation and help to those in need, to respect the liberty and property of others, to fulfil all we have covenanted to fulfil towards spouses, children, etc., the obligations gathered together under the title of 'natural law' by theistic moralists, and whose violation constitutes the ἀδικία so much discussed by the Greeks. The critics of utilitarianism have been right in recognizing the fact that these obligations (which are, of course, provisional or *prima facie*) must often take precedence over obligations to augment welfare, and sometimes over obligations to avoid augmenting pain and other forms of ill-being. For the essential form of impersonality comes out more clearly in these bridging deliverances of justice than in imperatives concerned with the good or ill of particular persons. On the other hand, as stressed previously, it is clear that the form of justice becomes a hollow shell if it ceases to organize well-being or ill-being: hence there will always be situations where the ill created, or good reduced, by fulfilling certain obligations is sufficient to suspend or nullify them. Where this point lies involves the reaction of what we have called a man's moral individuality, as well as an appeal to general principles, and this reaction will yield, in favourable cases, a decision wholly right *for* the individual concerned, though not necessarily valid for others. Such a situation must be accepted philosophically by philosophers as it is by ordinary persons.

If we turn to the sphere of punitive and rewarding requital, the curiously equivocal, but still resistant, character of the values and disvalues involved, generates imperatives themselves equivocal and liable to suspension, but majestically overriding all in a small range of cases. Rewarding requital would appear to lie largely in the hortatory dimension, especially when involving difficulty or personal remoteness: a smile or a word of praise is all the meed that can be demanded of us for generosities performed in Cathay. On the other hand, when we ourselves are the beneficiaries of even an uncovenanted kindness, there would appear almost a minatory obligation to requite it, if only in token fashion: to be deeply ungrateful is to be insensible to the verge of wickedness. It is not easy to justify these requirements, except perhaps as

364   VALUES AND INTENTIONS

revealing an understanding among persons too subtle to be enforced or even formulated, a covenant to be reciprocally kind in uncovenanted ways. Punitive requital can so readily fail of its symbolic purpose and become a mere infliction of injury, that it is best left, in all subtle cases of injustice, to the person concerned, with token encouragement in the form of coldness, withdrawal of favour, etc. etc. Only in the case of the gross injustices utterly subversive of co-operative living, in whose case prevention and deterrence buttress the claims of requital, can such requital become enjoined by a minatory imperative, whose basic character demands execution by the impersonal organization set up to ensure basic stability, i.e. the state. And even here the equivocal character of punitive requital demands the suspension of such an imperative wherever means not involving the deliberate creation of evil can be found. It is not our task here to enter into the immensely complex casuistry of punitive justice. We enter into its forecourts only to dispel the error that it is possible to study the form of ethical valuations without studying its concrete application, or that it is possible even to understand the meaning of terms like 'justice', 'right', 'duty', 'impartial', etc., without entering into such detail.

As we have not yet considered the difficult and complex values and disvalues connected with virtue and its contrary, we shall postpone the sketching of their peculiar deontological status, of the extent to which they generate hortatory and minatory imperatives, which apply to virtue in ourselves, in our neighbours, and in remote persons. We may acknowledge the mixture of platitude, vagueness and personal predilection in the above section, the nearest to practice in the whole book. The character of the mixture springs from the nature of the subject: that it does not permit a diremption into an abiding form, and varying, arbitrary content. It is not merely that one is not clear when one is blending the responses of one's own moral individuality with a universally binding deontological framework: it is that it is in principle impossible to hive these off cleanly. Where there is borderline *fusion*, there cannot be confusion. One finds in fact that, in the attempt to be most detached from one's own individuality, one most signally gives expression to it, and it is no doubt the case that the attempt of this author to sketch the firmament of duty has betrayed his own somewhat frivolous individuality at every

DUTY AND MORAL VALUE 365

point. All this calls neither for excuses nor regrets. The determination of duty is an oracular task hedged round with demands that one cannot be sure of fulfilling correctly: one can at best aspire, make a valiant attempt, etc. etc. But at a higher level one may see that one *has* performed the task correctly, since the earnest response of one's moral individuality is the only way to fulfil it. And this fulfilment, though personal, does not lack impersonal intelligibility, since it *individualizes* what can be seen to require just such individualization.

(IV) MORAL GOODNESS AND BADNESS

So far we have confined our attention to the various things that are objects of an impersonally approvable practical pursuit and satisfaction, without including among such objects this impersonally approvable practical pursuit and satisfaction itself. To take the step which includes this pursuit and satisfaction among its own objects, or rather (to avoid type-confusions) among the objects of a pursuit and satisfaction otherwise similar, but of higher order, is not only natural but inevitable. For, if we are impersonally to cherish such features of things as satisfactions, cognitive penetration, equal distribution, requital, etc. etc., then we are also committed to pursuing the practical pursuit of such things, and to being averse from their neglect or destruction. In the same way, if we are impersonally to be averse from features of things such as pain, error, arbitrarily unequal distributions, mutual incomprehension among persons, etc. etc., then we are also, by the same logic, to be averse from the practical pursuit of these things, wherever it may occur, or from the neglect to resist or prevent them, etc. etc. And if various impersonal cherishings and aversions can be expressed, too, in the more dynamic mode of what we have called hortatory and minatory imperatives, which tell us that it is our duty to realize this or that, whether in provisional (*prima facie*) or unqualified fashion, then we are led logically to cherish lines of practice that conform to such imperatives, and to be averse from such as flout them, and to direct to both new imperatives which prescribe duties of higher order. That the logic requiring this step has no formal force, does not make it less compelling. And if by 'practice' we mean not *any* production of results, but one that circulates through and is

366 VALUES AND INTENTIONS

throughout modified by our conscious awareness of things, then we are obliged, again not by a formal bond of entailment, to value such practice in no merely derivative or instrumental way, but in an underived, 'intrinsic' manner. For the *conscious* pursuit of anything so deeply incorporates the character of what it pursues in its own character and description, so deeply, in a sense, is 'identified' with the latter, that it 'makes no sense' to value X and not to value the *conscious* pursuit of X, or to shrink in horror from Y, and yet not to shrink in horror, and to warn men off, from the *conscious* pursuit of Y. We arrive therefore at a peculiar kind of value and disvalue, generating its own qualified and unqualified duties, to which the name of *moral value and disvalue* is appropriate, and which largely coincides in application with the terms 'virtue' and 'vice' ('wickedness'), though these last have perhaps too close a connection with the ingrained and habitual. It is now our task to consider the factors affecting this species of value and disvalue, the imperatives it generates, and how these stand as regards precedence in the final determination of obligation and duty.

Moral value and disvalue pertains, as we said, to the *conscious* pursuit or *conscious* production of this or that valuable or disvaluable features, or to the conscious fulfilment of this or that hortatory or minatory imperative: it does not pertain to any *non*-conscious productions or fulfilments, or to tendencies to non-conscious production or fulfilment, whose relation to what they produce (or tend to produce) is of an external, 'non-intentional' sort. Instrumentally we may shun, or seek to destroy, the mechanical source of pain, ignorance, maldistribution of welfare, etc. etc., but the instrument will not take the *taint* of what it produces as must be the case in regard to what consciously *aims* at evil. From this limitation to conscious production or intention follow all the usual provisos regarding ignorance or total absence of awareness: that no moral value or disvalue attaches to a man's production or attempted production of something he did not and could not readily have surmised to be a likely product of his actions, or to his production of something in circumstances of which he knew nothing, and of which he could not easily have known anything, etc. etc. From this it also follows that only those descriptions of a man's action are relevant to the assessment of his moral value, which he himself could give of them, which

DUTY AND MORAL VALUE 367

represent his own practical knowledge of them, that he is, e.g., signing a will, unlocking the door of his flat, giving a patient a sedative, etc. etc.—and not such descriptions, even if correct, as are remote from what he knows or conceives, that he is, e.g., unwittingly signing a confession, unlocking the door of someone else's flat, giving a patient poison, etc. etc. And only such consequences of what he supposes himself to be doing will be relevant in such assessments as he himself regards as certain or probable.

Within the bounds of this practical knowledge or conception must be further included, with a slight straining of usage, the values and disvalues, the imperatives and duties, that for a man pertain to the outcomes he supposes himself to be realizing, or that would so pertain if he gave the matter thought. And such values and imperatives as lie *wholly* beyond his purview, entail in him ignorance of 'the quality of his act', and so make him, to the extent that *they* are concerned, no fit subject for moral valuation. Obviously it is not only an act seen in its full cognitive, but also in its full apparent axiological and deontological shading, for a particular person, that enters into moral valuation. This is not to say that its value will entirely depend on what it seems to its agent to be.

The moral value or disvalue to be attributed to an action will further obviously be proportioned to the *distinctness* and *definiteness* with which its various value-relevant features, and their attendant values, are known or conceived. If moral value or disvalue only comes into question to the extent that something is a matter for consciousness, it will obviously come into question more emphatically, the more distinct and definite such consciousness is. This distinctness and definiteness, and the contrary qualities, cover a large range of different cases, all meriting close and discriminating attention, which it is impossible to give them here. It covers all cases of cognitive clearness and unclearness, in the sense given to these terms in the second chapter of this work: where we attend to, take note of, pay heed to, or keep something in mind, what we are aware of is much more relevant to the determination of our moral value and disvalue, than where we proceed heedlessly, inadvertently, absent-mindedly, recklessly, automatically, etc. etc. It also covers all cases of cognitive fulfil-ment and non-fulfilment, again in the sense given to the terms

368 VALUES AND INTENTIONS

in a previous chapter: to perpetrate cruelty in the full imaginative envisagement of the dismay and suffering it entails, is rightly judged more heinous than to do it with only a dry, verbal acknowledgement of the existence and intensity of such suffering. And it covers all degrees of nearness of realization: the deeply buried awareness of some circumstance, which can be brought to actual consciousness only by an effort, affects moral values less gravely than the awareness ready on a slight impulse to tremble into life. It will further cover all degrees of belief and degrees of approvability of belief: what seems to us only faintly likely, or what should seem only faintly likely, has obviously much less relevance for assessments of the moral value of our acts, than what seems to us, in a certain context, imminent, or what might rightly be thought such. The fact that an approvable level of belief is one that belief has, by its nature, some tendency to take, and that it could not otherwise be approvable, nor have attraction nor authority, makes it not absurd to include such an approvable level in our assessments.

All the factors we have mentioned apply, *mutatis mutandis*, to our practical knowledge, in the special sense of one's holding to well-founded values and imperatives. It is possible to have a firmament filled with many fine values and requirements, and yet to pay very varying degrees of heed to them. It is also possible to make concrete one's sense of the worth or unworth or imperativeness of something with very different degrees of imaginative envisagement, or of practical or emotional engagement. It is possible to carry out such a sense in some submerged, inaccessible segment of one's responsive repertoire, or in some fully manifest segment. And it is possible to have given such a sense fixity by the application of techniques which are also those which largely validate and guarantee it: techniques of careful reconsideration, techniques of consultation, techniques of sympathetic self-projection, etc. etc. Obviously all these factors are relevant to an assessment of moral value or disvalue: an act may be adjudged morally vile because done with an emphatic, vivid, well-pondered consciousness of the badness of what it produces, whereas it would be perhaps pardonable if this consciousness were marginal, sketchy and with no tests to lend it firmness.

It is here, too, that we may dispose of the difficult issue of the subjective and objective standards of duty and value, so insoluble

DUTY AND MORAL VALUE 369

from the standpoint of a non-naturalistic intuitionism, and so soluble from the standpoint of our non-rigorous, developmental *a priori*. Were objective values and imperatives simply 'out there' in some peculiar sphere or dimension, to which their subjective images conformed or did not conform in a largely chance manner, there could only be an internal and an external way to criticize our value-estimates, with nothing to give the one authority over the other. As we have seen the matter, however, the 'true values', 'true imperatives', etc., merely represent a carrying towards the limit of aspirations and techniques present in relatively undeveloped valuations, which have entered the sphere of discussion among persons, and so have implicitly submitted themselves to the tests involved in being impersonal. It makes sense, therefore, to judge an act in the light of its *own* unsatisfactory inner standards only because they are on the way towards standards that will approve themselves more completely, and it is possible to judge it in the light of these more ultimate standards because they represent a more thorough carrying out of its own. Were the 'right result' not somehow implicit in the 'wrong' one, and obscurely aimed at in it, it would be a gross impertinence and irrelevance to judge the one in terms of the other: it would be like condemning German because it failed to be good Dutch. Strictly speaking, moral valuation involves not the use of either standard separately, but of both together. A man's own actual standards must be brought in, since no standard can be a standard *for* anyone which is not also acknowledged by him, but what count as limiting standards must also be brought in, since it is only in a framework which includes these that a man's standards can be made an object of criticism. A man's own standards must, in fact, be brought in as being his own best approximation, or not-so-good approximation, to standards inescapably involved in and presupposed by the fact that we all enter into moral discussion with one another, and that such an enterprise is not merely an exercise in personal magic. On many accounts, it can of course be nothing else, even if its verbal shell may suggest something different: we, however, have found meat within the verbal shell.

It is easy to see, further, that moral value and disvalue must vary according to the precise *way* in which a valuable or disvaluable objective is pursued, or a qualified or unqualified duty

370 VALUES AND INTENTIONS

carried out. Some modes of pursuit involve much more conscious causality than others, and since conscious causality is the specific object of moral valuation, this latter will climb to higher levels when the former is more emphatically present. There are cases where there is indeed an awareness of a wide sweep of facts and consolidated values, but where this awareness has only a slight working influence on choice and action: actions done on impulse, in hot blood, under obsessive spells of various sorts, in circumstances of paralysing disarray, etc. etc. Sometimes we can say truthfully that such a wide awareness *could* only have had a small influence: what we may call the party of comprehension has had enough energy left it by the remaining forces of the mind, to rally itself to a judgement, but not to an effective decision. In all such cases where conscious causality is reduced, and where action is exclusively steered by a narrow range of considerations and values, the latter perhaps mere projections of passing excitements, moral value and disvalue must be attenuated. The taint of an evil outcome, or the perfume of a good one, will not cling to a conscious life which has had little to do with its production.

Similar limitations apply to all acts issuing from low-grade or high-grade routines, even from 'principles' left behind them by highly conscious decisions, but which now channel action automatically without being further inquired into. To the extent that such principles abbreviate and simplify the self-immersion in facts and the emotional and imaginative reliving of values, they lessen the effect of conscious causality, and to this extent reduce moral value. All this would seem to controvert the Aristotelian view, with its great charm for common sense, that it is only when right attitudes are quite ingrained, when there is no longer any wish to run counter to them, when their dominion is pleasant and involves no strain, that virtue or moral value is perfected. This view would seem to exalt the routinized, half-conscious pursuit of the good or performance of duty, above the fully, often painfully conscious pursuit or performance. In so far as this implication obtains, the view would seem to be misguided: it has preferred an efficient instrumentality, which does not take the *dye* of what it produces, to a conscious causality, which, by virtue of its intentionality, can and must do so. But the view need not be thought to have the implication in question. For perfected virtue, while not indulging in emotional heroics and reflective

DUTY AND MORAL VALUE 371

approfondissements on any and every occasion, may yet be *very ready* to do so, when the occasion really warrants it, and to back its depth of feeling with the required amount of practical effort. And the sort of practice out of which it arose need not have been one of unquestioning imitation of current social patterns, but may have involved many hard pushings of feeling and behaviour on to an impersonal plane, continuous appeals to reflection, and many difficult and keenly conscious choices, whose force may be held to carry over into the present, and which a man in action relives and builds upon. The possession of a good character, of a firm set of dispositions to do or pursue what one should, is in one sense one of the least intrinsically precious of things, in another one of the most precious. If it is neither the echo of clearly conscious, difficult elevation to an impersonal plane of choice, and if it no longer serves as the taking-off point for repeated and similar, or for new and dissimilar elevations, then it is a thing having only a utilitarian or perhaps aesthetic significance. Whereas if it represents the firm but temporary perch between past and future flights, all involving great outlays of conscious causality, and as deeply dependent on the former as the latter will depend upon it, then it may be allowed to take on the hues of the moral excellence into which it is ready, at any moment, to expand. If the possession of power is, as we have seen, intrinsically precious, then the possession of powers which, as it were, consolidate past moral progress, and place us at a definite and higher stage on the moral ladder, will be intrinsically precious, and precious because so intimately one with what is facilitated, and with what itself is so intrinsically precious. The techniques which establish our impersonal values and imperatives must be such as to enable us to condemn as 'errors' many widely held valuations, and it is among these that any high valuation of unreflective, habitual virtue must be placed.

Conscious causality is, however, at its most plain in the coolly taken voluntary decision or whole-minded wish or considered endorsement, and it is to these accordingly that moral value and disvalue will attach. The 'movement into coolness' means precisely that all features which affect the personal or impersonal worth of a situation are brought into clear consciousness, and made capable of modifying the direction of action: it means also that the impulsive and emotional forces in our being, while denied

372   VALUES AND INTENTIONS

direct expression, yet affect action indirectly through what may be called their conscious images. Instead of, that is, being attracted or moved by this or that first-order property, we become attracted or moved by this personal attractiveness or motive power itself, in the light of which an object may continue to be seen as 'offering advantage' (or the reverse) even in the absence of first-order urges towards it. Such determination by personal values instead of by first-order properties represents an increase in conscious causality, both because of its step into a higher universality, and because it transforms an urge *a tergo*, of which, and whose relation to other similar urges, we need not be clearly conscious, into a well-lit goal which lures us on *a fronte*, and whose relation to similar goals is likewise well lit and evident. And to be moved by those inescapable, impersonal attractive-nesses and motive powers which we call 'absolute values', is to carry yet further this exercise of conscious causality, since it is to make conscious a set of goals implicit in all conscious endeavour. Cool, whole-minded decisions and parallel forms therefore represent the highest strain of conscious causality, and it is to these accordingly that moral valuation, which sees values repeated, as it were, in the state of mind that consciously produces them or aims at them, will supremely attach. And decisions and parallel forms will be more accessible to moral valuation according as they are pondered and *deliberated*, i.e. precisely according as they involve a higher degree of consciousness and conscious causality. All this must not be taken as endorsing the doctrine that we can only choose contrary to our view of the best through inattention, forgetfulness, or a temporary blurring of vision. That we act in full consciousness has no tendency to show that we shall act on impersonal rather than personal values, nor even that we shall pursue our overall interest rather than some will-of-the-wisp to which we momentarily and capriciously attach importance. To choose coolly and in clear consciousness what we neither imagine to be best in itself nor best even for ourselves, lies unhappily in our repertoire: it is what gives the notions of wickedness and perversity definite application. But it is equally what gives application to their contraries, the notions of virtue and prudence, since by a conscious causality we mean a causality informed by insight into fact and value, but not one whose direction is uniquely determined by such information.

DUTY AND MORAL VALUE

373

By a conscious causality we mean, in fact, a causality characterized in its operation by one of the unique properties of conscious experience, its power to condense, and hold together in unity, a number of widely radiating conscious directions, so that neither these, nor their objects, can be conceived as making wholly separate contributions, and so that *no* mechanical model can explain their joint influence. An object or situation, if studiously contemplated, leaves behind it a unique conscious impression, whose character grows out of the elements studied, and sums them up, and yet adds to them its own unforeseeable emphases and groupings. And by the inherent tendency of conscious aliveness always to 'go one better' than itself, it must necessarily move in unforeseen directions. How such a conscious unity will operate accordingly eludes all definite computation, since it cannot be broken up into distinct functions or factors. Its growth out of its antecedents is necessarily in part 'creative', and so will be the emergence of whatever grows out of it. If this is the case even in regard to our humblest conscious impressions, which like irridescent bubbles form and burst on the surface of consciousness, how much more will it be the case in regard to those great gatherings together of all we want and know, so as to win from all a single resultant resolution? We are led irresistibly, as argued previously, to a view of our voluntary resolutions as more or less 'free' in the sense which many philosophers find so unacceptable, i.e. as *not* following according to some rigid rule from the fact that such and such factors and features are antecedently present, and assembled in this or that manner. This freedom, as emphasized before, is not to be taken as a negation of causality, but as a specific form of it: influences passing through the focus of conscious unity may emerge from it in a number of different directions, and we expect them to do so in greater degree the more profound the unity. There is an unmistakable oddity, a sustained originality, in the deliverances of anyone who *thinks* as he acts, and is deeply attentive to what he is doing, and it is in fact this quality that disturbs and slightly shocks the unthinking. In the deliberate decisions of a deeply reflective person, e.g. a judge or administrator, this quality is particularly obvious. While we may be extremely clear as to what such a person will *not* do, and this channels our expectations like the walls of a great canyon, the course of what he will do within these walls remains full of

374 VALUES AND INTENTIONS

subtle turnings, not merely adjusted to the windings of circumstance, but revealing a delicate spontaneity.

Such spontaneity may be imitated, but not effectively feigned: nothing shows itself up more instantly than the spontaneous *voulu*. And it is grossly wrong to assimilate it to *chance*, i.e. to situations where a number of factors interact externally, and produce results which shift incalculably from one moment to the next. Conscious spontaneity has a continuity, a decisiveness and an appropriateness which cannot be counterfeited by the randomizer: it is a plain case of *one factor acting variously*, not of a number of factors producing varied results through their intermixture. It is something we recognize even in a brief segment of action, and through which we can reliably discern our conscious contemporaries from the many cunningly built robots with which the daedal skill of science has surrounded us. And it is something, moreover, in which we recognize a more and a less, though this is not to be estimated by the grossness with which conscious choices flout our expectations. A grossly unexpected choice normally betrays the working of some grossly intrusive factor: a pistol pressed in the back, a secret signal, etc. etc. It is in cases where the choice falls within the outline of our expectations, and yet subtly complicates this, or where the choice involves a revolutionary adjustment to some new 'challenge', that the evidence of creativity is most salient. Imperfect as may be our analyses of situations where we recognize the spontaneous, it is plain that we do often recognize it, and that the recognition coheres with the expanding fabric of our knowledge.

What is important to note here is that, to the extent that choice and action reveal the spontaneous, they become accessible to moral valuation, such valuation being concerned with the consciously caused, to what can add its taint or perfume to what consciously intends it. The more spontaneously, the more gratuitously, we espouse the approvably good or evil, the greater will be our moral value or disvalue, a principle according to which we do in fact judge. Such gratuitousness will not mean that a man must be acting 'out of character' to be morally good or bad: he must be acting 'in character', since a man's considered conscious choice necessarily relives his past decisions, even if this reliving be also a rescission. Only if by 'character' be meant a set of patterns *exhaustively* manifest in what has been done up

DUTY AND MORAL VALUE 375

to the present, and not open to modification in future conscious syntheses, then there can be no act of conscious choice that is not more or less 'out of character', a touch of the uncharacteristic being a dominant mark of conscious causality.

If the conscious choice of what corresponds to a man's clearest notion of the approvably good or bad is the main object of moral valuation, this latter will obviously have purchase according as this approvably good or bad is more or less *directly* pursued. Here it is first obvious that the *merely instrumental* pursuit or production of what is recognized to be an approvable good must be *pro tanto* of smaller moral value than the final, unconditional pursuit of the same, or its pursuit 'for its own sake'. In the same way, the merely instrumental pursuit of the approvably bad, and of what is recognized as such, is obviously less heinously bad than the pursuit of the approvably bad for its own sake. The reason in both cases is obvious, that a conscious causality that only takes in a good or an evil on its way, as it were, will be less 'perfumed' or 'tainted' by it than one consciously intent upon good or evil. But while most thinkers would admit the soundness of the latter principle, many would question the former: they would hold there to be absolutely *no* moral value in pursuing the approvably good (which is recognized as such) if it be pursued *only* for the sake of something else, or with an 'ulterior motive'. This last position may, however, be queried. For obviously a man who is prepared to do the approvably good for an ulterior motive, must at least be *partially* moved by its approvable goodness: so much is involved in *recognizing* it be good and approvably good at all. And it is clear, further, that his practice is better than that of a man (perhaps no more than a type of diabolism) who would *not* be prepared to do what is approvably good even to achieve his own personal ends. If we blame a man for being willing to do what he recognizes to be evil for personal ends that are not in themselves evil, we should in logic be willing to praise a man for being willing to do what he recognizes to be good for personal ends that are not themselves good.

Passing from a point too abstract to be profitably discussed, we may next establish the more obvious point that the pursuit or production of the approvably good *for* its approvable goodness, and the pursuit or production of the approvably bad *for* its approvable badness, must rank, in respect of moral value or

376 VALUES AND INTENTIONS

disvalue, above the simple pursuit and production of what is recognized to be approvably good or evil, but is not pursued or produced *for* its approvable goodness or badness. Some may doubt whether *anyone* can pursue the approvably bad *for* its approvable badness (if 'badness' be not given some merely conventional meaning) and would regard it merely as an emptily logical or verbal 'possibility'. The thugs and jailers of Nazism have at least performed this service to morals: they have shown such attitudes to be possible because actual in their case. And it is plain, lastly, that moral value will vary according as a man is or is not willing to subordinate the various partial or qualified imperatives (which tell him, other things being equal, to pursue this or that species of good, or avoid this or that species of evil) to the overriding unqualified imperatives, which tell a man what is good on the whole or good for him, which in short set forth his fully obtaining minatory or hortatory *duties*. For to pursue approvable goodness (or avoid the approvably bad) only in *certain* specific forms, and to be willing to sacrifice all other forms to these, is in a sense *not* to love the approvably good for its own sake, but to have a personal, if noble, passion for what does not necessarily coincide with it. And while we need not deny that passions for truth, fairness, beauty, etc., pursued without qualification, and in total disregard of other valid claims, in a sense deserve the name of 'virtues', we may also say of them, what Augustine said of the virtues of the pagans, that they are really only 'splendid vices'.

Plainly it will be the love of duty, in the sense of self-submission to *overriding* hortatory and minatory imperatives, that will be the supreme determinant of moral value and disvalue, though the fission into two radically different classes of duties slightly complicates the traditional picture. In general, we may say that the violation of minatory imperatives is *per se* determinative of moral baseness or wickedness, while their fulfilment is as such a matter of near-indifference or mere correctness. We may say also that, while the non-fulfilment of hortatory imperatives is as such determinative of near-indifference or mere non-praiseworthiness, their fulfilment is in varying degrees praiseworthy, and the more so the more purely hortatory the imperative. We are most praised and also most blamed for doing what we need least do, and all this follows from the very nature of the imperatives in question.

DUTY AND MORAL VALUE 377

The situation is, however, much complicated in the concrete, and it is this that we must now turn to consider.

Obviously one of the supreme determinants of moral value and disvalue is summed up in such words as 'difficulty', 'cost', 'sacrifice', 'devotion', on the one hand, and by 'ease', 'gain', 'advantage', 'inertia', on the other. If what is impersonally valuable, or impersonally valuable in an agent's perspective, is pursued by him *against* the personal grain, in other words, at personal cost or at personal sacrifice, or if the pursuit involves hardship or difficulty, and is carried on with conspicuous devotion, then the pursuit has a much higher moral value than a similar pursuit which 'comes easy' to the person, which involves little sacrifice, and perhaps promises gain or advantage, or which is done perfunctorily and without zeal or effort. It is not therefore solely the (putative) value of what is produced or striven after that determines the moral value of an effort, but the greatness of this effort. If the outcome is poor, but represents the best the agent can achieve, one may see in it a great manifestation of moral value. The same applies where the state achieved has no positive value whatever, but merely avoids an important evil: if the state in question is achieved with profound personal difficulty and sacrifice, the moral value may be as great as where the result is positively good. Similar things apply if we turn to the case of disvalues. If evils are produced with positive ease, and accord entirely with a man's natural grain, and if it would in fact involve difficult self-suppression *not* to produce them, then we attribute less moral disvalue to their production than if this production involves effort and personal self-discipline. 'Temptation', we hold, softens, and thereby excuses, misdemeanours, as it hardens, and thereby exalts, deliberate wickednesses. The same applies to evils produced by outside causes, where it goes against someone's inertia to interfere with them: wickedness is much less in the case of such moral sloth, than if one deliberately crushes some preventive impulse. If the notion of a devoted self-suppression in the cause of evil might seem without application, the useful Nazis have served to instantiate it.

The 'hard' and 'easy', then, in one sense of these adjectives, are of central importance in determining moral value and disvalue. It is in clarifying the precise sense given to these words in this connection, that we may hope to understand this importance.

378 VALUES AND INTENTIONS

Plainly the 'hard' does not mean that which demands great energy, or opposes formidable resistances: to scale a wall in terror or passion is hard in this sense, but it is not hard in the sense relevant to moral value. The 'easy', in the same context, means, not a mere absence of impediments or a need for effort: it is the peculiar ease of a descent to Avernus, which may in many ways be a lively progress. It is plain, in fact, that the use of 'hard' in the sense relevant to moral value connects with the use of 'hardship', and implies a thoroughly dualistic psychology: the 'hardness' in question is one that involves difficulty, but not hardship, for what may be called our 'higher nature', and hardship for our lower. In the same manner, the ease relevant to moral value is in one sense the mere absence or diminution of the hardness just mentioned: in another sense it is a positive ease, involving neither difficulty nor hardship for our higher nature, but release, decontrol, satisfaction for the lower. The 'higher' and 'lower' natures are not hard to identify. The 'higher' is simply conscious causality in its more developed, integrated form of voluntary decision and considered wish and approval, the causality provoked by the mere thought of something as being a personal or impersonal motive for action, in a complete setting of similar motives, while the 'lower' is conscious causality in its more primitive, purblind diremption, where there are separate urges each moving to its specific goal, without full regard to circumstances or consequences, or to ends projected by other similar urges. And our whole manner of valuation has—it is not new to maintain—the plainest indeterministic implications. For while there is nothing remarkable in our thinking it *hard* for our higher, integrated conscious causality to encounter resistance from lower, less integrated forms, and *easy* for it to operate *without* such resistance, it *is* remarkable that we should think it *easy* for this higher conscious causality to *give up* the struggle with its less integrated opponents, and to *submit* itself to their dominion. What this tends to suggest is that our higher conscious causality has something gratuitous about it: what it expends it could also withhold, and often *more readily* than it expends it. In other words, the source of the hardness encountered by our higher conscious causality lies not in circumstance but itself: to do the hard thing is for it to depart more and more widely from its own median line of inertia, and to approach more and more closely to

DUTY AND MORAL VALUE 379

what represents for it the impossible. All this makes good sense in our ordinary talk about these matters: which does not shirk from holding that a thing may, without outer provocation, exert itself in a number of distinct ways, each with a different distance from certainty and impossibility. Only the long rule of deterministic nineteenth-century science, which applies to all things the categories best applied to unconscious things in space, has made all this seem so difficult. From the view taken by us of conscious causality, it is not obscure why we should value the difficult above the easy choice, and why by the 'difficult' we should mean the more gratuitous. For the hard, gratuitous choice is the one best expressive of a causality free from particular pressures, and engaged in perpetual revisionary movement over the whole firmament of what it knows and wants.

(V) DEVELOPMENTS OF THE ABOVE PRINCIPLES

We have laid down so far that moral value or disvalue will be proportionate to the value or disvalue impersonally attributed by a man to what he strives for or produces, with many qualifications as to the directness or indirectness of such striving, its partial regard for certain values or disvalues only, or its impartial regard for them all, and the degree to which it represents a man's most 'earnest' attempt to achieve an impersonal assessment. We have also laid down that moral values and disvalues will be proportioned to what we may call generally the *difficulty* or *ease* of the pursuit or production of what is judged impersonally good or evil, covering by the term 'difficulty' the amount of energy or effort which must be put forth at the cool, conscious, integrated level, which represents the output of strictly conscious causality, and covering by the term 'ease', not merely the reduced need of any output of this sort, but also the added presence of forms of causality *not* operative at this level, but in unconscious nature, or in the less reason-guided segment of a man's own nature, and all tending to the outcome in question. What we may call the determination of merit-demerit by the value-disvalue axis, on the one hand, and by the difficulty-ease axis on the other, are not, however, independent, but exhibit an interesting interplay, leading to results as complex and orderly as are the curves of co-ordinate geometry. Merit-demerit may in fact be represented

380 VALUES AND INTENTIONS

by a three-dimensional curve, oriented about the two intersecting axes mentioned above, Ease-Difficulty and Value-Disvalue, and divided by these into four importantly different segments: (a) that of the striving towards and the production of results that are positively valuable and that also involve personal difficulty; (b) that of the striving towards, and production of results positively disvaluable and also difficult for the agent; (c) that of strivings towards, and productions of, what is positively valuable and also easy; (d) that of strivings towards, and productions of what is positively disvaluable and also easy. The behaviour of this curve in each of these segments may now be briefly studied.

In the segment (a), or the difficult pursuit of the positively valuable, it seems plain that merit or moral value does not depend simply on the two factors of degree of positive value aimed at, and degree of difficulty in realizing this. It involves also the principle that the degree of positive value aimed at must *justify* the amount of difficulty and personal sacrifice undergone for its sake: not *every* degree of positive value will justify *any* degree of personal difficulty and sacrifice. It would not, e.g., be justifiable, and therefore not meritorious, to do a day's research in order to give someone a trivial piece of information, though it might be justifiable and meritorious to think for a moment on the matter, or to look it up in an available work of reference. Likewise, to take a charming example of Meinong's, it would not be justifiable to risk one's life to rescue a lady's pocket-handkerchief, though it might be reasonable to risk getting one's feet wet in the same cause. Efforts of conscious causality not proportioned to the good to be achieved are not meritorious at all, but mildly or seriously blameworthy: we apply to them such words as 'quixotic', 'fanatical', '*outré*', etc. etc. The reason for this kind of judgement is not far to seek. The difficulties surmounted in doing something may testify to a man's devotion to impersonal values, but they also involve discomfort, pain, frustration for himself, or they would not be difficulties, and as such they are impersonally disvaluable. It is not unreasonable, therefore, to feel that they will 'tip the scale' if increased continuously, and that (to vary the metaphor) from taking the 'perfume' of the value they make possible, they may begin at a point to 'taint' the latter with *their* evil, and this will be the point where the highest merit swings over into quixotism. Where this 'tipping' or 'tainting' point lies

DUTY AND MORAL VALUE 381

is, of course, a matter for individual reaction and discernment, and will differ from individual to individual—there are persons given to 'gestures' and persons not so given—being lifted into impersonality by the fact that it *does* represent each individual's profoundest reaction. What is not personal, however, is the existence of *some* such tip- or taint-point, and also that it will be further advanced the more valuable the outcome aimed at. A *very* valuable outcome obviously justifies considerable hardship and sacrifice. The apex of merit in the direction of increasing difficulty lies further *just on the brink of quixotism*: we behave most excellently when we realize some project at the maximum justifiable difficulty or sacrifice.

If we now turn to consider cases where difficulty remains constant but value increases, we arrive at the somewhat paradoxical principle that it is more meritorious to realize a *lower* value at a given level of difficulty—such a realization being justifiable—than to realize a *higher* one. This principle is not absurd, for it does not entail that we should realize lower values in preference to higher ones *in order* to be more meritorious. One's own merit, as we shall see later, is only, in fact, an indirect and secondary object of legitimate moral pursuit. Nor does it entail that, in a situation where two courses are open to us, one terminating in a higher and one in a lower value, it would be meritorious to choose the latter. What it does mean is that a man willing to make considerable effort for a lower degree of value, not in competition with a higher degree, is to that extent more value-regarding than one only willing to make the same effort for a higher degree of value, and he is so because *we take it for granted* that one willing to make an effort E for a lower value will automatically make it for a higher. If this were not the case, the principle would lose all claim to validity. The amount of difficulty a man is capable of facing, or effort he is capable of making, has, moreover, an absolute upper limit, and, somewhat paradoxically again, we shall have to hold that it is more meritorious to make this maximum effort (supposing it to be justifiable at all) for an outcome or project of lower value than for one of higher value. If we are only willing to exert ourselves maximally for outcomes of high value, we have less merit than those willing to exert themselves maximally for much poorer prizes. The paradox of this principle is removed if we assume that one willing to make the maximum exertion for

382 VALUES AND INTENTIONS

projects or outcomes of less value will automatically make it where outcomes of higher value are concerned. We may, in fact, hold that what conditions merit is not solely the effort *actually* put forth on behalf of a given value, but also the effort that the man *was prepared to put forth* had the value been less than it is. Thus a man who makes an effort E for a value V_1, may have all the merit of someone who makes the same effort for a lesser value V_2, provided that he was *prepared* to make the effort E for V_2. (We avoid the verb 'would'—'would have been prepared', etc.—as we do not wish to connect what we say with a man's long-term character, but with the *contemporary* state of his fully conscious causality.)

It may be argued, further, that for every degree of positive value there is a degree of effort which it would be, not a matter of indifference, but *shameful* not to make, should we know such effort to be probably effective. For small positive values, it is perhaps not shameful to make no effort at all, but a point must be reached (differently fixed for the earnest and the frivolous) where it is shameful to make absolutely no effort. For lower degrees of value above this point there will be a fairly low degree of effort that it will be shameful not to make—again provided such effort would have a good chance of achieving its result—whereas for higher degrees of value there will obviously be a much higher degree of effort which it would be shameful not to make, until we come to values so high that it would be shameful not to make the maximum practically useful effort to realize them. At this point the point of shame and the apical point of merit for *that* degree of value— coincide: we achieve the highest merit possible for that value *if* we realize it, and it would be shameful *not* to realize it. But where values are lower, it may be far from shameful not to make the maximum effort to realize them, and may even be quixotic to do so. And the apical point of merit in realizing them, whether at the maximum of effort or below it, may be separated by a considerable span of effort from the point of shame. In such a zone, imperatives will be hortatory, and the more purely so the more removed from the point of shame, though merit will be greater in heeding whispers so gentle. Whereas, near the point of shame, impersonal indications will lose fixed direction like a mariner's compass near the poles, and merit and demerit will alike vanish, though below this point indications will of course slew round to a minatory pose, to whose non-fulfilment demerit will attach.

DUTY AND MORAL VALUE 383

The topography of this sector (*a*) may now be briefly sketched. It will be more or less diagonally divided by a high ridge, each of whose points represents the maximum of effort legitimate for a given value and also the maximum merit for achieving that value. On the one side this ridge, like the Andean cordilleras, descends precipitously to the deep Pacific of quixotic demerit, where more effort has been expended on a project than its absolute worth justifies: on the other side it will, at the lower levels of value, decline more slowly, as an effort less than the maximum permitted is expended, until, after a fair spell in the less and less meritorious, it at length sinks beneath the tides of shame. But as values rise, and the point of maximum difficulty is reached, the point of shame will come close to that of apical merit: there will be the steepest of plunges from one to the other. (The analogy with South American geography here loses application.) As to the topography of the top of the ridge, it is not easy to give it. Shall we say that to make the maximum effort justified by some outcome is always equally meritorious, though both value and legitimate difficulty are varied? Is it the proportioning of effort to value that alone determines merit, or does absolute value itself count, whether in a depressing or buoyant fashion? And once the point of maximum difficulty is reached, shall we say that merit declines or rises or remains constant the more valuable the objective achieved? Our difficulties are increased by the fact, noted above, that moral value and disvalue depend also on a man's *preparedness* to exert effort even if he does not in fact exert it. There is no point in pursuing these conundrums farther: the field of moral values will perhaps not yield the wealth of precise theorems found in less subjectively warped territories. It is important to raise them only to show that the notions involved in this field exhibit many curious interrelations, giving rise to many highly precise questions, to which only partially definite replies can be given.

The topography of the remaining fields of merit and demerit may be more briefly sketched. The sector (*b*), the sector of actions done with difficulty and some sacrifice, and for ends known to be evil, may be called the sector of the *diabolical*. Had the S.S. men and other Nazis not provided us with living examples, we might have doubted whether this sector had occupants. There would seem to be no peculiarities in its structure, nothing comparable to the justifiability of sacrifice which distinguishes the

384 VALUES AND INTENTIONS

two sub-sections of (*a*). Our sector descends into the abyss, whether we follow lines of increasing disvalue or of difficulty, and the only things that arrest this descent are the limits of human effort, on the one hand, and the limits of human horror on the other. Both limits seem to have been reached by the German S.S.

The sector (*c*) is likewise somewhat uninteresting: in it the positive valuable is achieved, but achieved without difficulty, and by forces that have nothing to do with the higher forms of conscious causality. It has been held to be a region of moral indifference, where an action is done *in accordance with*, but not *out of regard for*, the law. We, however, may remember the proviso that it is not difficulty actually faced, but difficulty that someone is prepared to face, that determines merit. Hence a man for whom some value-productive action comes easy, on account of inclination, habit, circumstance, etc. etc., may yet have merit if he remains *geared* for effort should effort be required of him. It may, however, be questioned whether even an *acquiescence* in the realization of good, and a non-interference in its production, or a preparedness to use it instrumentally, such as might have been shown by a conscientious Nazi, may not have some slight merit: if so, this merit will be greater, the greater the amount of not-striven-for good that a person thus tolerates. And if the tendencies towards good which a man tolerates without encouragement are his own, there is no doubt that some savour of the good tolerated will perfume the will that tolerates it. Corrupted natures, it is not sentimentally held, may be purged and redeemed through their amiable weaknesses.

The sector (*d*) is more interesting. It covers acts productive of disvaluable results, and recognized as such, but done with 'ease', i.e. done under the pressure of forms of causality not of the integrated, purely conscious type. It covers the cases where we are 'tempted', led astray, bewitched, subject to duress, etc. etc. This region has the same diagonal division as sector (*a*), but less exciting contours: the diagonal separates a region of *total innocence*, where the temptation duress, etc., was so severe as completely to *excuse* the production of something evil, from a region where such exculpation is imperfect, and where we have varied degrees of culpability. It must be noted that the degree of temptation required to excuse the choice of something bad increases steadily with the

DUTY AND MORAL VALUE 385

badness of what is chosen. One must be more sorely tempted to sign an unjust death-warrant excusably than to tell a relatively undamaging social lie. Even though a man *could* have resisted certain temptations, it may have been unreasonable, in view of the small evil avoided, to incommode himself to that extent: such faults are, therefore, wholly venial. But, with an increase in evil, the inconvenience involved in resisting it becomes less exculpating, until, in the cases of major evils, it is proper to resist them with *all* the force of our being—provided, of course, that this resistance will be effective, or not improbably so—or else incur serious blame. There would seem only to be a dubious merit in a resistance to evil which is certainly vain: if it has merit, this can only be for its inspirational effect, or for its maintenance of a spirit which may not be so vain in other cases. We may note, further, that there is, for each man, a degree of temptation of duress— certainly not lightly to be presumed—beyond which counter-effort is impossible: such temptation or duress will be *wholly* exculpatory, no matter how evil the outcome. The demerit of producing evils under conditions of temptation or duress will, further, slope down continuously from all points and on all lines starting from the bounding line of the barely excusable. The gradient is easy if, for a given degree of temptation, the evil of an outcome increases, but it becomes steep if evil remains constant and temptation is reduced, until, with temptation altogether removed, we pass out of our sector into that of diabolical wickedness.

(VI) VIRTUE AND VICE: DUTY AND MORAL VALUE

We have completed our scholastic study of the meritorious and the wicked, more to give the savour of its undoubted near-tautologies, than to work it out in a finally satisfactory manner. What we have said might have been recast in terms of hortatory and minatory imperatives, and full-fledged duties, sector (*a*) being mainly that of difficult fulfilments of the hortatory, sector (*b*) of difficult violations of the minatory, sector (*c*) of easy fulfilment of the hortatory, and sector (*d*) of easy violation of the minatory. It now remains our task to consider two matters: the relation of the *actual* moral value or disvalue we have been dealing with to the more dispositional values enshrined in the terms

N

386 VALUES AND INTENTIONS

'virtue', 'vice' and their plurals, and also the various fundamental imperatives and duties connected with moral values and disvalues.

As regards the former question, it seems plain that one must impersonally prize (or misprize), not merely *exercises* of conscious causality directed to what is valuable or disvaluable, but also the various ingrained habits of mind and soul which make such exercises easy and agreeable to the person concerned, or, on the other hand, disagreeable and difficult. Such habits of mind and soul are hard, if not palpable facts about a man, and they must certainly take the perfume or taint of what they issue in, and of what enters into their description, even if not in the living, intimate fashion in which a thing consciously aimed at enters into the description of one's endeavours. They also represent powers which facilitate, or obstacles which hinder, the achievement of the impersonally valuable, or the ascent to *higher* rungs on the ladder of moral values, and powers, as we have seen, are intrinsically to be approved of, as impediments to power are intrinsically to be disapproved of. The habits of mind and soul whose manifestations are good may be called 'virtue' or the 'virtues', while the habits of mind and soul whose manifestations are bad may be called 'vice' or the 'vices'. Such habits may be the canalized forms of conscious causality operating below the cool, integrated, strictly conscious level: they may also be the channels left by exercises of strictly conscious causality in choice, which now make similar exercises easy, and a mere matter of course. And they may be *partial*, directed to this or that sort of valuable outcome, e.g. increase of affection and sympathy, etc., in which case we tend to speak *plurally* of vices and virtues, or they may represent an integrated direction to what is best done on the whole, and by the person concerned, to what, in short, is his full minatory and hortatory duty, in which case we speak of *virtue* in general and of its contrary *wickedness*. There is, further, another well-known contrary to organized virtue, which consists solely in disintegration and confusion of soul, the failure to co-ordinate strands of purblind impulse into an integrated, fully conscious synthesis.

As to all these cases of valuable or disvaluable spiritual strength and disvaluable weakness, it may be held generally that they are not too closely related to the values attaching to *actual exercises* of conscious causality, and that it is perhaps misleading (if convenient) to use the same terms 'moral value' and 'moral

DUTY AND MORAL VALUE 387

disvalue', or 'virtue' and 'vice', to cover both. There is even, as often observed, a certain antagonism among them. For with the perfecting of habits, the occasions for strenuous exercises of strictly conscious causality must diminish, at least in the directions covered by such habits, and, while they may be sought in other directions, it is at least thinkable that they may not be sought at all. We may have samurai, sahibs, καλοὶ καὶ ἀγαθοί, etc., relatively hidebound, practical exponents of good codes, not thirsting for novel exercises in the disinterested. And if we are to choose impersonally between what may be called well practised and active virtue, there is no doubt where the preference must lie. Practised virtue involves precisely that surrender to the empirical and the existent, that reduction of strictly conscious causality, which impersonality, the last fruit of conscious causality, must deplore, and with such reduction must go a blurring of sensitiveness to the finer, growing points of value, which will make moral improvement difficult. The well trained in goodness have notoriously blocked and delayed the reception of many most imperative, ethical developments, and have made moral reflection an activity of prophets, revolutionaries, reformers, etc., instead of one in constant and daily use. Active virtue is, however, not the only thing to be impersonally valued, and will frequently be inconvenient, uncomfortable and destructive of other values. One would not wish the whole fabric of a smoothly functioning way of life to be constantly disrupted to afford occasions for heroic virtue. Habitual virtue has its place if the absolute firmament of values, even if this may not be the high one allotted to it by the complacency of Aristotle.

From this contrast between different forms or senses of virtue, we pass on to consider the *duties* connected with either. We must here deal with an extraordinary moralistic tradition, which holds virtue, whether in act or habit, to be *incomparably* more valuable than any other sort of valuable thing, or to be perhaps the *only* unconditionally valuable thing in the universe, other things only having value as its complement or accompaniment. Similar remarks apply, *mutatis mutandis*, in the case of wickedness and moral weakness. From this it would seem to follow that the duty to promote virtue, and expunge vice, whether in ourselves or others, takes precedence over all other duties.

That virtue, whether in act or disposition, has a unique place

388 VALUES AND INTENTIONS

in the value-firmament need not be doubted, since all forms of value have this uniqueness, and are not replaceable by other forms. But that it occupies such a *supreme* place in the value-firmament as is commonly supposed may be gravely questioned: it is of forms of value the least capable of independent existence, and seems as much subject to cheapening by multiplication as any other form of value. That it is least capable of independent existence follows from all we have so far said, since the conscious pursuit of what is valuable or disvaluable could obviously have no value or disvalue, were there not values or disvalues, other than its own, that could attach to the objects it aimed at. And a habit of soul can have value or disvalue only as productive of valuable or disvaluable outcomes, which cannot, without an inadmissible regress, themselves *all* be valuable or disvaluable habits of soul. And if virtue, actual or habitual, is thus parasitic on other values, it suffers even more acutely than they do when cut off from other forms of value. If asked, in Moorean fashion, where the preference lies between a world of individuals possessed always of admirable intentions, but enjoying little satisfaction, understanding little clearly, contemplating hardly anything well formed, etc. etc., and a world of individuals enjoying all these latter advantages, and yet being largely slothful, self-interested and imperfectly scrupulous, it is not clear that the superiority would lie plainly on the former side. *Many* features of action and experience merit impersonal approval, but for different reasons: there can be no clear ground why *one* such reason, even if it in a sense presupposes all others, should take precedence over them. The graver forms of wickedness certainly may be ranked among important evils, both for the horror of what they compass, and for the clear consciousness and perhaps gratuitousness with which they compass it, but it is not clear why they should be regarded as *infinitely* worse than the worst forms of agony or spiritual degradation. And the forms of virtue which consist mainly in being free from these forms of wickedness, or in having no taste for them, would not seem to rank among the most highly precious things. And if merely habitual virtue is inferior to what we have called virtue in act, it would seem also inferior to other impersonally approvable spiritual activities: to the creation and contemplation of the beautiful, the entering into profound communion with others, etc. etc. If virtue, actual and habitual, became, further, more and

DUTY AND MORAL VALUE   389

more abundantly realized, while other values were allowed to fall
into decay and neglect, as has repeatedly happened in the world's
history, e.g. under monkish asceticism, Victorian strenuousness,
Communist discipline, etc. etc., can it be doubted that such 'over-
production' would both justifiably and inevitably produce the sort
of 'transvaluation' that occurred at the Renaissance, in our own
1890's and 1920's, etc. etc.? The unified conscious causality to
which moral values attach may be the crowning form of our
conscious life, but this makes it *less* basic, *more* dependent on other
types of value than they are in relation to it.

If moral good and evil are not, therefore, supremely good or
evil, they are none the less genuinely and indefeasibly so, and as
such they must have imperatives, hortatory or minatory, directed
to them, which will in some situations be overriding, constituting
full-strength duties or obligations. Some of these duties will be
directed towards moral values in a man's own person, some
towards similar values in his neighbours or in remote persons. We
shall attempt briefly to suggest what these duties are, and whether
predominantly hortatory or minatory in cast.

Moral evil, we saw, attaches to the non-realization of the not
too hardly realizable good: it attaches also to the not too sorely
tempted realization of evil, and, pre-eminently, to the dedicated,
difficult realization of what is evil. In all these cases it involves
a flouting of minatory imperatives, and becomes accordingly, by
infection with what it intends, itself the object of minatory
imperatives. We are warned off, not merely from various bad
outcomes, or bad absences of good outcomes, but from the
spiritual poses in which such outcomes are intended, and from
the ingrained habits which make such poses easy. It is our duty,
and our duty in the minatory sense, to avoid framing wicked
intentions, or carrying out wicked performances at the level of
unified conscious causality: it is likewise our duty to avoid
fostering various forms of less purely conscious causality, and the
dispositions or spiritual slants from which these spring. These
duties have, however, certain curious features which have been
often noted: it is often redundant, and sometimes self-defeating,
to seek to fulfil them. It is redundant to the extent that the duty
which warns us off from realizing some evil outcome is precisely
adjusted to the moral badness we shall amass *if* we realize it, and
to the difficulty of realizing or not realizing it, or the contrary

VALUES AND INTENTIONS

'ease'. If it is positively difficult for us to achieve an evil, we are warned off from achieving it most stringently, and our demerit in achieving it is correspondingly atrocious, whereas if 'temptation' makes it positively easy for us to achieve an evil, and correspondingly difficult to avoid it, we are warned off from it only mildly—the voice of duty does not confirm to a deterrent theory of moral disapproval—and the demerit in realizing it is correspondingly lightened. It follows that, if we wish to heed the imperatives bidding us minimize demerit in our actions—we are not considering the accumulation of merit—we cannot do better than do *our ordinary primary duty*, which is concerned with avoiding disvaluable outcomes, in which our own personal demerit does not figure. If we do our ordinary primary duty, in avoiding or attempting to avoid the production of evil, we shall, without giving the matter further heed, *also* fulfil our higher-order duty of avoiding demerit for ourselves. But if, on the other hand, our concern for the cleanness of our hands, and the purity of our heart, becomes obsessive, and we seek to achieve these independently, and for their own sake—which means, if it means anything, in ways *other* than those demanded by primary duty, if we should seek, e.g., rather to remove a relatively unimportant, but highly recalcitrant evil, than one gross and palpable, but not so hard to remove, in order to be more zealous against evil—then we shall have chosen as we are warned off by our primary duty from choosing, and shall have *failed* to achieve the cleanness of heart and hand that was our aim. The effective avoidance of moral badness in ourselves is therefore best promoted by giving relatively little thought to it, a proposition well known to Christian people at all times, who have been deeply aware of the subtle corruptions attendant on the observances of the Pharisees, or on the hand-washing of Pontius Pilate, but not brought to the notice of philosophers before the time of Max Scheler.

What we have said about the avoidance of demerit applies, *mutatis mutandis*, to the accumulation of merit. We acquire merit by being willing to heed even the stiller, more purely hortatory, promptings of duty, and to do so even in the face of opposing difficulty, but again a too zealous attention to the merit gained by attention to such slight whisperings may cancel it altogether. For we may be led to seek merit in doing the uncalled for, handsome, remotely generous thing, in preference to the humdrum duty which

DUTY AND MORAL VALUE 391

is urgent, inglorious and lies close at hand. And to do the uncalled for, handsome, generous thing in such circumstances is to exalt the hortatory above the minatory, instead of letting the former, as its nature demands, supplement the latter non-competitively: such inversion, violating a basic minatory imperative, cancels all merit. It is therefore intrinsic to moral value that it should be realized only 'by the way': our duty is to achieve it in the course of doing our primary duties. The most that we could do to realize it independently would be to go in quest of real-life situations that will provide occasions for it, situations of corruption, pain, injustice, etc. etc., a course regularly followed by reformers, saints, heroes, penitents, etc. etc. But it would be wholly repugnant to 'rig' or multiply or prolong these provoking situations in order to create room for personal heroics. The truly meritorious person must acquiesce happily in the vanishing of those evils which provoked his heroism, and must retire to his friends, his books, his garden, and other serener pursuits. This is yet another proof of the equivocal character of moral value: it has, as Hegel shows in the *Phenomenology*, a tendency to be double-faced, to seek hypocritically to preserve the evils whose attrition gives it employment. The preservation or creation of evils as spurs to moral value is not, however, anything that can be impersonally countenanced, however genuine the resultant virtue. To attribute such designs to God, as is sometimes done, is to make Him the cosmic miscreant whose crimes provoke other people's valuable police or rescue work.

Beside what may be called the first-class moral value of deliberate, difficult self-dedication to promoting the good and uprooting the evil, there is also the second-class moral value of having wants and habits *trained* in the direction of goodness and away from evil. Such wants and habits we certainly have a duty to promote, both for the sake of the goods regularly produced and evils avoided, but also for their own sake, as things coloured with the tinge of what they are dispositionally 'of', and as fixed rungs in the ladder from which ascents into first-class moral value may be made. That we have such a duty bears witness, also, to the limited importance of first-class moral value, for, as our habits and wants become more firmly espaliered to the framing walls of the good, we shall have less and less occasion for the large efforts involved in first-class moral value. If Aristotle was wrong in

392 VALUES AND INTENTIONS

valuing sound moral training above unreliable, difficult, moral decisions, there are situations where his is the right preference, where we pass with relief from struggles that improved circumstances have rendered superfluous to tidy interiors, regular personal relations and the ease and fragrance of good living. And sometimes our duty to acquire such habits will be minatory, and the habits themselves indispensable rather than valuable: veracity, punctuality, courtesy, etc., will fall into this class. But at other times the duty to acquire such habits will be hortatory, and the habits themselves rare and excellent: we have a hortatory duty to acquire increased generosity, deeper sympathy, equanimity in the face of difficulties, better 'motives' and spiritual stances in general. All these duties are to some extent independent of our primary duties: we may very well do some gratuitous character-building and training of moral muscle, sometimes in specially rigged, even make-believe circumstances, when primary duty is lacking. The danger of Pharisaism no doubt exists in this case too, if the justification of moral muscle is not seen in its use for deontically justified blows, but it is not endemic and intrinsic as in the case of the direct pursuit of meritorious actions and choices. Nothing, further, suggests that one cannot have 'too much of a good thing' in excessively pursued 'character building', and that it must cheapen itself, and thereby raise the price of unstrained activity and enjoyment.

If we turn now to the case of moral value *for others*, it is plain that this must generate many hortatory and minatory duties for ourselves, which are free from the self-defeating difficulties found in the direct pursuit of such values for ourselves. We are plainly warned off from leading others into temptation of a sort likely not to be withstood but weakly assented to: we are more strongly warned off from offering counsel or encouragement which may lead to the gratuitous, even difficult choice of the bad. If moral evil is, with pain, injustices, etc., rightly ranked among the great evils, there must be stern imperatives against furnishing the occasion or the instruments for its development. There is also a much weaker imperative, further weakened by remoteness, and becoming hortatory instead of minatory, exhorting us to do what we can towards *preventing* such moral evil. This imperative is weak, since the prevention demanded is both difficult and delicate: it must not grossly interfere with outer performance—

DUTY AND MORAL VALUE 393

though this may be interfered with for *other* reasons—since to stop a man from realizing an evil intention is not to stop him from forming it, nor must it penetrate into the counsel chamber of fully conscious causality, or must do so only *as* offering counsel. The slowly operating machinery of legal punishment may, by its very impersonality, speak to the impersonal segment in a man, and put certain valuations over to him, and it may for that reason (among others) be the duty of those placed to inflict it to do so: for the private outsider, the duty is one of coldness, unforthcomingness, withdrawal of all but obligatory co-operation, all, in short, that a man can do, without forcibly intruding on another, to bring home to him the unfavourable verdict passed on him by a non-partisan jury. This is a duty hard to perform, and readily admixed with Pharisaic zest, but in some cases better ill performed than not at all. There is also a duty, sometimes minatory, but more often hortatory, to seek unintrusively to *win* a man from evil courses, by exhibiting the contrary good ones unostentatiously, by favouring those who follow these contrary courses, and so insinuating pledges of favour to him *if* he reforms, etc. etc. The contemporary incapacity for moral *finesse* makes many think these not duties at all: many, certainly, would perform them so bunglingly as to be better advised to leave them unperformed. As to the encouragement of dispensable excellence in others—increased generosity, cultivation of aesthetic and other sensibilities, etc.—it is plain that the duties being hortatory for the agent himself, or minatory, only in cases of strong vocation—they will be far more mildly hortatory for the outside agent, who can with difficulty avoid bungling intrusion in seeking to carry them out. And as to the promotion of second-class moral value in others—the value of good habits, right moral opinions, etc.—it seems plain that the one case where it enters the sphere of minatory duty is that of the education of the immature. There indeed we should be ready to mould, retreating to gentler forms of suasion as soon as there appear signs of counter-moulding from within. (It is easy to dismiss such Froebelian delicacy of approach as an expression of bourgeois individualism: the separateness of persons, however late discovered, is, however, *the* basic fact for morals.) It is not our task here to write an essay on the detailed ethics of betterment, but only to suggest that such an ethics necessarily flows from the impersonality central to

N*

VALUES AND INTENTIONS

morality, though the difficulty of influencing from without, what must come freely from within, becomes ever more formidable on a deeper acquaintance with men and issues. That many betterers have been bunglers does not mean that we should, or indeed may, abandon the enterprise.

Of the duties to requite and punish, in so far as these can be separated from the duties to better our neighbours or ourselves, or to promote or prevent certain outcomes, we need for completeness briefly make mention. Punitive duty comes, as we said, at the very end of the 'queue', on account of its admixture with evil, whose smallest excess, like the blood in Shylock's pound of flesh, suspends duty altogether: it can exercise its indefeasible claim only when practically no other claim is there to contest it. The duties to reward are almost wholly hortatory, and are closely and necessarily admixed with the duties to better.

We have now completed our sketch of the two firmaments of value and duty, being content to show the family connections of their various members, and their varied specification of the same elusive but fruitful central principle. We have also sought to show the strange changing logic of their precedence in varying situations and for varying individuals, and its sensitiveness to the abundant and the rare, and to individual taste and preference, in a manner well understood in economics, but not often thought relevant in the moral sphere. But the laws regulating the rise and fall of prices of economic commodities reflect the fundamental form and life of consciousness, and these too, therefore, will obtain in the realm of impersonal ends and duties. The firmament of ends and duties, even more than the firmament of stars, twinkles and glitters perpetually, never ceasing to brighten where it was previously dim, nor to become dull where it was previously bright, and sometimes in quite new regions of the heavens. Such 'glitter' is inevitable where notions and attitudes are linked together by flexible relations of kinship, rather than by axioms and rules.

CHAPTER IX

EPILOGUE ON RELIGION

We have practically completed our sketch of the firmament of impersonal values, and of the directives and duties with which they guide conscious action. One crowning set of values remains over for consideration: the peculiar merits attaching to the objects of *religious worship* or *piety*, and the values of the notions, acts, beliefs and feelings connected with these. The peculiar objects of religion plainly tend to have the qualities that we value, whether personally or impersonally, attributed to them, and attributed to them in a supreme and superlative form. Were they not thus decked out in all that we find most precious, they would plainly not qualify at all readily for the deference we accord to them: it would be odd to defer religiously to what we considered mean, sordid, ill-formed, dishonest, base, etc. etc. The supreme or superlative sense in which religious objects have these valued features attributed to them has indeed something queer and 'numinous' about it. They do not merely possess the highest forms or degrees of the qualities we value: there is also a strange twist to the sense or manner in which they possess them, which transforms the palpable into the thin, the lucidly intelligible into the tantalizing and obscure, the straightforwardly gracious and good into what often has a touch of the terrible and sinister about it. But, however transformed, the values credited to religious objects have a lineal descent from the values credited to things, persons and conditions in common experience, and their very queerness or numinousness has itself such a lineal descent, being remotely derived from the values attaching to the novel, the pregnant and the pointed which we have seen to flow from drifts native to our conscious life. And not only does a peculiar nimbus of values surround the various peculiar objects of religion: it also encircles the persons and acts of those dedicated or devoted to such objects. They too manifest in lessened degree the transformed excellences attributed to the objects of their concern. They are more or less *holy* as it is entirely holy, and they body forth this holiness in forms of bliss, insight, ravished contemplation, love, devotion to duty, etc. etc., which are recognizably cases of the 'values' of satisfaction,

396 VALUES AND INTENTIONS

cognitive penetration, etc., which recommended themselves to our impersonal approval, and which are additionally approvable (for reasons yet to be investigated) in virtue of their specific religious style or manner. Every style or pattern of desirable living would seem to have what may be called its 'consecrated mode', and these modes together enter into a general pattern of consecrated living, or into several distinct patterns of such living, which are as much (and more than as much) objects of impersonal valuation, as are the forms of life which they consecrate. It is these consecrated modes of action and experience to which, with the objects which inspire them, we must now devote attention.

The religious sphere we are now entering is best characterized in terms of a governing attitude, which may be said to be one of deference become superlative or 'carried to the limit'. There is a wide range of feelings, patterns of action, even patterns of theory, rightly termed 'religious', and it is not necessary to find one clearly marked-off thing common to them all: all may, however, be said to have something extraordinary, extreme, 'set apart' in their manner of approach, which reflects itself in their object, or in the 'light' in which they view their object. What we regard religiously provokes a sharp fall of all personal insistence and self-confidence, temporarily lames our interest in, and our concern with, objects other than itself, weakens the zeal or zest felt in our favourite projects, enfeebles the confidence of our normal pretensions, and makes ourselves, and the things we normally care for, small and trivial in the face of something whose degree of superiority we feel powerless to assess. At the same time, and in virtue of the same deeply deferential attitude, what we bow to religiously comes before us as not belonging to the common run of things, as having virtues and properties of a quite extraordinary and surpassing sort, even if not revealed in what stands palpably before us, as extending in fact beyond what is palpable into a mysterious, not wholly accessible region or dimension. And if a passing touch of religious awe manifests all these strangely subduing, enhancing properties, its established hold on the mind must carry these farther yet. A religious 'spirit' must tend to organize the life of a man about some central object or objective, to subordinate his contemplative and practical interests to itself, if its object is thought of as having plans or wishes, it must tend to make these the man's own, and to subordinate his other

EPILOGUE ON RELIGION

wishes to them, and it must tend to do this *lastingly* as well as *unreservedly*. Religion, in short, where it gains a foothold in someone, must in some measure show itself to be an absolute, jealous passion, which aspires to take increasing charge of a man's purposes, which tolerates nothing alien to, or not infected by itself, which permits nothing half-hearted or Laodicean, which has something of the magisterial, rule-arrogating character that Butler attributed to his Conscience. And a religious attitude must tend further towards an *intellectual justification* of the esteem in which it holds its object, towards the finding or invention of operations, acts, manifestations, features which will support a splendid view of it, towards the framing of concepts making it easier for us to view it favourably, towards its widespread use in explanation and in organizing the fabric of knowledge. And it must tend, further, towards spreading its view and its fervour to others, towards enlisting them in the service of its *numen*, towards the fullest measure of proselytism and evangelism. If *all* valuations tend to be extended over the surrounding space of persons, this will be particularly the case—barring contingent limitations—in the case of valuations whose tendency is to take charge of the whole man, and to do so unreservedly. What seeks to rule all of a man, will seek by a natural extension to rule all men.

What we have done so far is no more than sketch the make-up of an attitude or mental drift of which there are certainly many actual examples, and of which the traits enumerated above can be seen to 'belong together', and to draw each other on in actual existence, even if, in the given case, they may not occur in company. How such an attitude may be formed in the individual, historic case is not anything we need go into deeply, or on which we can hope to pronounce accurately. Some awe must of necessity be engendered by the boundless environment about us, at least in some of its moods: so much is involved in its connection with compulsive experience and with the immense indifference presupposed by all belief. A world is something that can be believed in, and as such it must involve that dwarfing of our frail selves, and of our passing purposes, which must furnish some of the materials for an awe in germ religious. In the same way, the very roots of our social experience involve the believing encounter with a whole world of experience, or rather a whole galaxy of such worlds, all quite severed from our own, and obeying rhythms

398   VALUES AND INTENTIONS

and patterns with which we can only have partial sympathy: here too is a necessary source of awe, of which the religious is but a further extension. And as the first encounter with social space is normally that of a being without formed views, abilities or values, with a range of beings surpassingly mature, informed, agreed, secure, decided, powerful and in general benign, it is not hard to see how the religious attitude and view must naturally develop, while the security and succour it gives even when the childhood world is disrupted, explains its further continuance. However this may be, it seems plain that the development of a system of impersonal values cannot but find something allied or akin in the numinous transcendences of religion, while these latter cannot reach their full stature except in alliance with a system of impersonal values. While the springs of the fervent self-prostrations of religion may lie far from those of the cool self-transcendence of impersonal valuation, and while this difference of source necessarily involves tensions among them, yet in both the 'naughting' of the particular person constitutes a profound kinship, which must lead on to an alliance of mutual strengthening and completion in which each finds its developed form in the other.

That this is so needs no very elaborate demonstration. Religion with its absolute deference for its object must tend to move away from objects not vastly exceeding the worshipper in such qualities as he values, or from objects whose claim to exceed the worshipper is not capable of further substantiation, or destroyed on a 'daylight' examination. Natural objects or parts of nature, particular animals or species of animals, special persons or classes of person, special artefacts of various types, special utterances, writings, performances, etc. etc., may all be deferred to religiously, and in such deference they may seem to the devotee to be centres of power and virtue passing all observation or description. To the extent, however, that no backing can be given to such claims, nor a connection with qualities genuinely esteemed, even if only in symbolic or suggestive fashion, and to the extent that further examination makes the object appear narrow, feeble, paltry, circumscribed, ordinary, etc., it is plain that the religious attitude must move on to objects more plainly possessing eminence in valued qualities than such initial ones. And it is plain, further, that, since the claim of the religious object to be venerated must be

EPILOGUE ON RELIGION

399

capable, in virtue of the sheer absoluteness of religion, of being communicated to ever-widening circles of persons, the religious object must come more and more to be decked out with qualities *impersonally* approved, and that it must tend more and more towards the pattern of a detached, suprapersonal, norm-setting *mind*. It is not, therefore, a matter of empirical accident that objects of religion should progress from the merely physical, vegetable or bestial to the human and conscious, and that they should progress from perverse, bloodthirsty, arbitrary gods of restricted sympathies to gods bodying forth all forms of tireless benignity, redemptive passion, purity of intent, depth of perspicacity and of other impersonally valued qualities.

If religion can be seen thus to be intrinsically moralizable, it is easy to see, conversely, that the impersonal life of morality tends intrinsically towards religion. For our impersonal valuations are nothing if not synthetic and endlessly expansive. They arise out of a bringing together and an experiencing in one—even if only imaginatively—of varying sorts of interests, and of interests belonging to varied individuals, and they are, as we saw, always revaluing objects in new contexts, so that, e.g., what is supremely valuable in a context of rarity becomes continuously cheapened by superabundance or monotony, or what is valueless by itself becomes valuable as complementing something else, etc. etc. Our impersonal valuations therefore work towards a limiting ideal of a valuation which will do justice to every possible interest in every possible context, much as our theoretical judgements work towards a corresponding ideal of systematic truth. And the mind in which all such valuations are supposed actual, will itself necessarily attract supreme valuation: it will be a mind enjoying every conceivable species of valuable experience, and carrying out in relation to them all an unimprovably good design. Such a mind and its determinations, always going beyond anything achievable or conceivable by us, must necessarily enlist the supreme unquestioning deference called 'religious'.

We may note, further, that there is yet another direction in which our impersonal valuations find an extension and support in religion. For religion in its absoluteness must come to demand that the object of its deference should be subject to no *external* force or influence, and have nothing whatever *outside* of it. We cannot defer unreservedly to what is merely one among others, to what

400 VALUES AND INTENTIONS

derives its power from others, or is limited in its power by them. Religion moves along a groove of moral necessity towards having an object on which *all* other objects are dependent for their existence, from which they derive their virtues and excellences, which permits nothing excellent or powerful or even actual which is not an extension of itself. And when this limit is reached, and when it coincides with the limit of our impersonal valuations, the latter will acquire an immense security and strength. For when everything in the world depends for its existence and properties on an object absolutely good, we are assured that things work for the best, that, despite appearances, evil will not triumph, that our efforts to achieve the best of outcomes, and to be ourselves the best of persons, is not wholly a vain venture. Just as we can only carry out the demands of science in a world that has to a large extent honoured them in the past, and which we feel sure will honour them in the future, so we can only carry out the imperatives set by our various impersonal values if things have assisted our endeavours, and will do so in future. Religion, therefore, not only consummates but also buttresses morality. What we have maintained are all points of great triteness; but what must be stressed is that they represent developments of certain attitudes which are both natural and logical, not logical in the sense of being entailed by defined meanings, nor natural in the sense of being frequently found together, but both in the sense of following lines of deep affinity which afford grounds for reasoned expectation.

What we may now point to is the existence of a deep antinomy, capable of no ready cure, and certainly not cured by some facile separation or divorce, which infects the natural marriage of religion with our impersonal valuations. What we defer to religiously is of necessity thought of as existent: it must be a thing believed in, having some connection, not necessarily understood or obvious, with the things impinging on us in compulsive experience, and must compel us analogously. We cannot defer unconditionally to a bracketed phantom, a thing seen as entering into the description of certain ideas, thoughts and aspirations, but as having no status beyond such descriptions. The ideals representing the term of our impersonal valuations are such, however, as necessarily to outstrip and outsoar anything having the one-sided, definitely placed, unique, positive, fully carried out, individuated compulsiveness, which is necessarily involved in anything that can be

EPILOGUE ON RELIGION 401

believed in or counted as existent. A marriage between such parties must necessarily involve disastrous accommodations for one or the other. We must here remember the intrinsic indefiniteness of the family of ends projected by the general attitude of impersonality, and the absence of any order among them into which purely personal preference does not enter. X is best *for* someone, not absolutely and *simpliciter*. This might seem to accord well with the notion of an arbitrary 'Supreme Will', which can fill in the indefinitenesses of the impersonal order with its own personal decrees. We might have God, in His contingent nature or Logos, completing God in His sempiternal, paternal necessity. Such contingent decrees can, however, only be right for the Supreme Will in question, and not for any other wills in the world (if admitted at all), who will have the same right as the Supreme Will to their own personal rendering and ordering of impersonal values. (Perhaps this is why it is forgivable to blaspheme against 'the Son', or contingent nature of God, but not against the inescapable 'Father' and universally diffused 'Spirit'.) But even if this personal element in the ordering of values be ignored, it remains obvious that it is not possible to realize *all* good possibilities, since many of them remain obdurately incompatible with each other. Even if 'infinite things in infinite ways' flow from the nature of the Supreme Religious Object, it is still impossible that *all* things in *all* ways should flow from this nature, since if some are realized by it or included in it, others are thereby precluded from existing. It is part of what we ordinarily mean by 'existence' that it should add something to the infinite possibilities projected by notions which classify or describe, and that this something should somehow resolve the deadlock among incompatible possibilities, should 'decide' or 'choose' among them. The thought of something as existing is, in short, bound up with the thought of countless other possible things not existing, it is in short bound up with the thought that what exists need not be, that it is *non*-necessary or contingent. We are thus brought up against the crux of the matter: that the coincidence of what shall receive supreme religious deference, and what shall focus in itself the entire firmament of values, can be found only in an object at once existent, and as such exclusive of many possibilities, and also necessary, in the sense of being exclusive of *no* possibility, as admitting no possible state of affairs, and certainly no *good* state of affairs, from

402 VALUES AND INTENTIONS

which it is, or would be, excluded. And since this coincidence involves a conflict, it follows that an Object placed on its intersecting co-ordinates must itself be incapable of existence, and that the quest for something satisfactory to *both* religion and morality, and *finally* satisfactory to *either* (since each requires the other) is accordingly vain.

The considerations embodied in the above argument are so extremely simple, so formally logical, that they may be strengthened by some varied restatement. It seems plain that no object could *deserve* the unconditional deference in which both religion and impersonal values culminate, if it were merely *one* instance of excellent qualities, if there were *other* instances of such qualities, perhaps vastly or infinitely (if the word means anything in the context) inferior, or if there even *could* be such instances. There may be a being or beings vastly exceeding ourselves in excellence and power, and perhaps causally responsible for our existence and such excellent qualities as we possess, and meriting therefore the greatest respect, admiration, deference, gratitude and co-operation on our part. If, however, such a being or beings can be flanked, even in thought, by *other* instances of their excellent qualities, however inferior, then we are bound to reserve for such *other* instances, even if merely hypothetical, some part of our devotion and our deference, and our deference for the object or objects in question cannot be unconditional, absolute or in other words truly religious. To revere such a being or beings would in fact be to revere an image or illustration, however eminent, of the values we impersonally admire, and what could such a worship of images be but the old sin of idolatry? The object of approvable religion must in short be one from which all actual and possible good things derive their goodness, and without which they *cannot* be: it must itself have or *be* the goodness of all good things, and this puts it into a position impossible for something held actually to exist, which is not a mere abstract or limit helping in the description of other objects. We may go further and hold that anything that merely *happens* to exist, and to be creatively responsible for what exists in and makes up 'the world', but which can be flanked in thought by other non-theistic universes, or by universes dependent on other types of creator, is entirely unfit for supreme or religious deference, since some of this deference must be diverted to the alternative creators in question, or to the good

EPILOGUE ON RELIGION 403

men labouring in non-theistic universes. The object of approvable religion must in short be One Whose non-existence is inconceivable, Whose Essence involves Existence. This is the notion which rightly recommended itself to the religious sense of Anselm of Canterbury, but was also rightly seen by Aquinas and Kant to be incapable of an intelligible working out, though both shrank from drawing the appropriate conclusion: that approvable religion can have no existent object, and that, since it is of its essence to demand such an object, there can be no fully approvable religion. Or rather, that it would be only if the ontological argument were irrefragable that religion could be wholly approvable, and that, since it is not irrefragable, religion can be approved only in a transformed or modified form. While the ends set up by the operative spirit of impersonality may be said to form a 'kingdom', and to culminate in a 'crown' or a 'throne', the crown must, therefore, by its nature remain unworn, and the throne be untenanted, since nothing whatever that is actual, or that represents a decision among divergent possibilities, could conceivably be worthy of it.

The conflict here arrived at is not one that can be evaded by some simple expedient, such as the mere jettisoning of religion and its ultimate consecrations. For the lines of our impersonal purposes *do* intersect in something religious, and the more clearly so the more that we clarify and develop them. Religious objects are no dispensable luxury, but are essential to the description and actual existence of our life of impersonal valuation, which can neither be thought of nor be except as pointing towards them. If such objects are non-existent, they are not for that reason to be ignored or misprized: *their* non-existence is in some sense an infinitely important sort of non-existence, more important than the *being* of the orientations which involve them in their description. Since such objects *cannot but not exist*, and since they remain moving goals for all that, this inspiring non-existence may be regarded, by a suitable change of perspective, as their own peculiar form of being, which they cannot be without. But that what we supremely reverence should lack the *ordinary* existence which worshipful deference presupposes, is at first dismaying and disarraying, and must lead, as do all situations of conflict, to several attempted solutions, some crude and one-sided, some subtle and delicately balanced. It is in examining these that we

404 VALUES AND INTENTIONS

shall best see how the conflict should be faced, and where and how the various forms of consecrated living that religion offers, and their opposed disvalues, should find a place in our firmament of values.

One of the ways to counter the conflicts of the religion-cum-impersonal-value situation may be called the 'subsistential': it is that which purges its object of the shame of non-existence by maintaining it not to be the sort of thing of which existence can be significantly asserted, and so not in the same case as the griffin or the round square, which we at least *want* to assign to the realm of existence. It is, it may be said, an 'ideal object', one extruded, as it were, in the activity of one-sidedly looking at and describing particular objects, and being itself capable of being made the focus of similar one-sided regards and descriptions, but by itself giving us the machinery for thinking and talking about a world, rather than forming part of such a world. But, though ideal, it remains infinitely important, for our religious and other value-orientations are all directed towards it. To deny it existence is not in a sense to deny it power, since conscious being may be said to 'tend' towards it, and if it does not draw them, it is certainly *as if* it did so. And if a preparation for conscious activity be extended into the unconscious or inorganic world, as on many considerations it must, then the whole world, conscious or unconscious, may be allowed to 'tend' towards an ideal object or objects, which will none the less not be among the members of that world. Such subsistential solutions are characteristic of Platonizing philosophers at all times in the history of thought: they are characteristic, too, of those religious creators who are ready, on small provocation, to frame a whole pantheon out of a few abstractions, to turn a few dry theological concepts into a procession of 'Aeons', or a series of moral perfections into a Heaven peopled by 'Dhyani-Buddhas'. What is wrong with such religious transformations lies in their thinness and facility: they add little or nothing to the values that they seek to consecrate. To practise kindness and purity of purpose in imitation of Shakyamuni who died long ago among the blossoming Sala-trees, has little added to it by being done through the grace of Kwanyin or Amida or any other facile Mahayanist projection. If religious forms of bliss, vision, love, zeal, etc., are to have a profound importance, they must enrich the ordinary forms of these

EPILOGUE ON RELIGION 405

excellences with a unique glory of their own: they must not merely blur their outline with clouds of supererogatory incense.

Another way out of the profound religious impasse lies in accepting the non-existence of its object and seeking to make of this a majestic and glorious thing. This is the path probably trodden by Plato in his view of the Good as transcending the definite being of the Forms both in seniority and in power, and his identification of it with a principle of Unity, which from one point of view is exclusive of all determination or characterization, as from another point of view it is inclusively open to all, and which, together with another elusive Principle of Indefinite Quantity (the Great and Small)—a capacity both for indefinite multiplication and expansion as for indefinite division and diminution—'generates' the whole firmament of the numerically conceived Forms. Whatever the detailed interpretation of these doctrines—arguably more important than the analytic refinements of the dialogues—it is plain that they place the zenith of excellence, like the nadir of badness, at a point covered by conflicting requirements, or at a point *requiring* conceptual occupation rather than conceptually occupied. At such a point we in a sense conceive nothing, and yet *have* to perform this seemingly nugatory operation in order to conceive other definite and intelligible contents. Like the tautology and contradiction of Wittgenstein which, while 'saying nothing', are yet 'parts of the language', and necessary to its completeness, the Platonic One and its dark Opposite are necessary to our conception of the whole range of geometric, organic and psychic patterns, whose freedom from unclearness or conflict justifies us in saying that they *are*, whereas we cannot say this of their unclear, conflict-ridden originals.

That what is, from one point of view, empty and absurd, can, from another point of view, be inexhaustibly fertile and significant is, of course, something that many would contest. It can be defended only in the context of a full-fledged intentionalism which recognizes the thought *of* what cannot be (because involving incompatible and hence unrealizable requirements) as yet being a genuine and significant thought, and perhaps having an ordering role among thoughts which can and do terminate on actual objects. Whether or not the doctrine of the superessential One was that of Plato, is not interesting for our purpose. It was certainly the doctrine of many Platonists and Neoplatonists,

406 VALUES AND INTENTIONS

and through them the doctrine of many 'negative theologians' of the Middle Ages. It is perhaps implicit even in the orthodox identification of God with Being-in-general or Being-as-such, that passage of being into *a* being and of *a* being into being whose pursuit puts all our thought-habits at variance with one another. And it was certainly the doctrine of many modern idealists, and it lost Fichte his Jena professorship. But while in the west it has been mainly professed by philosophers, in the east it has had an authentic religious existence, where, to the passion for transcending existence, has been added the passion for putting an end to the restless movement of consciousness, to the endless variegation and frustration of conscious life, and to its basic differentiation into an objective and subjective aspect. The consecrated forms of bliss, insight, love and moral endeavour have there been directed, not to some supreme all-comprehensive intensification of the values present in conscious life, but to the comprehensive elimination of them all: the Upanishadic identifications of self with Brahman in which even knowledge becomes superfluous, the absolute freedom from minding anything which is the last *kaivalyam* of yoga, the final fading out of the Buddhist *Nibbāna*, where a whole series of states, each more rapturously free of definite content than the last—states of being aware of nothing beyond the infiniity of space, states of being aware of nothing beyond the infinity of mind, states which are blissful about nothing in particular, and states which are not even contaminated by bliss—lead on to the wholly blessed extinction, not only of the actuality, but even of the possibility of future conscious experience.

The evils of the nihilism and negativism just sketched must not be exaggerated. For the objects or states which they seek to describe, are not objects or states of the middle distance, possessed of the solid values attaching to things capable of being handled or to the actual handling of these. They may be said to be objects or states 'of the horizon', incapable of being moved from that horizon, since on their endlessly remote position depends their essential 'lure'. And, as limits to endeavour, they might as readily be described, and are in fact frequently described, in a rich spate of incompatible affirmations. Brahman is not only described as 'Not thus!' but as knowledge, mind, life, sight, hearing, earth, water, wind, ether, etc. etc., and *Nibbāna* is described by the Buddhist illuminati as blissful, undying, a çity, a

EPILOGUE ON RELIGION 407

refuge, an island, etc. etc. The non-existence of every recognizable form of being and experience becomes itself seen as a new form of being and experience, endowed with everything we regard as excellent, but in a new and secure form. This sort of approach has at least the merit of not sullying impersonal values with extraneous additions: the religious values lie so entirely beyond the ordinary sphere, that they have no true content beyond what lies in inspiring the highest forms of selflessness, detachment, compassion, insight and other approvable states and attitudes. Gotama Buddha, the most extreme in the depth and simplicity of his negations, may also be said to have founded the most unadmixedly good of religions, and to have been himself the least deluded of religious teachers, just as, by omitting transcendent personal claims, he became the most superlative in his virtues. But for religious values to live in a medium so divorced from existence and conscious life has, however, defects and dangers as well as advantages. For it depresses by contrast the whole range of ordinary experience and human relationships, and makes these seem of small account, when in fact *all* value resides in such experiences and relationships, or represents an extension of them, being nothing more than the *self*-approval and *self*-endorsement of our impersonal conscious life. And it tends to magnify the evils inherent in conscious living, and to see their values as merely contributing to such evils, rather than to dwell upon opposed, encouraging perspectives. And by belittling and denigrating ordinary experience and relationships it tends to build a divided society, given over, on the one hand, to self-cheapening monkish austerities, and, on the other hand, to social rigidities, unmoving technologies and popular religions fraught with superstition and delusion. And it is a prey to its own bad delusions since there is nothing worthy of the most momentary flicker of interest in ceasing to be conscious, or in ceasing to be. It in fact transforms a cessation which can be procured quite cheaply by turning on the gas, or by swallowing an overdose of barbiturates, into a thing to be laboured for by every device of meditative concentration, of austere self-punishment, and by an infinitely zealous self-purging of unworthy personal motives. Such errors must be countered by Spinoza's magnificent dictum: that the meditation of the wise is one of life, not of death.

At the opposite pole from such nihilistic solutions lie the

408   VALUES AND INTENTIONS

whole-heartedly existential ones, those that do not fear the scandal of particularity, of identifying the *numen* with something *not* inclusive in its being, something that exemplifies *certain* excellent qualities and not others, and that is bound up with particular objects and events in space and time much more closely than with others. We have here mainly the 'historicistic', Semitic religions to consider, our own Christian religion, its Jewish parent and Islam. These religions have the supreme merit of satisfying, or of seeming to satisfy, the demand that the various requirements embodied in a supreme religious object should enjoy more than a bracketed, merely intended status, that they should have some direct connection with the believable reality that we encounter in compulsive experience, that they should not merely lure us from the horizon, but in some manner 'come down' into the middle distance of the things and persons with whom we have actual dealings. And, for this 'coming down' to signify anything, it must be selective, discriminating, peculiar, sometimes marvellous. The Godhead must appear in the Burning Bush more directly than it appears in ordinary bushes, the Chosen People must be in a unique and special sense God's people, to be tried, used and redeemed in a quite special way, the words and voices heard by Patriarch and Prophet must derive from the Godhead more directly than do the words and voices representing their ordinary or extraordinary thoughts, the Messianic Kingdom, glorious in sensuous as well as in spiritual fashion, must be due at a date in the near future, perhaps before the disciples can complete their round of the cities of Israel, the person of Jesus and the Sacrament of the Altar must involve God's 'real presence' in a manner more signal than the ordinary round of cosmic phenomena, and the special character of such 'theophanies' must be often marked by discontinuities and perturbations of the natural order. No one can doubt that religions which exploit the special and marvellous have the advantage over religions, even nobler and purer, that do so in a lesser degree. It is clear, likewise, that there is an approvable aspect to their domination, the value that 'comes down' into the blemished here and now being preferable to that which remains an unblemished phantasm on the horizon. And it is clear, further, that the 'coming down' of the religious object to the middle distances also gives a unique definiteness and urgency to the pronouncements of duty, a

EPILOGUE ON RELIGION 409

definiteness and urgency which we have seen that they must have, if they are not to be vacant through generality. Abraham must *now* make the strange, difficult decision of leaving the comfortable corruptions of Ur for the as yet nebulous Land of Promise, the apostles must *now* follow Christ and not defer this to a more convenient moment when their commitments have been cleared up, the Virgins must *now* hasten to their assignment with the Heavenly Bridegroom, Saul must *now* reverse all his previous beliefs and ways, and accept a new apostolic vocation, etc. etc. In all these stories or histories the individual character of duty is stressed: its validity *for* an individual in a unique, temporal situation, and the unquestioning personal acceptance of it, which in part makes it right. Other natural consequences of this urgent realism are the excoriation of half-heartedness, lip-service and sloth, through which impersonality is whipped up into its purest, most devoted form. The positiveness of this dominant spirit is, however, such as freely to permit and encourage whatever does not set itself against it: even the most personal and fleshly wishes may be given consecration in relation to a *numen* which does not disdain the personal and the fleshly. On such a basis powerful, assertive civilizations may be built up: the Catholic civilization with its superb subordination of Aristotle and Vitruvius to its own unclassical purposes, the Protestant civilization with its scientific and practical flair, its romantic and analytical ingenuity, Islam with its unsubtle but varied brilliance and resource, and the dispersed Jewish civilization with its intense and anguished inwardness.

The coin has, however, its reverse side, and this more deeply offensive to our impersonal valuations than the reverse side of other religious solutions. The existential solution necessarily gives value and consecration to things for which no impersonal warrant can be claimed, and it necessarily withholds value and consecration from things for which such an impersonal warrant holds. And by its one-sided zeal for the localized, the uniquely dated and the special, it necessarily distorts its whole perspective of the field of values. The attempted identification of what is impersonally authoritative and desirable, with what is thus local, dated and special, must incline it, however much tempered by natural mildness, to the unremitting persecution of forms of value remote from, or independent of, those on which its consecration

410 VALUES AND INTENTIONS

has fallen. The existential religions tend therefore always to have an element of the vain and senseless, and that not adventitiously, but by their very nature as existential. To locate one's *numen* among particular realities, to give it a special relation to this or that actually existent thing, having these or those special properties, and this or that place and date in the cosmos, is necessarily to give an undue emphasis for which no impersonal warrant can be claimed. It is necessarily to be committed to loyalties which may, in the limiting case, become cruel, inequitable and evil. The will of Yahweh was not satisfied by inspiring His people to just and merciful living, nor in guiding them to a land where such living would be possible: He had to put Abraham through the essentially religious test of demanding of him the sacrifice of Isaac, a test which later inspired the actual sacrifice of Regina Olsen. The Messianic Kingdom's precise date stimulated the wise virgins to be present at the marriage feast, but the foolish virgins, who were vague about dates, had a shocking reception. And when this Kingdom failed to eventuate through a change of heart among the stiffnecked Jews, it was held necessary to bring it about by the violent magic of a contrived, voluntary death, staged in all the trappings of the prophetic writings, perhaps exceeding all other human events in its pity, but quite failing of edification, since carried out for a morally senseless, eschatological purpose. The speciality and existentialism of the coming Kingdom and its heroic Victim were then transferred to the society founded on His sacrifice, and in His name the barbarians were civilized and the Albigenses extirpated, both fruits of the impossible marriage between absolute values and particular existence. And if the marvellous feat of the Thomist theology was to have transformed the grossly particular existence of traditional theism into an existence indistinguishable from the ideal being of various forms of perfection—a transformation helped by a transformed use of Aristotle's notion of 'analogy'—yet the effect of this feat was not so much to enlist religion in the service of absolute values, as to enlist absolute values in the service of the grossest particularism. Protestant 'inwardness' may have dismissed most of the traditions, practices, rules, etc., of the Catholic faith as superstitious and vain, but became itself more desperately superstitious as regard to such of them as it retained. From a relatively comfortable ethic, which had a place for laxity as well as rigour, and which

EPILOGUE ON RELIGION   411

set limits to man's religious and secular obligations, there was a shift to an infinitely anxious ethic where there was room for nothing but wholly rigorous obligation, and where the most secular duty was also sacred. And from a view of human nature as fundamentally good, and restored to self through God's redemptive activity, there was a shift to a view of this nature as hopelessly corrupt, and redeemable only in arbitrary and external fashion. This ethic reduces itself to the painful and absurd in the teaching and example of Kierkegaard. And if we turn to the Jews, we find that pertinacious difference, and a 'chosenness' resting on no distinction of excellence, ends by becoming only a distinction in misery, and provokes natural wickedness to unnatural excesses. If Islam has, after much initial havoc, been more free from evils done or suffered, this has been only on account of the relative shallowness of its inspiration, and the comparatively untransfigured character of its founder. What must be seen is that *all* existential religion, which gives to its object a vestige of particularity or of actual existence, or which ties it up with special characters and choices, or with things and happenings in space and time, must necessarily end by affronting morality. The non-existence, rather than the existence, of the Divine, would appear, in fact, to be a 'practical postulate'.

It appears, then, that the demands of a religion which seeks to combine the full round of value with anything that can without abuse be called 'existence', involves a profound contradiction, and that their attempted fulfilment, if pursued far, can occur only in a number of equally uncomfortable, imperfect ways. This is, in a measure, frustrating, but this frustration, like others springing from contradiction, also has a favourable aspect, and can readily transform itself into an acquiescence. For, if it is shocking and painful that there can be no complete existent embodiment of the whole round of approvable values, how much more shocking and painful would it be to encounter such an embodiment, and what havoc would it wreak on our impersonal valuations? When the sacrilegious Titus stepped into the Holy of Holies at Jerusalem, hoping to see the Most High seated among the Cherubim, how much more shocking would it have been had he actually encountered some particular object, rather than the mystical void that stretched before him? And when some sacred congregation meets to debate an issue central of faith

412 VALUES AND INTENTIONS

and morals, and each member prayerfully exerts himself to heed every prompting of the Spirit, how shocking and how suspect it would be were the issue to be resolved by some fluttering dove-like appearance, perhaps making announcements at variance with the wisdom and conscience of the members? Plainly the Divine is not to be thought of as a being alongside of other beings, nor as a person among persons.

It is plain, further, that the denial of existence to a Supreme Religious Object has not the disastrous effect that it would have in the case of types of thing of which there both can be, and also can *not* be, an instance. Since the Supreme Religious Object is by its constitution not this sort of thing, its non-being can occasion no regret and no scandal. And its role of supreme inspirer of action would be incompatible with its being any sort of particular existent. Its role of inspirer means, further, that, like other objects which have a merely intended status, it enters not only into the description, but into the explanation, of many facts in the world. The whole conscious life of man may be understandable in terms of its convergence towards a Religious Goal, and, if the unconscious life of man and things is best understood as leading up to the conscious, it too may be illuminated by the same Goal. And we may say, if we like, that, as inspiring, uplifting and redeeming conscious beings, and as working *in* them while not being exhaustively *of* them, the *numen* has its characteristic 'mode of being', which is not less important than that of the transitory beings it inspires and uplifts. It is plain, in fact, that this is a case where so many balancing considerations are involved, that the most carefully balanced, multiply suggestive language is in place: we must make plain that while truly numinous objects cannot be said to exist as do houses, trees, etc., their explanatory and directive role puts them in a different class from illusions, mirages and fictions. And we may note, lastly, that to leave the throne of heaven empty, does not prevent us from multiplying presences near the throne. We may assume the existence of as many wise, powerful, and, in a measure, holy beings, embodied or disembodied, in all orders and grades, as we can conceive to our own satisfaction, and find necessary for our personal and moral security. Very possibly the world is prevented from foundering in a morass of misery, error and wickedness owing to the continued efforts of a vast number of sanctifying

EPILOGUE ON RELIGION 413

agents, of varying degrees of insight, power and holiness, in whose work we may be privileged to share. If Religion is, therefore, by its nature self-eliminating, its elimination is still one in which its spirit and style may be essentially 'preserved'.

Our aim in this chapter is not, however, to sketch a metaphysical theology, nor to provide a substitute for it, but to consider the special values and duties connected with religion, a task seldom attempted since the days of the *philosophes* and deists of the eighteenth century. The attempt might, however, appear vain, since quite obviously a man's religious duties must cohere with his actual religious beliefs and philosophy, and it would be empty and arrogant to lay down duties for him that spring from the particular views expounded in this book. The Supreme Object of Deference or Worship may be infected with the conflicts we have mentioned, but is not ordinarily thought to be so, and it would seem a senseless use of terms to say that a man should do things fitting in with the, to him, unknown or unacceptable philosophy we have set forth, rather than with a philosophy he understands and accepts. A Buddhist, lay or religious, plainly has a duty to follow the precepts, hortatory or minatory, involved in the Buddha's Eightfold Way—a Catholic, a minatory duty to fulfil many special obligations to God, prescribed for him by his Church, rather than to act in accordance with the views of a fallible, quite confused and certainly not holy person. And the duties of the Buddhist or the Catholic are their true duties *whatever* one's scheme of impersonal values may be, since a man's duties are personal to himself, and cannot, even in an impersonal context, be profitably divorced from his view of the world, his personal vocation and his accepted scheme of values. But it is none the less everyone's duty, through persuasion and submission to persuasion, to work towards greater agreement in respect of his impersonal valuations, such willingness being inherent in the very slant of mind known as 'impersonal'. And it also is the duty of the holder of a particular moral philosophy to work out a code of duties implied by that philosophy even for those who do not accept it, in the hope either of influencing them to such acceptance, or of being himself persuaded to find theirs the better way. Every thinker has therefore the right and the duty to tell others what would be their duty were they to see things as he sees them, which also seems to him what an impartial judge would judge,

414 VALUES AND INTENTIONS

and though this is not really the duty of those he addresses in the stage at which they find themselves, it represents an attempt to sketch their duty in situations of better illumination and of ideally thorough trial. The absurdity of prescribing to others may further be mitigated by finding analogues of what one thus prescribes in *their own* counter-prescriptions: one can make one's prescriptions as unarrogant as possible, by showing that others too accept a version of them. And one can find support, too, for one's view of religious duties, by considering the actual practice of stable governments, since Caesar, with his overall view of human claims and interests, is more often able to judge equitably of what should be rendered unto God, than are God's accredited devotees or ministers.

These provisos having been made, we may begin by laying down that our religious duties are in the main *purely hortatory* (though not for that reason less important), that the neglect of religion is like the neglect of beauty, the loss of a precious inspiration and reinforcement, and that it is not at all like a lie, or a betrayal, or an infringement of justice. The Divine, not being a person among persons, and not even a being among beings, cannot be wronged or hurt by our disregard: it is we who suffer loss by it. We are all desired, by our nature as impersonal beings, to direct our regard to the point of convergence of all our impersonal valuations, to organize our life about this point, and in this way to give consecration to our existence. We are required to assess and correct our attempts at benevolence by comparison with an ever more exquisite kindness, our endeavours at intellectual penetration by endeavours indefinitely more refined and scrupulous, our attempts at justice by a justice infinitely more comprehensive and impartial, and our pursuit of different kinds of valuable objective in the light of a plan that gives them all their place. And a faint note of the minatory enters into this requirement, in so far as, without some such aspiring idealism, our various endeavours will fall apart into the purblind and the piecemeal, will become tarnished by sloth, or silted up by complacency. Such idealism need have no note of the hysterical: the purblind and piecemeal are needed if there is to be fuel to burn in the religious focus, and the focus must not become ubiquitous, since religion is there to perfect and not subvert life. How far this unqualified idealism should be carried is in part a matter of

EPILOGUE ON RELIGION 415

vocation. There are dedicated, priestly types of soul whose vocation lies near the co-ordinating focus, just as there are souls naturally purblind and piecemeal whose contributions would go gravely awry were they to devote much thought to 'higher things'. Each individual must discover or decide where he may best stand in the radiant, freely formed structure, and while there are penalties for misguided decisions, the rewards for correct ones are vastly more important.

As to the precise manner in which we may keep alive our religious idealism, there can be no uniform directives. A man may pursue the consecrated life by means of special acts of meditation or petitionary prayer, special acts of recollection or endeavour, special outward performances, whether social or solitary, traditional or free: he may also pursue it through no special acts at all, but merely by carrying out his ordinary duties and activities in a specially consecrated or religious manner. The latter form of consecration or *karma yoga* is of course as open to the atheist as to the professing devotee. It obviously depends on the individual how religious objects will best acquire purchase on his soul and dominion over his life. In this connection the claims may be urged of the various established religions—Judaism, Taoism, Hinduism, Buddhism, Christianity, Mohammedanism, etc. It is by no means an easy thing for a mere ideal, and one incapable of full realization, to gain a grip on a man's mind and reorganize his behaviour, especially against strongly resistant personal intents, even if that ideal is the necessary outcome of our impersonal, interpersonal life. Whereas the established faiths turn this ideal into a believable reality, attached by fable or fable-encrusted history to the objects around us, or to historical happenings in the past or future, they give its requirements a definiteness which makes it possible to put them into practice, they remove from it the conflicts which embarrass the soul, and they spread it over a compact community of believers, which represent a wider extension of a man's purely personal interests as well as something that satisfies his impersonal ones. Through all these means established religions enable the divine to transform the soul, in a manner which would be well-nigh impossible without them. And, though there is no security to be had in either the moral or the religious enterprise, they provide a seeming security behind which morality and religion can gather strength, much as the

416 VALUES AND INTENTIONS

home provides a seeming security behind which children can learn to face the precariousness of adult existence. And through the misplaced *urgency* of many religions, and their wide use of minatory instead of hortatory notes, religions have often gained a hearing for imperatives that would otherwise have remained mere whispers. The sword of the conquering Arabs imposed humility, mercy and justice on countless millions, the terrors of Hell brought mildness to the barbarian invaders, and the self-torments of devout Protestants inspired the splendidly gratuitous achievements of Northern European civilization. For all these reasons established religions deserve use as means of grace. And they deserve use, further, because they are mostly creations of genius, and successful because they were such. The religions preached by Comte, Rousseau, Krishnamurti and others have admirable foundations, but a total lack of genius, and hardly anyone has been spiritually transformed by them. Buddhism with its paradoxical inversions and its appeal to profound death-instincts, and Christianity with its transfigured, glorious use of a symbolism of blood, have consecrated the lives of millions. The vocation of most religious men lies within such established folds, even if some must wander outside of them.

If a man has duties, mainly hortatory, but in part minatory, to cultivate religion in himself, and these involve taking up attitudes to the established religions around him, he has also duties, to a greater extent minatory, to the persons who profess such religions. These duties are minatory, since the whole security and moral progress of many persons is inwrought with the maintenance of their religion, and to subvert the latter is to menace the former. Respectful tolerance and abstinence from words or deeds that will cause religious shock or dismay, are plainly in most cases as obligatory as any abstinence from physical violence. But the tolerance to be shown to religions has yet another motive. It aims obscurely at preserving the multiplicity of religious approaches, each of which will compensate for the others' one-sided needs and existential definitenesses. It is above all directed against the emergence of anything *oecumenical,* in which there would be no check on the inventions, prescriptions and inquisitions of a particular system. Whatever may be openly said, everyone feels happier if surrounded by *some* respectable persons who do not share their faith, and nowhere are faiths purer than where they

EPILOGUE ON RELIGION

confront each other in sincere difference, and each feels a 'deeper unity' extending under the other's errors. It is clear, further, that sceptics, atheists, iconoclasts and other religious dissidents are to be encouraged, not merely as the emphasizers of piecemeal values without which religious values would be empty, but also as the necessary purifiers of religion from existential particularity. Iconoclastic laughter is the best agent for eliciting the 'deeper meaning' of historic performances, commands, etc., and separating this from its useful husk, and happy the religion that sustains such antibodies in its organism. There is even, quite plainly, a sceptical or iconoclastic vocation which can itself take on a religious colouring, the imponderables of personal integrity, scholarly scruple, scientific rigour, etc., being gathered together in a Manichaean struggle against superstitious contamination. Place must be found, in saintly histories, for the Blessed St François Marie Arouet's fight with the *infâme*, or for John Stuart Mill's vision of Liberty. Between a more and more deeply spiritual religion and the anti-superstitious pursuit of the highest values, there can, in the end, be only a difference of origin and approach.

It is not necessary for us to enter further into the complex, largely individual question of religious duty. What we have said harmonizes curiously with the pronouncement of Hume's Cleanthes: 'The proper office of religion is to regulate the heart of men, humanize their conduct, infuse the spirit of temperance, order and obedience . . . when it distinguishes itself and acts as a separate principle over them, it has departed from its proper sphere'. We may paraphrase this by saying that our religious duties lie in the performance of our ordinary duties in a special spirit, and that, when this spirit detaches itself from these ordinary duties, and becomes attached to new and special performances and objects, it is developing dangerously. Obviously, however, one does not wish to move towards that eighteenth-century impossibility, religion without enthusiasm, for such a movement tends to destroy living religion altogether, or to provoke its recrudescence in stridently existential or minatory form. If it be said that the principles we have invoked all depend on a particular philosophical position, it may be pointed out that these principles are in fact the ones followed in communities recognized as civilized, where there is most abundance of the things agreed to be good. Settled civilizations are precisely those where religion has this

418   VALUES AND INTENTIONS

general consecrating function—not necessarily stabilizing the *status quo*—rather than a special perturbing or interfering one. And they are principles acted upon, and to some extent acknowledged, even by those professing highly particularist views. Enlightened adherents of such religions distinguish the deliverances of the 'natural light' from their own special revelation, they admit the existence of 'invincible ignorance', and the special dispensations to those suffering under it, they respect consciences they think misguided, etc. etc. In all this they make a step from their side which balances the step of the infidel who sees in their values and prescriptions wrongly particularized forms of acceptable principles. It is the place of the particularist, existential element that alone is in question, the faithful holding those to be invincibly ignorant who fail to see its importance, while the faithless hold the faithful invincibly superstitious in believing in this importance. The intractable character of this dispute removes it from the sphere of the discussable, and in what remains there is profound agreement.

We have now completed our inadequate study of the special values and duties connected with religion. Religion, it is plain, has a tendency at once to perfect and crown, and also to corrupt and destroy, our impersonal values, so that the duties connected with it are of necessity complex. It tends, moreover, to be so inwound with man's impersonal values, and so liable to destroy them in its destruction, as to be pruned and cut back only at immense peril, and yet often obliging us to undertake such pruning if it is not to overgrow the entire structure of our rational life. Whatever operation we undertake against religion must be respectfully, even religiously undertaken, and the result of such operations must be to leave intact those varied forms of consecrated wisdom, love, service, etc., which obviously represent the extreme of value in the universe.

APPENDIX

HENRIETTA HERTZ LECTURE

THE STRUCTURE OF THE KINGDOM OF ENDS

By J. N. FINDLAY

Fellow of the British Academy

Read at the British Academy, 20 March 1957

I wish to speak this evening, with great comprehensiveness and some inexactness, on a subject on which I do not usually speak at all: the subject of the final ends of action, of the extent to which these may be given an agreed content, and of the degree to which they may be fitted into a system. I have borrowed my title, not from the ethical writings of Kant, where it properly belongs, but from the concluding passage of Professor Braithwaite's 1950 British Academy lecture, entitled 'Moral Principles and Inductive Policies'. There Professor Braithwaite ends by saying that 'the empiricist if he wishes may perfectly well use teleological language, and speak of pursuing $\epsilon \vec{v} \delta a \iota \mu o \nu i a$ or of pursuing happiness, using these abstract nouns not to denote unique and nebulous concepts, but in a way in which Aristotle and Mill seem frequently to have used them, as collective names for the Kingdom of all final Ends. In this 'Kingdom', he goes on to say, 'there are many mansions'. It is my purpose this evening to consider some of the many mansions into which this Kingdom of Ends naturally divides itself, and what, if anything, can be profitably said regarding the architecture of the whole mass of building.

I am braving this subject because I believe that the almost total contemporary neglect of it by philosophers is not due to the fact that everything philosophically significant, everything vertebral or (shall I say) osseous, has already been laid bare in it, and what now remains are merely the fleshy or horny scraps best left for the scavenging activities of edifiers and men of action. I believe, in fact, that some of the main formal bones of the subject are as yet inadequately exposed, much as some of the elementary notions of logic had to wait till the nineteenth century for an adequate exposure. I believe too, that some of these bones are so near the surface that they may readily be exposed and scraped even by the rough hacksaw methods of the present occasion. I

VALUES AND INTENTIONS

am glad, also, of an opportunity to speak roughly and largely on a topic that both deserves and allows of the most precise and detailed treatment. There is, I think, at the present stage of philosophy, mainly place for two sorts of philosophizing, both Aristotelian in their inspiration; one that proceeds with painstaking, piecemeal slowness and lack of system, infinitely sensitive to the varying ring of actual terms and usages, and deliberately myopic in its love of fine-grained detail, the other consciously pursuing what Wittgenstein called *Übersichtlichkeit*, the more distant view in which details are allowed to lose themselves in a blur, or to rearrange themselves in simplifying patterns, and which permits itself also the occasional Platonic purple patch, in which it gives voice to its sense of the importance of what it is doing. Both styles may be serviceable, provided one understands one's own performance in either case. Last year you had from Professor Austin an address in the former manner, one for which I have the highest admiration, since while never saying anything that was not obvious and incontestable, he yet always managed to be astonishing and profound. This year you will have to bear with a distinction-confounding, pattern-educing talk from me. I shall hope, however, that, when stripped of whatever may initially sound sweeping and astonishing, it too may be found to contain something that is incontestable and obvious.

To deal with so concrete a subject as the ends of action is for several reasons suspect. Moral philosophy, it is now thought, should be in its main scope meta-ethical. It should listen in to ethical talk, and should dissect its phrases and uses, without becoming involved in it. It should consider the working of such typically ethical expressions as 'really desirable', 'morally obliged', 'morally earnest', 'within one's rights', 'quite heinous and improper', and so on—it will be noted that I do not give a fashionable list of expressions—as employed by people who either have made or might make statements by their means, rather than use them in special statements of its own. It is not for moral philosophy, an analytical and critical study, to increase the range and difficulty of its own material, by claiming or exercising a special liberty of prophesying. It must itself abstain from applying ethical terms to anything, except for purely illustrative purposes—and here the extremely bad current examples of ethical discourse will serve as well as more acceptable ones—and it must likewise ignore the applications made by others, except in so far as there is something distinctive or remarkable in the *manner* in which they are used. We may allow ourselves perhaps to say such general things as that pronouncements of *moral* desirability or suitability differ from *other* pronouncements of desirability or suitability in that they are specially concerned with what is practicable, with what is within our power or control; perhaps we may limit them to what we

APPENDIX 421

are prepared, more or less solemnly, to impose on ourselves on future occasions, or on other persons similarly circumstanced to ourselves. However this may be, it is assumed that the distinguishing marks of the specifically *moral* uses of our various evaluative expressions are comparatively simple and circumscribed, that it is easy to pick them out and list them, and that their implications and 'influence' fall within narrow limits, beyond which nothing whatever can be said to 'follow' from their application. Everything further then becomes a matter for personal filling-in or filling-out, for a man's own judgement and decision.

This kind of approach to ethical terms and notions is, however, an instance of a radically wrong approach to notions in general, we may say to meanings of any sort whatever, whether these be meanings of isolated expressions, or of whole sentences in which they occur. This radically wrong approach lies in looking only for what notions or meanings undoubtedly include or exclude, for the minimum conditions of their use, as it were, while ignoring the many links of symptomatic suggestion, of counting for and counting against, of support and non-support by and for other notions, in which, we may say, the 'comprehension' of notions principally consists. Being A may involve being B as part of its undoubted content, but it may also favour or be favoured by being C, and be unfavourably related to being D, and this in varying degrees in either direction. Thus while it is undoubtedly central to what we mean by 'understanding' that a man who understands something should be able to go on correctly according to some governing rule or rubric, there is none the less an intrinsic connection between understanding and experiences of the 'Aha!' and 'Oho!' variety, which testify to understanding without being unquestionably part of it. There is, in short, a species of probability or probabilification, quite ignored by official practitioners of the subject, which holds between notions or meanings as such, rather than between the classes of happenings which instantiate them. Such probabilifications are part of the import, if not of the content, of any live and interesting idea. This probabilistic nimbus of our notions must not, however, be confused with their 'open texture' or their marginal vagueness, of which so much has been heard in recent times: the way in which the sense of 'understanding' extends problematically to cover the having of experiences of illumination, is not the way in which the sense of 'baldness' extends problematically to the having of a definite number of hairs. In the latter case it is obscure just what the notion involves, in the former case the notion involves certain things problematically or obscurely. The cutting off of a notion's mere vagueness will usually better it, whereas the cutting off of its symptomatic extension will deprive it of its life. We may say, further,

420 VALUES AND INTENTIONS

that while the symptomatic bonds between notions are for the most part
a reflection of the inductive bonds connecting the classes of their
instances—such and such a feature being a mark of such and such a
condition, because it has frequently gone with it in past experience—
the probabilistic connection is, in other cases, merely a 'relation of ideas',
one that rests on a felt affinity among our meanings, and not on any
past frequency of joint embodiment. The notional connection between
understanding and illumination seems mainly to be a connection of the
second type.

It is, further, by virtue of their obscure intrinsic probabilifications
that notions frequently change and develop, what is symptomatic and
marginal becoming nuclear and essential, and vice versa. Shifts of
meaning are not always accidentally and externally conditioned: they
are at times so cognate to a certain notion or meaning, that it is not unfit
to speak of the *same* notion as having developed, or as having become
more explicit. It is not necessarily confused to talk *in the singular* of
variations or developments in *the concept* of this or that. All this being
allowed, it is not absurd to look on the minimum meaning of our various
evaluative expressions, what is undoubtedly entailed by their use, as
the least interesting part of their import. What is *not* entailed by their
use may be more or less conformable to what can only be called their
'spirit', and by virtue of such conformability notional marks will tend
to be brought into, or to drop out of, a notion's central focus. If what I
am saying sounds like an attempt to rehabilitate the Hegelian 'universal
in action' or the 'concrete and dominant universal', I shall not deny the
impeachment. I shall only say that I think this notion can be given a
suitably clear as well as an obfuscating or woolly use, and that it might
even lend itself to some sort of exact topological treatment.

I suggest, therefore, that the contemporary pursuit of meta-ethics at
the expense of ethics, the attempt to study the working of ethical terms
while ignoring the things to which we apply them, is a largely self-
frustrating procedure, as impolitic as the purely syntactical study of
logic and language which was favoured in the 'thirties. (I am not
suggesting that the parallel is an exact one, only that it has some point.)
Just as it proved impossible to explain some of the key-notions of
logic in terms of what were derisorily called 'rules of consequence'—the
rules in question being the permission to write down certain strings of
marks once one, or a demon simultaneously employing an infinitude of
pens, had written down certain other strings of marks—so it seems
impossible to study the import of the evaluative expressions of morals
without descending, to an almost indefinite extent, into considering
the kind of application their use tends to favour or not to favour, the
sort of detailed case-content that is or is not conformable to it. It seems

APPENDIX 423

clear, in short, to use old-fashioned language, that the indispensable *form* of our ethical assertions is such as to call for, to favour, a certain sort of content, a point recognized by Kant when he passed from his first purely formal statement of the categorical imperative to the two subsequent forms which give it an appropriate content, which do not coincide with it in meaning, but which none the less may be said to continue it, and to fit in with it. It will therefore be my task to show that a certain organized framework of ends of action is in some way a *natural* projection of the attitudes behind our ethical pronouncements, and that this framework is no matter for personal judgement and decision. The scope for personal intervention in morals is immense and indefeasible. But it falls within a framework determined by the moral character of our judgements, which, like some space of complex curvature, biases the form and course of whatever is placed in it, and which cannot, without grave distortion, be regarded as simply omnirecipient.

There is, however, an older source of objection to the study of the ends of action than our contemporary meta-ethical preoccupations. This lies in the acceptance of an ethics of rule, which is concerned rather with the comparatively narrow range of the things that a man can immediately do, or effect by his doing, than with the vastly wider range of things that he can approve of or wish for, which things in fact crowd the interstices of his doing, as well as providing its context. In pre-scribing for doing this ethics is afraid to look far into the confused darkness surrounding action, lest it should thereby lose its firmness of touch and step. A little of the context of action it must consider, if it is to characterize what should be done in a relevant and significant fashion, but it prefers not to exceed the minimum look. All ethical determinations lie within an 'horizon' of some sort, whether this be an horizon fixed by practical urgencies, or by the limits of what is profitable to imagine: but the horizon of the ethics of rule is the beam of a farthing rushlight, while everything beyond is extruded into an alien wilderness of 'conse-quences', which it is not merely irrelevant but positively dangerous to contemplate.

It is not my task to probe into the causes of this strange purblindness, which gives a prominent place in moral philosophy to such interesting but minor questions as the return of a borrowed book, the writing of a testimonial, or the fulfilment of obligations peculiar to a certain society or even a definite social stratum. Possibly it represents the reverse side of the great courage of Protestantism, which, in casting aside the flexible guidance of authority, was afraid to exercise an equally flexible guidance of its own. That it represents an unfortunate limitation is, in my judge-ment, evident: it treats the question 'What shall I do or avoid?' as if it were a question different in kind from and unrelated to the question

424 VALUES AND INTENTIONS

'What shall I in all earnestness wish or not wish?', whereas, from a reasonably withdrawn standpoint, they are questions altogether of the same sort, and certainly not questions one can profitably consider apart from one another. The ends of action are not remote irrelevancies foisted on our practical dealings from without, nor springing from some alien and corrupting source: they are remoter, wider objectives of the same sort as the objectives we are in an immediate position to realize, nor is a considered turning of the mind or the will to the one more impossible or difficult to compass than its considered turning to the other. We can be as whole-heartedly *for* some objective beyond the range of our practical production, as we can be for something we are immediately able to put into practice. As Brentano said in a well-known passage: 'Sorrow—longing for the absent good—hope that it will fall to our share—desire to produce it for ourselves—courage to undertake the attempt—decision to do the deed. The one extreme of the series is a feeling, the other an act of will, and they seem to be widely separated from each other. But if we consider the intermediate terms, and only compare with each other those that are neighbouring, do we not see the most intimate connection and almost imperceptible transition?' I do not wish to deny that for *some* purposes it might be extremely important to stress the *differences* of the various terms in Brentano's series: I only wish to emphasize that for other purposes it may be right to stress their affinity, and perhaps to coin special philosophical terms or uses to cover it. The one word *Placet*, it pleases me, is not at all unfit to cover any term of the series: it would cover a request, a command, a decision, a quiet state of acquiescence or one of fervent satisfaction. I am extremely glad to see that Mr Hare recognizes this serial affinity in the valuable 'analytical model' which he develops at the end of his *Language of Morals*, and which is, in my view, the best thing in his book. I very much admire his overriding of linguistic barriers, little as I can like the strange pidgin English of the sentence: 'All mules being barren, please.'

There is yet another fashion in which an ethics of rule has made an ethics of ends seem unplausible and unacceptable. The ethics of rule has mainly limited itself to stating what may be called *minatory* rules or *minatory* imperatives or rules which *threaten*, in which there is always a concealed 'or else', an implicit note of menace. Its 'shalts', 'shoulds', and 'oughts' express rules of strict obligation, to deviate from which is to incur a fault, to merit censure or reprobation, and to have produced something which must either have been presupposed as, or which must now be consequentially reckoned as, evil. In its constant stress on what is obligatory, and its assimilation of all prescriptions to statements of obligation, it has ignored the close and one-sided tie-up of the obligatory with the bad, and its comparatively loose tie-up with what

APPENDIX   425

is good, which is evident even in the non-moral uses of the concept. For we say that we are obliged to swerve to the left to avoid a collision, or that we are obliged to take an umbrella to avoid being drenched by a thunderstorm: we do not say that we are obliged to do the former to demonstrate our driving skill or the latter to look like a city-gentleman. In making all its imperatives minatory, the ethics of rule has ignored the extent to which, in ordinary usage, there are what may be called *hortatory* imperatives or hortatory prescriptions, imperatives which urge, lure, or win us rather than goad us into action by warnings or threats. Our childhood is full of such sentences as: 'You really *should* get your hair cut, though I suppose it won't matter if it waits another week', and so on. Or if the ethics of rule has taken account of such prescriptions at the ethical level, it has tried to force them into minatory form, thereby ignoring or discounting their wide independence of functioning and their largely antithetical role. For in ordinary usage and practice the one generally takes up where the other leaves off, or slackens when the other is intensified. We seldom or never seek to wind up or clinch a protreptic discourse by warning people off from the non-performance or non-pursuit of what we are recommending, nor do we normally end a warning sermon against something, by speaking cajolingly of the absence of what it warns against. The mood of the two is too essentially antithetical. We may say, further, that the positive demand that something should be, and delight in its presence, is not entailingly, not even favouringly, but rather unfavouringly related to the warning that something should not be, or to positive pain in its absence. In the same way, warnings against something's failure to be there are not closely correlated with positive pursuit of or pleasure in its presence. *Seinsfreude*, as the Austrian analysts have indicated, is not always directly but often inversely related to *Nichtseinsleid*, and *Nichtseinsfreude* to *Seinsleid*. We do not for instance congratulate ourselves on the presence of water or common truthfulness, or on freedom from the tortures of Belsen, nor do we lament the absence of things lying at the opposite pole of excellence.

The minatory interests of the ethics of rule meant, however, that, to the extent that it *did* acknowledge hortatory imperatives, it had to recast them in minatory form, force them into the mould of strict obligations, and not place them in quite another dimension. These simplifying presuppositions produced absurdity and disaster in the systems of nineteenth- and twentieth-century utilitarianism. These assimilated the essentially minatory imperative which warns us against creating evil or suffering to the largely hortatory imperative which bids us spread happiness and other forms of well-being among our fellows, thereby obliterating one of the deepest gulfs in morals. They further framed

o*

426 VALUES AND INTENTIONS

their requirements in ruthlessly levelling quantitative form, and, being unable to find any pre-eminent number between nought and infinity, felt bound to opt for the latter, making it obligatory for each and all of us to go as far as we can in the direction of infinity in the sheer multiplication of welfare. Bentham sought to frighten away his ascetic conscience which he regarded as a bogey, but he replaced it by a bogey infinitely more frightening: the horrible haunting fear of having failed to realize a possible throb of pleasure for someone. Moore merely made the decrees of this bogey harder to understand, while also dignifying them with *a priori* synthetic status. At the risk of seeming crudely assertive, I shall here simply say that to me, so far from it seeming analytically or otherwise evident that I ought, on pain of incurring a fault, to seek to achieve the greatest possible sum of good or welfare, it seems rather to follow from the meaning of the words 'obliged' and 'good' that I am not obliged to seek to achieve the smallest particle of *mere* good of any sort whatsoever. Only to the extent that the absence of a good is regarded as evil, which is by no means always the case, does the notion of obligation, as ordinarily employed, enter into the discussion. I am not, of course, denying the obligatory character of much so-called 'doing good' which is really the removal of crying evil, nor yet perhaps of the higher-order obligation to do at least *some* things which are not, taken by themselves, obligatory. My point only is that 'obliged to' and 'bad not to' or 'bad if not' stand in an intimate and logical relation, whereas 'obliged to' and 'good if' or 'good to' do not. It is hortatory imperatives, oughts devoid of obligation, which delimit the upper reaches of what is excellent, just as minatory imperatives plumb the abysses of what is bad. And if Reformation-anxiety is, in all probability, responsible for the extraordinary distortions which have beset the development, in modern times, of a sound teleological ethics, then it would seem that the Counter-reformation has done something towards remedying them. I shall here merely give it as my opinion that the moralists of the Society of Jesus—whatever one may think of their dogmatic background—are alone among philosophers in having written liberally and sensibly on the topic of obligation, and in conformity with our actual judgements and practice.

My listing of the hindrances to what I shall call a complete, as opposed to a purblind ethics, does not of course imply that much valuable work on the ends of action has not been done since the Reformation, or indeed in the present century. The present century saw, in this country, the great work of Moore, whom I shall here praise for those now largely unread portions of *Principia Ethica* which are concerned with 'the ideal', which are thought to reflect merely the prepossesions and prejudices of a small, artificially segregated Cambridge

APPENDIX 427

and Bloomsbury clique. These are, I think, as valuable to moral philosophy as the analyses whose reputation is as justified as it is immense. It also saw the production of Rashdall's *Theory of Good and Evil*, as of much in the ethical writings of Sir David Ross. And on the Continent it not only saw the production of Brentano's address and treatise on ethics, but also Meinong's remarkable writings on Value-Theory, all with the dust now gathering upon them, despite their penetrating distinctions between the role of feeling as attached to the act and to the content of our presentations and judgements. In this century Scheler, too, wrote his magnificent *Der Formalismus in der Ethik und die materiale Wertethik*, and Hartmann his widely ranging phenomenological *Ethics*. In general, however, the works of this period suffer from a major fault: they proceed in a manner which some would call intuitive, others dogmatic, but which I shall simply call 'quasi-empirical'. They all train their eyes, as it were, on the skyline of the Kingdom of Ends, and simply tell us what they see there: that contemplation of beauty and personal affection are incomparably the most towering eminences in sight, that the highest floor of the mansion of pleasure lies well below the lowest window in the mansion of virtue, that there is or is not a special mansion of just distributions as distinct from the floor in the mansion of virtue reserved for just distributors, and so on. Unfortunately the protocols of these high-minded observers often fail to tally or even to be consistent, without any decision-procedure to adjust their differences. Obviously the possession of an excellent moral character does not (as Aristotle thought it should) ensure the possession of a penetrating ethical eye. The confusion thus engendered led by an inevitable process to the modern doctrine which makes ethical principles matters for personal decision, a doctrine which only gains plausibility by exploiting the ambiguities of the word 'decision', confusing the general direction characteristic of ethical concern as such with the specific directions to which we feel our way under its influence, and both with the various particular determinations which fall under them, having their force behind them. By confusing these various senses of 'decision', and assimilating them all to the last, this doctrine makes nonsense of all ethical discourse whatsoever. Plainly a new start must be made. The various specific directions of ethical pursuit and preference must be shown, in some sense, to 'flow' from the general direction of ethical concern as such: if they are not part of its undoubted focus, they must still fall within its penumbra. And there must be something of the same absurdity in running counter to them as in developing one's probability-talk in an eccentric manner, saying for instance that it is highly probable that p will be the case while also saying that it is highly probable that its contradictory not-p

428   VALUES AND INTENTIONS

will be the case. Such modes of speech are not indeed impossible, but they involve an internal unease and are for that reason unstable and self-eliminating.

I have now reached the point where I must show my hand, where I must offer you a blue-print of my realm of ends and counter-ends. I shall assume, without offering more argument, that the ethical problem is best formulated, not as a problem of making considered decisions, but as a problem of forming a sort of considered wishes, wishes which range beyond what is immediately practicable, and perhaps beyond what will ever be practicable for anyone. Being a problem concerned with wishes in general, it is also a problem concerning satisfied wishes, with the sorts of things that we should *like* if we saw them realized. It is a problem which may be put in the words, 'What things should really be or not be?', or, equivalently but more misleadingly (since ethical pronouncements need not refer to the speaker), 'What things should I—or rather should one—seriously wish or not wish for?', and its answers might take the forms, 'Let X, on reflection, really be', or, 'Would, in all earnestness, that X might have been' and so on, etc. etc. (The inclusion of expressions of earnestness, seriousness, considered-ness, etc., is in my view essential to what we mean by 'ethical', though most recent writers have disregarded it.) I formulate the ethical problem in this manner because I find it more illuminating to regard the problem of practical choice as a special case of the problem of considered wishing, a case in which a for once not stepmotherly nature translates wishes into reality, than to regard the problem of rational wishing as a problem as to what one would choose to realize were one in the position of omnipotence. I do so because, as I said, what we wish or do not wish for fills the interstices and provides the background of conduct, and because, for all developed ethical views, it is as important what we wish for in our hearts as what we do in the market-place. I do so further, because wishes can, without abuse of language, be said to persist in their satisfactions: when satisfied, we say that things are as we wish though it is true we sometimes say that we then have nothing to wish for. Wishes span the gulf between means and ends, between the possible and the impossible, the actual and the non-actual, the practicable and the impracticable, and they are impervious, save as regards grammatical expression, to the temporal distinctions of present, past and future. If wishing provides an unbounded horizon for idle fantasy, it also provides an horizon where rationality may range unfettered.

It is obvious, however, as I have already made plain, that the wishes towards whose formation the ethical problem is directed are not any and every sort of idle wish: they must be wishes of a highly peculiar sort,

APPENDIX   429

Fully to characterize them would be impossible this evening. It would not, however, do violence to one's habits of speech and thought to say that they must be deeply considered wishes, framed in the most comprehensive factual framework available, and conceived as circumstantially as possible. It would likewise not be odd to say that they must be wishes having that not readily analysable whole-heartedness that Meinong called *Ernst*, and that they must, further, be existential wishes, wishes concerned with what really is to be or not to be, and not merely with the show or surface of things as occurs in play or art. Lastly and most importantly, they must be wishes that one would characterize as in some measure, or at least in intention, 'disinterested', 'impartial', 'impersonal': they must be the sort of wishes that, as is said, *one* forms, or that one *should* form, not merely the sort of wishes that I personally form. This note of impersonality in what one demands or is pleased with seems itself to be demanded in whatever behests, pronouncements, approvals, resolutions, performances, could be rightly denominated 'ethical', though of course it is not confined to the latter. This, I think, is as much part of uncultivated usage as of the special talk of philosophers. Impersonality, taken together with the other mentioned marks of earnest, desiderative, reflective, existential intention, would seem in fact to be the operative universal which binds all ethical pronouncements together.

By this impersonality I mean a character which I can only describe by saying that I show it when I speak *for* others, or *on behalf of others*, as well as *for* myself; in the extreme of ethical development I show it by speaking *for* everyone or *on behalf of everyone*. I can, it is plain, in some sense speak for others as well as for myself, whether in the field of judgement or the field of demand and wish: even if my utterance contains no first-person plural pronoun, it can in some sense be a collective, or would-be collective utterance, something claiming to be said for an 'us', and by a 'we'. What is involved in such collective speaking presents difficulties for analysis. It involves, no doubt, some obscure picturing of the attitudes of others, whether accurate or inaccurate. It also involves the absence of any felt division between one's attitude and theirs, the sort of situation described by saying that one 'identifies' oneself with their attitude, or that one feels sympathetically 'at one' with it. What really is the analysis of such situations I shall not attempt to say, except that I feel profoundly dissatisfied with attempts to explain them in terms of mechanisms of projection, empathy, sympathy, and what not. 'We', it seems to me, is as simple and straightforward a pronoun as 'I': its use does not demand the aetiology it has often received. Impersonality, moreover, is in no sense peculiar to the moral realm: it occurs as much in the assured judgements of sense-perception and science. A man who

430 VALUES AND INTENTIONS

has examined something carefully with the appropriate sense-organs and instruments goes on to speak about it, not merely for himself, but for all competent and normal observers. A scientific theorist, likwise, makes statements on behalf of the whole company of scientifically minded persons, who employ the methods approved of in his 'culture-circle'.

To speak impersonally, as a 'we' rather than as an 'I', would further be wholly misrepresented, as being a statement *about* what a certain collection opines or wishes: in impersonal speech we strive to *voice* the opinions and attitudes of a collection, without at all referring to it. There is, however, *this* analogy between speaking *for* a collection and speaking *about* a collection, that one feels almost equally mortified if one says *that* one's collection has attitudes that it actually has not, or if one voices attitudes on their behalf which they turn out not to share. If I speak for others, and they fail to endorse my utterances, I may not have been refuted, but I have certainly been stripped of my mantle of authority, and, if I wish to wear it again, either they or I must change our tune. It is clear, further, that to speak *for* others is quite different from speaking *to* others, even should my utterances take the form of a universal prescription. To order everyone to do as I do or intend to do is certainly a magisterial act, but it is an abuse of language to characterize it as moral. In the same way to tell others what one likes, and then to beseech them to find it so also, is a form of utterance often practised, but far removed from the impersonal *assurance* characteristic of morality. What I am saying is anything less than new. It is to be found more or less in what Butler says about his conscience, or Adam Smith about his impartial spectator, in what Rousseau says about the *volonté générale*, or in Kant's faithful transformation of the latter into the dictates of his self-legislating will. It is present in Hegel's identification of the Self or Ego with *die Absolute Negativität*, or again with *das thätige Allgemeine*, the Universal in Action. It is strangely absent from the analyses of Stevenson and Hare, perhaps owing to a commendable wish to stress the neglected relations of ethical pronouncements to those which are not ethical.

My reference to Hegel's attribution of *activity* to what is impartial and universal has the advantage of enabling me to pass to my next point: that impersonality is by its nature contagious. It obeys a 'logic', and that logic is to spread, to level farther and farther, to become more and more absolute. Once speak for *some*, and one will find oneself readily forced into speaking for more, until, in all situations not warped by personal bias, one comes to speak for all: impersonality resembles the scriptural mustard-seed in whose branches the fowls of the air ultimately find their accommodation. *What* one says when one pronounces impersonally is, moreover, profoundly affected and shaped by

APPENDIX 431

the impersonality of one's utterance, as I shall have occasion to show in what follows. There is nothing *formal* in this spread of universality. Formally, the mere presence of universally quantified variables constitutes universality, however full of anomaly, hiatus, arbitrariness, disjoined multiplicity the accompanying content may be. One is wishing with the widest universality if one demands that everyone with red hair should have his head cut off, while all those with other colourings should be given a public dinner. There is no sense of speaking of one unrestrictedly universal principle as being *more* universal than another, and no sense consequently in speaking of a tendency for the less universal principle to pass over into the more universal. Our actual talk, however, gives a perfectly good sense to such degrees of universality, and it tends itself to slide naturally from ways of speaking that are arbitrarily restricted to others that are less so.

I have now to show how *das thätige Allgemeine* can be genuinely active in shaping the ends and counter-ends of considered living, how impersonality and impartiality can somehow give us a concrete way of life, and not merely a containing form into which almost anything can be fitted. I shall approach this point by considering one feature of practically all teleological systems of ethics: the unquestioned place given to pleasure and satisfaction among the ends of living, and to dissatisfaction and pain among its counter-ends. Has it not seemed strange to anyone that such ends should be so unanimously chosen? Why should so empty, so almost meaningless an abstraction as pleasure or pain be regarded as an end or counter-end of living, while other ends more palpable, and more consciously chosen, are not so much as mentioned? Is it not strange that no moral philosopher has listed a good wife or a good dinner among the undoubted ends of living, that he has not troubled to write a gastronomic or a nuptial chapter? Aristotle's anaemic discussion of friendship is no substitute for the latter. The reason for the restriction is, however, plain. The impersonal standpoint of the moral philosopher forbids him to include among his ends of pursuit or avoidance even such as it would be *logically* possible for someone to find uninteresting, though all or most men find them extremely so. When we speak ethically (at least in the more developed forms of such speech) we speak not merely for our human associates with their incredible variety of taste, but also for any possible beings as might not care either to replenish themselves with food, or to marry or give in marriage. At the level of impersonality no concrete source of satisfaction can be impersonally satisfactory except in so far as it *is* satisfactory to someone. Only the satisfactory or the pleasant becomes the end to be aimed at, and the dissatisfying or the painful the counter-end to be avoided. It is therefore not out of piglike materialism or *folie*

432 VALUES AND INTENTIONS

de la boue that hedonistic moralists have set up their two ultimate terms of reference, but rather out of an excess of disinterested formalism and impartial universality. What pleases must be pursued, and what pains must be avoided, because, at this impersonal level, there is nothing else left to pursue or avoid.

It might appear now that our task was ended as soon as it was begun, and that no further ends or counter-ends of living could be prescribed beyond what is satisfactory, on the one hand, and what is unsatisfactory, on the other. This is, however, far from being the case. Impersonality in attitude, by an internal logic which is not the less genuine because not based on any formal entailment, necessarily presses on to many higher-order objectives besides the first-order objectives recognized by hedonism. Since an impersonal attitude aims at detachment from purely personal aims, and since it seeks to speak for others as much as for the speaker, and in a manner that they will not derisively repudiate, it must, by the internal logic just mentioned, come to prefer such objects of pursuit, and also such satisfactions of pursuit, as are themselves infected with its own impersonality. These will be for it the *higher* objects of satisfaction, and the satisfactions of higher order, as opposed to the objects and satisfactions of lowest level.

It is not hard to list some of the directions in which impersonality will thus pursue itself and take pleasure in itself. They are, in fact, the directions recognized by the moral philosophers of the present century, even if in the adventitious, quasi-empirical way we disapproved of. Obviously, in the first place, the impersonality evinced in our moral attitudes and pronouncements will find something congenial, and accordingly worthy of pursuit and satisfaction, in the impersonal achievements of every judgement of perception, in which there is always a systematic discounting of appearances that vary from one observer to another. In much the same way, it cannot help finding something congenial in that impartial use of evidence, from whatever source derived, which is characteristic of empirical science, and the systematic discounting of data not capable of a *public* exhibition or repetition. The impersonality which seeks, as we say, to obtain a *true* view of the natural world, seems wholly analogous to the impersonality displayed in our moral attitudes and utterances, and must of necessity recommend itself to the latter. Obviously, too, such scientific or observational performances will be valued according to the skill, the zeal, and the success that they show. In the same way it seems clear that there is a characteristic impartiality of impersonality present in the austere satisfactions of the picture gallery or the concert chamber, even though it is not now fashionable to talk about 'aesthetic distance', nor to talk generally about anything aesthetic. The object or product admired in

APPENDIX   433

these difficult enjoyments must plainly bring out a character or a meaning in a manner perspicuous *to all*, and not merely gratifying to the tastes and predilections of the individual at some particular phase of the enjoyment. Good art is, and should be, mortifying to the natural man, and therefore satisfying from an impersonal level: though it only achieves impersonality in the realm of show, it must necessarily recommend itself to the kindred impersonality of our moral attitudes. Lastly, the impersonality of our moral attitudes must obviously approve of itself, whether manifested in the judge or speaker himself, or in the conduct and attitude of other persons. It must approve of its own skill or success in achieving non-arbitrary adjustments of personal interests, of its own zeal in attempting to achieve them, or of its own deep earnestness in wishing for them. It is indeed not tautologically necessary that morality should be one of its own interests, much less, as some philosophers have claimed, that it should be its only interest: it is nonetheless 'logical' in some sense that it should approve of itself among other ends of living. And the impersonality involved in morality must approve also of the impersonality evinced in certain deep forms of love and affection: even Adam Smith admits that sympathy must be more readily sympathetic to sympathy than it is to antipathy. All this is the merest sketch of a 'deduction': I have painted vague portraits of various widely recognized goods, and tried to exhibit the logic that holds them together. I leave you to paint similar portraits, and to work out similar deductions, of what is bad. All that I have been concerned to show you is that to wish for the ends in question, and to wish for them together, is in no sense an arbitrary matter.

So far I have spoken merely of the members of the Kingdom of Ends: I have yet to assemble them into a body. Here I shall content myself with the briefest indications. It is clear, at least, that we should *not* follow any purely quantitative or Benthamite model such as has been adopted with modifications by Moore, Rashdall and Ross. We cannot legitimately balance the bad, whose removal or avoidance is obligatory, against the good, which is the proper object of a hortatory demand. Nor can we merely barter one positive good against another, at a fixed rate of exchange, selling out in knowledge in order to acquire bonds of love, or surrendering stocks of pleasure while preserving holdings in virtue. Since the directions in which impersonality may be exercised are varied and incomparable, it is absurd to treat their differences as unimportant, and their special characteristics as interchangeable and commensurable. Faced with the problem of choosing among them, we can but say with Plato: 'Give us both' (or rather 'Give us all'), and then proceed to solve the practical problem as richly as possible. Since the imperatives connected with the good are hortatory, this problem is not so agonizing as the words suggest.

434 VALUES AND INTENTIONS

The Kingdom of Ends is, in short, a body, or, if you like it, a mystical body: it certainly cannot be dismembered and reprocessed in a manner suitable to a stock-yard. Nor can it, for the same and other reasons, permit unmeasured growth towards infinity in any direction. The rational economic principles which govern the abundant and the rare apply also here: the over-produced end must necessarily lose in value, while the under-produced end must become correspondingly more precious. It is indeed strange that a period which gave birth both to ethical utilitarianism and to classical economics could make use of such flexible notions as that of marginal utility in the one case, and employ only rigid notions in the other. Yet it is plain that we do judge morally according to such flexible principles, and also that, since impersonality involves a non-arbitrary attitude to the ends of living, we are right to judge so. I need not here again comment on the deep absurdity of holding, not merely that it is desirable, but also that it is obligatory for us to strive towards the greatest possible total of good, a rule that would condemn even God to an endless senseless multiplication of excellence. If a good life is devoid of jealousy, it must likewise be devoid of greed, above all of a greed which would cheapen the best.

You may feel at this point that my Kingdom of Ends wears a somewhat totalitarian aspect. Having started with the meagre concept of impersonality, I have now ended up in an all-comprehensive ethical system which leaves place neither for argument nor divergence. I am unrepentant on this issue: I do hold that impersonality works in a definite direction, and that while a vast range of prescriptions and wishes may be denominated 'moral', there are some that remain more paradigmatically moral than others. Something like this seems to me to be covertly claimed in all forms of ethical talk, and I for one should cease to make ethical judgements and decisions if I did not think it could be given a good sense. What one *ought* ethically to wish, or how one *should* ethically judge, is to me simply the limit towards which ethical wishes and judgements, by virtue of what they are, inevitably move. Were deeply scrupulous and not merely rule-of-thumb moralists as common as are deeply scrupulous and not merely rule-of-thumb scientists, I do not think that my contentions would sound at all strange. That I may have failed to characterize the direction of our ethical attitudes adequately, does not mean that it is not actual and operative, even within the limits of the present account. But even within the limits of the present account there is still abundant room for divergences in the judgements and wishes which may still, by virtue of their impersonality, claim to be moral. And there is even further possible divergence in the application of the ground-plan of morals to the detail of actual life and personal preference, an application which has been wrongly

APPENDIX 435

represented as a mysterious exercise of intuition, but which may rightly be represented as the free and legitimate exercise of choice. For moral decisions in this sense there must always be unlimited scope.

I wish, in conclusion, to apologize for two features of this lecture: its kaleidoscopic character and its *ex cathedra* air. The former is due to the fact that I have thought much about ethics without writing about it over a long period: you have therefore had to hear me whole. The *ex cathedra* air is mainly due to the fact that I have had to indicate the character of the arguments I might give for certain positions without actually giving them: it does not reflect any great confidence in my own opinions. My main aim has been to suggest that ethics, as it has been traditionally conceived, has been neither abolished nor exhausted, that modern lexicographical and linguistic techniques have neither solved nor dissolved its problems. They have merely removed the aerial perspective that made those problems seem simpler than they really are.

INDEX

Abnormality (sexual), 278
Absolute values, 250, 372
Abstract beauty, 247
Abstraction, 63, 78
Achievement preferences, 163
Achtung, 216
Acte gratuit, 218
Action, 189
Activity, 50, 136
—, mental, 137–45
Activity-wants, 158
Aesthetic debasement, 253–4
— feebleness, 252
— individuality, 347
— reality, 252
— value, 228, 249–50
— wants, 157
Affinity, 32, 50, 422
Agitators, 362
Agreement, 230, 272
Albigenses, 410
Amphibiousness, 32
Ampliative inference, 106–7
Analogy, 79
— of inner experience, 27, 51, 73, 220, 260
Angelico, Fra, 253
Angels, 234
Anglo-Hegelians, 43, 106
Animal consciousness, 62, 68, 102, 111, 147, 150, 297, 310, 322, 348
Anscombe, E., 142 *n.*
Antinomy, 134
—, in religion, 400
Apartheid, 362
Appropriation (of punishment), 314
Approvability of belief, 113–34
— of valuation, 211–12, 225
Approval, 189
Aquinas, T., 403
Arbitrariness, 204, 232, 259, 263, 285
Arguments in punishment, 321
Aristotle, 36, 54, 82, 142, 151, 172, 179, 201, 270, 346, 350, 370, 387, 391, 409–10, 419–20, 427, 431
Asceticism, 266, 280
As-if explanation, 150–1
Aspects, 77–8
Assent (in belief), 100, 186, 225
'Atmosphere', 30
Augustine, St, 376
Aussereinander, 31
Austin, J., 17, 192, 194, 420
Authenticity, 256
Aversion, *see* Not-wanting

Bad, 222
Badness, aesthetic, 252–3
—, of injustice, 289
— and obligation, 426
Baseness, 333–4
Beauty, 244, 256
—, abstract, 247
Behaviour, 32, 34, 50–1, 60, 69–70, 270
Behaviourism, 273
Belief, 93–134, 181, 184–5, 264
Benevolence, 274–5
Bentham, J., 22, 235–7, 329, 426, 433
Berkeley, G., 260
Bernoulli, J., 125
Bertrand's problem, 127
Better, 222
Betterment, 325–6, 393–4
Bewährung, 116
'Bleen', 122
Bodily knowledge, 172–3
Body, 174
Bosanquet, B., 90
Bosch, Hieronymus, 327
Bracketing, 101–2, 107, 109–10, 184, 254, 400
Brahman, 269, 406
Braithwaite, R. B., 419
Brentano, F., 16, 25, 35–43, 93, 136, 155–6, 424, 427
Buddhism, 166, 277, 320, 406, 416
Butler, J., 191, 221, 397

Caprice, 187, 219
Categorical attractiveness, 336
— imperative, 312, 423
Catholicism, 409–10, 413
Causality, 141–5, 176, 198–200, 285–6, 373
Chances, Theory of, 117, 121, 128–9, 134, 288, 293
Character, 183, 186–7, 371
— building, 392
Cheapening, 248, 329, 355, 434
Chisholm, R., 95 *n.*
Choice, 163, 185, 190, 194
Christianity, 320, 358, 390, 408, 416
Clash of interests, 306–7
Clearness, conscious, 47–51, 58–9, 241, 246
Cognition, 45–6, 95, 175, 180, 207–8, 228, 230, 235, 241–2, 261
Coherence, 104–7, 118, 122, 261–3
Common sense, 130
Communication, 88–9, 130, 220, 224, 258

438   VALUES AND INTENTIONS

Compensation, 315–16
Compulsion, 295–6
Compulsive experience, 102–4, 107–8, 112, 114, 116, 118–19, 121–2, 127–8, 130, 132–3, 140, 143, 184, 220, 222, 254, 257–8, 400
Comte, A., 416
Condensation (concentration), 30, 165, 171, 270, 373
Conflicts, 83–4
Conformity to the given, 82
Conscience, 346–7
Conscious causality, 318, 335, 370–2
— light, *see* 'light'
— pursuit, 366–8
Consciousness, 46–7, 57
— of action, 136
Consecrated mode of values, 396
Consent, 100, 185, 190, 225, 323
Contemplative values, 228
— wants, 157
Context, Principle of, 351
Contract, Social, 307
Coolness, in belief, 112
—, in wanting, 166, 179–85, 195–6, 371
Corrective justice, 313–14
Correctness of value-judgements, 223
Corroboration, 116
Courtesy preference, 164
Creativity, 373
Cruelty, 240, 279

Dante, 328
Death, 237, 310, 407
Decision, 24, 189, 204, 346, 372, 427, 435
Deference (religious), 396–9
Degradation (sexual), 279–80
Deists, 413
Deliberation, 186–7, 218, 372
Descartes, R., 17, 33, 74, 80, 260
Descriptions, theory of, 41–2
Desirability, 208, 212, 222, 227, 287–8
Detail (empirical), 119–20
Determination, 85–6
Determining tendency, 179
Determinism, 182, 194, 202, 379
Deterrence, 316–17
Difficulty (of decision and action), 196–7, 261, 290, 357–8, 360, 377–9
Diogenes, 296
Directedness, mental, *see* Intentionality
Disapprovability (of beliefs), 113, 115
Disharmony of interests, 306–7
Disjunction (of minds, persons), 72–3, 268, 293–4, 306
Disposition, 48, 55, 59
Disrespect, 278

Dissatisfaction, 228, 238
Distributive justice, 298–9
Disvalue and minatory oughts, 340
Disvalues of cognition, 264
— of impotence, 284
— of personal transcendence, 278–9
Diversity, range of, 126–7
Duty, 16, 341

Ease, 377–9
Economics and ethics, 434
Ecstatic awareness, 67
— emotion, 276
Education, 297
Emotion, 165–73, 208, 222–4
Emotional presentation, 175
Emphatic use of 'feeling', 173–4
Endorsement, 214, 231, 244
Entailment, 84–5
Entrails, functions of, 169
Epistemic evils, 265
— preferences, 163
— values, 228
— wants, 157–8
Equality, 299–302, 329
Equalization, 89–90
Equity, 125–9, 259
Esse apparens, 47, 101
Ethics of rule, 20, 423
Evidence, 104, 118, 121, 259
Evil, lower limit of, 358
Evils of belief and knowledge, 264
— of injustice, 289–90
Evincing (of emotions), 336
Excluded middle, 20
Exculpation, 384–5
Existence, 400–2
Expansion of wants, 167–8
Experience (personal), 26–34
Experience-preferences, 163
— -wants, 158
Exquisiteness of satisfaction, 154
Extrapolation, 267

Fairness, *see* Justice
Falsifiability, 120
Family Relations, 15, 17, 45, 94
Fantasy, 184–5, 246
Fascism, 329
Fatigue, 248
Favouring, 198, 420
Feeling, 100, 112, 137, 140, 146, 155, 165–6, 171–8, 207–8, 222–4, 230
Fichte, J. G., 406
Fiction, 101, 412
Fixation, 151
Flagellation, 248–9
Flaubert, G., 357
Fly-bottle, 199–200
Form (Wittgenstein), 29

INDEX

439

Freedom, 191–5, 198–200, 228, 285–6, 297–8, 304–5, 373
Frege, G. W., 41, 58, 61–2
French Revolution, 295
Frequency, 111, 117, 127–8, 259
Freud, S., 361
Frustration of Meaning, 160
Fulfilment, 31, 51–8, 81, 83–4, 102, 116, 118, 139, 158–9, 241, 246–7, 267, 269

Gauguin, P., 356
Genuineness, 256
Gestalt psychology, 242
Gide, A., 219
'Glitter' (of value-firmament), 394
Goodman, N., 122
Goodness, 213
Gotama Buddha, 277, 281, 407
Gratuitousness, 284, 318, 341

Habit, 153, 163, 371, 386–7, 391–2
Hare, R., 17, 424, 430
Hartmann, N., 16, 427
Hedonic knowledge, 236
— values, 228, 240
Hedonism, 233
Hegel, G. W. F., 17, 25, 44, 61, 84, 106, 120, 124–5, 221, 295, 307, 324, 327–8, 347, 391, 422, 430
Heidegger, M., 17
Heraclitus, 33
Higher welfare, 241
Himmler, H., 327
Historicism, 408
Hobbes, T., 162, 307
Horizon, 20, 286, 328, 338, 351–2, 423
Hortatory imperatives (oughts), 339, 353–7, 361–4, 376, 385, 425
Hume, D., 20, 55, 96, 144, 166, 176, 179, 208, 417
Husserl, E., 16, 25, 31, 51, 54, 64, 66, 102
Hypocrisy (moral), 391

Idealism, 132–3, 151, 414–15
Idolatry, 402
Illfare, 354, 357–8
Images, 54, 119
Impartiality, 221, 225, 243, 259, 263, 272, 293, 326
Imperatives, 336–7
Impersonality, 16, 130, 214–27, 231–3, 241–2, 248, 250, 256–61, 272, 290, 295, 299, 307–8, 326, 345, 363, 399–400, 429–30
Impotence, 284
Indeterminism, 188, 218, 378
Indifference, 126, 164, 243, 256, 279, 290, 344

Induction, intuitive, 104, 107
—, problem of, 128–30
Inequality, 302–3, 308–9, 315, 329
Inexistence (intentional), 35, 63, 101, 196
Inference, 105
Injustice, 239, 288–331, 361–3
Inner life states, 26, 32, 102–3, 270
Insincerity, 349
Instrumental spread, 147–8, 151–2, 375
Intentionality, 35, 36, 39–41, 43, 101–2, 196, 231
—, sidelong, 75, 136
Intentional objects, 147, 149, 152
Interiorization, 40
Internal relations, 23, 43, 106–7
Interstitial values, 288
Intuition, 213, 222, 260
Islam, 408–9, 411

Jesuits, 22, 344, 426
Jesus, 281, 408
Jews, 408–9, 411
Judgement, 93, 102
— of value, 211, 222, 225, 370
Justice, 229, 263, 265, 288–331
Justification of difficulty and sacrifice, 380
— of emotions, 170, 215
— of valuations, 215, 223

Kant, I., 17, 25, 71, 76, 79, 87, 108, 125, 132–3, 216, 226, 242, 251, 260, 281, 312, 320, 337–8, 403, 419, 423, 430
Karma yoga, 415
Keynes, J. M., 127
Kierkegaard, S., 271, 411
Kingdom of Ends, 419
Kinship, 15, 132, 117
Knowledge, 131–2, 181, 284
—, bodily, 172–3
—, desiderative, 149
—, emotional, 170–1, 259
—, hedonic, 236
—, how and that, 270
—, of other minds, 266–9
—, practical 142–3, 259, 367–8

Laming effect of pain, 303, 356
Law of Excluded Middle, 85
Lawrence, D. H., 253
Legitimation, 231
'Light' (conscious), 57–66, 110, 112, 114–15, 139, 170, 208–9, 211, 222, 241, 334–5
Likelihood, *see* Probability
Likeness, 123–6, 232, 329

440 VALUES AND INTENTIONS

Limit of actual and approvable, 203
— of aspiration, 369
— of deference, 396
— of injustice, 289–90
— of sharing, 328
— of wanting, 185
Limiting frequency, 117
— view, 108, 112
Locke, J., 307
Logic, 31–2, 51, 75, 84–5, 106, 129, 180–1, 201, 212, 221, 225, 227, 229–30, 232, 237, 261, 272, 286, 298–9, 317, 323, 365–6, 394, 400, 430, 432
Logical values, 228
Love, 275–8, 294

Mahayana, 404
Malevolence, 279
Marx, K., 261, 301
Materialism, 133
Mathematics, 103, 106
Meaning, 61–2, 98–9, 111, 160, 165, 246–7
Meinong, A., 16, 175, 380, 427, 429
Méré, Chevalier de, 126
Messianic Kingdom, 408, 410
Meta-ethics, 23, 227, 420, 422
Metaphysics, 103, 108, 116, 273
Mill, J. S., 93, 234, 287, 417, 419
Minatory imperatives (oughts), 338–9, 354–5, 357–8, 361–4, 376, 385, 424–5
Modality, 65, 176
Monadic separateness, 297, 299
Monotony, 237, 240, 356
Moore, G. E., 16, 23–4, 36, 54, 130, 137, 193, 209, 320, 351, 388, 426, 433
Moral individuality, 348–50, 363–4, 378
— values (disvalues), 229, 325, 333–4, 365–9, 375–80, 388–9
Moralism, 387
Motivation, 142, 147, 335
Mythology (of inner experience), 27, 34

Naturalism (ethical), 203
Nazis, 279, 284, 327–8, 330, 376–7, 384
Neoplatonism, 405
Nerval, G. de, 281
Newman, J. H., 100
Nibbana, 406
Normative values, 205, 207–8, 218, 287
Notional compulsion, 266
Not-wanting, 155, 159–63

Objective and subjective values, 369
Obligation, 16, 20–2, 131–2, 293, 341–4, 424–6
Obsession, 359–60
Ockham, W. of, 47, 100
Ontological Argument, 403
Opacity, referential, 37
Openness of belief, 99–100, 102, 258
— of personal transcendence, 266
— of universality, 225
— of will, 192–201
Opinion, 93, 102
Opportunity, 304–5
Organic Wholes, Principle of, 320, 350
Other minds, 71–2
Ought, 222, 332–44

Pain, 172–3, 230, 238, 261, 303, 322, 358–9
Partial belief, 109–11, 186
Partial-mindedness, 186
Passivity, 50, 140–1
Pater, W., 253
Paul, St, 191
Peirce, C. S., 102, 104, 108, 118
Permission, 21, 116, 190, 231, 242
Perspicuity, 245–6, 252
Perversity, 187–8, 196, 232, 306
Pharisaism, 390–3
Phenomenology, 335
Philosophes (eighteenth century), 413
Philosophy, 324
Placet, 155, 424
Plato, 79, 123, 125, 155, 179, 218, 233, 243, 251, 271, 288, 301, 327–8, 331, 405
Platonic justice, 327–31
Pleasure, 177–8, 229–30, 431–2
Poignancy, 245, 248–9, 260, 262
Policy (in emotions), 169
Polyadicity of belief (Russell), 42
Popper, K. R., 17, 116, 120
Posterity, 237
Power, 228, 280–6, 297–8, 304–5
Practical knowledge, 142–3, 197
— syllogism, 151
Pragmatic paradoxes, 25
Pre-established harmony, 137
Pre-existent meanings, 65
Preference, 162–5, 191
Presumptions of emotions, 169–70
Presupposition of existence in justice, 300
Prevention, 316–17, 360–1
Prima facie duties (oughts, right-nesses), 337
Prior, A. N., 202 n.
Prior probability, 121
Probabilification of notions, 421–2

INDEX

441

Probabilistic *a priori*, 44
Probability, 110, 113–17, 119, 121, 127–8, 134, 254–5, 258–9, 288, 293, 331
Prolongation of pattern, 137–8, 143, 147–8
Promises, 310
Proselytism, 397
Protestantism, 409–11, 423–4
Provisional duties, 340
Prussianism, 328
Psychognosy, 25
Publicity values, 271
Punitive correction, 313

Quality (in mental states), 96, 171–2, 176–7, 233
Quasi-empiricism, 24, 427
Quasi-wants, 178
Quixotism, 380–1

Randomness, 107, 117, 123–4
Rashdall, H., 16, 24, 427, 433
Readiness, 38–9, 99, 102, 164
Reality, 105, 108, 112, 184, 256–7
— -indifference, 156
— -preference, 163–4
Realizability, 127–8, 259
Realization, 270
Reasons, 19, 23, 142, 149–50, 165, 179, 196, 203, 216–17, 229
Recklessness, 187
Redistribution, 315
Reductio ad absurdum (punishment), 320–1
Referential opacity, 37
Reflexive use of words, 61–2
Reflexiveness of consciousness, 66–70, 74, 86, 144, 175–6, 260
Relation-like (character of mental reference), 35–6
Relations, 36, 77
Religion, 395–418
Remoteness, 361
Representativeness (of action), 186–7
Requital, 318–19, 363–4, 394
Resentment, 279, 291, 302, 327
Respect, 272–4
Response (practical) and belief, 94–6
Responsibility, 191–2
Reward, 313
Rightness, 213, 222, 292–3, 338–9
Ross, Sir D., 16, 24, 337, 427, 433
Rousseau, J. J., 416, 430
Ruin (spiritual), 357, 359
Rule, ethics of, 20, 423
— (in Kant), 79
Ruskin, J., 341
Russell, B., 41–2, 65
Ryle, G., 25, 172

Sacrament, 408
Sacrifice, 275, 377
Same-mindedness, 288
Sartre, J. P., 17
Satiety, 248
Satisfaction, 154–8, 189, 228–30, 233–40
Scepticism (religious), 417
Scheler, M., 16, 279, 390, 427
Scientific preferences, 163
— wants, 157–8
Self, obligations to, 343–4
Selflessness, 266
Sense (= meaning), 41, 61–2
Sense-data, 54–5, 80
Sense-experience, 53–6, 82, 102–3, 116, 118, 140, 172
Sense, inner, 69
Sensory surface (aesthetic), 246–7
Seriousness, 101, 165–6, 186, 213
Sex, 277–8
Shakyamuni, 404
Sharpening, 86
Sidelong intentionality, 75, 99, 136
Sincerity, 206, 216
Smith, A., 221, 272, 430, 433
Social contract, 307
Socrates, 209, 320
Solipsism, 273
Space of persons, 71, 88, 210, 212–13, 215, 219–20, 280, 306–7, 398
Space of possibilities, 111, 114
Spheres of right, 307–12
Spielraum, 111–12
Spinoza, B., 34, 100, 106, 407
Spontaneity, 285–6, 374
Statistics, 107
Stevenson, C. S., 213, 430
Stoics, 100, 166, 179
Stout, G. F., 93, 136–7, 144
Strength of belief, 111
— of wanting, 162
Stretching experiences, 261
Structure of the Kingdom of Ends, 16
Subjective rightness, 369
Subsistence, 404
Substitution, 151
Summation of pleasures, 235
— of values, 350
Suppositio simplex, 61
Syllogism, practical, 151
Symbolism of punishment, 322
Sympathy, 210, 220–1, 224, 270, 272, 294, 330
Symptomatic suggestion, 421
Synechism, 104, 107, 122–5, 128–9, 262
Synthetic *a priori*, 107
— character of consciousness, 76, 78

442 VALUES AND INTENTIONS

Tautology, 106, 178, 212, 230
Teleology, 34, 131, 335
Temptation, 384–5, 392
Tertullian, 104
Tetens, N., 168
Titchener, E. B., 172
Time, 144–5, 201–2, 235, 237, 239
Titus, Caesar, 411
Tolerance, religious, 416
Totalitarianism, 330–1
Transcendence of the personal, 265–6, 271, 328
Transcendental deduction, 17, 76, 87, 225
Tristan und Isolde, 277
Truth, 254–5
Trying, 145–6

Unconscious, the, 150
Understanding, 40, 228, 232, 294, 306–8, 342–3
Universality, 66, 91–2, 151, 225, 312, 422, 431
Unfreedom, 286
Unserious wants, 165–6
Utilitarianism, 22, 363

Validity of valuation, 223, 227
Valuation, 203–9, 244, 257, 276
Value-judgements, 211, 222
Value-movement, 218
Values, 134, 203, 218, 255–6, 340, 372
Verbal determination of action, 179, 182
— expression of value, 208
— expression and conscious light, 62–4

Verbal magic, 127, 208
Verification, 56
Virtue (vice), 333–4, 386–7
Vitals, language of, 168
Vitruvius, 409
Vividness, 223–4
Vocation, 249, 263, 356, 361, 415
Voluntariness, 191–2
Voltaire, F. M. A., 417

Wanting, 147–59
—, rationalized, 203–5
— and freedom, 285–6
— and justice, 295–6
Warmth of feeling, 174–5
— of wanting, 166, 168, 207
'We', 429–30
Weakness, 284
—, moral, 386
Welfare, 228
— and justice, 296–7, 353–7
Whole-mindedness, 186–90, 205, 324, 337–8, 349
Wickedness, 386
Wish, 20, 31, 159, 189, 204, 206–7, 428
Wittgenstein, L., 17, 28–9, 55, 94, 106, 247, 260, 267, 269, 405, 420
Wittingness, 324
Worthwhileness, 332
Wrong, 292–3, 340–1
— determination of duty, 348–9
Würzburg School, 260

Zeno of Elea, 201
Zest, 217–20, 291